D1190304

melancholy order

Columbia Studies in International and Global History

Columbia Studies in International and Global History

The idea of "globalization" has become a commonplace, but we lack good histories that can explain the transnational processes that have shaped the contemporary era. Columbia Studies in International and Global History will encourage serious scholarship that is not confined to a single country or continent. Grounded in empirical research, the titles in the series will provide fresh perspectives on the making of our world.

Cemil Aydin, *The Politics of Anti-Westernism in Asia; Visions of World Order in Pan-Islamic and Pan-Asian Thought*

Patrick Manning, *The African Diaspora: A History Through Culture*

MELANCHOLY ORDER

Asian Migration and the Globalization of Borders

ADAM M. McKEOWN

COLUMBIA UNIVERSITY PRESS   *New York*

COLUMBIA UNIVERSITY PRESS

Publishers Since 1893

NEW YORK   CHICHESTER, WEST SUSSEX

Copyright © 2008 Adam McKeown

Library of Congress Cataloging-in-Publication Data
McKeown, Adam, Ph.D.
  Melancholy order : Asian migration and the globalization of borders / Adam McKeown.
    p.   cm. — (Columbia studies in international and global history)
  Includes bibliographical references and index.
  ISBN 978-0-231-14076-8 (hardcover : alk. paper)—ISBN 978-0-231-51171-1 (e-book)
  1. Asia—Emigration and immigration. 2.   Globalization—Asia. 3.   Boundaries—Political
aspects. 4.   Emigration and immigration—Government policy. 5.   Passports.   I.   Title.
II.   Series.
  JV8490.M44 2008
  325'.25—dc22   2008022230

♾

Columbia University Press books are printed on permanent and durable acid-free paper.

Printed in the United States of America

c 10 9 8 7 6 5 4 3 2 1

For Gina,
my treasure of coerced migration

Contents

Tables and Figures

Tables

Figures

Acknowledgments

Writing is painful. Thinking and research are pleasures. A National Endowment for the Humanities Summer Stipend, junior faculty development grants from Northeastern and Columbia universities, and a Social Science Research Council Postdoctoral Fellowship in International Migration allowed me to indulge my pleasures. Visiting fellowships at the Russell Sage Foundation in New York and the Asia Research Institute at the National University of Singapore greatly eased my pain.

Many people have assisted in the development of this book through a diverse range of contributions, including commenting on drafts, pointing out errors, providing logistical support and sources, or making offhand remarks that crucially shaped my thinking. After writing a book about identification and categorization, I am acutely aware of the inadequacy of any attempt to properly classify their contributions. So I will express thanks through the simplest and most egalitarian method that I know, alphabetical order:

Jerry Bentley, Lauren Benton, Ulbe Bosma, Adrian Carton, Pär Cassel, Henry Chan, Diego Lin Chou, Matt Connelly, David Cook-Martin, Nicola Di Cosmo, Peter Dimock, Nicholas Evans, David Feldman, John Fitzgerald, Lisa Ford, Donna Gabaccia, Julian Go, Mike Grossberg, Eric Han, Dirk Hoerder, Walter Huamaní, Paul Jones, Ira Katznelson, Doug Knox, Adam Kosto, Philip Kuhn, Marilyn Lake, Eugenia Lean, Erika Lee, Steven Legomsky, Liu Hong, Leo Lucassen, Greg Mann, Patrick Manning, Sucheta Mazumdar, Leslie Page Moch, Prabhu Mohapatra, Brian Moloughney, José Moya, David Northrup, Pablo Piccato, Meha Priyadarshini, Qiu Liben, Anupama Rao, Humberto Rodríguez Pastor, Anthony Reid, Anne Routon, Saskia Sassen, John Scanlan, Elizabeth Sinn, Lok Siu, Neil Thomsen, Charles Tilly, Tiffany Trimmer, Mika Toyota, Gray Tuttle, Theresa Ventura, Michael Williams, John Witt, Xiang Biao, Yang Bin, and Henry Yu.

Of course, even the most rationalized method of classification cannot systematically recognize every feature of a complex reality. Thus a mass expression of gratitude must go out to the many audience members who have listened and commented on various manifestations of this book. The students of my graduate seminar, "International Orders," also read a rough draft of the entire manuscript in the fall of 2005 and influenced my thinking more than they probably know. Finally, a special expression of nepotistic gratitude must be reserved for Cecily and Gerri McKeown. I am afraid that the final product will not even partially make up for their sacrifices in making it possible.

Before the Law stands a doorkeeper. To this doorkeeper there comes a man from the country who begs for admittance to the Law. But the doorkeeper says that he cannot admit the man at the moment. The man, on reflection, asks if he will be allowed, then, to enter later. "It is possible," answers the doorkeeper, "but not at this moment." Since the door leading into the Law stands open as usual and the doorkeeper steps to one side, the man bends down to peer through the entrance. When the doorkeeper sees that, he laughs and says: "If you are so strongly tempted, try to get in without my permission. But note that I am powerful. And I am only the lowest doorkeeper. From hall to hall, keepers stand at every door, one more powerful than the other. And the sight of the third man is already more than even I can stand." There are difficulties which the man from the country has not expected to meet, the Law, he thinks, should be accessible to every man and at all times, but when he looks more closely at the doorkeeper in his furred robe, with his huge pointed nose and long thin Tartar beard, he decides that he had better wait until he gets permission to enter. The doorkeeper gives him a stool and lets him sit down at the side of the door. There he sits waiting for days and years. He makes many attempts to be allowed in and wearies the doorkeeper with his importunity. . . . The man, who has equipped himself with many things for his journey, parts with all he has, however valuable, in the hope of bribing the doorkeeper. The doorkeeper accepts it all, saying, however, as he takes each gift: "I take this only to keep you from feeling that you have left something undone." . . . During all these long years the man watches the doorkeeper almost incessantly. He forgets about the other doorkeepers, and this one seems to him the only barrier between himself and the Law. In the first years he curses his evil fate aloud; later, as he grows old, he only mutters to himself. . . . Finally his eyes grow dim and he does not know whether the world is really darkening around him or whether his eyes are only deceiving him. But in the darkness he can now perceive a radiance that streams inextinguishably from the door to the Law. Now his life is drawing to a close. Before he dies, all that he has experienced during the whole time of his sojourn condenses in his mind into one question, which he has never yet put to the doorkeeper. He beckons the doorkeeper, since he can no longer raise his stiffening body. The doorkeeper has to bend far down to hear him, for the difference in size between them has increased very much to the man's disadvantage. "What do you want to know now?" asks the doorkeeper, "you are insatiable." "Everyone strives to attain the Law," answers the man, "how does it come about, then, that in all these years no one has come seeking admittance but me?" The doorkeeper perceives that the man is nearing his end and his hearing is failing, so he bellows in his ear: "No one but you could gain admittance through this door, since this door was intended for you. I am now going to shut it."

—Kafka, *The Trial*

melancholy order

Introduction

The Globalization of Identities

The modern passport is a palpable manifestation of an idealized global order. It is a tangible link between the two main sources of modern identity: the individual and the state. It specifies a unique individual within a matrix of standardized physical categories, and it guarantees that identification with the marks and seals of a recognized nation state. It embodies both the most private and the most bureaucratically alienating of identities, being an object of intense personal attachment even as it is a tool of global regulation and standardization. The photograph, accumulated visas, seals, and amendments further enrich it as a token of personal history even as they entrench the bearer more deeply within the files and machinery of state surveillance.[1]

The modern passport is addressed to a global audience; other documents can establish the link between nation and individual for domestic purposes. The passport announces to other states that the issuing state will take responsibility for the identified individual. To cross international borders without such a document (in the absence of special agreements to the contrary) makes one "illegal," "irregular," or a stateless person who must depend on the mercy of others. The efficacy of the document depends on recognition of the issuing entity as part of an interlocked order of nation states. The ability to generate standardized forms of identity is, in turn, an important part of obtaining this recognition. Although the passport claims merely to be official recognition of a preexisting individuality, the act of documentation itself makes nations and individuals into realities.

Of course, this model obscures as much as it reveals. Both individuals and nations still reserve many powers for themselves. Every person thinks there is more to himself or herself than can be embodied in a document. And nations rarely consider passports to be conclusive proof of nationality. Most accept passports only as a matter of comity and insist that they are under no legal compulsion to do so. Passports provide few guarantees other than a state's promise to accept the bearers when they return. This model is especially misleading in its insistence on the equality of individuals and of nations.[2] Entry visas (or the privilege of moving across borders without one) and residence permits make finer distinctions beneath these formal claims of equality. They enforce distinctions of wealth, politics, and occupation and categorize individuals according to kinship, marriage, education, money, job, language, race, religion, intentions, and experience of persecution. Much of the actual documentary proof of identity is produced not by states and individuals, but by companies, political parties, friends, families, brokers, and lawyers. But despite these ever-proliferating participants and categories, the possible public identities are remarkably standardized around the world. The individual remains the final object of identification, and states still monopolize the authority to stipulate forms of evidence and make final decisions.[3]

What kind of world has made possible these passports, visas, and permits? They do not merely record a preexisting reality. They emerged as part of a global process of creating stable, documentable identities for individuals, and dividing those individuals across an international system of nation states. More specifically in terms of regulating global mobility, a multitude of new institutions, technologies, legal structures, and categories have constructed international borders as the primary site of regulation. Indeed, the ideas that border control is a foundation of sovereignty and that sovereignty entails a power to unilaterally regulate human entries have become basic principles of the international system, even as the institutions and techniques to exert this control have diffused and standardized across those borders. The very possibility of identifying an immigrant at the border, before he or she has been inserted into a web of domestic identification, depends on the legibility and reliability of documents and identities produced by foreign nations. In turn, the ability and willingness to produce such documents has become one of the many qualifications necessary for recognition as a state within the international system.

The global system of migrant identification and control is not inherent to the existence of an international system. It was a fairly late development, the specifics of which emerged from a series of historical contingencies in the continuing suppression of nonstate sources of identity and unregulated cross-border mobility. In particular, most of the basic principles of border control and techniques for identifying personal status were developed from the 1880s to 1910s through the exclusion of Asians from white settler nations.[4] In other words, migration control did not emerge as a logical or structural necessity of the international system, but out of attempts to exclude people from that system. But by the 1930s these practices that were developed to fortify the edges of the international system had become universalized as the foundation of sovereignty and migration control for all states within the system. And far from being the repression of natural freedoms, this universalization was grounded in the expansion of institutions and ideals that have made it possible for us and even compel us to imagine ourselves as free, autonomous, self-governing individuals.

Globalization of Borders

The history of modern international identity documentation is a global history, inseparable from processes of human mobility and the proliferation of modern nation states. As such, it should be part of the history of globalization over the past two centuries. This assertion is not as simple as it may first appear because globalization is often understood as a process of increasing interaction. Passports, borders, and migration controls are often perceived as obstacles against integration and the very principles of free exchange that are at the foundation of an interactive world. But regulation and flows are inseparable. Identity documents and migration regulations were often established with the intention to both protect and hinder movement, or, to put it more precisely, to facilitate and block certain kinds of mobility.[5] Indeed, to be a "free" migrant is possible only in conditions of extensive government suppression of private coercion and other activities that may hinder safe passage. Much of the work of passports and bounded national territories is to provide precisely this kind of suppression and encourage mobility. The history of globalization as interaction is inseparable from the globalization of borders.

Globalization is a fundamentally time-based process. But most understandings of globalization distort the relevance of history, precisely because of the tendency to see globalization as something that overcomes rather than interacts with borders. Globalization is often defined as increasing flows, expanding interconnections and fragmentations, or time-space compression that overcomes older separations and distinctions. In this perspective, flows and interactions are historically dynamic. Cultural and political borders are static and unitary, necessary foils to globalization. They mark off "traditional" units that are prior to and outside of globalization, bereft of any significant historical dynamic other than as obstructions that are increasingly transcended, penetrated, or undermined. This kind of global history—whether written in 1848, 1898, 1948, or 2008—often begins in the recent past of no more than twenty to thirty years, leaving earlier history to the hegemony of national territorialism, immobility, stable identities, and tradition.[6] "As a result," explains David Ludden, "we imagine that mobility is border crossing, as though borders came first, and mobility second."[7]

Scholarship on globalization has generated a powerful vocabulary of networks, diasporas, nodes, fields, unbundling, deterritorialization, scapes, and systems to describe interactions across diffused and transregional spaces. But these concepts have remained static, situated within the unhistorical epoch of the "new."[8] Defined against the static past of borders, debates over globalization have often revolved around question of whether flows of goods, information, and especially people are undermining the sovereign state. From a historical perspective, this is an odd question because migration and the consolidation of an international system of nation states have emerged symbiotically over the past two hundred years. They were and still are complementary processes. To be sure, flows and borders are often in tension, but it is precisely this tension that is the most important source of historical dynamism.

Attempts to write a deeper history of globalization usually describe a linear process that germinated in Europe as far back as the medieval period and then gradually expanded to engulf the world.[9] These are histories of unilateral diffusion rather than globalization. They leave no place for the processes of mutual interaction that are key to most understandings of contemporary globalization, as if the digestion of intervening contacts with the rest of the world had little impact on the processes themselves. Histories of the international nation state system also take this tack, finding its origins in medieval cities, the Protestant Reformation, and the establishment of a "Westphalian System" of territorial sovereignty in sixteenth- and seventeenth-century Europe. The subsequent global spread of this system without significant modifications is then a fait accompli.[10]

Interest in globalization has nonetheless stimulated pathbreaking historical research on the global movement of goods, people, and ideas beyond Europe. There is a growing awareness that writing history from the perspective of nation-based containers has obscured historical processes of interaction. Even in terms of simple measurement of interactions, the flows of goods and people from the 1890s to 1910s reached per capita levels similar to the present.[11] These histories tend not to describe a linear process, but cycles of expansion and retreat. The cycles are sometimes depicted as periods of penetration and resistance (by those who are suspicious of globalization), or as a "belle époque" and backlash (by those who are not). The methods of economists, excellently suited to measure movement, exchange, and market integration, often dominate these understandings of globalization.[12] However these flows are interpreted, these global narratives still tend to be about quantity, placing material flows in a unique position of historical agency.

Given the extent to which borders have been taken for granted in histories of globalization, attempts to write global histories framed as anything other than an expanding West tend to be fragmented and incoherent, an endless string of comparisons between nations and regions. But starting points for a more nuanced history can be found in analyses of contemporary globalization that envision mutually constitutive processes of homogenization and differentiation.[13] Contact generates not only assimilation and convergence, but also new ways for people to distinguish themselves from each other and from what they perceive to be a homogenizing universalism. Interaction also generates standardized categories for framing difference, such as ethnicity, nationality, race, rights, or even loyalty to a sports team. To appropriate these symbols and institutions is to claim participation in a wider social field by selectively asserting the terms of difference that will be recognized by other groups and not mark one as backwards. Roland Robertson has schematized these processes into four basic ways of identifying and belonging in the world: individual nations, an international system, individual selves, and humankind as a whole. These are experienced (but not necessarily acknowledged) as in tension with each other: society vs. individuality, geopolitical competition between states vs. a harmonious international system, the relativization of cultures vs. common sentiments of humanity, universal human rights vs. national self-determination.[14] These tensions are key mechanisms of change within the global field.

This approach can be the basis of a rich global history grounded in the mutual entanglement of flows and borders. For example, as late as the turn of the twentieth century, the world political map still contained a multiplicity of political units: nation states, city states, princedoms, federations, empires old and new, protectorates, colonies, dominions, extraterritorial enclaves, customs receiverships, clans, and other kin-based units, with a broad spectrum of subordination and autonomy among them all. When we follow flows of information after the mid-nineteenth century, we find that two of the most widely diffused kinds of knowledge were of (1) the institutions and attitudes that constituted a sovereign, independent nation state; and (2) the institutions and attitudes that constituted a sovereign, free individual (discussed more in the following section). By the early 1960s a mosaic of nation states with similar institutions and similar claims to autonomy covered most of the world. It was a spectacular diffusion and homogenization of political forms.[15] These forms are now taken for granted as precisely the opposite of globalization, the basic units of a fragmented, preglobalized world. Yet they are themselves the products and vehicles of global interaction.

In global histories of flows, the consolidation of states and borders is sometimes explained as a backlash against nineteenth-century globalization, a retreat into protectionism, nationalism, and racism impelled by the insecurities and change brought by interaction.[16] Such an account is helpful but hardly sufficient. The flows of information and power that helped to establish these borders were inseparable from the knowledge and practices that facilitated and guaranteed the flows of goods and peoples in the first place. Those latter flows were made possible by institutions that enforced customs laws in predictable ways, adhered to standardized means of diplomatic and commercial interaction, implemented international agreements, and provided predictable legal and commercial protections. State monopolization of the means of mass violence; the suppression of pirates, bandits, and autonomous lords; the consolidation of territory; and the policing of borders and jurisdictions were the very means by which states protected those flows.[17] The more that state institutions conformed to internationally familiar standards of consolidated borders and power exerted over individuals, the more fully they could participate in global interaction. If they did not participate voluntarily, gunboats and colonial conquest made it mandatory. It was a story of standardization, but without convergence into a single polity. Many parts of this story have already been told in the context of national and colonial histories; international identity documentation and migration control provide material to write the story as a global history.

Regulating Migrant Identities

Modern border control and international identity documentation emerged in the late nineteenth century as part of the expanding global industrial economy. More direct causes included the rise of the international state system, mass mobility, and new technologies of generating and organizing data such as fingerprints, photographs, and sophisticated filing systems. Emergent ideals of individual rights, equality before law, national unity, self-rule, and the free movement of goods, money, and people were also part of the package. These ideals can be glossed as liberal principles or, in a term more appropriate to the late nineteenth century, the standards of civilization. But any label runs the risk of obscuring the many contradictions within these ideals. The total compatibility between individual freedoms and the management of society for the "greater good" theorized by men like John Stuart Mill has rarely worked out so smoothly in practice. Of particular relevance for migration was the fact that self-rule, a crucial source of freedoms, was inseparable from the conceptualization of a "people." A polity capable of self-government was one that respected individual freedoms and had institutions that preserved individual rights. An effective political community of and for the people was the main guarantor of these individual freedoms. This often required membership controls, whether to protect the existence of liberal institutions or merely as the right of a free, self-governing people.[18] In practice, the vigilance of membership controls often grew in direct proportion to the egalitarianism of the community, coming in tension with ideals of free mobility and the universality of individual rights. These tensions were mitigated and obscured through categories such as race or "illegal" aliens that could justify unequal treatment.[19]

In the 1860s and 1870s the scale was tipping in favor of laissez-faire ideals of free movement. It was increasingly difficult to justify the control of human movement except in exceptional circumstances of threat and subversion. Great pressure was placed on Asian nations and colonies to partake of these ideals. But at the same time new controls started emerged in the 1880s to restrict the mobility of Asians to white settler nations. Unlike earlier controls, these new controls focused on entry rather than exit, concentrated on the border as the main site of enforcement, and developed extensive mechanisms to distinguish individual identities, which proved at the time to be even more difficult than distinguishing races. Tellingly, the controls were created by white settler nations around the Pacific that saw themselves as the forefront of the liberal freedoms of the nineteenth century. These nations were the sites of multiple innovations in democratic governance and self-rule, such as secret ballots, women's suffrage, universal education, and progressive labor laws. Ideals and practices of self-rule were also the foundation of exclusionary policies. Modern border controls are not a remnant of an "illiberal" political tradition, but a product of self-conscious pioneers of political freedoms and self-rule.

The erection of border controls gave a physical presence not only to national borders, but to the cultural macro categories that divided the world into East and West, civilized and uncivilized. These macro divisions justified border control, even as border control transformed them from imagination into reality. The administrative cordon around the Pacific demarcated the line between progressive democracies and "stagnant" Asian polities, between free migrants and coolies. Asians' unfree condition demanded exclusion, selection, and surveillance. This, in turn, generated opportunities for evasion that prompted investigations that even further demonstrated the extent to which Asians did not live up to ideals of free migration and displaced the blame for harsh enforcement onto the migrants themselves.

Pressures from Asian nations and proponents of free mobility and racial equality eventually caused these controls to be reformulated in ways that appeared nondiscriminatory and accommodating of individual freedoms. This developed in the context of three seemingly irreconcilable challenges: (1) the justification of migration controls in the context of liberal ideals and extraterritoriality in Asia; (2) the development of modes of control that were compatible with and could even produce "free" movement and intercourse, both as a universal right and as a condition for economic growth; and (3) the standardization of identification procedures and migration norms around the globe, which included an insistence on the sovereign right of a nation to control entry as it pleased.

Migration and Self-rule

On the surface, demands that Asia be "opened" to foreign trade and travel existed uncomfortably alongside the movement to exclude Chinese from the white settler nations. But within the broader logic of "civilization" that framed many global encounters, both demands could be made perfectly compatible. Extraterritoriality in Asia was the flip side of self-rule. The principles that justified the exclusion of Asians from the white settler colonies could also be used to justify the penetration of Europeans into Asia, and vice-versa. Liberal ideals were often formulated in opposition to images of a tyrannical European past. Peoples beyond the North Atlantic were similarly conceived as nations in their nonage: uncivilized savages, Asian despotisms, people enthralled by superstitious customs or otherwise incapable of self-rule.[20] They did not provide rights and equality before law, or even basic protections of life and property. To obtain these rights and protections in Asia, foreigners had to be subject to their own law if they were to properly exercise the universal right of intercourse. And only through intercourse and learning could these nations be brought out of their nonage. Few contemporaries linked settler self-rule and extraterritoriality as complementary aspects of the same ideals, but both of these locally specific practices were presented as necessary consequences of broad global distinctions between peoples. The rhetoric of "civilization" was ideally suited to this task, encapsulating a vision of deep institutional differences that could be simultaneously characterized as deep historical cultures and as stages along a common trajectory of progress. The very vagueness of the contents of civilization made it an ideal tool to simultaneously assert separateness and the need to adhere to common global standards.[21]

In the context of multiple diplomatic, administrative, and legal pressures, however, it took finesse to develop the practical institutions of migration control in ways that simultaneously justified extraterritoriality and exclusion. This was resolved by asserting that free mobility in the interior of nations and equal access to law were features that distinguished the civilized states from barbaric and despotic ones. The lack of these features in Asia justified intervention. Their presence in the white settler nations, however, could justify exclusion of the uncivilized because liberal institutions of self-rule may collapse under the weight of so many children of despotism who were ignorant of republican virtues. The need to uphold liberal institutions meant that Asians within the border were promised (but not always given) free movement and equal access to law, but only on the condition that those outside the border had no necessary rights at all and could be hindered from entering at will.

In this way, the basic legal and political justifications of modern migration control did not develop out of intercourse between formally equal nations and peoples. Rather, they developed in the context of isolating particular peoples from participation in the modern world. Universal liberal ideals were no longer derived from the mere existence as a human, but from the existence of state institutions that could enforce them. By the early twentieth century, these principles were promulgated as the norms for interactions between all peoples and nations. This was possible because diplomatic pressures and the consciousness that these principles could potentially be applied to non-Asian migrants produced a tendency to replace the vocabulary of race and distinction with legal phraseology that was self-consciously race neutral and ostensibly universal in its application. This neutralized language obscured the racial origins of migration control and projected them into the universal standards of the international system. This broader promulgation also entailed breaking the more general idea of free intercourse—fundamental to mid-nineteenth-century liberalism—into component parts of migration and commerce (diplomacy having already broken away earlier in the century). To this day, strong ideologies still promote free commerce and exchange of information as a global good and something that should be subject to international negotiation and pressure. Few people make similar claims about unhampered international migration. Migration control was also broken into different aspects: excessive restrictions of domestic movement and departure are still strongly criticized as infringements on human rights, but few critics ever question a nation's collective right to protect its borders by limiting entry as it chooses, although some critics may insist that a liberal state should exercise those powers sparingly.[22]

Regulating Free Migration

At the very least, an acceptable immigrant was expected to be "free." Such a demand was unavoidable in the wake of the suppression of the slave trade and the decline of European indenture, but it was far from clear what a "free" migrant might be. This issue was debated endlessly in nineteenth-century discussions about the status of labor contracts. Was the ability to bind one's own labor for a certain period of time a fundamental expression of freedom or a subversion of it? At a more fundamental level, the emerging ideal of the free migrant drew on a deep mistrust in liberal thought of all factions, special interests, privileges, intriguers, cabals, conspiracies, and partial societies that intervene between the sovereign individual and the public interest.[23] The disrepute of bonded migration was part of a broader attack on the private organization of movement and violence. Legitimate migration was to be uncoerced, voluntary, undertaken as a result of individual decisions and for the sake of a better life. From this perspective, transportation agents, brokers, and recruiters of all kinds were potential abusers and rightful targets of suppression unless they collaborated with government regulation.

But the private exploitation of migration was often difficult to disentangle from family and village networks or the dealings of any entrepreneur who operated beyond the reach of a single government. In this context, social networks and guarantors that had once been the main producers of identity became increasingly unworkable. Identities linked to ancestry, caste, class, title, or ranks of nobility were also increasingly suspect as well as being of little utility in differentiating between the many equally poor and undistinguished people in the mass migrations of the nineteenth century. New methods of identification had to be developed.

This challenge was met by isolating the individual as the agent of migration, possessor of rights, and object of regulation. The creation of the free individual migrant was not only a moral imperative but a regulatory imperative, the best means of extracting a mobile population from one set of institutions and power relations and depositing it in another. Migrants were torn out of informal social networks and institutions and repositioned as individual bearers of distinguishable qualities and documentation that could be fixed within a matrix of standardized categories and cross-referenced files. Intermediary organizations were gradually pushed out or criminalized, except for large transportation companies and other organizations that collaborated with government supervision. Identity became less a function of who one knew or could claim as a relative than of the ability to fulfill carefully defined categories of family, status, occupation, nationality, and race. This helped create actual migration patterns that more closely approximated the ideal of free migrants making independent choices to better their own lives and that of their families. Individuals and their families even came to be seen as the natural units of migration that existed prior to rather than as a product of regulation. Regulations then claimed to select and protect these free individual migrants from the abuses of private interests. Increased regulation could thus be presented as a means of fulfilling rather than impinging on free movement and individual rights.

In the minds of many, the free migrant, not hampered by obstructive regulations and custom, was also an imperative for economic and social development. Only when government obstacles to movement were removed would the economy and individual abilities achieve their full potential. This perspective was troubled with contradictions when applied to particular situations. For example, under what conditions could Asian migrants be understood as free when it was believed that tyranny and servility were the very conditions of their existence? Also, the "free" movement of people was possible only under certain protections against abuses and illegitimate contracts, all of which could easily be interpreted as the interference of government power. In practice, the very possibility of a free migrant was inseparable from forms of government surveillance. From medical inspections to the regulation of steamships, from contract laws to "liable to become a public charge" clauses, migrants were distinguished into those who were part of the global engine of intercourse and those who were a potential threat or dead weight. The individual under government surveillance was the foundation of the idea of the free migrant and of the new migration laws and identification techniques that emerged at the end of the nineteenth century.

Standardization

Merely isolating the individual was not enough to generate an identity. In fact it made the process more difficult. How was it possible to fix and verify an identity not grounded in a network of mutually accountable relationships? The very act of trying to identify an individual at the border made the development of new techniques into an inescapable necessity. Any previous identity produced by evasive and potentially exploitative social networks was inherently unreliable. A new identity had to be generated on the spot. Indeed, the very construction of the "free" migrants was the act of ripping them out of previous social networks and reinserting them into new matrices of bureaucratic power.

The new identity needed to be categorized and easily accessible, that is to say standardized, if it were to be an effective means of regulation. This took two forms: the characterization of each person as a unique, physical object, and the development of technical, testable categories of status, occupation, and family that could be standardized within and across nations. Technologies like photography, fingerprinting, and anthropometric measurement helped to define persons as unique objects. But mere measurement and representation were of limited usefulness without the development of complex relational filing systems. Identification of the corporeal human was of little social significance if it could not be embedded in an institutional memory as retrievable data. Through files and forms organized according to well-defined categories of race, occupation, nationality, and family, identities could be fixed and the information made available to multiple officers and institutions. Individuals themselves had to repeatedly reproduce their recorded identity in order to obtain institutionalized benefits and rights. Technical identification became social and personal identity.[24]

Many of these techniques were first exercised on international migrants through the regulation of Chinese, especially to North America, through the enforcement of Chinese exclusion laws. These laws specified categories of Chinese who could and could not enter. Bureaucrats had to develop techniques to systematically sift through massive numbers of migrants one by one, determine the truth of each claim for admission, and apply a status that could fit each applicant within prefabricated social categories. These included standardized interrogations, the systematic collection of documentary and corroborating evidence, and the evaluation of signs on the individual's body and bearing. This evidence had to be arranged in methodical order with transparent interpretations. But even these technical procedures would have been ineffective without the collaboration of other officials and lawyers around the world in the production of standardized paperwork. Pressure was especially exerted on the Chinese government to clarify the proper authorities and methods of issuing documents and to suppress brokers and agents that might subvert proper identification.

The techniques designed to control Asians became the template for practical workings of general immigration laws in the white settler nations, and ultimately around the world. By the 1920s, appropriation of these laws by particular nations was driven less by practical needs than by the need to produce the documentation expected by other nations and to live up to international standards of a well-governed nation state. States often claimed that immigration law was a domestic concern, not subject to international negotiation. But this very assertion of a unilateral prerogative was part of a broader diffusion and standardization of principles about what it meant to be a sovereign state within an international system.

The History of International Identification and Identities

The entire history of global migration control and identity documentation, not to mention the globalization of borders, is an extremely broad topic. This book focuses on the documentation of status and the formulation of the border as a site of control, arguing that basic principles were developed through the control of migration from Asia to the white settler nations in the late nineteenth century. Less attention is given to other equally important and arguably more fundamental procedures, such as the global development of medical inspections and technologies of physical identification, including photography and fingerprints. In particular, the creation of that other East-West divide, the one separating Europe from the Ottoman Empire and (sometimes) Russia, was a crucial nexus for the creation of modern sanitary cordons, medical inspections, and refugee policies. And the development of physical identification technologies such as fingerprints took place on a global scale in which colonies were very prominent sites.[25]

Also, the public debates and political coalitions that are the meat and potatoes of most nationally based studies of migration policy are not prominent
in this analysis. Such approaches are very relevant for understanding the timing and specifics of certain migration policies but rarely look at the effects of
those policies, begging the question of how politics and legislation matter.
They also take for granted the broader principles of border control that have
framed those debates and policies, and were more the products of enforcement than of political debate. Of course, race and its role in ordering the
world is the crucial context for understanding both migration policy and its
enforcement in the nineteenth century.[26] If race seems to be downplayed in
this work in favor of a focus on "civilization" and technical discussions of law
and administration, this is only because I want to emphasize the extent to
which seemingly neutral vocabulary can redeploy principles of hierarchy and
discrimination even as it claims to overcome them.

My analysis is strongly influenced by Michel Foucault's microphysics of
power and institutions that actively produce knowledge and individual identities, especially through the disciplines of examination, enclosure, and standardization. Many other studies have emphasized the role of migration laws
in creating racial and sexual identities, a few drawing explicitly on Foucault.[27]
But they have largely focused on the racial and sexual categories that marginalized and excluded migrants from the national body. Very often, they
imply that once we unmask the technologies of the state we can recover a
more equitable social justice or more radical individuality. In other words,
the assertion of individuality and incorporative ideals of the nation are taken
as the standpoint from which to critique power rather than as the exercise of
power. To be sure, categorization, distribution, and normalizing judgments
are important aspects of the microphysics of power. But the particular categories themselves are of less significance than the processes of individualization and categorization. The specific racial, occupational, kin, and political
contents of migration categories have shifted over time and across nations,
always contested even from their very inception. The individualities and nations that are the objects and frames of these categories, however, are almost
never questioned.

In the words of Foucault,

Perhaps, we should abandon a whole tradition that allows us to imagine
that knowledge can exist only where the power relations are suspended
and that knowledge can develop only outside its injunctions, its demands

and its interests. . . . We must cease once and for all to describe the effects of power in negative terms: it "excludes," it "represses," it "censors," it "abstracts," it "masks," it "conceals." In fact power produces; it produces reality; it produces domains of objects and rituals of truth.[28]

Foucault suggests that we think of "not the 'centre of power,' not a network of forces, but a multiple network of diverse elements."[29] Migrants were not only the objects of monolithic state regulation, but one of the diverse elements that created the knowledge and regulation of mobility. To critique the repressive activities of migration categories is precisely to demand the gentleness, humanity, and inclusivity that are the hallmark of modern power, to re-create the liberal tradition of fearing power as an external imposition. I follow Foucault in emphasizing the modern human soul as the primary product of power rather than the site of critique, but I go beyond him in situating this power globally.

The book is divided into four parts. Part 1 takes a broad look at the rise of mass migration and new processes of regulation up to the 1870s. The four chapters in this part focus, respectively, on premodern regulation, patterns of global migration, the surveillance of Asian indenture, and the centralization of regulation. Six related themes are developed: (1) the ways in which Asian migrations have been forgotten and placed outside progressive trends of world history through the creation of borders across the Pacific, thus obscuring the hierarchies within globalization; (2) the simplification of multiple sites of regulation in favor of national borders and centralized controls; (3) the privileging of individuals and their families as the natural units of migration; (4) the creation of the "free" migrant as the main object of regulation; (5) the suppression of private forms of organization other than those that are willing to collaborate closely with the government, and the importance of the latter in developing new forms of state regulation; and (6) the rise of laissez-faire ideals as inseparable from the formation of an international system and centralized controls. In sum, part 1 argues that the mass mobility of "free" migrants has been inseparable from the emergence of new forms of control, with threads of power extending from ideologies of world order and inequality, to national borders, through charitable organizations, transportation companies, brokers, and migrant businesses, and down to the surveillance of individual bodies and our deepest feelings of social and personal identity.

Part 2 takes up the narrative of how the principles of modern migration control were produced out of the restriction of Asian migration to the white settler nations in the late nineteenth century. It begins with a discussion of the administrative, political, and ideological difficulties of initial attempts to control Chinese migration in the middle of the century. Different nations, departments, and individuals disagreed on how to interpret the laws and who had the authority to interpret them. Continuing international crises with China in the late 1880s over migration and indemnification, and struggles between central and local enforcement institutions in the white settler nations, led to the first unambiguous legal decisions and diplomatic policies that justified border control in the context of liberal ideology. The nation and "civilization" replaced the individual as the site of "universal" rights, and the border marked the limit of where such rights needed to be recognized. Many of the documents used in this section are familiar from the specific histories of Chinese exclusion in each nation. Rather than reconstitute the details of each of those histories, the account constructs the story as an international process and emphasizes the emergence of general principles from these encounters.

Part 3 analyzes the practical enforcement of the new principles of border control through the administration of the U.S. Chinese exclusion laws at the turn of the twentieth century. The United States is particularly important because, unlike British dominions, it was an independent nation state dealing directly with Asian nations and was repeatedly compelled to justify the policy and practice of migration control within an international system. As a result, the U.S. laws were also compelled to make the clearest distinctions between certain kinds of people who were and were not allowed to move: those that embodied the progressive promise of intercourse and those that threatened to undermine liberal institutions. Five processes are emphasized: (1) the extraction of individuals from their social networks and reinsertion into new administrative categories and cross-referenced files; (2) the establishment of what Aristide Zolberg has felicitously called "remote control" by consuls in China;[30] (3) the standardization of procedures within the United States and across nations; (4) the continuing failure of migration control to achieve its stated objectives and the reasons for those failures; and (5) the symbolic power of border encounters in asserting an international order of states and hierarchies.

Taken together, parts 2 and 3 describe the creation of an institutional trajectory for modern migration control in a world of nations and individuals. Some of the prominent features of this creation included:

- **Bureaucratic procedure as a nexus of interests and power.** In speaking of identity documents and migration control, it is easy to fall into an analytic rhetoric of state power and invasive bureaucracies versus the freedom and rights of the individual. Conventional narratives of national migration control policies are often plotted as a story of democratic rights gradually chipped away by relentless and unaccountable bureaucracies. But in practice, democratic and popular institutions were often more willing to completely disregard migrant rights than were the bureaucrats and executive institutions that were responsive to multiple domestic and international pressures. The need to participate in an international system and negotiate multiple demands ultimately proved stronger than constitutional protections and rule of law in preserving the last vestiges of migrant rights.

Actual migration procedures emerged at the nexus of several competing interests and were generated from innumerable decisions, encounters, pressures, and expedient compromises around the world. The participants included migrants and lawyers evading rules, exploiting loopholes, challenging procedures, or demanding by-the-book interpretations; clerks and midlevel officials making daily decisions; departmental officials constructing definitions, writing regulations, and justifying policy; diplomatic officials insisting on the need to exercise control with a sensitivity toward broader international concerns; and public remonstrations and sensationalistic media that highlighted both ineffective enforcement and inhumane cases of red tape. All participants complained about the obscure and inefficient procedures yet constantly reinforced them by insisting on rigorous adherence in the interest of their own immediate benefits or of greater long-term predictability. Endless contestation and compromises produced procedures that did not serve any one interest but became the very arena that shaped the possibility of further interaction, even as bureaucratization itself became the common nemesis and scapegoat for all.

- **Asia as problem.** The establishment of modern migration control entailed a systematic attack on nonofficial sources of identity and organization of migration. It was also an endless process of disciplining civil servants as well as the migrants themselves. But officials framed their explanations of the consistent failures of migration control as a fight not against international networks, failed regulations, and errant civil servants, but against the corruption of the Chinese state and culture. Thus, the divide between civilized and uncivilized was privileged as the main obstacle to global intercourse and rule of law.

• **Migration control as ceremony.** Complex and technical procedures almost never achieved their stated intention of ascertaining the "truth" and "rights" of each individual case. Quite the opposite, they even entrenched and facilitated the reproduction of fraud. Officials were aware of these short-comings, but their reforms continued to reinforce precisely those procedures that generated fraud in the first place. This is because the main achievement of identification procedures was not to document identities but to produce them. Thus, the suppression of "fraud" and discovery of "real" identities was much less important than the process of compelling migrants to appropriate and continually reproduce new identities that were now entrenched within new cross-referenced networks of surveillance. This was not only a mechanical process, but a symbolic act of situating migrants within new social relations and hierarchies. As such, the procedures were increasingly effective the more they took on a ceremonial and even ritualized quality. Migrant procedure was a physical and symbolic orchestration of social relationships that situated the participants in relation to each other and to greater "truths" about rule of law and the nature of global order.

Part 4 looks at the global diffusion of these principles and practices during the early twentieth century. Even social movements that opposed immigration laws, such as the Chinese anti-American boycott of 1905 and Gandhi's satyagraha movement in Africa, reinforced the general principles of migration control while criticizing only specific aspects. They helped internalize those principles through intense physical, intellectual, and spiritual mobilization, transforming the protection of national borders into an exercise of individual and collective self-discipline, purity, procedural egalitarianism, and national regeneration. Ultimately, the main objection against immigration laws was that they should not humiliate legal migrants or permit discrimination after entry on any basis except admission status, objections that played an important role in the further refinement and expansion of migration controls. By the 1910s, standardized templates of migration control began to diffuse across the world, partly as a result of the need to conform to international documentation standards, but mostly as a demonstration of the ability to adopt modern international institutions.

The conclusion discusses how these principles and procedures—and the continued forgetting of the history that produced them—still shape contemporary migration control and possibilities of reform. No constructive suggestions for the future are offered.

Part I

Borders in Transformation

Many aver that the story confers no right on anyone to pass judgment on the doorkeeper. Whatever he may seem to us, he is yet a servant of the Law; that is, he belongs to the law and as such is beyond human judgment.

There also exists an interpretation which claims that the deluded person is really the doorkeeper. . . . The argument is that he does not know the law from inside, he knows only the way that leads to it, where he patrols up and down. His ideas of the interior are assumed to be childish, and it is supposed that he himself is afraid of the other guardians whom he holds up as bogies before the man. Indeed, he fears them more than the man does, since the man is determined to enter after hearing about the dreadful guardians of the interior.

He is deceived also about his relation to the man from the country, for he is inferior to the man and does not know it. In the first place, a bondman is always subject to a free man. Now the man from the country is really free, he can go where he likes, it is only the Law that is closed to him, and access to the Law is forbidden him only by one individual, the doorkeeper. When he sits down on the stool by the side of the door and stays there for the rest of his life, he does it of his own free will; in the story there is no mention of any compulsion. But the doorkeeper is bound to his post by his very office, he does not dare go out into the country, nor apparently may he go into the interior of the Law, even should he wish to.　　　　—Kafka, *The Trial*

1

Consolidating Identities,
Sixteenth to Nineteenth Centuries

Passports and the regulation of human mobility are nothing new in world history. State and nonstate institutions have compelled, promoted, and hindered movement on the basis of language, culture, occupation, status, wealth, family, property, race, religion, or any number of other qualities since at least the beginning of written records. Contemporary methods of control were built on these historical practices. But since the eighteenth century, the great heterogeneity of past techniques and identities has been distilled into two fundamental principles: the individual and the nation. Other categories of control have persisted, especially health, family, wealth, occupation, race, and political orientation. But unlike nationality and the individual, they are constantly challenged and debated, with critics and defenders alike appealing to individual rights and national interest as both the sources and the objects of better regulation.

Changes in the regulation of mobility are apparent in the very sources used to measure migration. Before the nineteenth century, regulations were designed, among other things, to protect trade and occupational privileges, control labor, collect taxes, limit access to local communal property, defend private property, distinguish between classes, and monitor vagrants, bandits, and other subversives. Knowledge of that migration comes from bills of lading, indenture contracts, trading licenses, town registration rolls, genealogies, shipping rosters, corvée rosters, deportation records, vagrancy arrests, safe-passages, and letters of recommendation. By the middle of the nineteenth century, migrants were counted almost entirely as a consequence of crossing state borders and encountering national governments. Migration statistics were generated by government officials at transportation hubs who counted individuals and fitted them to predetermined categories of nationality, health, occupation, and race. These statistics and files continued to serve many of the purposes of earlier controls, but access to rights and privileges increasingly revolved around the single issue of the conditions under which individuals crossed national borders and were recorded into these databases. The diverse and complex range of communal, relational, and networked identities were rendered increasingly irrelevant.

The simplification of mobility regulation after the mid-nineteenth century took place in the context of two developments: the centralization of state power and emergent ideals of free mobility. National states and the institutions of freedom found common cause in the attack on local powers, corporate privileges, and the private organization of labor through slavery, indenture, and master-servant laws. The liberation of the individual migrant firmly relocated the migrant under the jurisdiction of public rather than private institutions. Even as old forms of control were finally dismantled around the Atlantic by the 1860s, new ones were constructed, such as medical exams at the border, surveillance of transportation agents, the citizen-alien distinction, and racial exclusions, all of which had to be formulated and justified in the name of preserving freedoms. This gradual process is best described not in terms of intensification or reduction of surveillance but in terms of transformations in the methods of control and identification. Overlapping jurisdictions, corporate privileges, and the extension of personal protection were replaced by territorial borders and the citizen-alien distinction as the main sites of regulation, all grounded in the twin languages of individual freedom and national interest.

Migration in the Law of Nations

Before the nineteenth century, European writings on the law of nations grounded discussions of human mobility in concerns over the proper relationships between the rights of the free individual and the national community. Some of the strongest statements on the need for states to respect the natural right of free mobility were produced in the sixteenth century. Over time, these were qualified with more nuanced discussions of the exercise of natural rights made possible by the existence of a stable political community, and of the acceptable limits of policing that community against unconstrained mobility. By the end of the eighteenth century, the need for state self-preservation had largely superseded the rights of mobility and duties of hospitality. These principles, however, only had a tenuous relationship with actual practices of mobility and control. They were more an account of how things *should* be than of how they were. But many of the specific formulations that justified both free movement and control proved quite enduring, far beyond the context that produced them. By the mid-nineteenth century, the phraseology of the law of nations pervaded diplomatic and legal relations around the world, even as the original reasoning behind them was forgotten or rejected.

A burst of learned assertions about the natural rights of free movement and trade accompanied European expansion into Asia and the Americas in the sixteenth century. Francisco de Vitoria's 1539 critique of Spanish conquests in the Americas contained one of the most influential assertions ever of a fundamental right of free movement and commerce that existed prior to the laws of man. He began by insisting that the Indians had true dominion over themselves much like any European nation, and that the Spanish had no right to make war on them merely because they were barbarians, unbelievers, and sinners. On the other hand, the Spanish did have a just cause for war if the Indians refused the Spaniards' right to travel and dwell peacefully among them. These rights were an aspect of divine law, as Vitoria demonstrated through scriptural passages that enjoined men to treat strangers with hospitality. They also had precedents in human law and custom, as demonstrated by existing practices of free mobility between France and Spain and between barbarian nations. Vitoria framed the bulk of his argument, however, in terms of natural law. This meant that the right of free mobility was rooted in (1) reasoning about that which was of greatest benefit to all mankind, leading to the conclusion that it was "inhuman to treat strangers and travelers badly without some special cause"; (2) the fundamental idea that all things not harmful or detrimental to others are lawful; and (3) the natural freedom of man at the beginning of the world, from which it could be derived that, "When all things were held in common, everyone was allowed to visit and travel through any land he wished. This right was clearly not taken away by the division of property." Any human enactment that barred the peaceful enjoyment of this natural right "would be inhumane and unreasonable, and therefore without force of law."[1]

In his 1588 work, *On Nature in the New World,* Spanish scholar José de Acosta extended this same logic to China. He wrote that the Chinese death penalty for foreigners entering without royal orders was unfair and inhuman, adding that "nothing is more deeply engraved in human nature than the love for learning and the right to experience new things."[2] And in 1608 Dutch lawyer Hugo Grotius began his *Freedom of the Seas,* a polemic against

Portuguese claims to exclusive rights over the Indian Ocean trade, with an assertion that the right of free trade and travel was a "most specific and unimpeachable axiom of the Law of Nations . . . the spirit of which is self-evident and immutable." This axiom could be empirically observed in God's work:

> God Himself says this spellbind through the voice of nature; and inasmuch as it is not His will to have Nature supply every place with all the necessaries of life, He ordains that some nations excel in one art and others in another. Why is this his will, except it be that He wished human friendships to be engendered by mutual needs and resources, lest individuals deeming themselves entirely sufficient unto themselves should for that very reason be rendered unsociable.[3]

These declarations of the inalienable right of free mobility were mostly written as challenges from expansive new polities against previously established powers and claims. Over the next two centuries, as the law of nations grew more concerned with international relations in Europe, it focused more on the creation of a stable political community as the source of human well-being. Assertions of the natural rights of mobility were increasingly qualified by an overriding concern with allegiance and the mutual obligations of individuals and states. The prestige of the natural law tradition continued to grow, but the conditions found in a hypothetical state of nature became less relevant than the need for self-protection through civil society. The long-term interests of the individual were best achieved by restraining the wanton fulfillment of desires through the promotion of sociability and harmonious cooperation under the protection of a state. As Samuel Pufendorf explained in *The Law of Nature and Nations* in 1688, states were established for the safety of men and would be imperiled if men could come and go without recognizing this sovereignty. Thus, "it is understood as a common law of all states that, whoever has passed into the territory of any state, and all the more if he wishes to enjoy its advantages, is held to have given up his natural liberty, and to have subjected himself to the sovereignty of that state."[4] From there, the work of the law of nations was to discover the most rational ordering of harmony and stability between states.

Although strongly committed to the idea of natural law, Pufendorf explicitly disagreed with Vitoria on the need to admit all foreigners for trade and travel, saying that the duty of hospitality should be recognized as a free gift rather than an obligation. He admitted that it was a duty of humanity for a state to admit strangers and provide them with shelter and hospitality. But this duty was grounded more in the benefits that intercourse could bring to the state than in the inalienable right of mobility. States had a perfect right to exclude strangers who had "no honorable or necessary reason for being away from home," were not upright, or were not able to pay for their own lodging (3:3, §9). He recognized man's natural freedom to migrate at pleasure and be a "citizen of the world" like Socrates (8:11, §2). But he assumed that most individuals would not choose this path unless the state in which they resided did not adequately provide for their welfare. Moreover, if a nation did not desire to visit other nations, it was not obliged to receive strangers without good reason. In this vein, he disagreed with contemporaries who found China's exclusive policies to be arrogant, inhospitable, and overcautious.[5] China and Sparta were examples of nations that, "wishing to prevent the corruption and debasing of their ancient customs by contact with such sightseers," legitimately doubted that hospitality was part of natural law (3:3, §9).

Writing in 1764, Christian Wolff developed this logic into a stronger and more clearly formulated stance in favor of a state's right to exclude at will, again using China as a key example. A nation's duty to foster commerce and migration was grounded entirely in the benefits and wealth that could accrue through such exchanges. The Chinese state was exemplary in its enlightened regard for the welfare of its people and had the resources to provide for its own needs. Thus it had little obligation to foster interactions and could devote its entire energies to self-protection:

> The Chinese, when they wished to introduce the best form of a state, so far as they could, and therefore to perfect the same perpetually more and more, and to preserve the morals of their nation pure and uncorrupted, prohibited all commerce with other nations; nor did they allow access to their lands by foreigners, although they had an abundance of the things suitable for engaging in commerce with other nations. Nor can it be said that therein they violated the natural law of nations. For the obstacles had to be removed which could prevent them from perfecting themselves and their condition as it ought to be done.[6]

Swiss jurist Emerich de Vattel's 1758 work *The Law of Nations* carried these ideas into the twentieth century through frequent citation by diplomats and lawyers. Vattel wrote with a practical clarity on migration, taking a middle path between the demands of free mobility and states' rights. In the spirit of his contemporaries, he based his work on the fundamental principle that "The aim of civil society is to procure for its citizens the necessities, the comforts, and the pleasures of life, and in general their happiness; to secure to each the peaceful enjoyment of his property and a sure means of obtaining justice; and finally to defend the whole body against all external violence." As such, it was morally "bound to preserve its corporate existence."[7] He admitted the premises of Vitoria and Grotius that nature "intended earth to be man's dwelling-place," but,

> If in the abstract this right is a necessary and perfect one, it must be observed that it is only an imperfect one relative to each individual country; for, on the other hand, every Nation has the right to refuse to admit an alien into its territory when to do so would expose it to evident danger or cause it serious trouble. This right is based upon a care for its own security which it owes as a duty to itself. By reason of its natural liberty it is for each Nation to decide whether it is or is not in a position to receive an alien (1:§229–30).

Nineteenth-century proponents of immigration restriction frequently cited Vattel's statement that "The owner of a territory can forbid entrance into it, or grant the privilege upon such conditions as he thinks fit to impose" (2:§135). But they rarely acknowledged Vattel's subsequent discussion of the duties and "right in conscience" of the owner in the application of such restrictions. To forbid the entry and residence of foreigners without specific or important reasons was to abuse the right of exclusion. A nation also had a duty to provide inns, fair treatment, and hospitality to strangers. "In doing so each citizen will fulfill his duties towards mankind and will at the same time be of service to his country. Honor is the certain reward of virtue, and the good-will which is won by kindness often produces results which are of great importance to the State" (2:§139). He also insisted that to except one nation from rights granted to others "is a discrimination which would constitute an injury, since it could only proceed from ill-will or contempt" (2:§137). In sum, Vattel staked out a somewhat ambiguous ground within which each state had to decide for itself the proper balance between honor and sovereign prerogative.

The rights of immigration were of much less interest to legal theorists than what Vattel called the "celebrated question" of the right of emigration. This latter was more directly linked to the pressing issues of defining a social compact and civil society. All authors recognized a variety of practices among states. Most agreed that the best state policies required permission for departure but easily granted that permission except during periods of crisis or if the individual had outstanding debts. Wolff went furthest in supporting the right to limit departure entirely, arguing that the right of emigration did not exist as a natural right prior to the formation of states because the civil society from which an individual could depart did not exist in the state of nature.[8] North American political thinkers such as Benjamin Franklin and Thomas Jefferson swung to the other extreme, insisting that people should be free to depart without permission in order to choose the state that could best provide for their welfare and self-preservation.[9]

Vattel again staked a middle ground, following John Locke's argument that every man was born free and could, upon reaching the age of reason, decide "whether it is well for him to join the society in which he happens to be by birth."[10] Vattel explained that a choice to depart would carry a debt of gratitude to recompense the state for the protection and education already received, and that it must not endanger the welfare of society. Still, an honorable man would depart permanently only under the conditions in which an absolute right of renunciation existed: an inability to obtain subsistence, a state that did not discharge its obligations to him, or a changing of the social compact without his consent. From the perspective of the state, to allow free departure with little or no good reason was contrary to its welfare and safety. Such a privilege would "only be suffered to exist in a country which is without resources and is unable to supply the needs of its inhabitants. In such a country there can only be an imperfect society" (1:§222). In other words, a state that allowed free departure was the kind of incompetent state from which a person had a right to depart freely in the first place.

Writers on the law of nations generally spoke of migration either as the temporary passage and residence of individuals for the sake of business, study, or curiosity, or as an issue of exile and allegiance. They did not conceive of migration as the mass labor migrations of the nineteenth century or, for that matter, even the labor migrations, seasonal travel, and self-regulating trade diasporas of the early modern era. Grotius argued that mass emigration was illegal, "for if such migration were permissible the civil society could not exist."[11] Pufendorf disagreed, reasoning that "The destruction of one [civil society] is the creation of another, and the decrease of one works to the increase of another. After mankind had multiplied nature desired that it be gathered into civil societies, but she never commanded that this or that state endure and flourish forever" (8:11, §4). Neither formulation spoke to twentieth-century fears of mass immigration as more of a threat to the receiving state than to the sending state. In 1788 Georg Freidrich von Martens expressed the question of migration control in a way that highlighted the basic assumptions of his time. He argued that sovereign states had the right to forbid all entry, although in contemporary Europe no powers refused such passage, and most did not even require permission. Such a system was possible because "One of the principal objects of police is to hinder the subjects from emigrating in too great numbers."[12] In a world of states primarily concerned with regulating the political community through domestic controls and the restriction of exit, immigration control could indeed be limited to talk of hospitality, virtue, lodging, and the possible dangers posed by sightseers and dishonorable individuals.

Vattel's definition of emigrants as those who "take their families with them and all moveable property" (1:§224) seems to resonate with contemporary understandings of immigrants. For example, Black's Law Dictionary now defines an immigrant as "a person who arrives in a country with the intention of settling there permanently."[13] In neither case does the definition capture the temporary and uncertain nature of most mobility. And any perceived similarity also glosses over the specific context in which each assertion was produced. Vattel's definition emerged from his overriding concern with issues of exile, allegiance, and the maintenance of civic bonds and welfare that could be disrupted through indiscriminate departure. These concerns have become increasingly under attack and irrelevant since the nineteenth century, but the definition itself has persisted, written into migration laws and circulated as common knowledge about "true" or "traditional" immigration. It is often juxtaposed to the "undesirability" of more temporary intentions or the marginal position of "migrant labor." Vattel's definition has proven versatile enough to play an important role in the politics of modern national identity, but in the process of translation it has become abstracted into a description of migration per se, independent of political relationships. This depoliticized definition has come to define both the object and the proper product of regulation. This happened even as the ideas of the state of nature, the social compact, honor, obligation, and exile that had once generated this definition were gradually forgotten and replaced by the closely related concepts of sovereignty, self-preservation, the good of society, intercourse, contract, and consent. This would ultimately lead to a new vocabulary of selection, assimilation, and border control as the best expression of the problems of immigration in a modern world where states were taken for granted more than mobility.

Identification Networks

The law of nations depicted an ideal-type migration world of states and individuals that barely hinted at actual practices of migration and regulation. Nonstate groups such as guilds, religious orders, ethnic trading diasporas, and lineages were often most active and had most at stake in regulating their membership and mobility. These institutions controlled access to social and material resources and to the paraphernalia necessary to be identified as a member. As such, the identification and regulation of much premodern migration was part and parcel of the regulation of occupation, status, class, and property. Travel was difficult without the ability to make connections through bloodline, breeding, occupation, or learning, all of which could be documented through skills, clothing, manners, and personal introductions. Potential migrants who did not have these skills or social connections had to establish a relationship with those who did. This could mean anything from being born into an ethnic trading diaspora, to joining a religious order, finding a prominent patron who could provide travel documents, becoming a household member or domestic servant, or traveling under conditions of indenture or slavery.

Short-distance and seasonal movement was most likely to be channeled through networks of merchants, craftsmen, specialized laborers, and family. Skilled migrants, including herders and other nomadic groups, moved on specialized circuits through markets, towns, pastures, and estates in Asia, Europe, Africa, and even in a Russia bound by serfdom. They also shared (or guarded) knowledge about new markets, patrons, and natural resources. Entire villages often specialized in skills such as banking, stonemasonry, letter writing, or trade in particular products, sending members to ply their trade across regions, oceans, and continents. By the late sixteenth century, such networks spanned the world from Manila to Amsterdam and back. These networks could be regulated through guilds and trade associations, or more informally through ethnic trade diasporas in which trust and secrecy were reinforced by relatively closed networks of kin and ethnicity. Successful movement in pursuit of an occupation entailed participation in the norms and regulations of a network, participation that may well have been part of the family for generations. Distance could often weaken these obligations and controls, but other mechanisms could be used to create multiple layers of trust and obligation. Merchants used adoption and strategic marriage as a way to recruit reliable managers and local connections. Religious conversion could further strengthen those bonds as well as establish status in local societies, whether by obtaining patronage and protection by adopting a local religion or by reinforcing separation from local social obligations by adhering to a religion of outsiders. Miners, bandits, and merchants pooling money for long-distance expeditions also used written contracts, sworn oaths, and ritual to build trust and control.[14]

In all of these networks, it was possible to tell who belonged and who did not by their tools, speech, clothing, bearing, and knowledge. These markers often corresponded to class and status identities in local societies. This meant that migrants maintained signs and practices that could identify them to the outer world as well as to their peers. Merchants were often identifiable through their ethnic difference and exemption from many local obligations. Envoys, nobles, and officials could be recognized by their retinue, manners, clothes, knowledge of genealogies, personal familiarity with their peers, and skills in the arts of rulership. Intellectual workers such as Christian monks, Islamic legal scholars, and Chinese officials shared not only arcane knowledge but also the specialized languages of Latin, classical Arabic and Persian, and the language of the Chinese classics that could be used to identify themselves to local rulers as well as to each other. Pilgrims also moved through well-trodden routes with established infrastructures, generally in large groups that both protected them and identified them to outsiders.

Travel documents were as much letters of introduction as identification documents. They were just as important for who signed them as for who carried them, embedding the bearer in a network of human relationships. Documents that listed the specifics of a traveler focused less on personal characteristics than on status as the master of a ship, caravan, or retinue, noting all of the accompanying goods, animals, clothes, and followers. This emphasis on the outer paraphernalia could entirely replace any description of physical identity, and common stories of mistaken identity and kings traveling incognito testify to the possibility of one person usurping the outer trappings of another (although it was difficult to usurp the trappings of a skilled craftsman, scholar, merchant, or noble without great expense and effort).[15]

For many, contracts and bills of sale functioned as travel documents. The expensive and risky act of long-distance travel was possible only by subjection, willing or not, to somebody who had the resources to fund their mobility. This often meant that wealthy merchants, landowners, nobles, and agents of the state sponsored migrants as employees, indentures, slaves, soldiers, corvée laborers, and people under other forms of debt or labor obligations. Not only did merchants and states have the necessary resources to support this movement, but they could also treat their investments in terms of aggregate costs and benefits that could control for risk much better than an individual migrant for whom a long, expensive voyage could be an all-or-nothing proposition. The financiers further reduced their risks through a variety of legal and political protections, such as monopolies, contracts, and master-servant laws.[16] In all of these cases, the facilitation and control of mobility was most effective when state and private actors worked in collaboration—or were one and the same.

States and Mobility

It is almost the definition of a state that it is concerned with the regulation of population. This concern was often framed as the preservation of security, prosperity, or revenue. Censuses, tax rolls, registrations, travel permits, naturalization, inheritance laws, serfdom, and a variety of techniques for the distribution of rights and privileges were implemented to this end and often had significant implications for individual mobility. But states were only one aspect of a dense network of interlocking institutions. Effective mobility controls relied on the collaboration of local elites, communities, and other institutions described above. Even relatively strong and centralized states such as the Russian and Chinese empires delegated most of the work of surveillance and identification to estates, villages, lineages, religious institutions, and other corporate groups.[17] Enforcement was so entwined that it was often hard to make a clear distinction between state, local, and private regulation of movement (not to mention the very existence of these distinct spheres).

Despite the law of nations' focus on the relationship of states to exiles and traders, states were also quite involved in more elaborate ventures of mass mobility, such as relocating conquered populations, evacuating people from sensitive areas, promoting settlement of underpopulated areas, establishing garrisons, organizing labor corvées, and importing slaves and servants. Some of these movements were impelled by direct force, although long-term projects were most effectively implemented through collaboration with merchants, landowners, and other local elite, or even by directly granting incentives to migrants themselves. Such collaboration could take different forms and produce different results. For example, much of the work of settling western China after the devastation of the Ming to Qing transition in the mid-seventeenth century was delegated to merchant-dominated native place institutions. Settlement resulted in an extensive small landholding economy that was part of a broader trend toward easier mobility, commercialization, and taxation of individual households across the empire.[18] In contrast, the frontier of southern Russia was an area of continuing raids and warfare. Expansion relied on collaboration with military elites, who were rewarded with land grants and control over labor. Territorial expansion played an important role in the consolidation of serfdom, although the empire did make a concerted attempt to attract more independent settler groups with commercial and artisanal skills in the late eighteenth century by offering loans, land, and temporary tax exemptions. This latter project was only partially successful due to exit controls in most European countries.[19]

States relied on local institutions and elites because they had the most knowledge and influence over local society. In any case, few states ever had the resources to unilaterally regulate migrants beyond a limited number of individuals and groups that were directly connected to the central government. Collaboration with local institutions helped shoulder the expense and bear responsibility for errant individuals. In turn, local groups were happy to have state backing in monitoring their own membership. On the other hand, the delegation of power also created a space for local institutions to protect their subordinates, demand privileges, and develop systematic and often lucrative means of evading state regulation. In this context, it is not surprising that state regulations were often honored as much in the breach as in the observance. Collaboration was most effective when there was a convergence of interests between the state, the locality, and private interests, such as that between merchants, colonial planters, African rulers, and Western European property regimes to channel African slaves across the Atlantic.

Across long distances, states and sovereigns could act as yet one more of the many migration networks described in the last section. Official envoys, nobles, merchant caravans, and ships often carried papers addressed to foreign officials requesting free passage and protection for a specific journey. The utility of such a document depended on the prestige and power of the person who issued it. It was less important that a physical individual was properly identified than that a person who could guarantee the status and good conduct of the bearer embossed the proper seals of authority on it. A typical example is this Tibetan passport from 1688:

From the noble Lhassa, the Wheel of the Law. To those that are on the road as far as Arya Dèsa or India, to clerical, laical, noble, ignoble, monastic communities, lay communities; to residents of forts, stewards, managers of affairs, to Mongols, Tibetans, Turks and to dwellers in tents in the desert; to public messengers and ambassadors going to and fro; to keepers and precluders of bye-ways; to the headmen, subjects, all those charged with the responsibility of civil and military affairs; to all these is ordered. These four, guests of Phun-tschogs Lcang-lo-can in Lhassa Christian merchants, after having exchanged their merchandise, going back to their country, having with them sixteen loads on beasts, wherever they go, always assist them with whatever they need, especially compulsory horse transportation; and do not hinder, rob, or plunder them; but let them go to and fro in peace. Action with the above intention leads propitiously to bodhi.[20]

Similar in purpose, but appealing to different cultural norms, was a paper that the governor of Connecticut issued in 1805 to Benjamin Silliman, the president of Yale. It listed Silliman's titles and positions, noted his "respectable parentage," and concluded that

The said Professor Silliman is therefore Hereby Recommended to all nations & Countries to & through which He may have occasion to travel, for His safe Protection & Passport among all their People.—And He is hereby commended particularly to the kind notice, attention & assistance of all Literary & Scientific men, in the several Countries & Places, where he may visit or Reside.[21]

Professor Silliman probably had to rely on the goodwill of his hosts in responding to this request for passage and protection. But most such documents were simultaneously declarations of authority and promises of retaliation if the bearer was mistreated (or, in the Tibetan case, the promise of spiritual reward for good treatment). The bearers were a walking advertisement of a ruler's claim to be the final guarantor of safety and punishment across the land.[22] Local officials and lords often issued similar documents that were valid only in smaller realms within the broader domain. Of course, the authority of rulers did not always extend as far as the bearers of their documents. Then the bearers had to rely on the good intentions of their hosts and their evaluation of the threat of force that backed the document. Hostages and other pledges often proved to be more reliable guarantees of safe passage and residence than mere paper.[23]

Many states required international travelers to exchange their papers at the border for domestic papers that were addressed to local officials and marked out predetermined routes, although this often applied to wealthy convoys, ships, and envoys rather than laborers and petty merchants who posed less of a threat. Entry was frequently restricted to a limited number of port and border towns, where travelers could be confined until they received permission to travel further inland. The conditions varied greatly. In Korea, foreign traders were restricted to walled compounds with living expenses supported by the government.[24] In other cases, like that of Khoqandi merchants in Qing Central Asia in the 1830s, local headmen were tacitly permitted to govern themselves and collect taxes from all foreign merchants.[25] More formal arrangements included treaties signed between Russia and the Qing in 1689 and 1727 that established trading towns at the frontier and detailed arrangements by which Russian merchants could present a passport to Chinese officials at the border to be exchanged for Chinese documents for travel along a predetermined path to Beijing. On their return, Russian traders had to carry a passport issued by the Russian consul in Beijing. Russians who got into trouble were immediately sent back to Russia to be punished by Russian tribunals.[26] Other international treaties have allowed for the recognition of papers issued by foreign sovereigns rather than an exchange of papers at the border. For example, the treaty of friendship of commerce between Denmark and England in 1670, famed for containing the first formal use of the word "passport," described papers that would accompany ships and be recognized by officials in both kingdoms.[27] These practices were increasingly standardized across Eurasia up to the end of the eighteenth century, through treaties and customs that provided for foreign merchants to be subject to their own laws and deal with local officials through headmen—which generally meant rule by the customs of the merchant diaspora rather than any state.[28]

The use of documents to regulate inland travel required collaboration with local elites. For example, monks and merchants who arrived at the coastal borders of Song China (960–1279) needed to supplement their documents from home with the sponsorship of two guarantors in China and to inform officials along their route of their impending arrival in order to obtain entry.[29] In fifteenth-century Korea, a Japanese family on the nearby island of Tsushima was granted the power to issue passports to all Japanese ships, bypassing many Japanese noble families with greater claim to authority.[30] In the Atlantic, the ban against foreigners entering Spanish America was largely enforced by the merchant guilds of Seville, which had a large interest in protecting the monopoly of Spanish subjects in the colonial trade. They identified merchants who qualified for licenses-of-passage, essentially exercising the authority to define Spanish subjects as those who did not compete with their interests.[31]

Many states in Asia and the Atlantic also found common cause with local communities in domestic regulation through vagrancy and poor laws.[32] To local communities, vagrants and paupers were people without legitimate access to local resources. To states, they were potential bandits, sorcerers, tax evaders, and mischief makers. Imprisonment was a common but expensive penalty. An extensive web of vagrancy laws could make expulsion into a more attractive option that directed the vagrant back to a community with the obligation to care for him or her. Northern European towns and parishes sometimes experimented with deporting convicts and paupers to North American colonies that could not easily redeport them back home. The identification of vagrants and paupers was made possible by face-to-face relationships in towns, guilds, and trade diasporas. Any person who did not arrive with an indenture contract, good introductions, property, or skills was a potential burden on the community. Even in a city as large as eighteenth-century Boston, the agent charged with "warning out" indigent migrants could know nearly all of the residents on sight. Nonresidents found in "low circumstances" would be ordered to "depart speedily." Warning out rarely resulted in physical expulsion, but the close surveillance encouraged people to seek employment or depart voluntarily.[33]

When social pressures and threats failed, enforcement was generally difficult. Some North American colonies required licenses for aliens to reside for more than three weeks and for hosts to report strangers to the city authorities. But most laws focused on the shipmasters who imported paupers and convicts rather than on the migrants themselves.[34] For example, a Maryland law of 1676 forbid the entry of felons and convicted malefactors, "afterwards procured by masters of ships, merchants, sailors and others out of the common jails to import into this province and here to sell and dispose of such felons and malefactors as servants, to the great prejudice and grievance of the good people of this province."[35] It required shipmasters to file passenger manifests, post bonds, and swear an oath that they would not sell any such people. In theory, the shipowners had more vested interests and were more easily monitored at the ports. But in practice, they merely added the bonding fees and potential penalties onto the passage money. Even then it was difficult for municipalities to collect penalties from these highly mobile men, and the expenses of litigation deterred many attempts to do so—the same problems that plague migration control to this day.[36]

In all of these cases, territorial borders and the identification of aliens per se were rarely the most common or effective forms of mobility control. Indeed, mobility control was less often the primary object of regulation than a byproduct of efforts to impose taxation or to distribute rights, privileges, and discriminations. Differential taxes, land taxes, poor laws, master-servant laws, naturalization laws, property rights, military obligations, religious affiliation, or the granting of trade monopolies, tax farms, and other special offices were among the many kinds of regulation that had some impact on mobility. The distinction between subjects and foreigners was just one of many possible ways to distribute these rights. Before the late nineteenth century, many states even had difficulty defining a foreigner. In terms of access to rights and resources, nomads or people from a neighboring town could be as foreign as people from beyond the sovereign's jurisdiction. Criteria that had little to do with geographic provenance, such as lineage, occupation, trade, status, and personal connections, generally played the most important role in the distribution of travel privileges. Struggles over these rights were also a key site of interaction between states, localities, and other groups.

The regulation of mobility could be used to help consolidate political power across localities and groups. On market days in medieval England, agents of the king manned toll booths and operated courts of justice in the towns. This not only earned a healthy revenue for the king but also facilitated commerce across the island by providing both domestic and foreign merchants with consistent institutions for resolving disputes as they moved from fair to fair. As the fairs declined in the fourteenth century, the king began to issue patent letters to individual merchants that guaranteed certain rights and liberties across the realm in return for faith and allegiance to the king. These were often just reformulations of liberties that the merchants already possessed, but they opened a rhetorical door for a categorical distinction between aliens and natives through denization and naturalization that was defined by jurisdiction of the king or Parliament.[37] At the same time, the recruitment and naturalization of foreigners without local ties was, as in many other states, a way to obtain services from people whose primary loyalty was to the central sovereign and who would be less likely to rebel. This could even extend to the naturalization of bandits and frontier raiders, on the theory that obtaining access to land and other privileges would cause them to stop their predatory activities.[38]

Dense networks of domestic controls and local interests were a de facto method of controlling entry. Whatever the struggles and differences between different groups, all had an interest in controlling access to resources by outsiders. Common interests in exit control, however, were much more elusive, as could be seen in the persistent discussion of exit control in writings on the law of nations. At times states and local groups shared fears of people escaping their debts and labor obligations. Slavery, serfdom, and master-servant laws were a common method of restricting departures. But even free individuals could not obtain a passport to depart Virginia in the seventeenth century until they had posted a notice of their departure on the church door for two subsequent Sundays, thus giving potential creditors a chance to recover their debts.[39] But the idea of uncontrolled departures also generated in states many fears that were not so widely shared. States especially feared that subjects beyond the reach of domestic surveillance could plot rebellion, become bandits, engage in religious deviance, and drain the wealth of the nation. States also passed laws restricting the exit of people engaged in occupations thought necessary for the well-being of the realm, a concern that often ran against the interests of guilds and trade organizations that preferred to regulate their own wide-ranging connections. European states in the eighteenth century consolidated all of these fears into a general concern that population was part of the national wealth that should not be drained through emigration. It was not until the middle of the nineteenth century that Malthusian overpopulation fears and liberal ideologies of free movement and exit seriously challenged official depictions of emigrants as deserters and a moral evil.[40]

The lack of common interest made exit controls difficult to enforce. For example, Qing officials repeatedly warned that overseas merchants would grow their hair (thus losing the shaved head and queue that identified them as Qing subjects), collude with foreign kings, join foreign armies and pirate bands, sell rice and ships to foreigners, and abandon their filial duties. But the practical enforcement of exit controls was fraught with difficulties and reversals. From 1664 to 1683, with Ming loyalist forces concentrated in Taiwan, the Qing entirely evacuated the southern coast up to twenty miles inland. While effective, such intense militarization was difficult to maintain and undesirable in the long run. Controls were relaxed with the conquest of Taiwan, but new edicts to entirely ban departure from 1717 to 1727 only encouraged permanent departure, piracy, smuggling, and complaints from local officials that the lack of trade hurt local economies. In 1727 long-term overseas residents were granted amnesty if they returned immediately, and new edicts in 1728 granted short-term overseas trade licenses to merchants with good reputations, specific destinations, and bondsmen who could guarantee their return.

The government cultivated private collaboration by licensing special merchant organizations *(hang)* to regulate the trade and ensure proper conduct. But this arrangement guaranteed collusion of local officials with merchant interests more than it ensured the enforcement of Imperial laws.[41] The Great Qing State was no more effective than local North American ports at overcoming the perennial problems of systematic mobility control.

From Town to Nation

Given its focus on political community, it is not surprising that the understanding of migration in the law of nations was somewhat unrealistic. But even the ideas of political community were unclear in terms of the appropriate scale of reference. The emphasis on the social compact in natural law revolved around ideas of personal choice, duty, and gratitude that could be best expressed in a local setting. Indeed, local communities were most likely to make decisions about migration and membership. Yet it is much easier to read the law of nations in terms of large states with distant sovereigns who ruled through law and abstract allegiances. Both types of community existed throughout the early modern world, but the larger state wrested power over membership and migration control away from localities and private organizations by the end of nineteenth century. State centralization and the increased correspondence of territory, power, and social identity took place in polities around the world after the mid-eighteenth century.[42] The following account, however, will focus on the Atlantic world, drawing upon the more extensive research on changes in membership and mobility control.

The law of nations helped point the way toward this shift in the Atlantic world. But many of the key developments were grounded in the ideals of inalienable freedom, equality, and self-rule that the law of nations had increasingly relegated to a now-irrelevant state of nature. The growing attack on special privileges now recuperated these ideals within the framework of the popular state. Along the way, the citizen and alien opposition replaced those privileges as the fundamental legal and political distinction. Territory rather than status and allegiance increasingly defined the jurisdiction of the state, and restrictions on physical mobility within national borders were gradually loosened—although unhindered movement across those newly fortified borders had a much more erratic history.

The correlation of equality before law, territorial sovereignty, border control, free domestic mobility, and the privileging of national over local regulation has a certain logic in hindsight. But the specific results were hardly predetermined. Experimentation and uncertainty characterized much nineteenth-century alien regulation. Even the need for any regulation at all was subject to debate. Most significantly, local communities could deploy ideals of equality, freedom, and self-rule just as easily and often more convincingly than could national governments. Localities challenged national attempts to identify citizens and control mobility as infringements on rights that should belong to the local sphere. Nonetheless, national governments increasingly usurped the power to define and delegate responsibilities and, by the end of the nineteenth century, even monopolized their enforcement.

Before the early nineteenth century, central polities and local communities frequently engaged in a low-level but constant struggle over the identification and regulation of members. In Spain, for example, Aristotelian understandings of community and *jus commune* were invoked in defense of the right of a community to determine its own citizens and of individuals to choose their own community as a natural right of all men. Determination of local membership was grounded in sentiment and local relationships rather than legal distinctions or royal prerogative. These bases of citizenship were said to exist prior to the king's law and were often used to attack the king's right to naturalize courtiers and merchants who belonged to no local community. By and large, the royal government followed local determinations of membership in determining subjecthood, reasoning that the key qualifications of loyalty to the king and intention to obey the law were best indicated by submission to communal obligations.[43] In England and its colonies, local membership regimes were more legalistic, often centering on the "freeman" who could gain full membership rights through a variety of means, such as apprenticeship, redemption, office holding, patrimony, or special grant. The specifics varied from place to place, but they were similar enough to give the sense of common English tradition.[44] At the same time, it was precisely the values of "freedom" and self-rule thought to define this tradition that could justify resistance against the infringement of central power. For example, attempts by Parliament and the king to influence naturalization and migration laws in the North American colonies were key grievances leading to the rebellion.[45]

The French king had greater powers than other eighteenth-century West European sovereigns over the regulation of mobility and aliens. This centralization provided the framework for the mobility controls of the French Revolution, often cited as the birthplace of the modern passport. Inasmuch as the modern passport is an international document addressed to other states, the revolutionary passport does not live up to this claim. After briefly abolishing all movement controls from 1788 to 1792, the revolutionaries refined old regime techniques of limiting exit, controlling domestic movement through local officials, and issuing passports to foreigners entering at the border. The control of vagrancy and protection of the states against conspirators remained important public justifications of internal surveillance.[46] But the revolution was important in that it invested eighteenth-century centralization trends with new political value. Revolutionary France was not to be a monarch wielding his bureaucracy to manage a tangle of unequal privileges, estates, and cliques. It was to be a nation made up of citizens, each individual and equal before law. Accordingly, the passport was an official document of national belonging rather than a semipersonal letter of recommendation. The nation became a key criterion shaping an "us" and a "them"—albeit defined less by territory than by loyalty to the revolution. Even so, the criteria for defining us and them remained vague until the end of the nineteenth century. Indeed, the "them" who needed to be documented were just as likely to be workers and vagrants as foreigners.[47]

The German principalities and their more prosaic concerns of welfare financing deserve more credit for the development of the modern passport as an international document. The deportation of vagrants from one community to the next was especially troublesome in the small jurisdictions of Germany. Some German states expelled thousands of people a year, leading to a chaotic situation of deportation and counterdeportation. After 1816 many began to establish reciprocal deportation treaties in which each state promised to accept the return of its citizens who required poor relief. Similar treaties spread throughout western Europe after the 1860s. The effective working of these treaties depended on being able to reliably document the citizenship of deportees so that their home state would feel compelled to accept them, and to require individuals to carry these documents in their travels.[48]

Whether because of international negotiations, fear of disease and paupers, revolutionary ideology, or fear of revolutionary ideology, the citizen and alien distinction spread around the North Atlantic at the turn of the nineteenth century. Often, cities and towns were first to reframe their traditional membership criteria in terms of citizenship. The constitutions of the United States in 1787 and the Netherlands in 1796 were among the first to consolidate these local jurisdictions into national spaces with equal rights for all citizens, albeit via a framework to distribute powers between local and central governments rather than abolish local prerogatives. In other places, the rights of citizens came through the adoption of Napoleonic law codes in the wake of French conquests. Still other states erected national border controls, deportation and registration laws to protect themselves against revolutionary subversives. As in France, none of this necessarily meant a decisive transformation in the methods to identify subjects and control mobility. Napoleonic regulations often required laborers and artisans to carry workbooks in which their employment history was written, thus directly linking mobility to the needs of employers and industry. "Vagrancy" was also on the rise as a public problem. Whether or not vagrancy actually increased in this period, workhouses, poorhouses, and arrests and deportation of vagrants certainly did. These institutions required substantial outlays of public money, thus generating more concern to systematize the identification of migrants. The simple alien and citizen distinction was gradually refined into gradations such as citizens, residents, denizens, and temporary aliens that defined access to social welfare and whether one was subject to expulsion.[49]

Actual enforcement of alien, workbook, and deportation laws was scattershot. A bewildering variety of laws, papers, and notations were issued and monitored by a hodge-podge of local officials with distinct jurisdictions, variable competency, and frequent susceptibility to bribery. Enforcement could take place at borders, internal checkpoints, registration at inns, and through random encounters with police and soldiers on the road. For their part, employers and sympathetic local residents often helped aliens evade laws, access relief services, and avoid deportation. The intensification of surveillance over lower classes and potential revolutionaries also caused many well-to-do individuals to resent carrying papers, especially those that noted their physical characteristics, feeling that they were only for vagabonds and other disreputable types. By the 1830s, as fears of revolutionary subversion subsided, most elites traveled without passports.[50] By the middle of the nineteenth century, faster and cheaper transportation technologies also made surveillance even more difficult. A rising middle class with tourist ambitions joined the elites as people who expected to travel without obstacles, blurring the distinctions between rich and poor that had once made class profiling an effective tool of enforcement. At the same time, industrialists in search of labor wielded a potent laissez-faire ideology to condemn mobility controls at all levels.

Any new laws to regulate mobility had to be justified in terms of humanitarian concerns or hygiene. Many of the greatest advances in border regulation took place in the context of creating a barrier between Asia and Europe against the threat of medical contagion. In the 1770s Russia, building on its strengths in domestic mobility control, pioneered the creation of a systematic cordon across the Black Sea to prevent the entry of plague and later cholera from the Ottoman Empire. By the 1830s, a chain of stations was established along the Danube with systematic regulations, routine quarantine, and health certificate requirements.[51] Like most migration controls, this one was not effective in the long run. By the 1890s, the Germans felt compelled to help patrol the fortified border between Russia and Poland—originally established to restrict exit from Russia—to help stem the flow of cholera into Germany. Passenger laws to regulate shipboard conditions, such as those enacted in Britain and the United States from 1803 to the middle of the century, also justified government intervention into private enterprise. Even in midcentury England, dominated by laissez-faire ideology and fear of government expenditures, enforcement of the passenger laws led to the creation of the first expert bureaucracy in the country, one that rarely shied away from intervening in the private affairs of shippers and brokers. In New York, these concerns resulted in the creation of the government-run Castle Garden Immigration Station in 1855 to aid migrants and keep them out of the hands of unscrupulous runners.[52]

By and large, however, the second half of the nineteenth century was an era of limited border controls. The revolutionary uprisings of 1848 had caused a brief upsurge of migrant surveillance in western Europe, but from the 1860s to 1880s passport requirements and most internal document checks were abolished in countries around the Atlantic. The constitutions of Bolivia, Ecuador, Mexico, Peru, and Uruguay even stipulated that foreigners could travel freely without passports.[53] By the end of the century even Russia, often held up as the epitome of despotic surveillance, began to loosen its internal movement controls.[54] This did not mean that documents were unnecessary. In the United States, free persons of color often carried passports and letters of introduction to protect themselves from harassment by local officials.[55] Poorer travelers in Europe could show passports to avoid military conscription. Middle-class travelers even found them useful, if only to pick up packages at the local post office. Other travelers, however, found that carrying no documents could help them avoid deportation as fewer and fewer countries would accept deportees without clear evidence of nationality. In fact, even as borders went down, deportation was on the rise in some countries such as Belgium and Germany.[56] This moment of free mobility was not so much the abolition of controls, but an interlude in the repositioning of the power of identification from local to central authorities.

2

Global Migration, 1840–1940

The mass migrations of the nineteenth and early twentieth centuries were a worldwide phenomenon. From the North Atlantic to the South Pacific, hardly any corner of the globe was untouched by migration. These migrations were similar in quantity and organization, all linked through the processes of modern industry and globalization: new transportation technologies; the peopling of frontiers; the production, processing, shipment, and marketing of raw materials and manufactured goods; and the production of food, shelter, and clothing for people who worked in those industrial and distribution networks. It was a truly global process that grew simultaneously with the consolidation of an international state system.

Most histories have recounted the age of mass migration as a transatlantic phenomenon. When migrations beyond the Atlantic are remembered at all, it is usually as a limited number of indentured laborers pressed into the service of Europeans. This historical memory is not random. It is the foundation of the broadest of global identities: East and West, North and South, First and Third Worlds; and the liberal and illiberal regions of the modern international system. It corresponds with depictions of European migrants as pioneering settlers who opened frontiers and constructed new nations, bearing individual initiative and progress to the cutting edge of world history. Asians, in contrast, are remembered as backward and earthbound peasants unable to participate in the sweep of modern history except as impoverished sojourners compelled by external dynamism and coercive intervention.[1] In fact, however, Asian migrations were as numerous as the Atlantic migrations and organized through similar networks. In the middle of the nineteenth century, the large proportion of Asians traveling to the Americas and Australasia had the potential to create densely integrated patterns of global migration that linked the Eastern and Western hemispheres. By the end of the century, however, only a small fraction of Asian migrants traveled beyond Asia. State interventions and racially inspired migration controls had established a barrier across the Pacific, helping to segregate the world into distinct migration regions.

Migration patterns were segregated into regions even as the economic forces behind migration grew increasingly integrated around the world. Mechanisms to control Asian mobility gave concrete enforcement to the images and ideologies of difference that had inspired those controls in the first place. These images of a backward, immobile Asia helped erase Asian migrations from the historical memory and still shape understandings of Asian migration to this day. They have the effect of placing Asia outside of historical globalization, and of making inequalities appear to be the consequences of physical isolation and cultural difference rather than the product of interaction and state intervention. In fact, however, the segmentation of the world into unequal regions has been inseparable from the processes of integration.

Memories of Migration

It is easy to find assertions in state-of-the-field volumes on migration history that privilege the uniqueness of the transatlantic system. Many of these are simply statements of quantity, such as the assertion that "By chance or choice, almost half of these world-travelers settled in the United States."[2] Some go further and assert that transatlantic migration was also different in quality, such as the claim that it

> is North and South America in the nineteenth and twentieth centuries that provide the great stage for the migration drama, where migration assumes extraordinary dimensions. While for the other continents migration was a means of relieving demographic pressure by moving surplus population to regions of lower density, in North and South America the problem was one of providing a labor force to work the vast areas of open land waiting to be brought under cultivation.[3]

Other statements of transatlantic uniqueness are intended to highlight the increasingly global quality of contemporary migration, such as the assertion that "Although international migrants were not exclusively European, the overwhelming majority came from that continent. . . . Before 1925, 85 percent of all international migrants originated in Europe, but since 1960 Europe has contributed an increasingly small fraction of emigrants to world migration flows."[4] In *The Age of Mass Migration*, Hatton and Williamson justify their exclusive focus on the North Atlantic with an argument that the inherent qualities of the "present Third World" led to its isolation from the historical processes of globalization until recently. These regions "were segmented by discrimination, language, and custom. They were segmented by long distance and high migration cost. They were segmented by the poverty of the Third World labor-surplus areas, areas so poor that potential emigrants would have found it impossible to finance the move to the booming OECD labor markets anyway."[5] By placing migrations beyond the Atlantic outside of globalization, their argument that globalization leads to economic convergence becomes a tautology: globalization causes economic convergence because only places that converged are considered to be sites of globalization.

These citations could be dismissed as grounded in a lack of information. But the ready acceptance of these assumptions about Asian migration is the basic groundwork for this lack of knowledge. Few of these volumes give much attention to areas beyond the Atlantic except to confirm those basic assumptions, down to the very frameworks for collecting data. This can be seen in Pieter Emmer's comparative work that categorizes long-distance migration as being intercontinental or not. He includes Russians who crossed the Ural Mountains and French who migrated to Algeria as intercontinental, but not Chinese who went to Singapore or Hadhrami to Java. After counting five to six million intercontinental African and Asian migrants from 1800 to 1960, he concludes that "The study of migration as part of the process of European expansion and contraction clearly shows that Europeans have participated much more extensively in intercontinental migrations than Africans and Asians."[6] This distinction then becomes the basis for qualitative judgments. In his essay "Was Migration Beneficial?" he divides global migration into temperate and tropical plantation systems, the latter made up almost entirely of indentured Asians and Africans. He then suggests that it does not make much sense to ask if Asian migration was beneficial "given the relatively small volume of both internal and external migration," thus dismissing the relevance of much of the world in understanding global processes.[7]

Emmer's distinctions may seem crude, but the general assumption that Asians did not migrate and that those who did consisted almost entirely of indentured labor dominated by Europeans pervades much of the literature. This assumption is somewhat understandable for Indian migration given its relatively tight organization within the British Empire to work on European-owned plantations. Much more perplexing are the characterization of Chinese overseas migration as indentured and the consistently low estimations of Chinese migration in Western-language scholarship, ranging from 2 to 8 million (which, as we shall see, accounts for less than half of all Chinese emigration).[8] Most of these numbers were ultimately drawn from three studies by Chen Ta, Chen Zexuan, and Arnold Meagher, all of which were counting only contract labor migration.[9] But even the incomplete Chinese numbers in Ferenczi and Willcox's *International Migrations*, still the most widely used source of migration statistics, count 5.5 million immigrants to the Straits Settlements from 1881 to 1915, 3.7 million departing Chinese ports from 1876 to 1901, and 2.4 million leaving Hong Kong from 1900 to 1924. This already accounts for up to 8 million Chinese within a limited period, not including the indentures (mostly before 1874) that make up other estimates.[10] Extrapolation from these numbers could easily have provided a much larger figure for Chinese migration, if not for the assumption that Chinese did not migrate.

One recent history of global migration explains the causes of Chinese migration overseas and to Manchuria as "Imperial Chinese maladministration and revolts, overpopulation and natural disasters as well as colonial penetration."[11] Research on European migrations (as the author demonstrates elsewhere) has consistently argued that the first three causes rarely, if ever, explain the establishment of steady migration patterns from Europe. And "colonial penetration" is, of course, irrelevant for Europe. This explanation leaves the impression that Chinese did not migrate according to the same kinds of processes that produced European migration. Without European intervention, Asians would have remained tradition-bound, immobile peasants, subject only to Asian despotisms and crude Malthusian pressures. The overall effect is to render Asian migrations categorically different from the transatlantic migrations that were a crucible of the modern world.

Forgetting also happens in other parts of the world. For example, Chinese scholars generally consider the Manchurian migrations to be a form of domestic movement that is irrelevant to global comparison.[12] But the current Manchurian population of over 100 million suggests a demographic transition similar to those of European settler colonies in the Americas. Without these migrations, Manchuria might not be a part of China today, but part of Russia or Japan, or an independent nation like Mongolia. In this case, national borders have discouraged a broader understanding of global migration patterns and reinforced images of a stagnant East.

TABLE 2.1 Global Long-Distance Migration, 1840–1940

Destination	Origins	Amount (millions)	Auxiliary Origins
Americas	Europe	55–58	2.5 million from India, China, Japan, Africa
Southeast Asia, Indian Ocean Rim, Australasia	India S. China	48–52	5 million from Africa, Europe, NE Asia, Middle East
Manchuria, Siberia, Central Asia, Japan	NE Asia Russia	46–51	

Source: Adam McKeown, "Global Migration, 1846–1940," *Journal of World History* 15 (2004): 156.

Long-Distance Migration

Rather than start with assumptions about the distinctiveness of different systems, let us start with migration data. Port and customs statistics from around the world support an estimate of at least 150 million long-distance voyages from 1840 to 1940, spread over much of the world (table 2.1).[13] This number mostly counts ship passengers who traveled in third class or steerage, people categorized as "immigrants," "emigrants," or "laborers," and migrants who registered under officially sponsored colonization schemes like those from Russia to Siberia and Central Asia. Data for return voyages are less readily available, so (as with most migration statistics) this estimate includes multiple trips by single individuals. It does not count people who traveled overland or in first class, or those who avoided inspection and enumeration. The prevalence of these evasions is apparent in comparing numbers from emigration and immigration ports that sometimes vary by 20 percent or more.[14] Thus, estimates like this can only describe general trends but are still useful as a basis for broad comparisons.

The bulk of these long-distance migrations can be classified according to three systems that were similar in quantity and connected major sending and receiving regions: transatlantic migration from Europe to the Americas; migration from India and South China to a region centered on Southeast Asia but extending across the rims of the Indian Ocean and the South Pacific; and migration from Russia, North China, and Korea into the broad expanse of North Asia stretching from the Russian steppes to Siberia and Manchuria. The three destinations were the great frontier settlement regions of the modern world. Smaller auxiliary flows moved across these systems but accounted for less than 5 percent of the total movement.

Transatlantic

The movement of Europeans to the Americas is the best known of these migrations. Nearly 65 percent went to the United States, with the bulk of the remainder divided between Argentina (which had the largest proportion of foreign-born residents), Canada, Brazil, and, to a lesser extent, Cuba and Uruguay.[15] Over half of the emigration before the 1870s was from the British Isles, with much of the remainder from northwestern Europe. As migration increased along with new transportation technologies in the 1880s, regions of intensive emigration spread south and east as far as Portugal, Russia, and Syria. Up to 2.5 million migrants from South and East Asia also traveled to the Americas, mostly to the frontiers of western North America or the plantations of the Caribbean, Peru, and Brazil. Half of the Asian migration took place from 1850 to 1885, after which the decline of indentured labor recruitment and the rise of anti-Asian immigration laws took effect.

Southeast Asia–Indian Ocean

Migration to Southeast Asia and lands around the Indian Ocean and South Pacific consisted of over 29 million Indians, at least 19 million Chinese, and about 4.5 million Europeans, mostly to Australia, New Zealand, and South Africa. Most migration from India was to colonies throughout the British Empire. Nearly 4 million Indians traveled to Malaya, more than 8 million to Ceylon, more than 15 million to Burma, and about a million to Africa, other parts of Southeast Asia, and islands throughout the Indian and Pacific oceans. Despite the notoriety of and extensive debates over Indian indenture, less than 8 percent of total migration from India was indentured at the time of departure, mostly before 1908 to distant places in the Americas, Africa, and Fiji. The majority of Indian migrants to Southeast Asia did work on European-owned plantations, usually recruited with some form of assistance or debt through native *kangani* and *maistry* recruiters. Up to 2 million migrated as merchants or travelers not intending to work as laborers.[16]

The vast majority of Chinese migrants came from the southern provinces of Guangdong and Fujian. Up to 11 million traveled from China to Singapore and Penang, from where more than a third of these transshipped to the

Dutch Indies, Borneo, Burma, and places further west. Nearly 4 million traveled directly from China to Siam, between 2 and 3 million to French Indochina, over a million directly to the Dutch Indies (for a total of over 4 million if transshipments from Singapore are included), less than a million to the Philippines, and about half a million to Australia, New Zealand, Hawaii, and other islands in the Pacific and Indian oceans.[17] Given the wide variety of labor recruitment and financing schemes and the fact that many migrants were trained to tell inspectors that they had not signed a contract, it is difficult to determine the number of migrants who migrated with labor contracts. Less than three quarters of a million Chinese migrants signed indenture contracts with European employers, including a quarter million to Latin America and the Caribbean before 1874, a quarter million to Sumatra from the 1880s to the 1910s, and a smaller number to mines, plantations, and islands scattered throughout Malaya and the Pacific and Indian oceans. From 1881 to 1913, 776,457 Chinese who had not paid their own passage signed labor contracts in front of the Protector of Chinese in Singapore, and most of these migrants went to work for Chinese employers in mines and plantations.[18] Many, if not most, Chinese paid for their own passage or borrowed money from relatives and friends. Others had their original passage paid by wealthy Chinese under the "credit-ticket" system, although the terms of repayment varied and the migrants were not necessarily bound to work for their creditors. In all cases, the organization of migration was largely independent of European regulation but deeply linked to the expansion of a Europe-centered global economy.

Northern Asia

Migrants had trickled into Central Asia, Siberia, and Manchuria for hundreds of years before the Qing government's gradual relaxation of restrictions against movement into Manchuria after the 1850s and the emancipation of serfs and opening of Siberia by Russia in 1861. Both governments actively encouraged settlement with homesteading policies in the 1880s, each attempting to counter territorial encroachment by the other. Railroad construction in the 1890s further strengthened the migrant flows. At least 13 million Russians moved into Central Asia and Siberia. This briefly reversed in the 1920s as local policies were erected against Russian settlers, but resumed familiar eastward patterns by the mid-1920s when central directives overrode local policies.[19] Between 28 and 33 million Chinese migrated into Manchuria and Siberia, along with nearly 2 million Koreans. Another 2.5 million Koreans migrated to

TABLE 2.2 World Population Growth, 1850–1950 (millions)

	1850 Population	1950 Population	Average Annual Growth (%)
Receiving			
Americas	59	325	1.72
North Asia	22	104	1.57
SE Asia	42	177	1.45
Sending			
Europe	265	515	0.67
South Asia	230	445	0.66
China	420	520	0.21
Africa	81	205	0.93
World	1,200	2,500	0.74

Source: Colin McEvedy and Richard Jones, Atlas of World Population History (London: Penguin, 1978).

Japan, especially in the 1930s, and over 2 million Japanese moved into Korea and Manchuria. In addition, up to a million northern Chinese, Koreans, and Japanese migrated to a diverse range of destinations, including much of the Americas, Hawaii, Southeast Asia, South Africa, and Europe.[20]

Taken together, these migrations caused a significant redistribution of the world's population. All three destination regions experienced massive population growth, with their populations increasing by factors of 4 to 5.5 from 1850 to 1950 (table 2.2). Growth rates in these areas were over twice that for world population as a whole. In comparison, growth rates in the sending regions were lower than world population growth and less than half of those in the receiving regions. Taken together, the three main destination regions accounted for 10 percent of the world's population in 1850 and 24 percent in 1950. The Americas and northern Asia grew more quickly than Southeast Asia with its smaller area, tropical environment, and more entrenched native population. Nonetheless, from 1870 to 1930 approximately 35 million migrants moved into the 4.1 million square kilometers of Southeast Asia, compared with the 39 million migrants who moved into the 9.8 million square kilometers of the United States.

At first glance, 19 million overseas emigrants from China or 29 million from India seems like a drop in the bucket compared with the several millions from much smaller countries like Italy, Norway, Ireland, and England.[21] But if we adjust the focus to regions of comparable size and population, the rates are very similar. Some peak rates of overseas emigration from Europe in the 1910s are 10.8 emigrants per 1,000 population in Italy, 8.3 from Norway, and 7 from Ireland.[22] In comparison, the annual average overseas emigration rate from Guangdong province in South China, which had a slightly larger geographic area and slightly smaller population than Italy, was at least 9.6 per 1,000 in the peak years of the 1920s. Hebei and Shandong provinces (sources of migration to Manchuria) had an even higher rate of 10 per 1,000 during that same decade.[23] In terms of broader regional population, emigration from Europe from 1846 to 1940 accounted for 15.4 percent of the European population in 1900, compared with 11.3 in China and 10.4 in South Asia. This latter difference is not insignificant (and only tentative, given our lack of knowledge of internal and overland migration), but it certainly does not justify a categorical distinction between quantity and quality of migration in the different regions.

Other Migrations

Transoceanic migration in these three systems was only the tip of the iceberg. Other migration moved in and out of places such as Africa and the Middle East that were at the interstices of the main long-distance systems. Overland and domestic migration, much of it within the main sending and receiving regions, also generally escaped the web of enumerators and inspectors. Perhaps the great majority of global migration was seasonal and temporary movement to nearby cities, towns, factories, mines, agricultural regions, and unused lands.

The transatlantic migrations could be extended to include over 13 million people who moved to the western frontiers of North America, first primarily across the United States and then into the western plains of Canada. This process also included the relocation of great numbers of Native Americans and the migration of over 2.5 million Mexicans to the agricultural areas of the Southwest in the early twentieth century. The industrial centers of the northeastern United States also attracted over 2.5 million Canadians, and then over a million African Americans and Mexicans in the early twentieth century.[24] In other parts of the Americas, great numbers of Andean and other peoples moved to coastal plantations and cities, and more than 300,000 Caribbean peoples migrated to plantations in Central America and Cuba, to the Panama Canal Zone, and to the United States.[25] Migrants also moved within Southeast Asia and the South Pacific. These included up to 500,000 Javanese traveling to plantations in Sumatra and the Southeast Asian mainland, and, in what may have been some of the densest outmigrations ever, more than 300,000 Melanesians and Micronesians who worked on plantations and as seamen throughout the region.[26]

Massive internal migration also took place within the major sending regions of long-distance migration. In Europe, migrants from Ireland traveled to England for work, and from eastern and southern Europe and Belgium to the industrial areas of northwestern Europe, especially France and Germany. Within Russia, migrants moved into the growing cities and southern agricultural areas.[27] Within India they moved to tea plantations in the South and Northeast, to the mines and textile producing regions of Bengal, and to newly irrigated lands and urban areas throughout the subcontinent.[28] In China, they migrated to growing coastal cities, to areas of the Yangtze basin left underpopulated by the Taiping Rebellion, and to borderland areas of the Northwest and Southwest, including overland migration to Burma.[29] Each of these regions hosted at least 20 million journeys.

Africa experienced net transoceanic immigration, but in much smaller numbers than other main destinations and from a wider variety of origins. The immigrants included more than 3 million French and Italians into North Africa and up to a million other Europeans, Syrians, Lebanese, Arabs, Indians, and Chinese throughout the continent.[30] The end of the transatlantic slave trade led to increased movement of slaves into the western Sudan, Middle East, and areas bordering the Indian Ocean in the late nineteenth century. Labor migration to plantations and mines in southern and central Africa increased through the late nineteenth and twentieth centuries, as did movement to agricultural areas and coastal cities in western and eastern Africa. Millions of people took part in these movements, some of whom were coerced or otherwise went to work for European enterprises, but many of whom also found independent occupations.[31]

The Middle East and ex-Ottoman lands were also at the interstices of the main long-distance flows described above. Projects such as the Suez Canal and development of cotton cultivation in Egypt attracted large amounts of local migration, while Lebanon and Syria experienced some of the highest overseas emigration rates in the world. Conflicts surrounding the dissolution of the Ottoman Empire also generated refugee and state-fostered migrations that were a foretaste of processes that would become increasingly common over the twentieth century. By the 1920s, 4 to 6 million people were dislocated in population exchanges between Turkey, on the one hand, and the Balkans, Greece, and Russia, on the other, with Christians moving north and Muslims moving south. Around a million Armenians were expelled from Turkey to points around the world, and nearly 400,000 Jews moved to Palestine in the early twentieth century.[32] Mass movement of refugees would extend to other parts of Europe in the wake of World War I and the Russian Revolution, including the movement of 3 million Russians, Poles, and Germans out of the Soviet Union. In a different kind of movement, millions of people also took part in the *hajj* to Mecca, including nearly 700,000 from the Dutch Indies after the 1870s, a predecessor of the twentieth-century explosion of long-distance tourism.[33]

In addition to the migration of settlers and workers, merchant diasporas continued to flourish. For centuries before the 1800s these ethnic networks were some of the most prominent exemplars of long-distance migration. Their importance was diminished or transformed under the economic changes and new labor migrations wrought by industrialization. Jewish merchant networks were subsumed into the operations of European capital, while Armenian merchant networks were decimated by the traumas of genocide. But other old and new diasporas flourished and expanded, often at the frontiers of globally expanding credit and trading networks where they adapted long-standing forms of commercial organization for the needs of the new economy. They often developed reputations as "middlemen," but more than just fitting into preexisting social gaps, their activities created market and social relationships that had not existed before. For example, Chinese merchant networks were often at the cutting edge of an expanding world economy. They channeled labor throughout Southeast Asia and pioneered dense networks of shops and services in places as distant as the Amazon rubber groves, South Pacific atolls, and upriver Borneo. They also provided services to other migrants and workers in plantations and urban neighborhoods throughout the world. Merchants from India similarly expanded trade networks into Central Asia, Africa, and Southeast Asia. Chettiars from South India expanded along with the British into Burma, and Parsis facilitated the India-China trade using some of the capital they earned to establish textile mills in India. Sindworkies from the town of Hyderabad in what is now Pakistan spread around the globe from Japan to the Panama Canal and Tierra del Fuego, establishing upscale "curio" shops for international tourists and becoming prominent carriers of Japanese trade in the Dutch Indies. Other merchant diasporas such as the Hadhramis from Yemen, Hausa in western Africa, and Lebanese Christians also joined this interface between expanding industrial enterprises and dispersed individual producers and consumers around the world.[34]

Historical Trends

The concurrent rise of migration around the world was not coincidental (fig. 2.1). The rise of rapid, inexpensive transportation, the growth of global markets and industrialization, the loosening of controls over internal migration, and the expansion into frontiers around the world all reinforced each other in a snowball effect. It was a world on the move, with people flowing into factories, construction projects, mines, plantations, agricultural frontiers, and commercial networks across the globe. Rice planters in Burma, tin miners in Malaya, rubber tappers in Borneo and the Amazon, and wheat farmers in Manchuria were as much a part of this global economy as steel factories in Pittsburgh, sugar plantations in Cuba, merchants in Calcutta and Singapore, and ranchers in the plains of North America and Argentina. Foodstuffs and resources from frontiers near and far supplied growing immigrant populations in industrial centers, trade entrepots and mining frontiers. Inexpensive steamships crossed the oceans of the world after the 1850s, as railways crossed North America and North Asia. This, in turn, attracted more immigrants, who produced more goods that generated more trade, more movement, cheaper transportation prices, and more disruptive commercialization of agricultural areas around the world that generated more immigration. Where mass transport did not extend, its agents did, supplying information and access. All were linked through the worldwide processes of economic globalization, and industrial transformation.

These migrations increased more quickly than world population. Migration involved 0.36 percent of the world's population in the 1850s, rising to 0.96 percent in the 1880s, 1.67 percent in the 1900s, and then declining to 1.58 percent in the 1920s. The overall growth in long-distance migration was punctuated by short-term regional ebbs and flows that corresponded with business cycles and job opportunities. After a North American depression of the late 1870s, transatlantic migration boomed and clearly surpassed migration from and within Asia for the first time. This boom corresponded with a greater concentration of migrants in industrial and trading occupations in

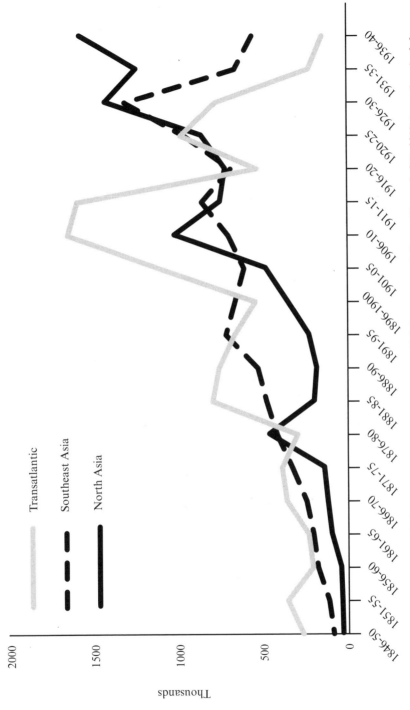

FIGURE 2.1. Global Migration, 1846–1940. [Source: Adam McKeown, "Global Migration, 1846–1940," *Journal of World History* 15 (2004): 165.]

towns and cities, a pattern that would be followed in North Asia at a fifteen-to twenty-year delay. Migration from South China expanded at the same time as transatlantic migration, although Indian migration remained stagnant until after the turn of the century, except for a crest in the early 1890s. Rural populations continued to grow more rapidly than urban ones in Southeast Asia, but Asian migrants increasingly took up work as independent traders, small-holders, and craftspeople rather than laborers.

Migration around the world boomed at the turn of the century, more than doubling in the decade after 1900 to over 3 million a year. Transatlantic migration reached a spectacular peak of over 2.1 million in 1913, and migration to Southeast and North Asia also reached unprecedented peaks of nearly 1.1 million a year from 1911 to 1913. World War I caused a global decline in migration, hitting the Atlantic region the hardest. But global migration once again reached peaks of over 3 million a year in the late 1920s, with Asian migration reaching new highs of 1.25 million migrants to Southeast Asia in 1927 and 1.5 million to North Asia in 1929. Transatlantic migration recovered to 1.2 million migrants in 1924, after which immigration quotas in the United States severely curtailed migration from southern and eastern Europe. The Great Depression put a stop to much migration, with the exception of the command economies of Japan and the Soviet Union, where coercion and government promotion produced rates of up to 1.8 million migrants a year.

Regionalizing World Migration

Even as migrants covered the world along with economic globalization, they were also increasingly divided into separate regions. In the middle of the nineteenth century, global migration patterns pointed toward the creation of a single global system. By the end of the century, short-term migration cycles around the world were increasingly similar, suggesting that the economic forces shaping migration were increasingly integrated. But by this time, the patterns of migration had become segregated into three separate systems. Globalization generated difference even as it brought the world together.

Short-term migration cycles and return rates correlate well with employment cycles. The more the employment opportunities abroad, the lower the return rates. By the 1890s, return rates to South China, India, and Europe had begun to converge, not only in their timing but in absolute numbers (fig. 2.2). The global economy shaping migration was clearly becoming more integrated.

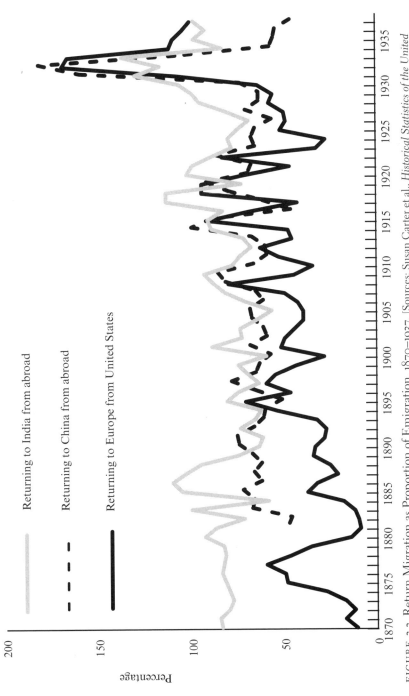

FIGURE 2.2. Return Migration as Proportion of Emigration, 1870–1937. [Sources: Susan Carter et al., *Historical Statistics of the United States* (New York: Cambridge UP, 2006); Kingsley Davis, *The Population of India and Pakistan* (New York: Russell and Russell, 1951), 100; Adam McKeown, "Global Migration, 1846–1940," *Journal of World History* 15 (2004): 186–89.]

Legend:

Returning to India from abroad

Returning to China from abroad

Returning to Europe from United States

But at the same time as short-term cycles grew more identical, the patterns and destinations of migration had become highly segregated. This increasing segmentation is especially clear in the distribution of Asian migration. At least 227,000 migrants from South China traveled to the Americas and Australia in the 1850s. Numbers for Southeast Asia in this period are speculative, but migration to non-Asian destinations amounted to at least 40 percent of all emigration from South China. Indentured migrants, mostly to Cuba and Peru, accounted for about 90,000 of these migrants. The remaining 135,000 went mostly to the gold fields of California and Australia, with nearly 50,000 Chinese traveling to California in just the period from 1851 to 1855. These gold-rush migrants were funded and organized by Chinese capital and depended on Chinese mining skills. But as Chinese migration continued to expand, movement beyond Asia remained stagnant. It declined to 6 percent of total emigration in the late 1880s and remained at that level over the next five decades (fig. 2.3) The subsequent stagnation was not a consequence of inadequate resources, earthbound peasant mentalities, or any other distinction that made Chinese migrants categorically different from European emigrants. It was a result of exclusionary laws and the scarcity of inexpensive direct transportation to Latin America after the end of indenture.

Shifts in the proportions of Indian migration beyond Asia are not so dramatic, but Indians' exclusion from non-Asian destinations was much more complete (fig. 2.4). About a quarter of all Indian overseas migration in the 1840s and 1850s was to non-Asian destinations, most of it under indenture contracts. Migration beyond Asia then retained a steady average of about 16,000 migrants a year until the decline of indenture after the turn of the century. But by the 1880s, the proportion of migration beyond Asia had already declined to about 5 percent of total migration. Unlike the Chinese, even the absolute number of Indians beyond Asia declined to an insignificant trickle after the restriction of indenture contracts in 1908 and their abolishment in 1920. Most indentured Indians had traveled to islands with few economic opportunities beyond the plantations, reducing the attraction for new migrants and making it difficult to build migration networks. The few who traveled to North America after the turn of the century were unable to establish strong migration networks before the imposition of exclusionary measures, implemented with great efficiency by local governments that had learned from their experiences in regulating Chinese and Japanese immigrants. South Africa and colonies in eastern Africa were the only non-Asian destinations with established Indian communities and economic opportunities to attract new

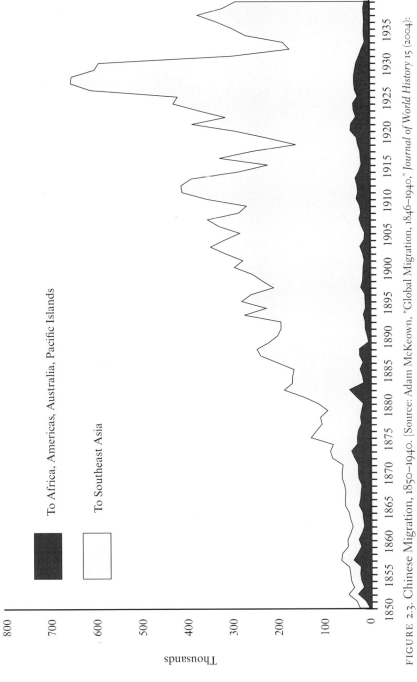

FIGURE 2.3. Chinese Migration, 1850–1940. [Source: Adam McKeown, "Global Migration, 1846–1940," *Journal of World History* 15 (2004): 188–189.]

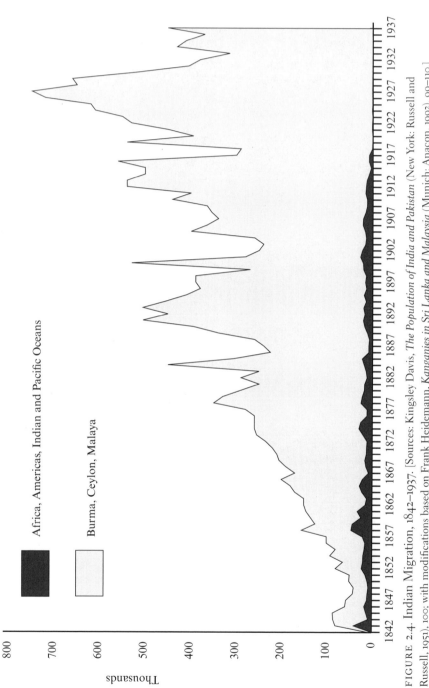

FIGURE 2.4. Indian Migration, 1842–1937. [Sources: Kingsley Davis, *The Population of India and Pakistan* (New York: Russell and Russell, 1951), 100; with modifications based on Frank Heidemann, *Kanganies in Sri Lanka and Malaysia* (Munich: Anacon, 1992), 99–110.]

migrants in the early twentieth century. But by the 1900s, South Africa was also cordoned off behind exclusionary legislation.

Regulation and the consolidation of borders not only blocked migration, but also encouraged and directed it. Nearly all Indian migration took place within the British Empire despite the resistance of white settler colonies. In response, white colonists and officials often promoted white migration to settlements throughout the empire, although with limited success due to the competing allure of the United States. French and Italians were encouraged to migrate to North Africa in the name of imperial interests, as were the Japanese to Korea and Manchuria. Indeed, the North Asian migration system was largely shaped by Russian, Chinese, and Japanese policies that encouraged migration as a way to claim, fortify, and develop territory, making the North Asian system the most insular of the three major systems. The fact that the Russian and Chinese projects are so often forgotten is perhaps the greatest mark of their success. Both Siberia and Manchuria are now considered integral parts of the home nations of the immigrants who populated them, and the movements have been subsumed under national rather than international histories.

Regional Dynamics

A global comparative perspective can show that the patterns and organization of migration were broadly similar around the world. Each specific flow existed at a specific nexus of common global forces that came together to produce particular yet broadly shared experiences of mobility.[35] Little evidence supports a broad distinction between a progressive Atlantic region and an earthbound Asia. Low rates of female migration and high rates of return migration in Asia are often presented as evidence that Asians were sojourners, unlike the pioneering families who crossed the Atlantic and assimilated into the emerging new nations.[36] Quantitative evidence does not support this distinction, especially if analyzed over time rather than as hundred-year averages. It does, however, suggest that transatlantic migrations were more dynamic than those elsewhere over the long run, with greater shifts in sending regions and more long-term variability in rates of return and female migration. The Atlantic world was clearly an area in transformation, whereas Asian migration systems were much less dynamic. Globalization generated divergence as well as convergence.

In Europe, the main migrant homelands shifted broadly from northwestern to southeastern Europe between 1840 and 1940. No similar shift can be found in Asia. In South China and India, despite local shifts between counties and villages, the main migrant-sending regions of the 1850s were still the main migrant-sending regions of the 1930s. In China, the proportion of migrants departing from different ports remained almost constant from the 1870s to the early 1920s, after which Hong Kong started to increase slightly.

Overall proportions of women migrants were much lower to Southeast Asia than to the United States. But they also fluctuated much less, exhibiting steady growth rather than shifts. Annual proportions of women migrating to the United States were as low as 20 percent in the early nineteenth century. They rose to 40 percent in the 1860s, where they remained until a sudden drop to 30 percent in 1900. They remained at this level until 1914, after which they gradually increased to 54 percent by the late 1930s. In contrast, the proportion of women leaving Hong Kong grew steadily from 6 percent in the 1860s to 18 percent in the late 1920s, then doubled to 36 percent by the late 1930, an increase that mirrored that from Europe, if at a lower proportion.[37] Data on the migration of Indian women are less readily available, but such migration rarely rose above 20 percent before the 1930s. Return migration from the United States also fluctuated much more strongly than that from Southeast Asia before the general convergence of return cycles in the 1890s (fig. 2.2).

Shifts in female and return migration to Europe may be partly explained by increased emigration from regions with larger stem families, as argued by Donna Gabaccia.[38] Nuclear families predominated in northwestern Europe, the source of most midcentury transatlantic migrants. Husband and wife depended on each other for subsistence, and many women had experience in market activities. In comparison, migrants from southern and eastern Europe, as well as China and India, tended toward multigenerational patrilineal families. The migration and wages of individual members were an investment in the maintenance of this larger structure. Women often remained with their husbands' families to continue contributing to this larger economic unit rather than just the nuclear family. The men journeyed abroad as a kind of investment, expected to send much of their earnings back to this larger unit and eventually returning home themselves. Return rates were indeed much higher from southeastern Europe, ranging from 50–60 percent for southern Italians, Greeks, and Slovaks to a high of 90 percent for Bulgarians and Serbs.

But differences in family form still draw attention to the dynamic shift in emigration sources within Europe, where migration from northeastern Europe eventually declined. Migration in Asia continued to be a multigenerational strategy that endured and expanded among the same villages and towns for more than a century. One reason for the decline in migration flows from certain parts of Europe was the convergence in wages across the Atlantic. In Asia, however, wages did not converge, and they may even have diverged in places.[39] Rural conditions in China and India, although highly commercialized, remained static, as did occupational structures in Southeast Asia. In contrast, shifting European emigration patterns corresponded with the spread of industrialization and urbanization across both the Americas and Europe.

On the receiving end, shifting proportions of female and return migration from the Americas corresponded with changing conditions of frontier settlement, urbanization, and shifting industrial occupations that increasingly preferred male over female workers. Even northern Europeans, who made up the bulk of mid-nineteenth-century settlers, had larger rates of return and male migration by the end of the century.[40] In contrast, in the late nineteenth century, females predominated in short-distance migration to the cities of western Europe, where, like Irish women who migrated to the Americas in the mid-nineteenth century, they found ready employment in service occupations.[41] Return rates from Canada and especially Brazil, with their somewhat more constricted economic opportunities, also tended to be higher than those from the United States. Returns from Australia also changed dramatically, declining from 60 percent in the 1890s to 20 percent in the 1910s, as the British and Australian governments encouraged family relocation.[42] In comparison, Southeast Asia underwent minimal urbanization and economic development in this period.[43] The proportion of Chinese migrants working as agricultural proletariats and in artisanal, mercantile, and transport-related jobs gradually shifted toward the latter over time, but this was more a function of better entrenched migrant networks with greater access to commercial resources than of significant structural changes. None of these were occupations that employed high numbers of women. Only with the rise of Chinese small family retailers after the turn of the century did the proportion of Chinese women grow.[44]

Migration to industrializing North Asia developed more along the lines of migration to the Americas. Anecdotal evidence suggests that early years of migration to the temperate agricultural frontiers North Asia included relatively high proportions of women. Russian officials encouraged family migration to Siberia, and observers often commented on the sight of entire families on their way to Manchuria, especially during the North China famine of 1876–1879. By the 1920s, as the frontier was settled and industrial and mining jobs became more common, Chinese migration to Manchuria was 80 to 90 percent male after the 1890s, with return rates of more than 65 percent. Like in the Atlantic, these return rates underwent volatile swings, but these swings did not correspond to those in the Americas and Southeast Asia, possibly due to much stronger state intervention into both migration and the economies.[45]

Differences in settlement rates between the Americas and Southeast Asia are often attributed to differences in return and female migration. But return rates to Manchuria were the same as those to South China, and female migration was even lower. Yet Manchuria is now even more dominated by descendants of Chinese than North America is by descendants of European immigrants. A more significant cause of the ability to leave descendants is migration to tropical areas with complex native societies and plantation economies versus migration to temperate frontiers and urban areas where native populations largely died out. Nearly all southern Chinese and Indians migrated to tropical areas within or near well-established native states. But still, in some places their descendants make up more than 30 percent of the population, such as in contemporary Malaysia, Sri Lanka, and scattered islands around the world. Calculations that account for intermarriage and assimilation with natives could make the numbers much higher. By comparison, European migrants have fared much worse in tropical areas. Costa Rica, Cuba, Venezuela, and Colombia are the only tropical countries with populations of European descent at all comparable to those of Asian and African descent in Southeast Asia and tropical America.

Of course, this is as much a story about power as it is about numbers and physical environment. As Qiu Liben has argued in critiques of the Sinocentrism of his Chinese colleagues, Chinese migration has shaped the modern world much less than European migrations have. The 30 million Chinese and descendants of Chinese who could be found around the world in the early 1990s amounted to nothing near the number of descendants of European migrants around the world—indeed, they amount to little more than the European-descended population in Canada. Chinese and other Asians did travel the world, Qiu argues, but modern world history is still the story of Europeans and Western capitalism.[46] Asian merchants in Fiji and Haiti, miners and agriculturalists in Southeast Asia and Africa, and railroad laborers in Siberia, Manchuria, and California all undertook their work in the context of financial, political, and military power concentrated in the hands of Europeans and Japanese. Chinese did not replace indigenous peoples on the temperate frontiers of the Americas and Australia in great numbers because they did not have the power to shape the laws and opportunities in their favor—unlike in Manchuria where the early stages of migration were shaped by the Chinese state. The builders of those borders set the narratives and standards by which migrations are evaluated. The success of those narratives in characterizing distinctions between Asian and Atlantic migrations indicates the deep success of past institutions in producing knowledge about where migration took place, what it was, and what it should be. And this is ultimately knowledge about global order, and the role of different peoples in that order.

3

Creating the Free Migrant

As U.S. commissioner-general of immigration from 1902 to 1908, Frank Sargent was one of the main architects of modern immigration control. He saw his work as a tool for benevolent deeds rather than oppression, enforcing humanitarian laws that safeguarded the national interest while protecting free migrants from the exploitation of unfettered capital, unscrupulous brokers and coercive Old World governments. In an article written for the *Annals of the American Academy of Political and Social Science,* he explained that the subjects of migration law "are not inanimate like merchandise; they are human beings. They have aspirations, hopes, fears and frailties." For their benefit and the benefit of the nation,

> It has become an established principle of this Government to frown upon the efforts of foreign countries and of interested individuals and corporations to bring to the United States, to become burdens thereupon, the indigent, the morally depraved, the physically and mentally diseased, the shiftless, and all those who are induced to leave their own country, not by their own independent volition and their own natural ambition to seek a larger and more promising field of individual enterprise, but by some selfish scheme, devised either to take undue advantage of some classes of our own people, or for other improper purpose.[1]

By the turn of the century, to be "free" had become a touchstone for the evaluation of migration. The free migrant was an autonomous individual, making personal choices without the pressure of extraneous obligations or coercion. The meaning and desirability of free migration was self-evident to its many proponents. But the correlation of freedom with actual human mobility remained elusive. The tensions are apparent even in Sargent's own assertion of the need for government intervention that would sift out the undesirable migrants while protecting the "independent volition" of desirable migrants from the seductions and abuses of "selfish" and "interested" private organizers of migration. The very possibility of free migration depended on suppression of certain migrant activities.

Ideals of free migration in the middle of the nineteenth century were shaped both by the abolition of the African slave trade and the rise of the principles of free trade and intercourse. Both shared a commitment to the idea of individual choice and free volition but could be in conflict about how best to obtain that choice and volition. Abolitionist rhetoric rested on a polarized opposition between slavery and freedom that left little room for intermediary conditions. In their quest of absolute freedom, many (but not all) abolitionists found the laissez-faire toleration of the power of property and contracts to be an unacceptable infringement on individual freedoms. In turn, proponents of free trade remained opposed to the kinds of government regulation frequently proposed by humanitarians and labor organizations. The struggles between the proponents of different freedoms could become quite heated but rarely disturbed the conviction of any participants that migration could and should be free.

The commitment to free migration grew especially complex in the consideration of Asian migration. The decline of the slave trade had led to an increase after the 1830s in Asians indentured under multiyear contracts to plantations in the Americas and islands in the Indian Ocean. Even though this was a minor portion of Asian migration, it dominated the imagination of both Europeans and Asians about the nature of Asian migration. Debates over the "freedom" of Asian migration were incoherent and contradictory, but they were critical in generating an image of Asians as backward and impoverished people, ignorant of their own rights and incapable of mobility without coercion or the assistance of indenture. Given these conditions, most observers ultimately agreed that some level of government surveillance was necessary to suppress private abuses and guarantee some level of freedom. This surveillance flourished within the embrace of the British Empire. Chinese indenture, on the other hand, took place in an international space that was not easily subjected to regulation. Although the lack of regulation could ostensibly be understood as a measure of freedom, the British believed it generated abuses and oppression, leading them to spearhead a morally charged suppression of the Chinese indenture trade.

The regulation of Asian indenture not only was an important part of the structure of institutions that came to distinguish East from West, but ultimately helped shape the understandings and institutions that make up migration control around the world. In particular, accounts of Asian indenture generated a well-articulated suspicion of unregulated intermediaries, recruiters, and transportation companies as sources of unfreedom. The autonomy of planters and shippers was gradually restricted, while unregulated brokers, ethnic labor recruiters, informal credit arrangements, and even village and family networks were pushed underground and criminalized. They were replaced by government institutions that attempted to isolate individual decision makers as the object of regulation. The free individual migrant, far from being a natural pheomenon that emerged most fully in the absence of government regulation, was the product of extensive intervention into the organization of human mobility.

Free Contract, Free Labor

In the eighteenth century, migrants were largely carried across the Atlantic as commerce: slaves, indentured servants, convicts whose labor was for sale, and other passengers held onboard like cargo until relatives or prospective employers paid off their passage costs (these latter sometimes known as "free willers").[2] The decline of migration as commerce in the mid-nineteenth century was part of a larger struggle over the meaning of a free citizen and free labor. Critics attacked the potential for abuse by employers, ship captains, and other entrepreneurs who, under cover of property laws, misused and exploited their power over others. A free man was to be a man with power over his own labor, and only free men could be the foundation of a free nation. At the same time, the meaning of the contract changed from an instrument of subjection and dependence into an act of personal freedom and consent. A valid labor agreement no longer implied a transfer of property in the form of labor across a hierarchical relationship from employee to employer. Rather, it implied an agreement between equals, each with the freedom to live up to their own promises.[3] Although the ideals of free contract and free labor rested on similar foundations, they would become one of the main fissures of ideological and political struggle around the world during the nineteenth century.

At the turn of the century, some defenders of European indenture made their case in terms of paternalistic benevolence. They claimed that indenture offered an opportunity to the industrious poor, prevented them from becoming public charges after arrival, and allowed them to gradually integrate into the community. As late as 1835, as part of a larger screed against uncontrolled Irish immigration, Alexander Everett wrote in *North American Review* that indenture embedded the migrant in a web of mutual obligations, guaranteeing his service to the community and acting as insurance against his own destitution. The very willingness to indenture one's self even helped select migrants with an industrious character. During his indenture the migrant, "being thus supplied with immediate occupation, and placed in direct subordination to the habits, genius, and character of American society, he is provided with a species of national education, acquires a real as well as a legal citizenship, and in many instances obtains an interest in the rights of property as well as of persons."[4]

By this date it was a losing argument. It could not stand against the anti-slavery argument that freedom was a prerequisite for political participation, and that self-command of one's own labor was a key marker of freedom. In 1830 public opinion had already helped scuttle an attempt to import five thousand indentured Europeans to Jamaica in 1830, denouncing it as "white slavery."[5] To sign away a portion of one's liberty, even for a temporary period of indenture, was to be treated like property and little better than a slave. Anything less than complete freedom was not freedom at all. But Everett's position was also rendered irrelevant by new understandings of the meaning of a contract. Even among supporters of extended labor contracts, the contract was to be understood as an expression of free will and consent, not an instrument of patriarchal and community control. The ability to commit to a contract was both a measure and a consequence of freedom and power over one's own person. Even a contract of temporary indenture was justified if entered on the basis of an informed calculation of self-interest. The virtue of a contract was to be found in mutual advantage rather than social integration. To restrict the scope of possible contracts by banning indenture was to place limits on personal freedom.

Despite a broad consensus that contracts should be instruments of consent and legal equality, disagreements over the qualities that made a contract free or unfree only intensified by the middle of the nineteenth century. In the anglophone Atlantic of the early nineteenth century, the terms of engagement made all of the difference. A contract was free if entered into voluntarily, without coercion and in full knowledge of the consequences. But an alternative interpretation existed, especially in the northern U.S. states and among labor unions, that focused on the terms of enforcement. The use of physical restraint or penal sanctions to enforce a contract could render it unfree.

This was especially the case if one party was subject to penal sanctions while the other was subject only to civil and pecuniary penalties. The length of a contract was also a common means of defining an unfree contract, but it rarely was incorporated into legal definitions. By the 1870s, most states around the North Atlantic had begun to prohibit the enforcement of labor contracts through anything other than civil and pecuniary penalties.[6]

This shift in the understanding and use of contracts did not take place in labor relations between Europeans and non-Europeans. The basic issues of disagreement (among Europeans, at least) over Asian indenture were quite similar to those in the North Atlantic region. These disagreements settled into a relatively stable set of labor contracting laws and norms by the 1860s, but under very different terms from those of European labor contracts. Long-term indenture contracts were common in Asia and Africa, contracts could often be transferred between employers without the consent of the laborer, and freedom of contract continued be measured by the terms of engagement rather than enforcement. Most laws stipulating criminal enforcement of Asian indenture contracts were not repealed or modified until the first half of the twentieth century. The differences in contract regimes were framed by common assumptions about the difference of "Asiatics" themselves. Both pro- and anti-indenture publicists agreed that Asians were mired in outmoded customs under stagnant despotisms, not entirely capable of self-rule and certainly not free. It was premature, if not totally inapplicable, to expect Asians to exercise "freedom" on their own. For proof, one only need look at the fact that Asians continued to submit themselves to indenture, whether because they were too ignorant and servile to desire their own freedom or because they did not enjoy the material conditions to achieve their own freedom.

Both pro- and anti-indenture activists claimed that they could improve the lot of Asians, but they differed on whether indenture was an effective midwife for their liberation. Pro-indenture publicists emphasized the opportunities that migration offered to escape tyranny and poverty at home. Indenture would compel migrants to be industrious and productive rather than idle vagrants. Anti-indenture publicists were equally dismayed at idleness and lack of opportunity in Asia and equally convinced that Asians did not have the capability to emancipate themselves. But they mistrusted the ability of planters and labor recruiters, tainted by the history of slavery, to be agents of emancipation. Education and Christian missions were a much better solution. For both, however, government surveillance to protect the rights of indentured migrants was doubly justifiable on the belief that Asians could not understand or protect their own rights.

Debates over the benefits and conditions of Asian indenture have continued over the past 170 years. They have also continued to be framed by the terms of the Asian contract regime itself rather than interrogating those terms.[7] In particular, questions regarding the consensuality of the contracts have dominated these studies, suggesting that a distinct indenture regime could be justified to the extent that it allowed free, undeceived individuals to make uncoerced decisions and then deliver on those anticipated benefits. Were the laborers coerced, kidnapped, defrauded, or entrapped into debt? Did they fully understand the agreement that they made? Was government regulation effective? What were the gains and losses of indenture? Did they gain access to better wages? Were they subject to excessive punishments? What were the mortality rates? In the words of historian Marina Carter, such questions are driven by the conviction that "the minimization of mortality was to be the means by which a 'free' labour migration avoided degenerating into a '*coolie* trade.'"[8]

Taken as a whole, these studies and investigations have provided no clear answer to these questions. Whether because of partisan testimony in the evidence or the opacity of migration practices that could not easily fit into the binary of free and unfree, the amount of "freedom" enjoyed by indentured migrants remains controversial. Attempts to produce descriptions of indenture that conform to the categories of free and unfree have only succeeded in producing extremely ambivalent representations, the most concrete of which is the label of "pseudo-slavery."[9] But despite disagreements over the nature of the indenture experience and the effects of government supervision, there does seem to be general agreement that official surveillance of the conditions of contracting, transportation and labor is necessary to guarantee freedom. The optimal amount of freedom is subject to debate, but at the very least planters, humanitarians, officials, and the migrants themselves could all agree that they wanted migrants to be healthy and robust, recruited without deception and with little cause for violence. In other words, laissez-faire rhetoric or not, a government presence that restrained the actions of abusive private actors was seen as a main guarantor of both migrant rights and a robust labor market, a necessary condition for a "free migrant." Beyond this, however, understandings of freedom remained contested and internally contradictory.

Indenturing Indians

Plans to bring indentured Indians to sugar colonies in the Indian Ocean and Caribbean materialized immediately after the abolition of slavery in the British Empire in 1834. Criticisms of those plans emerged just as quickly. Both sides appealed to ideals of freedom, progress, and the greater interests of the empire. Pro-indenture activists spoke of how indenture was essential for the progress and prosperity of all parts of the empire. Contracts and cash advances "freed" impoverished migrants to circulate throughout the empire to places where they could work most effectively for the benefit of themselves and their employers. Indenture could alleviate poverty and overpopulation in India while assuaging labor shortages in the sugar colonies, allowing British plantations once again to be competitive with those in slave colonies like Cuba and Brazil. To suppress the right of Indians to move and enter into contracts freely was to undermine British ideals. As one Calcutta firm with an interest in emigration wrote to the Bengal government in 1838,

It is a question involving the rights of British subjects (in principle, of *all* British subjects) to carry their manual labor to the most productive market. . . . any other political doctrine, though practically extended for the present to only a particular class of men, must obviously be extensible to all classes alike; and to assert it, therefore, in this case, would be to establish a precedent of the most perilous nature to constitutional liberty.[10]

Anti-indenture activists drew on the ideals and institutions of the antislavery movement. They objected that the restrictions on personal liberty entailed in indenture contracts made them akin to slavery. No middle ground of partial freedom was acceptable. By infringing on freedom, the recruitment of indentured labor also infringed on humanity, family, and Christianity. The empire, they argued, had a responsibility to protect and assure the well-being of its colonial subjects. This was especially true for those who, whether due to ignorance or coercion, were unable to protect themselves against adventurers and self-interested capital.

In these early attempts at indenture, private companies were given almost complete freedom to recruit in India, required only to take potential migrants before a local magistrate who would assure that they were departing voluntarily. Almost nobody was satisfied with the operations of these companies. Only the Indian Ocean island of Mauritius was able to obtain a steady stream of labor. But even there planters complained of poor selectivity that left them with the "refuse of Indian bazaars."[11] Antislavery activists pointed out abuses such as kidnapping, deception, and high mortality on the voyage. The controversy and dissatisfaction was such that in 1838 the Colonial Office suspended recruitment pending an investigation into conditions in Mauritius and India (the same year that a pioneering commission was also sent to Canada to investigate conditions of the Atlantic passage). Members of the inquiry commission and of the Colonial Office in London were divided much along the same lines as the pro- and anti-indenture camps, and the resulting reports largely consolidated the arguments of each. After much delay, regulations were drawn up in 1842 that placed recruitment under government surveillance (the same year as a significantly revised passenger law was enacted for stronger surveillance over the Atlantic trade, albeit with much less controversy). Indentured emigration was first limited to Mauritius, but by the end of the decade it was extended to the Caribbean and Malaya, spurred by the gradual dismantling of British tariff preferences for colonial sugar that made Caribbean planters even more desperate to secure an inexpensive labor force.

As indenture became an established practice, the force of objections grew weaker. In part this was because the antislavery and anti-indenture movement was divided over the proper response to the removal of preferences and establishment of free trade. The decline of some sugar colonies after the end of slavery had undermined their claims about the superior virtue of free labor, and they found that most freed slaves (and colonized Asians) were reluctant to adopt "civilized" and Christian habits.[12] But more significant was the extent to which subsequent reports and official attitudes managed to set the terms of the debate in favor of regulated indenture. Pro-indenture arguments about the broad benefits of allowing contracts and the market to do the work of "freeing" potential migrants were presented as structural truths. Objections to indenture were disaggregated into a series of "abuses" that could be limited through surveillance and regulation. By 1864 the regulations of previous quarter century were consolidated into single law that continued to be revised through the 1880s. Its provisions included supervision by agents and "protectors" appointed by colonial governments; the establishment of depots at ports where migrants could be inspected and their distribution regulated; medical examinations; investigations by magistrates into the conditions under which the contract was signed; the listing of specific conditions to be included in the contracts; licensing of subrecruiters; regulation of shipboard conditions; and the specification of laws in destination colonies to be enacted before emigration would be permitted. Although the early indenture laws had grown simultaneously with British passenger laws focused on abuses in Liverpool, the Atlantic laws ultimately failed to expand beyond licensing brokers and the inspection of shipboard conditions and were enforced by a declining corps of officers. The progressive state first embraced Asia.[13]

These regulations did not establish direct government intervention so much as set parameters of acceptable health, voluntariness, responsibility, and transparency. Within this space abuses could be minimized, and participants could be seen as free and autonomous agents. As the lieutenant governor of Bengal instructed the protectors stationed in India, "The Protector should initiate no action. His authority should be limited to checking any abuse: to seeing that the laws and regulations in force are properly observed; and to securing the coolies from deception or violence. . . . The Agent [of the destination colonies] should see to the interests of the colonies; and the Protector to those of the coolie."[14] This position was formally framed as "benevolent neutrality," the idea that the proper role of government was a mild surveillance to ensure fair play and that none of the participants impinged on the freedom of each other or the market. This helped focus subsequent debate on the effectiveness of this regulation rather than the legitimacy of indenture itself. Repeated rounds of official inquiries only confirmed the "objectivity" of government surveillance by allowing pro- and anti-indenture proponents to fill the committees and have their say, with the government acting as impartial mediator. So long as the debate continued to be framed as a choice between slavery and freedom, new conceptualizations of indenture were discouraged, and any government action in favor of freedom helped maintain the premise that indenture was not a new form of slavery.

In 1875 the government of India briefly explored the possibility of more direct official encouragement and management of emigration. The secretary of state for India reformulated pro-indenture arguments to make the case that managed migration would be to the benefit of all:

From an Indian point of view, emigration properly regulated and accomplished by sufficient assurance of profitable employment and fair treatment seems a thing to be encouraged on grounds of humanity, with a view to promote the well-being of the poorer classes. We may also consider from an imperial point of view, the great advantage which must result from peopling the warmer British possessions, which are high in natural resources and only want of population by an intelligent and industrious race to whom the climate of these countries is well suited.[15]

Objections to this proposal came from officials who objected to emigration altogether and those who worried that overseas colonies competed against the needs of tea and coffee planters in India. A more general objection was that managed migration would only create a permanent subservient condition for Indian emigrants rather than "free" them into opportunities for upward mobility. Officials ultimately opted for the status quo. In 1877 the government of India explained that it did not want to involve itself in the enforcement of contracts in the colonies because "it would keep [the emigrant] in the state of helplessness and dependence upon the action of Government to which he is accustomed in this country, and from which it is one of the most desirable results of the emigration to free him."[16] A free market, properly regulated, was to be the school of experience that brought India out of its subservient state— although nobody thought to ask whether that subservience should be dated prior to or as a consequence of intensified British regulation.

Of course, not everybody was satisfied that government surveillance succeeded in curbing abuses and promoting the educational discipline of a free market. Increased competition between destination colonies encouraged deception and circumvention of regulations by agents in India. Emigrants often appeared before magistrates in groups, in which rote interviews and substitutions of examinees made the premise of any substantial investigation into the conditions of their contracts seem absurd. And even if colonial indenture laws were up to the standards demanded by India, it did not mean that they would be effectively implemented. Protectors and magistrates often blatantly failed to enforce them or interpreted them in favor of planter interests. And other colonial laws to police "vagrants," to establish expensive registration taxes and pass systems, and to restrict commercial activities and property holding for postindenture Indians often made it difficult for Asians to exist as anything but indentured laborers or potential criminals while abroad.

Some critics continued to blame rapacious capitalism for these problems, but most agreed with the government in directing the blame to the Indians themselves. Not only did Indians have a tendency to prey upon each other, but their ignorance and weakness made them unable to know and protect their own interests. Indian recruiters and subcontractors were widely believed to be the "worst kind of men," motivated purely by profit to defraud their compatriots and—despite their supposed subservience—to hide their activities from the government. They operated in labyrinthine ways far beyond the comprehension of any official. Their understanding and manipulation of the situations and needs of natives allowed them to bring potential migrants under their control and to exploit those in trouble by paying their debts and offering advances. But it was precisely their deviousness and inscrutability that were thought to make them so indispensable. European agents argued that they would never be able to penetrate the dense customs and social networks of the villages and cities without the assistance of these local recruiters.[17] Continuing discussion about the need to regulate or suppress these recruiters only convinced observers that Indians themselves, not the indenture system, were responsible for most of the abuses.

Although several times as many Indian migrants traveled and worked through informal recruitment networks, the attention given to indenture—measured in terms of reports, debates, descriptions, and historical analyses—dwarfs the attention given to self-organized migration. Indeed, overseas indenture was written into the very definition of emigration in the Emigration Act of 1883, which defined emigration as "Departure by sea out of British India of a Native of India under an agreement to labour for hire in some country beyond the limits of India other than the island of Ceylon or the Straits Settlements." Migration to coffee and tea plantations in Ceylon, dominated by *kangani* recruiters, attracted almost no attention in official correspondence until 1893 and no legislation until 1901, despite migration rates over four times higher than those to indentured destinations.[18] This lack of regulation was not merely a result of cultural and physical proximity. Indenture regulations for Assam in northeastern India were established in the 1860s almost as soon as migration was desired, as were recruiter licensing laws to Burma in the 1870s.[19] Apparently, all forms of regulation and organization could produce satisfactory labor markets. And all could become objects of critique when labor flows failed to meet demand. For example, the planters in Malaya encouraged *kangani* migration in the late nineteenth century as more "free" and "progressive" than indentured migration, and then in 1904 they tried unsuccessfully to supplant native recruiters with government recruitment when labor supplies hit another cycle of scarcity.[20] But knowledge about Indian migration, what it meant to be a free migrant, and rhetoric to characterize and critique all forms of Asian migration were definitely produced in the context of indenture.

Indenturing Chinese

Indian indenture prospered within the British Empire until the turn of the twentieth century. Attempts to indenture laborers from the Chinese Empire were much less successful. By the 1870s, just as the Indian indenture system was consolidated, Chinese indentured emigration was severely curtailed in the wake of abuses and bad publicity. British and Americans blamed most of the abuses on the incompetence of the Chinese government and the schemes and greed of nonanglophone recruiters. Ultimately, however, the biggest problem was that Chinese indenture did not take place within the surveillance of a single empire but across multiple frontiers, departing from China, Macao, and Hong Kong to a variety of destinations that included Hawaii, Peru, and British, Dutch, French, and Spanish colonies. In this international context, private recruiters could more easily evade regulations and shop for more favorable forums. International competition for laborers also facilitated waves of international accusations and publicity. On this global stage British and U.S. diplomats forsake "benevolent neutrality" in favor of condemnation of the "coolie trade" and collaboration with China to formulate a more restrictive set of regulations.[21]

Like India, China appeared to be a favorable site for labor recruitment because of a commercialized rural economy and dense population. But occasional attempts to recruit laborers from the 1810s to mid-1840s were largely unsuccessful. Restrictions on foreign merchants made it difficult for European recruiters to operate on the mainland, and competition from Chinese recruiters limited European activities even in Singapore. The establishment of Hong Kong and new treaty ports after the Opium War in 1842 led to renewed attempts to work from the mainland. In 1851 British officials began to look into the possibility of indenturing laborers from southern China to work in the Caribbean. Reports from a variety of sources were already aware of extensive Chinese-organized labor migration to mines and agricultural areas throughout Southeast Asia over the previous hundred years, and of prevalent financing schemes in which the migrants' passages were paid in advance in return for one year of labor abroad.[22] They often described this migration as "free," even comparing it favorably to European migration. As late as 1876, in response to questions posed by a California investigation into the conditions of Chinese migration, the U.S. minister in Beijing, William Williams, acknowledged that many migrants took out debts and other obligations to finance their migration, but he situated this as a positive effect of the market forces and political restraint of China and the United States as compared with the aristocracies, serfs, and deportations of Europe:

> There is no caste among the Chinese, no privileged class or titled aristocracy on the one hand claiming rights over serfs, or slaves on the other; and, consequently, no power inheres in the hands of one portion of society to get rid of their drones, their criminals, their paupers, or their useless slaves, by shipping them to other lands. Those who arrive in California are free men, poor, ignorant, and uncivilized indeed, easily governed and not disposed to make trouble in any way, but hoping to get a good price for their labor. . . . The imperial government can no more control the movement of its subjects, or keep them within its territory, than the President can restrain those of our citizens; neither power can control or limit emigration or travel.[23]

In 1853, the British Foreign Office asked its consuls on the South China coast if Chinese migration to the West Indies should be enticed through contracts and advances or left "wholly free and unfettered." The consuls unanimously agreed that a contract and cash advance were necessary to get Chinese to migrate to an unknown land.[24] The issue was not that Chinese were impoverished and ignorant of migration, but that they already had access to well-developed migration networks and strong commercial acumen. Recruitment for the West Indies would have to be competitive.

The first attempts at recruitment in Amoy (Xiamen), chosen for its long-standing practices of labor migration, not only failed to be competitive but caused riots against the Western companies that attempted them. The main complaints were that the Chinese recruiters engaged by the companies were outsiders who used kidnapping and deceit.[25] Indeed, such practices were probably necessary in order to recruit Chinese to unknown lands on terms much less favorable than those in Southeast Asia, although the influence of rumors spread by competing recruiters cannot be discounted. The British retrenched to Hong Kong, where, despite repeated efforts over the next fifteen years, they were never able to establish indenture recruitment on favorable terms and without "abuses."

To many Europeans, the Chinese state was a major obstacle to a smooth regime of free emigration. They saw it as excessively authoritarian and opposed to free intercourse, yet incapable of enforcing its own laws against emigration.

It was indeed difficult to engage Chinese officials on this topic because of the embarrassment of discussing the regulation of a migration that was officially prohibited. After the withdrawal from Amoy, the Colonial Office instructed Hong Kong Governor John Bowring to notify consuls in China that they were not to aid in the recruitment of coolies, but "if the Chinese subjects of their own free will should prefer to risk the penalty attached to the transgression of the law . . . you are not bound to prevent, or even ostensibly be cognizant of, such acts, for it is the duty of the Chinese government to enforce its own laws."[26] But this attitude did not prove sufficient to channel labor away from competing recruiters in China or Macao. Indeed, obtaining a steady supply of "free" emigrants in an international sphere beyond the regulatory efforts of any single government would prove elusive. An 1853 report from the Colonial Land and Emigration Commissioners feared that increased regulations in Hong Kong would drive recruiters to Macao and migrants to destinations outside of the British Empire. But they also worried, in reference to China, that it "would appear difficult to deal with abuses which take place in collecting foreign emigrants in a foreign country, having its own political and judicial organisation, and jealously alive to any interference with that organisation."[27]

At the same time, the presence of Chinese in Hong Kong, outside the control of Chinese state, was no guarantee of their freedom. Rather, it only generated new ways to depict the migrants as unfree and the cause of their own abuse. Already in the 1840s, Hong Kong officials who worried about their still tenuous control over the island argued that once Chinese were freed from the despotic control of the Chinese state, it could only be expected that a people with no habits of self-restraint would relapse into banditry and licentiousness. The very act of movement selected for such people. As Chinese Secretary Charles Gutzlaff wrote in 1846, "It is very natural that depraved, idle, and bad characters from the adjacent mainland and islands should flock to the colony where some money can be made. They are a roving set of beings, and committing depredations wherever it can be done with impunity; they cannot be considered as domesticated, and are in the habit of coming and going according to the state of the trade."[28] Governor Bowring borrowed this image to explain the Amoy riots, arguing that emigration had become such a habit that the town was overpopulated by "the idle, vagrant and profligate," that, when stimulated by greedy Western recruiters, made it impossible to establish "a quiet, steady and progressing system of well-digested emigration, giving time for the fit selection and becoming organization of proper bodies of Chinamen."[29]

British officials also identified Chinese customs and economic practices as problems working against a migration that was free from abuse, even when those customs seemed similar to the basic principles of free contracts. West Indian planters were adamant about the need for female emigrants to create a less "depraved" laboring population. James White, the emigration agent in China, argued that this would only be possible by offering bounties to men who traveled with their wives. This was based on the perceptions that there were cultural restrictions against female emigration and that the sale of women and children was pervasive in Chinese society. White concluded that the distinction between marriage and a market transaction was trivial, and slavery was indistinguishable from the patriarchal control over the household. Female emigrants could be obtained only by collaborating with local practices.[30] This led to some discussion over and ethnographic reports on whether proper marriage even existed in China. The Colonial Land and Emigration commissioners ultimately agreed with White, adding that "Whatever may be thought of the state of morality which renders this possible, we cannot but point out that, as far as the woman is concerned, the result will be to raise her from the state of slavery under Chinese, to that of freedom under British law. . . . We cannot help hoping that these considerations will be held to constitute a substantial difference between the proceedings recommended by Mr. White and the Slave Trade."[31] Hong Kong Governor George Bonham, however, objected that Mr. White's plan "would doubtless give rise [to] . . . a trade little different from the Slave Trade," arguing that "The offer of a premium, without some official check, is a dangerous experiment to try with so venal and money-grasping a people as the Chinese." He added that if such a plan were to be implemented,

> The British authority should inquire carefully into every case of marriage so performed; should have the parties brought up before him, and the woman narrowly and strictly examined previous to shipment, and a declaration made and signed by her, to the effect that she was a free and voluntary emigrant, that she freely and voluntarily married her present husband, and that no compulsion or any other agency had been set at work to induce her to do so. Without some official control of this nature, the plan would be a bad one, for the offer of a premium such as that suggested, without some official check, is a dangerous experiment to try with so venal and money-grasping a people as the Chinese.[32]

A system similar to Bonham's was finally adopted as a solution that was "less abhorrent to our notions of freedom and less suggestive of abuse."[33] In all perspectives, the Chinese condition in the absence of British intervention was conceived as degradation and slavery. Indeed, the very commercialization that framed the civilizing potential of indenture had become the source of Chinese corruption.

Beginning in 1855 the Hong Kong government also passed a series of passenger laws based on those in India and England to better regulate the indenture trade. They required that the harbormaster make sure that all passengers traveled voluntarily, that all brokers be licensed, and, after 1858, that British ships did not carry emigrants beyond the British Empire. As predicted by the Land and Emigration Commission, most of these measures just pushed recruiting operations into Macao, especially those for Cuba and Peru. The British military occupation of Guangdong from 1858 to 1861 during the Arrow War (also called the Second Opium War) created an opportunity that officials believed would provide "great facilities for conducting emigration on fair and humane principles."[34] Europeans worked with local Chinese officials to develop a system of surveillance similar to India's. Governor General Lao Chongguang issued orders to local magistrates in April 1859 to punish all kidnappers, to make sure that emigrants were aware of all the conditions of their contract, and to reassure migrants that the government had no objection to their departing with the foreigners once both parties had given their consent. Emigration depots were established in October, requiring at least a forty-eight-hour stay during which migrants were subjected to a joint examination by Chinese officers and emigration agents, and given a chance to think more carefully before signing a contract. A public proclamation from the governor general that month described the regulations and explained of the migrants that "Their emigration is voluntary, and wholly different from that which is conducted by the kidnapper who sells his fellow-man. In order that this villainy may be stopped, and the difference between it and the former made patent to the world, such means of investigation and of inspection should be provided as will plainly denote a distinction."[35]

Collaboration in the regulation of emigration not necessarily mean a common understanding. During the negotiations over proper regulations, Prince Gong of the Zongli Yamen (the Chinese foreign affairs office) had also distinguished labor emigrants from other migrants by insisting that, "Although they are employed by foreigners and received monthly salaries, they are not selling their labor to foreigners, they should be considered as if China were loaning them to foreign countries to use. Therefore, even though they have left their homeland, they are still entitled to protection from the Chinese government."[36] This new surveillance, which for the Europeans meant a guarantee of the emigrants' freedom, was for the Chinese a means of asserting government jurisdiction in the face of other powers and over migrants themselves. Those who departed without surveillance were not entitled to protection.

The legitimacy of these arrangements was recognized in a provision of the Treaty of Beijing signed between Britain and China in 1860 that declared that Chinese subjects "are at perfect liberty to enter into engagements with British subjects . . . and to ship themselves and their families onboard any British vessels at the open ports of China." Some local officials continued to accuse the foreigners of kidnapping, and an investigatory report noted local suspicions that Europeans would use lotion to lighten the emigrants' skin, curl their hair, and then conscript them into foreign armies.[37] But Beijing seemed satisfied with the new arrangements and began negotiations with Britain and France to formalize them under an international convention. China, Russia, the United States, and Prussia ratified the convention in 1866, but the French objected to stipulations that contracts be no longer than five years, that return passage be provided after the expiration of the contract, and that emigration depots could not be established without the permission of the Chinese government. The French convinced the British to join them in not ratifying the convention, but China insisted that the terms of the convention be enforced anyway for any recruitment within China.

International Surveillance

Surveillance was difficult to maintain in the international conditions of the South China coast. Chinese depots were rarely used because recruitment via Macao circumvented this system altogether. Portuguese authorities did promulgate regulations similar to those in India and China, but most observers claimed that enforcement was no more than a farce. By the late 1860s, Europeans and Chinese in Hong Kong frequently protested activities in Macao. As British ships were prohibited from carrying emigrants from Macao, the British had little interest in supporting the freedom of emigrants to depart from any port they wanted. In these conditions, accounts of Chinese indenture contracts grew overwhelmingly negative, depicting the indenture trade as an abuse and infringement on individual freedom and calling for government intervention that went far beyond the benevolent neutrality of the Indian government.

In 1867 Hong Kong Legislative Consul J. Whittall claimed that even the rigorously monitored emigration from Hong Kong should be banned because it was a stain on the reputation of the colony. Indenture contracts should also be made invalid in British courts because "they shift the responsibility of the miserable coolie's detention from the shoulders of his kidnappers to those of official authority. . . . Let voluntary emigration, pure and simple, be as uncontrolled from China as from Ireland, but let it be made criminal for British subjects to aid, abet, or in any way subserve, contracts of servitude for a term of years."[38] London officials, concerned with justifying Indian indenture, dismissed these objections. Acting Colonial Secretary Henry John Ball in London responded that, under existing arrangements, Chinese emigrants knew what they were getting themselves into. He blamed the problems on the severity of existing regulations and even hoped that "a uniform form of contract might perhaps be settled on terms more just to the planters than that adopted by the Peking Convention [of 1866], which has caused nearly all honest and open emigration to cease, and has thrown the trade into the hands of unscrupulous parties, who care nothing for the Chinese Government or their Convention, thus actually increasing the evils which it was intended to suppress."[39] In more moderate terms the colonial secretary, the duke of Buckingham, added that the suspension of emigration from Hong Kong would cause difficult international complications. He insisted that the British government fulfilled its duty to the migrants merely by ascertaining that they signed their contracts voluntarily and understood their decision.[40]

Opinions in Hong Kong were not so easily mollified. A series of scandals in the early 1870s resulted in British- and Chinese-led international pressure to stop the labor trade from Macao, especially to Cuba and Peru. In 1870 indentured laborers carried out of Macao on the French ship *Nouvelle Pénelope* rebelled and killed some sailors. The ship then docked in Hong Kong, where the justice of the peace declared that the emigrants had been taken against their wishes and were justified in their rebellion. Nonetheless, the French consul demanded that China pay restitution for the sailors who had been killed even if the rebels themselves were not to be punished. The British judge objected that the laws against slavery should be universal and respected by the French and the Chinese, but he ultimately admitted that he had no jurisdiction over relations between China and France. China agreed to pay the indemnity.[41] But that event and a riot on the *Dolores Ugarte* out of Macao that same year helped motivate officials of several countries to act against Macao. The governor of Hong Kong tried to stop all ships fitted in that colony from picking up Chinese passengers in Macao. In 1873 Governor General Ruilin in Canton attempted a blockade against Macao, and Beijing sent a commission to Cuba to inspect the condition of the emigrants. The governor of Macao responded with talk of the many local jobs that depended on the emigrant business and promised to review and reform the licensing procedure.[42] In 1874 Chinese passengers escaped from the Peruvian ship *María Luz* to a British vessel anchored in Japan's Yokohama harbor. Japanese authorities set up a tribunal to decide if they should be sent back to the *María Luz*, hearing opposing arguments by representatives from Britain and Peru. Appealing to both "universal law" and Japanese laws against slavery, the tribunal decided that the Chinese should not be forced to reembark against their will. Several European consuls in Japan (except Britain and the United States) protested against the irregularity of these proceedings and the lack of jurisdiction enjoyed by the Japanese, but the decision was not reversed.[43]

The publicity and diplomatic pressure generated by these incidents led Macao and Hong Kong to suppress contract labor altogether. China soon signed treaties of friendship and commerce with Peru and Spain that permitted free migration between their countries, although few migrants took advantage of this until after 1900. China continued to allow indentured emigration, but only in the context of bilateral agreements with rigorous conditions that made it an issue of international relations rather than one of property and private control. For Japan, its handling of the *Maria Luz* affair was an important step in its long climb to escape "Asia" and be considered as one of the civilized nations. The Japanese tribunal had assumed the power to determine the conditions of slavery and freedom, whereas India and China still depended on external surveillance.

Migration Obscured

Between the accusations and counteraccusations, the vested interests and the shifting of blame to crimps (local Asian recruiters) and subcontractors, it is hard to know how the actual recruitment of migrants took place. The practices of migration were lost under the rhetoric, never able to fit within the categories of voluntary or coerced. Recruiters were compelled to obscure their modes of organization in order to fulfill the formal needs of inquiries into their freedom. This further perpetuated an understanding of all Asian and especially Chinese migration as somehow illegitimate and unfree, and even obscured knowledge about the very existence of Chinese migration that was not indentured.

In 1854 the Hong Kong harbormaster wrote that the free emigrant and the coolie "are understood to be widely different, the former being a class of persons who have paid their passage, while the latter are understood to be those who have had their passage paid for them under an agreement."[44] But perhaps the great majority of migrants borrowed money from relatives, friends, companies, and crimps to pay their passages to destinations like California, Victoria, and Singapore without a formal contract. Most of these transactions went unnoticed by officials. Indeed, ignorance of the conditions of migration became the official stance of Hong Kong officials in the wake of the coolie scandals and regulation—much like the earlier disinclination of Chinese officials to discuss emigration. In 1881, in response to requests from Australia to report on the free or unfree nature of Chinese emigration, the attorney general of Hong Kong would only say that he had been consulted on the meaning of contract emigration and its relation to debt obligations many times. His answer was that he could only address concrete cases, not hypotheticals.[45] Only in 1910 did Hong Kong formally admit that many Chinese engaged in "kangany" emigration, in which a returned migrant gave assistance to new emigrants.[46]

The very act of ascertaining the "freedom" of emigrants served to push the actual organization of emigration underground. For example, after the passage of U.S. laws prohibiting the participation of U.S. ships in the coolie trade in 1862, consuls had to inspect every U.S. ship departing Hong Kong to make sure that all of the passengers were voluntary. At first, the consuls were perplexed by their charge. In 1869, confronted by more than two hundred Chinese recruited to work in southern sugar plantations, the U.S. consul wrote to the State Department asking, "What constitutes a free and voluntary migrant?" The State Department could give no advice.[47] By 1871, the consuls had developed a ritualized interaction similar to that designed to demonstrate freedom in India and Macao. The consul would board the ship immediately before departure and ask each migrant the following questions:

Q: Who induced you to go?

A: No one.

Q: Why do you go?

 . A: Because I wish to get higher wages and be a free man.

Q: Who sold you your ticket?

A: The elder.

Q: Did you sign any contract to work in America in payment for the ticket?

A: No.

Q: Have you make *any* arrangement with regard to your labor after arrival in California?

A: No.

Q: Then you declare unqualifiedly that you are under no obligations whatever to any persons, which will bind you to labor for any particular party in the United States?

A: I do.[48]

Russell Conwell, the Baptist minister who recorded this exchange, claimed that emigrants actually bought their tickets via brokers from local officials, pledging their families as guarantees of repayment. The brokers then trained the migrants how to answer the questions properly.[49] The very act of guaranteeing freedom had transformed migration into an act of evasion, regardless of the actual status of each migrant.

The ambiguities of migration were further exacerbated by brokers and recruiters who manipulated the vocabulary of coolies and freedom in their competition with each other and attempts to avoid surveillance. For example, in 1876 the Hawaiian government authorized two Chinese companies in Honolulu to recruit indentured laborers for the sugar plantations. By 1878, Chinese in Hong Kong and Canton were publicly criticizing the recruiters from Hawaii as slave traders. The Hong Kong government refused to grant them a recruiting license, and officials in Canton arrested two of them. In the meantime, contracted laborers were departing to Hawaii from the Chinese port of Whampoa on ships chartered by the Chinese-owned China Merchant Steam Navigation Company. Beijing ordered investigations by Minister Chen Lanbin in Honolulu and Governor General Liu Kunyi in Guangdong. The latter claimed that all the emigrants had paid their own passage and were departing under arrangements no different from those for emigrants who left for San Francisco or Singapore, although he did not clarify what those arrangements were. The press in Hong Kong and Hawaii, however, accused the China Merchant Steam Navigation Company of having manipulated public opinion and colluded with local Chinese officials to have its competitors arrested. Ultimately, nobody knew who was protecting whose interests or how these workers were recruited, except that they ended up with five-year contracts in Hawaii.[50]

In Singapore, officials, planters, and urban merchants had a more direct interest in strong flow of labor, and the coolie scandals ultimately translated into legislation aimed at regulating autonomous Chinese labor organization rather than indenture per se. Starting in 1868, several passenger and immigrant registration bills proposed in the Singapore legislature were defeated, largely by the argument that they would be a useless expense that interfered with growing local labor needs. All sides in the debate, however, including urban Chinese merchants who had petitioned for stronger migrant protections, agreed on the need to limit the power of "secret societies" and unregulated brokers over the migrants. A petition from European planters in 1873 insisted that the free market was the best protection because, once outside the influence of the secret societies, "the competition for labor is so great as to obtain for the newly arrived Immigrant perfect security from extortion or unfair labor bargains. The only danger which assails him is that he may be, either before landing or after, hurried and cajoled into engagements to work in countries outside of this Settlement, and in ignorance shipped away beyond the influence and protection of our laws."[51] The Chinese brokers, on the other hand, were more desirous of contracts and depots as a way to stop runaways. A commission appointed to investigate recruitment in 1874 was unconvinced that any serious abuses existed in the current system but nonetheless remained concerned about the lack of government surveillance,

The Government knows little or nothing of the Chinese, who are the industrial backbone of these Settlements; and the immense majority of them know nothing of the Government. We know that a certain number of Chinese arrive each year, and that a certain number go away; but how long they stay, how many come back a second time, what they think about and desire,—as to all this we know nothing. . . . We believe that the vast majority of the Chinamen who come to work in these Settlements return to their country not knowing clearly whether there is a Government in them or not.[52]

The legislature finally agreed on an ordinance to suppress secret societies in 1869 and the establishment of the Chinese Protectorate in 1877, which would manage an immigrant depot to supervise the signing of labor contracts by indebted migrants. The depots, however, were contracted out to private brokers, and less than 10 percent of the migrants ever used them, most routinely claiming that they paid their own passage. A later investigation in 1890, despite again concluding that "the abuses of the current system are more sentimental than real," still insisted that interventions by the Chinese government and unscrupulous actions of brokers of the "most worthless class" who exercised undue persuasion on the migrants disrupted the workings of a truly free market.[53] It asserted that "It is important that the coolly should be a free agent, at liberty to choose the employment and country he prefers."[54] To this end it proposed an extensive system of government-operated depots from China to Singapore that would channel migrants directly to their destinations after signing contracts in China.

In these debates, the very meaning of a "free" market or "free" labor became as obscure as the practices of migration themselves. But the characterization of Chinese as somehow an obstacle to freedom was increasingly unquestioned. This understanding became one of the main justifications for the creation of concrete boundaries that would divide the world into geographical arenas of free migrants and coolies. In 1879 David Bailey, once the U.S. consul in Hong Kong charged with keeping prostitutes from leaving and now stationed in Shanghai, selected material from ongoing debates about indenture and the sale of women and children to write a long treatise on Chinese slavery and concubinage, which he forwarded to the U.S. State Department with the comment, "If Chinese emigration to the United States is to continue and increase with slavery or *quasi* slavery, and concubinage, inbred and permeating its every feature and organization, so that they may be said to be an indissoluble part of its present system, is it not a subject to which American statesmen should turn their attention with some degree of anxiety?"[55] However conceived, slavery was a characteristic that was intrinsic to Chinese society.

By this time, committees and politicians in the United States no longer needed to be convinced. The image of the bound Asian coolie had become an indelible part of the public culture in white settler colonies. The very nature of Chinese society had made it impossible for Chinese to be free migrants. A freedom defined by commercial transactions may be sufficient for colonial planters and capitalist magnates, but not for residence in a civilized nation of self-governing equals. The very surveillance that officials and planters had found necessary to guarantee a minimal level of freedom had helped mark Asians as inherently incapable of exercising freedom on their own, as something other than "true" immigrants. To this day, the binary of free and enslaved continues to frame the project of writing Asians into the immigration histories of Western settler nations. It is merely turned on its head to cast as free individuals, dreaming to settle, yearning for liberty, releasing pent energies, and "breaking the cake of custom."[56] To depict them as indebted laborers, sojourners, or otherwise embedded in networks of obligation rather than individualistic liberty would be to "exclude them categorically from American immigration history."[57] The many alternatives between coolies and free, voluntaristic settler-immigrants are quietly erased, obscured under an aura of illegitimacy and embarrassment.[58]

4

Nationalization of Migration Control

The 1870s are generally considered the apex of laissez-faire migration around the Atlantic, if not the world. But even if direct restriction was at a nadir, this was also when the experimentation of the previous half century finally consolidated into the basic framework for modern migration control. The ideal of free migration replaced that of migration as commerce and the nation became the sole legitimate source of identification and control. In Asia, institutions to enforce free migration against the perceived abuses of despotic regimes and unscrupulous brokers were well consolidated. In the Atlantic world, the private organization of migration was increasingly illegitimate unless willing to collaborate with official surveillance. More than merely a period of limited government intervention, the 1870s were when acceptable forms of private and official regulation, and the distinction between the two, were firmly established.

The story of the national centralization of identities and mobility control is ultimately part of the much larger story about the creation of an international system of states and the rise of the modern citizen. The parts of this story that are of immediate relevance to migration control include the legal and political struggles against local and corporate regulation, the rise of the modern passport, and an attack on transnational migrant institutions and networks in favor of large transportation companies and formal charities as the most legitimate forms of private organization. In all of these cases, the imposition of national controls was justified by the insistence that migration was ultimately an international matter that should be regulated by national governments rather than local institutions with low accountability. This centralization was so successful that by the 1920s, national borders had even replaced other impediments such as distance, cost, and local institutions as the main obstacles to mobility. The sovereign nation state had become both the main building block and primary impediment of global integration.

Migration in International Law

The 1870s were also a period when the idea of intercourse was at its apex in international law, especially among anglophile lawyers. At the turn of the nineteenth century, intercourse was generally conceived as the entwined relationships of trade and diplomacy between nations. By the middle of the century, commerce and migration had become the heart of intercourse. Political relations were treated less as an aspect of intercourse than as the process by which the customs and usages of intercourse were transformed into treaties and law (or else undermined, if the politics were unenlightened). This reconceptualization of intercourse as a prelegal expression of natural phenomena was very much in tune with laissez-faire ideals. But rather than promoting an absence of regulation, international lawyers understood intercourse as a source of codifiable international law which, once discovered, could be put to the service of further perfecting intercourse. Many lawyers argued that the very possibility of international law depended on the existence of intercourse between states. But, as implied by this formulation, they were ultimately even more dependent on the existence of a community of discrete and equal sovereign states as the fundamental subject of international law. Indeed, the existence of states was taken as a given while the usages and laws of intercourse were seen as a work in progress. But this progress was never fulfilled, and by the end of the century deference to sovereign powers largely trumped the unrealized claims of intercourse.[1] But this new privileging of national sovereignty still had to be justified in terms of the virtues and necessity of intercourse.

Over the nineteenth century, international lawyers gradually diverged from their predecessors in at least two ways: decreased attention to the individual as a source of rights and object of law, and the replacement of natural law with positivist methodology. States retained the centrality that they had attained in the eighteenth century. But the earlier concern over the proper relationships of individuals to the state was relegated to the sphere of municipal law as international lawyers increasingly limited their own jurisdiction to interactions between states. Ironically, the growing emphasis on positivist methodology actually made it increasingly difficult for international lawyers to say anything concrete about those interactions. The job of a positivist lawyer was to observe and codify actual practice between states—what states did rather than what they *should* do. Truth and order were to be found in the school of experience, not in the fanciful speculations of natural law. The need for international law was still grounded in much the same arguments of natural law, that compromises, harmonious interaction, and stability served the long-term interests of everybody. But the older vocabulary of duty, honor, and obligation was replaced by one of consent, reciprocity, retaliation, and the necessity of progress as the sources of legal behavior. Well-established precedents and agreements were the meat and potatoes of positive international law, which could fill the generalities of intercourse with concrete legal guidelines. But in a period of change and uncertainty, few well-established modes of regulating migration existed beyond a diverse plethora of national and local laws. Ultimately, the mere existence and diffusion of national legislation became the only identifiable common usage.

Writing in 1788, Georg Friedrich von Martens, a pioneer of the resurgent positivist tradition, formulated the issue of commerce with a logic that would frame later discussions of intercourse and migration (and with a conciseness rarely reproduced in those later discussions): "Men being by nature obliged to assist each other reciprocally, there exists a sort of general obligation for them to carry on commerce with each other. This obligation, however, is only an imperfect one; it does not hinder a nation to consult its interests in the adoption of certain conditions or restrictions."[2] By the second half of the nineteenth century, migration was increasingly specified as an aspect of commerce that could be considered independently of trade. But discussion of migration actually declined in comparison to the eighteenth century, and any specifics beyond von Martens's general principle remained elusive in the face of empirical and theoretical difficulties. Discussion of the natural rights of exiles and travelers gave way before an almost exclusive emphasis on states. And jurists had almost nothing to say about freedom of exit other than the occasional remark that it was a matter of internal legislation or that exit restrictions seemed to be declining.[3] They were slightly more effusive on the question of entry. Most agreed that the right to exclude and expel aliens was a basic condition of sovereignty, but that certain limits on those powers were a practical necessity to reap the benefits of intercourse and avoid retaliation.[4]

In his *Introduction to International Law*, first published in 1860, Yale University President Theodore Woolsey posed questions that highlighted the ambiguous terrain staked out by the simultaneous emphasis on sovereignty and intercourse:

Sovereignty in the strictest sense authorizes a nation to decide upon what terms it will have intercourse with foreigners, and even to shut out all mankind from its borders. If a protective tariff, or the prohibition of certain articles is no violation of rights, it is hard to say how far one state may not go in refusing to have commerce with another. If foreigners may be placed under surveillance or may have various rights of citizens refused to them, why may they not be excluded from territory? If it be said that the destiny of separate states, as of separate families, is to be helpful to one another, that entire isolation is impossible, still the amount of intercourse must be let to the judgment of the party interested; and if a state, judging incorrectly, strives to live within itself as much as possible, is it to be forced to change its policy, any more than to modify its protective tariff? And yet some kind of intercourse of neighboring states is so natural, that it must have been coeval with their foundation, and with the origin of law; it is so necessary that to decline it involves often extreme inhumanity; it is so essential to the progress of mankind, that unjust wars have been blessings when they opened nations to one another. There could, of course, be no international law without it.[5]

In searching for a middle ground, Woolsey first deferred to state sovereignty by framing the problem in terms of choice rather than obligation,

> Intercourse, whether through travelers or merchants, is regulated by the free sovereign act of each state. Whether it will have a passport system, a protective tariff, special supervision of strangers; whether it will give superior commercial privileges to one nation over another; in short, whether it will be fair and liberal, or selfish and monopolizing, it must decide, like any private tradesman or master of a family, for itself. The law of nations does not interfere at this point with the will of the individual state (89).

But, like natural law theorists before him, Woolsey qualified the scope of free action by drawing attention to the undesirable consequences of poor choices that went against established usages. Thus, a state could not exclude the properly documented subjects of a friendly state without giving definite reasons. To a large extent this was merely a practical necessity to avoid retaliation and enjoy the benefits of intercourse. But Woolsey backed these utilitarian calculations with a charged vocabulary of progress and advancement. He taunted those who might reject international law with the threat of being left behind in the march of civilization, "Non-intercourse and restriction are fast disappearing from the commercial arrangements of the world, and jealousy of foreigners is vanishing from the minds of all the more civilized nations, in the East as well as in the West" (89). William Hall, a firm believer in states' "duty of sociability," wrote similarly, "The exercise of the right [to exclude] is necessarily tempered by the facts of modern civilization. For a state to exclude all aliens would be to withdraw from the brotherhood of civilized peoples; to exclude any without reasonable or at least plausible cause is regarded as vexatious and oppressive."[6]

Despite such statements, sociability and reciprocity still had insecure footing in positivist international law, something to be realized through progress rather than something that already existed. By 1905, Lassa Oppenheim, a noted synthesizer of prevalent opinions, wrote that

> all the consequences which are said to follow out of the right of intercourse are not at all consequences of a right, but nothing else than consequences of the fact that intercourse between the States is a condition without which a Law of Nations could not exist. The civilised States make a community of States because they are knit together through their common interests and the manifold intercourse which serves these interests. Through the intercourse with one another and with the growth of their common interests the Law of Nations has grown up among the civilised States. Where there is no intercourse there cannot be a community and a law for such community.[7]

Some commentators have cited this and similar passages as evidence of how positivists have exclusively privileged the rights of states over all else. But it can be better understood as an aspect of the broader positivist project toward discovering the proper laws to bind international society. Just as sovereign individuals could be the subjects of a well-formulated municipal law that actually cultivated rather than suppressed their freedoms, so sovereign states could be subjects of international law that enhanced rather than impinged on their sovereignty. But in the absence of an overarching power to enforce law, the creation of international law depended on the painstaking work of detailed observation, codification, and persuasion. For Oppenheim it was a work in progress, and all that could be said about migration at the time of his writing was that a state had no duty to admit all unobjectionable foreigners into its territory but could not "exclude foreigners altogether from its territory without violating the spirit of the Law of Nations and endangering its very member-ship of the Family of Nations." He insisted that this claim was grounded in the evidence that "no State actually does exclude foreigners altogether," even though all states had the right to do so.[8] As we shall see in the next chapter, this statement was possible only within the "Family of Nations," which, along with the rhetoric of "civilization," established the borders at which exclusion could take place with impunity.

Few lawyers were willing to be more specific than this on migration, espe-cially in the absence of the conventions, treaties, and widely shared practices that were the backbone of positivist international law. This offered great lee-way for discretion and ambiguity. Politicians, academics, administrators, and migrants filled this space with arguments ranging from an almost complete right of free movement to a nearly total power of exclusion. Participants in courtroom and political debate easily extracted quotes from the international law tomes that supported one extreme or another. In fact, most of the quoted authorities actually held both extremes to be true. Mobility was not a right, but it was a necessity if one were to be counted in the Family of Nations. The very act of framing the problem in this way served to entrench these extremes as the irreducible anchors of the problem, and to present all alterna-tives as compromises. This only made the problem seem increasingly fixed and intractable.

The problem persisted even with the decline of intercourse as a compel-ling motivation for international law. After the 1870s, the rhetoric of interstate reciprocity gradually displaced intercourse in discussions of international mo-bility, as can be seen in the citations from Oppenheim. After World War I, positivist methodology and the privileging of sovereignty fell into disfavor. But the new international law of the 1920s only consummated the privileging of states over intercourse by emphasizing the establishment of international structures to create and regulate agreements between nations.[9] By this time, the idea of intercourse had entirely disintegrated into its constituent parts of international relations, commerce, and migration. Trade has survived many of these shifts as an issue of sovereign prerogative that is commonly subjected to international conventions and agreement. But migration control has come to be seen as an indivisible aspect of sovereignty. In the 1920s and 1930s this was evident in the proliferation of both exit and entry controls. But by the sec-ond half of the twentieth century, the ethics of migration control were further disaggregated according to the direction of movement. Free exit and internal mobility are now asserted as universal norms and often linked to individual rights. The right of a state to control entry as it wishes, however, is almost never challenged.[10]

From Commerce to Migration

The rise of national power over mobility and identification was closely tied to the decline of migration as commerce. Structurally, this follows from the expansion of direct state power over individual citizens, which requires the suppression of local allegiances and the private control over people as property. But the actual historical development was not so straightforward. The attempt to relocate freedom as a national possession rather than an issue of local self-determination and property was especially difficult. The transformation played out with particular intensity in the United States, where conflicting ideological commitments to chattel slavery, individual freedom, and free intercourse were all deeply entrenched. The struggle between them often played out in clashes between central and local power. Local self-governance at the state and town level was the bulwark of republican freedom, even as it also remained the stronghold of slavery. States claimed the right to control migrants as a power of community policing that should rightfully be located in the local communities that dealt with migrants most directly. The federal government, on the other hand, claimed power over migration as part of its constitutional powers over commerce and the necessity of centralizing matters related to international intercourse and treaties. In this context where support of states' rights was strongly linked to the support of slavery, many abolitionists found themselves in the uncomfortable position of justifying expanded federal control over migration by characterizing that migration as a form of commerce in people. U.S. passenger laws monitoring conditions of transportation continued to refer to immigrants as "imports" through the middle of the century, despite objections that this word was not appropriate for a free and voluntary immigrant. To label them anything else might call into question the power of the federal government to enact the legislation in the first place. The inclusion of both commerce and migration within the broader category of intercourse helped facilitate the shift to federal regulation. But the final consolidation of national power over migration came only in the 1870s after the military defeat of the proslavery states in the Civil War.

In the first half of the nineteenth century, U.S. legal opinions on the power to regulate migration were as experimental and inconsistent as migration control in Europe.[11] In the 1824 case *Gibbon v. Ogden*, the Supreme Court confirmed federal power over commerce and the unconstitutionality of an intrastate passenger steamship monopoly granted by the state of New York. As part of the decision, Chief Justice John Marshall offered an expanded understanding of federal powers over commerce that defined it as more than just "buying and selling, or the interchange of commodities. . . . [It] is something more: it is intercourse. It describes the commercial intercourse between nations, and parts of the nations, in all its branches, and is regulated by prescribing rules for carrying on that intercourse."[12] In his confirming opinion, Justice William Johnson referred to the provision in the ninth section of the Constitution that forbade Congress from passing a law before 1808 that prohibited "the migration or importation of such person as any of the States, now existing, shall think proper to admit" as evidence that "transportation of both men and their goods, is not only incidental to, but actually of the essence of, the power to regulate commerce" (231). He justified this power by insisting on the continued elaboration of commerce as a crucial part of modern civilization, "Commerce, in its simplest signification, means an exchange of goods; but in the advancement of society, labor, transportation, intelligence, care, and various means of exchange, become commodities and enter into commerce" (229).

Even as Johnson wrote his opinion it was being defeated in the realm of practical politics. While sitting on the circuit court of appeals in 1823, he had declared a South Carolina law requiring the quarantine of all black seamen in local jails while their ship was in port to be unconstitutional and in contravention of treaties. State officials refused to enforce his decision. The British government appealed to Washington, where the State Department responded that police laws like this were under state jurisdiction and declined to intervene. Even though the British government could not formally negotiate with the South Carolina government, British consuls ultimately negotiated a bonding arrangement there in which black seamen could remain onboard ship rather than being held in local jails.[13] But the fundamental jurisdictional issues were unresolved, and they would remain so for nearly half a century as courts and lawyers made the most of the many ambiguities in the relation of commerce and migration.

Marshall's and Johnson's assertion of federal power over the regulation of passenger vessels left much latitude for interpreting how the people themselves could be regulated. State power to subject immigrants to quarantine was never challenged as an aspect of local police powers. In its 1837 decision on *City of New York v. Miln*, the Supreme Court also confirmed the state power to collect information about all arriving passengers with an eye to demanding bonds on behalf of those who seemed likely to become wards of the state. The court argued that the collection of information did not infringe upon the rights of commerce, and, more significantly, that upon landing passengers were transformed from articles of commerce into people subject to local law. International law widely recognized that aliens should conform to local laws. State bonding requirements were justifiable as measures of self-protection for much the same reasons as quarantines against physical pestilence, as "precautionary measures against the moral pestilence of paupers, vagabonds, and possibly convicts."[14]

The 1841 case *Groves v. Slaughter*, about the validity of a contract to import slaves to Mississippi despite a state constitutional provision against introducing slaves for sale, invited even more difficult speculation on the definition of human transportation. The Court found the contract of sale to be valid because the constitutional provision was not self-executing without explicit legislation. But this narrow interpretation did not stop attorneys and judges from expressing a hodgepodge of opinions on the relationship of migration and commerce. Northern abolitionist lawyers had argued that the contract was valid, in part because the Mississippi provision was an unconstitutional breach of federal powers over commerce. Opposing counsel Robert Walker argued that slaves were indeed property and subject to local laws. At the same time, slaves were not merely inanimate chattel but people, and, as decided in *Miln*, they could not be counted as articles of commerce once they were within national borders. Walker chided the abolitionists for their "strangely inconsistent" argument that, "Men are not property, and cannot be property . . . and yet that as such, commerce in them among the states may be regulated by congress and by congress alone."[15]

The majority opinion avoided the topic of federal powers over commerce, but abolitionist judge John McLean centered his dissent on that question. He argued that power over commerce did include vessels carrying passengers, but that slaves could not be counted as either merchandise or passengers. He reasoned that the logic of federal power over commerce was to guarantee free commerce between states, making it impossible for congress to pass a law prohibiting commerce to some states and not others. Yet slavery was permitted in some states and not others, so it clearly was not meant to come under the federal commerce provisions. If it did, states like Ohio would be unable to pass constitutional provisions that prohibited traffic in slaves. Instead, McLean

justified the Ohio constitution in terms of the traditional powers of community policing: "Each state has a right to protect itself against the avarice and
intrusion of the slave dealer; to guard its citizens against the inconveniences
and dangers of a slave population. The right to exercise this power, by a state,
is higher and deeper than the Constitution. . . . Its power to guard against, or
to remedy the evil, rests upon the law of self-preservation; a law vital to every
community, and especially to a sovereign state" (508). Dissenter Robert Taney
and, in an appended opinion, the majority judges merely stated without explanation that the federal government has no control over the interstate traffic in slaves. Only proslavery judge Henry Baldwin stood with the Northern
attorneys in favor of federal jurisdiction over the slave traffic. He argued that
slaves were described as objects of commerce in international treaties and as
potential "merchandise" for sale in the Mississippi constitution. As such, it
was impossible to deny that they were subject to federal regulation (512–13).

The mélange of diverse opinions continued to proliferate in the *Passenger Cases* of 1849. John McLean lived up to his assertion of federal power
over migration by writing the majority opinion for a divided court that denied
states the power to collect head taxes on all immigrants, both desirable and
undesirable. He argued that this was not a special police or quarantine act,
as in *Miln*, but a systematic tax on all passengers regardless of their threat
to the community. He justified federal power over migration by repeating
the increasingly common complaint that immigrant taxes hindered the free
movement of migrants to the sparsely populated western states that desired
them, while retaining the income for coastal states on the pretext of supporting indigent migrants in ports where they often did not remain. Taney dissented on the principle that as the taxes were used to establish a fund for the
support of indigent immigrants they still were an exercise of the states' power
to protect themselves against paupers, convicts and the stick. As a sidebar, he
also objected to how McLain followed Marshall in substituting intercourse
for commerce, thus incorporating the movement of private people into what
should be understood as a more limited movement of goods.[16]

The dissent of proslavery judge Peter Daniel explicitly argued a point that
remained implicit in McLean, that "passengers" and migration were a form
of intercourse that was categorically different than the traffic in slaves (although Marshall had included both voluntary and involuntary passengers
as intercourse). Daniel also openly characterized that difference in terms of
race. He then borrowed abolitionist vocabulary to vehemently object to the
classification of white immigrants as commerce:

[Commerce is] applicable only to articles of trade proper,—goods, chattels, property, subjects in their nature passive and having no volition,— not to men whose emigration is the result of will, and could not be accomplished without their cooperation, and is as much their own act as it is the act of others; nay, much more so. The conclusion, then, is undeniable, that alien passengers, rational beings, freemen carrying into execution their deliberate intentions, never can, without a singular perversion, be classed with the subjects of sale, barter, or traffic; or, in other words, with imports. (504–5)

Federal jurisdiction over migration control was ultimately imposed over the barrel of a gun. During the Civil War, Congress expanded its involvement in migration through the 1862 law prohibiting U.S. participation in the coolie trade and the 1864 act to encourage immigration (repealed in 1868), which was part of a larger project of Secretary of State William Seward to promote labor importation.[17] An 1866 congressional resolution also protested the deportation of paupers and criminals from Europe to the United States as "unfriendly and inconsistent with the comity of nations."[18] Even in California, the state supreme court struck down state legislation to impose a monthly head tax on Chinese as an encroachment on the federal prerogative to regulate immigration—although this was not the last of such legislation in California.[19]

Congress retreated from this assertion of jurisdiction in the immediate postwar years. But the reappearance of state legislation led to the definitive Supreme Court recognition of federal power over all aspects of immigration on March 20, 1876, with unanimous opinions on both *Henderson v. Mayor of New York* and *Chy Lung v. Freeman.* The former overturned a New York law that allowed bonding requirements to be commuted into a flat fee for all passengers, while the latter overturned a California law that gave the collector of customs broad discretion to demand bonds from "lewd and debauched" Chinese women. Both opinions had a brevity and assurance that ran roughshod over the complexities of earlier cases. In *Henderson*, the court cited Marshall's definition of commerce as intercourse to argue that federal jurisdiction includes the regulation of means of admission for both passengers and cargo.[20] Acknowledging the possibility that *Miln* could be interpreted differently, the Court justified itself in terms of the changing historical times in which the transportation of passengers from Europe had attained an economic significance as never before:

It has become a part of our commerce with foreign nations, of vast interest to this country, as well as to the immigrants who come among us to
find a welcome and home within our borders. In addition to the wealth
which some of them bring, they bring still more largely the labor which
we need to till our soil, build our railroads, and develop the latent resources of the country. . . . Can it be doubted that a law which prescribes
the terms on which vessels shall engage in [the transportation of mi-
grants] is a law regulating this branch of commerce?[21]

Other than the high discretion given to customs officers, the California
law overturned by *Chy Lung* was not much different from the kinds of bonding laws confirmed in *Miln*, in that it required bonds only from those who
might be deemed a burden on local society. But now the Court could draw
on the Fourteenth Amendment guarantee of equal protection to all persons to
declare the law unconstitutional. It also emphasized the international ramifications of migration control, specifically noting how the extensive discretion
granted to customs officials conflicted with the guarantee of free movement
in the 1868 treaty with China,

It is hardly possible to conceive a statute more skillfully framed, to place
in the hands of a single man the power to prevent entirely vessels engaged in a foreign trade, say with China, from carrying passengers, or to
compel them to submit to systematic extortion of the grossest kinds. . . . If
citizens of our own government were treated by any foreign nation as the
subjects of the Emperor of China have been actually treated under this
law, no administration could withstand the call for a demand on such
government for redress.[22]

The Court argued that under such laws, "A silly, obstinate, or a wicked commissioner may bring disgrace upon the whole country, the enmity of a powerful nation, or the loss of an equally powerful friend," while the federal government remained helpless and liable to international reclamations.[23]

The privileging of international intercourse was simultaneously an assertion that the proper scale of community and self-protection was to be the nation, not the locality. But even though the assumption of federal powers was
framed as an attack on obstructive local laws, even more restrictive national
laws would soon be enacted, accompanied by more concerted efforts to concentrate administrative discretion and evade international accountability.

Indeed, senators from California had already anticipated the *Chy Lung* decision by shepherding a bill through Congress in 1875 that excluded convicts, prostitutes, and Orientals who came without their free and voluntary consent from entry into the nation. And a large portion of the responsibility to enforce this law was delegated to U.S. consuls in Hong Kong, who improvised their own procedures far from any direct supervision or accountability.[24] Ultimately, the task of policing the borders of a national republic would be even more contested and difficult than that of policing local communities.

Passports

One of the most widely recognized markers of the shift to national control over identity was the transformation of the passport into an internationally standardized certificate of citizenship. In the early nineteenth century, passports were largely understood around the world either as a means to control domestic movement and departure or as documents requesting safe passage. The modern international passport was created alongside the suppression of local mobility controls, as well as increased state powers over conscription, deportation, and responsibility for nationals abroad. All of these activities generated interstate disputes that forced states to clarify who their citizens were and how they would be protected, and to do so in a way that was acceptable to other nations. In short, the modern passport emerged as an internationally recognized documentation of state responsibility for individuals abroad. This happened well before it became a sine qua non for entry into most states, and even before it was widely recognized as proof of citizenship within the state that issued it.

Before the general abolition of passport controls across the Atlantic in the 1860s, the use and recognition of passports was still highly fragmented. They were issued and monitored by an enormous variety of local governments, ministries, and personalities, and usually valid only for particular destinations and voyages, often under the terms of treaties or other reciprocal privileges.[25] As late as the 1860s, passports for international travel from the United States and Great Britain were still issued by mayors, magistrates, justices of the peace, state governments, and other respectable personages, to intended audiences that were also a mix of state and private individuals and institutions. Passports were also regularly issued to nonnationals, both for travel in the country of the issuing official and for travel in third countries. In Britain before 1858, many travelers leaving the country preferred to purchase their passports from the French or other consulates in England because passports issued by the British Foreign Office were expensive and issued only to people who were known to the secretary or state personally or through recommendations.[26]

International law texts rarely mentioned passports before the 1860s except as documents of safe passage in time of war. In part, this was because they were usually considered to be domestic rather than international documents. But over in the second half of the century, international lawyers began to hint at a new kind of passport that would be both a document of national citizenship and a tool to facilitate intercourse. In his commentary to the 1866 posthumous U.S. edition of Henry Wheaton's *Elements of International Law* (original 1836), Richard Dana discussed the "theory and practice" of peacetime passports in a way that described it as a document in transition:

> Each nation, as part of its internal system may withhold the right of transit through its territory. Permissions to foreigners to pass through it are properly passports; and, in strictness, a foreigner would be obliged to obtain a new passport at the boundaries of each nationality, and each national authority might subject him to an examination to ascertain his character and citizenship. To avoid these inconveniences, a system is adopted by which a citizen, leaving his own country for another, obtains from his own government what is called a passport, and is so, as respects a right to leave his own country; but, in respect to foreign countries, is rather a certificate of citizenship. . . . The most that can be claimed for it is, that it is a request to foreign governments to admit the bearer, with the privileges and obligations of a foreign citizen. It would seem plain, that a diplomatic officer abroad could give no passport to any person who did not stand in some relation with that officer's country; if not as a citizen or subject, perhaps as in its employment.[27]

Although framed as description, Dana's account was actually lobbying for a particular understanding in the face of a still chaotic practice and theory. The references for his account were all taken from the William Lawrence's edition of Wheaton published in London in 1857. Lawrence, however, had quoted the sources rather than summarizing them, making no attempt to reconcile the disagreements on who could issue passports and to whom, on whether they authorized entries or departures, and on whether they were certificates of nationality or personalized recommendations of free passage.[28] But Dana did not stand alone in his interpretation. Wheaton's tome was one of the most widely used and translated works of international law around the world in the nineteenth century, and Dana's version quickly became the authoritative edition, especially among U.S. diplomats. In a world of declining passport use, U.S. officials were among the most aggressive in promoting a new role for the passport as a universally recognized certificate of nationality and limited promise of responsibility.

Both the United States and Great Britain began to centralize their passport-issuing capacities in the late 1850s, even as passport requirements were abolished across the Atlantic. U.S. officials wanted to better monitor the departure of U.S. citizens because they were afraid that people abroad were naturalizing in other countries and avoiding their duty as citizens. In contrast, many European countries were increasingly permitting free exit and naturalization abroad so that they would not have to worry about diplomatic protection or dealing with impoverished returnees.[29] U.S. officials were especially troubled by the conscription of naturalized U.S. citizens during visits to their home countries.[30] Congress passed a law in 1856 that only the Department of State could issue passports, although state officials continued to issue passports into the 1860s. In 1873 the State Department tightened its peacetime policy to issue passports of limited duration (rarely more than two years) only to applicants who swore an oath of allegiance and who had not joined a foreign military or been naturalized by a foreign government.[31] In Britain, the Foreign Office reduced its price and made passports more readily available in 1858. This was instigated by an embarrassing incident in which an assassin had traveled on a French-issued document by falsely claiming to be a British subject, leading the French government to order the French consuls to issue no more passports to British subjects.[32] The increasing rejection of locally issued passports abroad also discouraged local officials from issuing them. Centralized documents were backed by the power and guarantee of a state, becoming a common currency in a world of expanding intercourse.

The acquisition of passports grew increasingly impersonal under centralized regimes, with paperwork replacing face-to-face relationships and generating new problems. Government officials worried that passports obtained by mail and through brokers would get in the hands of irresponsible and disloyal people who would use them for purely instrumental purposes. In 1893 the State Department suspended the renewal of passports abroad because "Unscrupulous persons while still abroad would send their old passports to agents in this country, who would present them to the Department, at the same time leading it to suppose, often by false statements, that the original holder was in this country at the time of the application."[33]

As they strengthened their domestic power over passports, U.S. officials also pressured other countries to accept U.S. passports as nearly uncontestable certificates of nationality. From 1893 to 1895 the U.S. government protested several cases in which the local authorities in the Austro-Hungarian Empire would not accept U.S. passports as evidence of naturalization and citizenship. Secretary of State John Gresham wrote to the Austro-Hungarian minister in 1893 that the issue at stake was the refusal of Austro-Hungarian authorities to "accord respect to the passport, duly issued by the lawful agencies of the United States as *prima facie* attestation of the citizenship of the bearer, and therefore, of his treaty rights." He continued that foreign officials were free to investigate the validity and genuineness of a document, but not to assert that the passport is useless as evidence per se and engage in their own investigation of citizenship. Such actions would be "wholly incompatible with the universally admitted doctrine that a state is the sole and ultimate judge of citizenship of its own dependents, and is, in its sovereign capacity, competent to certify the fact."[34]

The international problems encouraged more domestic centralization. In 1895 Secretary of State Richard Olney suggested that a greater uniformity of naturalization certificates between local courts might help avoid similar international incidents in the future.[35] The need to document travelers and more carefully define the citizen-alien distinction also inspired a wave of new and reformed nationality laws around the world at the turn of the century. The growing regulation of citizenship meant that by the early twentieth century most countries could demand a passport as a prerequisite for entry. But the insistence on its prima facie value as a certificate of citizenship also undermined its role as a means for states to sift potential entries. The receiving state was now left with few means of rejecting its claims and a high probability of causing an international incident if it did.

As the second-guessing of passports grew increasingly awkward, the work of regulating entry was left to the visa. In 1866 Dana described the *"visé"* stamped onto a passport as "assent to the bearer's passing through" that avoided the trouble of issuing a new passport at the border. The accumulated visas also gave officials a convenient record of the bearer's travels.[36] In 1898 U.S. Passport Clerk Gaillard Hunt downplayed the surveillance effect of the visa and merely described it as an endorsement issued by some countries, "denoting that the passport has been examined and is authentic, and that the bearer may be permitted to proceed on his journey."[37] Like the inspection of passports, U.S. officials recognized the right to issue visas, but only as a means of attesting to the genuineness of the document. Such inspections had to avoid any "unwarranted discrimination" against nationalities or individuals. For nearly two decades after 1895, U.S. officials protested against the Russian consul's interrogation of Americans as to their race and religion as a way to deny visas to Jews, even using this as an excuse to terminate a trade treaty in 1911.[38] But even as Hunt wrote, administrative changes in the issuing of U.S. consular visas in China would soon transform the visa into a certification that the issuing official had engaged in his own independent examination of qualifications for entry beyond those certified in the passport. The visa would become a central tool of migration control that made it possible to discriminate in terms of race, wealth, status, and occupation.

For a brief moment, however, the impulse to discriminate against Chinese also generated the last official U.S. objection to the idea of a passport as document of citizenship from the U.S. Bureau of Immigration in 1905. The bureau was not convinced that the State Department made sufficient investigation into citizenship claims (the State Department made the same criticism of bureau investigations) and balked at accepting passports as prima facie evidence of U.S. citizenship for Chinese. To legally justify this stance, the bureau argued that passports were political documents that demonstrated something less than the rights of citizenship,

> [The passport] is a document which, from its nature and object, is addressed to foreign powers, purporting only to be a request that the bearer of it may pass safely and freely, and is to be considered rather in the character of a political document, by which the bearer is recognized in foreign countries as an American citizen and which, by usage and law of nations, is recognized as evidence of the fact. But this is a very different light from that in which it is to be viewed in a court of justice, where the inquiry is as to the fact of citizenship. It is a mere ex parte certificate, and if founded upon any evidence produced to the Secretary of State, establishing the fact of citizenship, that evidence ought to be produced upon the trial, as higher and better evidence of the fact.[39]

After some discussion, the State Department agreed to issue passports only to Chinese who had already undergone bureau investigations.

By 1906, John Bassett Moore could confidently assert in his *Digest of International Law* that "A passport is the accepted international evidence of nationality," and that all other forms of *laissez passer* and letters of recommendation that had once proliferated under the name passport were only relevant to conditions of war or other particular cases.[40] Despite such assertions, the basic premises of the bureau's 1905 objections still hold. Passports are treated as citizenship documents only as a matter of international courtesy. They have little to no formal status in international law, or even in the legislation of many countries. Many states still reserve an arbitrary power to issue passports to anybody they choose and to refuse to recognize them as proof of citizenship.[41] The fact that states generally choose to honor the passport is testament to the extent to which even the idea of an unaccountable sovereignty is grounded in the norms of international system.

Entwined Enforcement

By the 1870s, governments also increasingly disassociated themselves from the business of assisting migration, be it local funding for the emigration of paupers and convicts or financial support for intracolonial emigration or resettlement. In large part this was a matter of fiscal frugality, of governments unwilling to bear the expenses of transportation or undertake responsibility for impoverished migrants. But this withdrawal was also justified through the free-trade argument that social processes such as migration reached their optimal equilibrium when left to their own devices. Both attitudes were explicitly expressed by British officials justifying the abandonment after the 1860s of government programs to assist migration to the colonies.[42] Social assistance, they argued, was most effective when left to private, voluntary, and mutual-aid associations.

This did not mean granting free rein to all private organization of migrants. Rather it meant a rising wave of new regulations that continued the suppression of private organization and assistance in favor of migrants defined by individual volition, and of regulation by large corporations and charities that collaborated with government regulation. Even these latter organizations often came under suspicion for improperly seducing and organizing impoverished and undesirable migrants who would never have moved if left to their own devices. Migration regulation was increasingly designed to make the activities of these organizations more limited and transparent. Ultimately, only private organizations willing to collaborate with government surveillance were tolerated, and even encouraged. This generally meant organizations with activities framed as philanthropy or mutual aid, as well as large transportation companies with good public relations. The actual distinctions between philanthropic societies, mutual aid associations, and labor recruitment operations were often quite blurry, shaped more by the public and official relations of key officers than by any absolute difference in the character of their operations. But the belief in a firm distinction between private and official regulation became a fundamental feature of modern migration control.

Since at least the seventeenth century, associations have existed around the world to provide assistance and information to migrants and colonists and to protect localities from the threat of vagrants. In the Americas, private associations were often established to provide information and assistance to newly arriving migrants. In mid-nineteenth-century Baltimore, a portion of the immigrant head taxes was even distributed to the German and Hiberian societies for this purpose.[43] In Europe, voluntary associations sometimes took up the responsibility to facilitate the departure of convicts and paupers, such as the German Prisoner's Aid Society in Würtemburg from 1860 to 1880, which supported the emigration of released convicts.[44] From 1850 to 1887, Mormons in Europe established a Perpetual Emigrating Fund that offered loans and pooled resources for emigration to the Americas.[45] In a slightly less direct mode, the Society for the Protection of Immigrants was established by local notables in the emigration port of Hamburg in 1851 to provide information about lodging and tickets. Concerned that swindlers would prey on inexperienced migrants and multiply the number of indigents and criminals in the city, the society convinced the government to ban runners and hucksters from the railway station and helped mediate disputes between emigrants and innkeepers.[46]

Many associations were established by migrants themselves. Their activities could include mutual aid, the regulation of commercial activities, and philanthropic ventures. Chinese merchant, native place, surname, and sworn brotherhood associations around the world often pooled resources to provide services like letter writing, remittance banking, temporary lodging, the distribution of employment information, and repatriation of the bones of the dead. Sometimes these institutions engaged in labor recruitment and business regulation, dominated by economic elites with a vested interest in the perpetuation of migrant labor. At other times they were vehicles of philanthropy that organized funds for hospitals, old people's homes, repatriation of destitute migrants, legal services, schools, disaster relief, and anti-Japanese activities in

China. Some of the larger associations also engaged in more formal kinds of regulation. For example, the Six Companies of San Francisco arranged with the Pacific Mail Steamship Company in the nineteenth century not to sell any tickets to Chinese passengers unless they had a Six Companies certificate testifying that they had paid all of their debts.[47]

Regulatory activities could extend to formal cooperation with governments. Umbrella organizations such as the Six Companies and United Chinese Association in Honolulu acted as informal representatives of the Chinese government before the establishment of formal diplomatic representation. Their activities often included issuing identity documents that were recognized by officials abroad and in China. In the 1870s the Tung Wah Hospital Board and Po Leung Kuk (an organization devoted to the protection of girls) in Hong Kong sent men to board departing ships to make sure that the migrants, especially women, emigrated voluntarily. With the enactment of the U.S. Page law in 1875, the U.S. consul developed an application form that required women to have their status investigated by the director of the Tung Wah Hospital. The Tung Wah board also worked with the governor general of Guangdong to repatriate Chinese who had been kidnapped. They sent the bill for repatriation to the registrar general of Hong Kong, who would then collect from the boarding house keeper charged with having originally seduced the migrant.[48] In a less cooperative mode, Six Company lawyers who were stockholders in the China Mail Steamship Company successfully used the company's influence to object to the appointment of certain immigration officers in the United States.[49]

Sooner or later, such organizations attracted suspicion from officials who worried that they facilitated undesirable immigration. Funds for the emigration of paupers, convicts, and Mormons ultimately collapsed under official pressure. Local governments also grew fearful of the informal power of Chinese associations, labeling them "city halls" or *imperium im imperio*. By the 1880s, the Tung Wah Hospital board had to circumscribe its activities because the white residents of Hong Kong were increasingly uncomfortable with its growing influence. Even government-sponsored recruitment could fall under suspicion. Attempts by the United States (1864–68) and Canada (1889–1906) to promote immigration through private companies (the American Emigration Company and the North Atlantic Trading Company, respectively) generated enormous suspicion among European governments and complaints from migrants about poor treatment and deception. Indeed, the Canadian arrangement potentially ran afoul of emigration laws in many countries, forcing Canadian agents to act in a nearly underground fashion and limit their activities to advice and information.[50]

Associations could adapt to satisfy official expectations. Jewish emigration associations often gained official approval by taking up the restriction of migration on their own initiative. In the 1880s up to a quarter of the applicants for assistance to all immigrant aid societies in Britain—many of which were Jewish associations that had expanded their operations to all immigrants—were repatriated to their native countries.[51] By the end of the century, philanthropic support had helped establish an extensive network of Jewish associations across Europe and the Atlantic. Many focused on helping Jews to leave Russia, but their work also included sending representatives to meet passengers at border towns and ports; helping migrants with temporary lodging and onward tickets to the Americas; ascertaining that they would be able to satisfy immigration restrictions and had the funds, skills, or family to support themselves abroad; and repatriating those who did not. They even sent circulars to home villages to persuade unsuitable migrants not to leave in the first place.[52] They organized group colonization efforts in Argentina and Canada that provided housing, tools, and cattle to qualified migrants, but also subjected those migrants to extensive investigations to demonstrate those qualifications. According to Major W. E. Evans-Gordon, who investigated these associations for a British Royal Commission in 1902, "It was realised that if people not so accredited were allowed to wander off to the Argentine, the settlements there would speedily become overcrowded and degraded, and that the respectable and capable settlers would suffer."[53] In the opinion of the United States Immigration Commission of 1907, these associations counseled rather than funded or encouraged potential migrants.[54] Through this mix of support and restriction, Jewish societies formulated their private activities in a way that conformed to state interests.

Both the British and U.S. investigations were preliminary to the establishment of new border controls. Before border control became the regulatory method of choice, however, most migration laws of the nineteenth century focused on regulating the means of transportation. Although sometimes intended as a method of reducing emigration, they were largely meant to limit perceived abuses by "unscrupulous" brokers and shippers. Framers also hoped that they might make particular ports more attractive in the competition for migrant traffic, although the taxes necessary to enforce these laws often offset the advantage of superior conditions.[55]

The English passenger laws of 1803 were a pioneering attempt to regulate the means of mobility. Despite numerous revisions and improved administration over the next half century, these laws proved impossible to enforce until the rise of steamship companies in the 1870s. Their greater long-term investment in a stable passenger traffic helped put an end to the more egregious forms of abuse. In the meantime, passenger laws were augmented by laws requiring the regulation of brokers and rooming houses in ports. One of the most notable of such laws was passed in New York in 1848 (cause of the *Passenger Cases*) in response to the spike in impoverished Irish emigrants fleeing the famine. It required licenses for boarding houses, established a quarantine hospital, set up immigrant enclosures where brokers were not allowed, and authorized the appointment of agents to help warn migrants against unscrupulous activities. Many shippers responded by carrying their passengers to Canada. Influence could also go the other way around. Shipping lobbies also encouraged the revision of passenger legislation to better harmonize the practices in different ports, whether they be across the Atlantic or between the many ports that sent pilgrimage ships to Mecca.[56]

Emigration laws in the second half of the nineteenth century increasingly focused on the regulation of brokers. France (1854) and Belgium (1876) pioneered laws that required the licensing of emigration agents, in part to seduce migrant traffic away from the German ports. Over time, the laws grew increasingly interventionist. The Swiss emigration law of 1888 was the first to prohibit advertising, impose bonds and penalties on emigration agencies, and require them to ascertain that passengers had the proper papers and would not be rejected at ports of arrival. It was a model for the comprehensive Japanese emigration law of 1896, the German law of 1897, and the Italian law of 1901. The latter required all emigrants to carry passports, regulated shipping rates, provided for official emigration agencies to be established abroad, and was enforced in collaboration with agents of the U.S. Marine Hospital Service in Italy to better assure that emigrants would pass U.S. health inspections. All of these laws were intended not to limit emigration so much as to generate a well-ordered departure of healthy, noncriminal individuals that maintained ties to home and projected a good image of their home nation abroad.[57] The Hungarian emigration law of 1903 was a culmination of these trends, placing the regulation of emigration directly under government control. The framers explained that migrants could be better protected from exploitation at home than by relying on philanthropy abroad. Such regulation would also ensure that emigration was not reckless but a true "quest for work," that migrants would be prevented from going to countries that were "dangerously unhealthy," that "their patriotism shall be kept alive, and that in every possible way their return to their native country may be assured."[58] Despite the high ideals, critics claimed that it was primarily a means to monopolize emigration business revenue. Civil servants were given a commission for each emigrant recruited and were accused of engaging in even more deception and corruption than the private agents.

An ever-changing synergy emerged over the nineteenth century between new laws and private regulation. The most successful private organizations readily accommodated the enforcement of migration laws. Indeed, collaboration could help them control an ever larger share of the market. But those that tried to collaborate were not always up to the task of increased responsibilities For example, in 1886 Thomas Cook & Son was granted a monopoly to supplant "unscrupulous brokers" and organize the pilgrim trade from India to Mecca. The company proved unequal to the task and had to relinquish its monopoly after seven years. German shippers, however, proved much more effective, demonstrating both the great expense required and the even greater profits that resulted from collaboration.[59]

The involvement of German shippers in the enforcement of migration laws began in 1892 when German officials worried that the increasing departure of poor Jews from Russia had caused the spread of cholera epidemics. Officials erected emigrant hostels in Hamburg and sent medical inspectors to the Russian border to implement quarantines. Fearful of losing passengers, the steamship companies Hapag and Lloyd petitioned the government to allow them to finance and operate disinfection stations at the Russian border. The companies also ascertained that migrants had sufficient money for onward tickets out of Germany and then carried them on nonstop trains to Hamburg and Bremen. The two companies flourished under the emigrant monopoly granted by the German government. In 1901 they built an enormous emigrant station in Hamburg, complete with segregated dormitories, churches and temples for all denominations, and kosher and nonkosher dining halls with orchestras. Medical inspections ensured that migrants conformed to the emigration laws of their destinations and thus avoid liability for a return journey and possibly a penalty. Some people even accused German border officials of abetting this monopoly by turning back emigrants who had outward tickets via France. Whatever the causes, competing routes were nearly decimated, especially those through England that did not engage in medical inspections and often had their passengers rejected at American ports.[60]

In his 1902 investigation, Major Evans-Gordon insisted that the facilities at Hamburg were a direct result of American laws: "The argument often advanced as to the American restrictive law being useless and ineffective falls to the ground. It is entirely clear, although the numbers rejected in America may be small, that this is entirely due to the elaborate precautions which are taken before the emigrants start to prevent the possibility of their rejection."[61] The U.S. Immigration Commission of 1907 was also impressed not only with Hamburg, but also with procedures established by French, Swiss, and Hungarian authorities (although emigrants from the latter country still often preferred to travel through Germany). On the basis of rejection rates at U.S. ports, the commission decided that the U.S. public health inspectors in Italy were even less effective in enforcing U.S. laws than most foreign governments and transportation companies (although Scandinavian migrants underwent no predeparture inspection and still had the lowest rejection rates at U.S. ports).[62] As a result of the investigation, diplomatic difficulties created by the stationing of health officials in foreign countries, and Bureau of Immigration claims that shipping companies had been using official inspections as an excuse to avoid the penalties for bringing ineligible migrants, U.S. public health officers were recalled from Japan, Hong Kong, and the Russian port of Libau in 1909. The Bureau of Immigration later claimed that trachoma cases from Asia even declined at American ports after shippers took responsibility for predeparture medical inspections.[63]

Creation of the Unfree Migrant

While some migrant-related organizations flourished, many others were pushed underground. The very act of migrating with outside assistance became cause for suspicion that the migrant himself was somewhat less than desirable. Less transparent forms of organization were stigmatized, usually by personalizing them as evil men, traffickers, padrones, and irresponsible immigrant bankers who exploited cultural ties and the ignorance of their countrymen for the sake of profit. In many ways this was an attack on the very possibility of migration. Migration would generally have been too expensive and risky without the information, opportunities, and other resources made available through recruiters, friends, and family. Attacks on these networks only pushed them further underground, reinforcing the idea that they had something to hide. Ultimately, this was a struggle over who had the right to control and benefit from migration.

Some migration did indeed take the "classic" form of individuals and families engaged in monodirectional relocation. Most created complex transnational spaces of geographically dispersed families, businesses, and other institutions.[64] Migration was often a kind of family investment, meaningful less as a chance for individual mobility than as a source of income for the family at home. It would have been a pointless endeavor without the networks of businesses, associations, and fellow villagers through which money and the fruits of migration could be transformed into status objects, material support, and other investments at home. Ultimately, some migrants and their families relocated entirely into the new communities. But for many others, migration was an economic strategy to be repeated through the generations, creating villages, families, and circuits of information and mobility that ranged far beyond any single locality.

These networks constrained opportunities as much as they created them. They circulated the information and assistance that made migration possible. But once established, it was difficult for an established network to access new job opportunities and new destinations, even if only rudimentary new skills were necessary and the economic benefits were high. The networks generated a social geography that was not congruent with physical geography. A potential migrant may have had more knowledge of distant Penang, Omsk, or Chicago than the nearby market town because that was where his uncles and cousins were. But perhaps more to the point was that many migrant elites had an interest in controlling and limiting information and opportunities in order to strengthen their own monopoly of these resources. These elites gained profit and prestige through their skills in negotiating borders, their knowledge of transportation, communication, and employment opportunities, and their ability operate across multiple borders. Migration itself became a source of sustenance and self-reproduction for these elites. In turn, the brokers tried to exclude their fellow migrants from developing similar knowledge and skills on their own. Contractual authority over workers, if it existed at all, was buttressed by claims of family ties, personal obligation, and manhood. It was the very density of these ties, many of which were not easily regulated, that made their activities appear threatening and potentially exploitative.

Migrant brokers were often the target of migration laws. In addition to those aimed at migration agents, laws that prohibited the importation of migrants under contract or other forms of prepaid assistance also helped suppress their activities. Such laws were generally enacted in nations with broad suffrage as a way to protect the domestic labor conditions against the operations of unfettered capital. Other nations, including many emigrant nations, encouraged contracts as an effective means of recruiting, controlling, and protecting migrants. Both state support and suppression, however, often led to the same result of marginalizing and demonizing the small and informal recruiters that evaded regulation and big capital. The Italian ambassador expressed this attitude well in 1894, when he urged the U.S. government to enforce its 1885 anticontract law more effectively against "padroni" labor contracting, calling it a system "by which Italian immigrants voluntarily surrender their individual liberty to designing men, in order to procure money to pay their passage to the United States . . . whereby they become personal serfs, controlled by rapacious men who rob them of a large part of the fruits of their labor."[65]

But enforcement of the U.S. law was fraught with contradictions and difficulties that made the very act of migration into one of deception and evasion. It was especially difficult to reconcile this law with the exclusion of paupers. In the words of the U.S. Industrial Commission report of 1901:

> The consequence is that the immigrant must summon all his ingenuity and subterfuge to dodge the two extremes. He strives to show that he can support himself, and he strives to show that he does not know of any job by which he can support himself. If he cannot support himself he is sent back as liable to become a public charge. If he has provided beforehand for the self-support he is sent back as liable to displace American workmen. The immigration inspectors are therefore reduced to a queer predicament. They must discover, first, whether the immigrant is sound in body and mind—that is whether he can compete successfully for a living with American workmen. If so, they admit him. They must discover, secondly, whether he really has a prospect of finding work, and thereby of competing with American workmen, and they exclude him if he gives the best of all evidence that he will compete successfully with American workmen.[66]

Court convictions were also difficult because many judges were reluctant to abrogate contracts entered by free individuals and because of the difficulty of obtaining irrefutable evidence from emigrants trained to deny that they had entered into a contract. The issue was also plagued by difficult questions about the extent to which verbal arrangements, vague promises of jobs, and the assistance of friends and families should be considered assisted immigration?[67]

Broker and recruitment networks also existed far beyond the control of any single government. Brokers could easily teach immigrants what to say to immigration officials and what kind of written evidence to avoid carrying on their person. Thus, regulation produced forms of evasion that justified further suspicion and demonization of brokers, and the depiction of migrants themselves as ignorant dupes driven by desperation. As Secretary of the Treasury John Carlisle explained in his response to the Italian ambassador, "These contracts are made in Italy with illiterate people in almost abject poverty, who willingly barter their personal liberty in order to procure the means necessary to enable them to come to America to better their condition."[68]

Characterizations of victimized migrants often expressed sympathy while still using the very fact of deception as evidence of their undesirability. As U.S. special immigration investigator Marcus Braun complained, the collusion among shipping companies, brokers, and migrants created an "unnatural immigration" that "consists of paupers and assisted immigrants, and is induced and brought about by the unscrupulous and greedy activity displayed by a large number of agencies and subagencies having well-established connections in the United States and abroad."[69] These problems were compounded because many desirable migrants who signed no contract may often have been deported as contract laborers because "the unfortunate emigrant becomes so confused by the manifold advices and instructions he receives prior to his arrival that he is made to believe things he has never intended to say."[70]

Padrones and other informal recruiters were often depicted as the vestiges of premodern forms of labor organization, exploiting personal loyalty and cultural obligations. But, as seen in the intimate ties between brokers and shipping companies investigated by Braun, they were actually very much a product of the industrial economies and mass migration of the nineteenth and twentieth centuries, flourishing in the interstices between villages and modern industries in need of labor. The fact that shipping companies often denied their ties to these brokers helps situate these forms of organization as adaptations to an environment with little legal or government support. The more effective brokers did manage to appropriate some of the legitimacy of their partners for themselves, although this could shift quickly along with political fortunes. In an example used by historian Gunther Peck, Italian labor broker Frank Cordasco arranged to supply the Canadian Pacific Railroad with

Italian labor in 1902.[71] At first railroad officials called this a cutting-edge form of employment that was "in vogue." They believed Cordasco could provide them with a flexible labor force and assume many of the responsibilities of organization and provisioning. After the arrangement went sour in 1904, Cordasco sued the railroad for not living up to its promises. In court, it came to light that Cordasco's recruiting activities extended far beyond the borders of Canada. The railroad minimized its arrangements with Cordasco, realizing that they went against the 1897 Alien Labor Act that made it illegal for anybody other than the North American Trade Company to solicit and import foreign laborer. Cordasco had also evaded Italian emigration laws by having migrants sign agreements in Chiasso, Switzerland. Once feted as "king of the workers," Cordasco was now attacked as an unscrupulous padrone who charged illicit fees and flouted the law. But Cordasco's declining reputation must also be understood as part of a losing political and public relations struggle. The Italian Immigrant Aid Society in Montreal, recently funded by the Italian government, had assisted in developing charges against Cordasco. But one of the leading members in the attack on Cordasco was his main competitor, Alberto Dini. It turned out that despite its official sponsorship, the society itself was deeply involved in sending unemployed Italians from Montreal to rural areas of Canada, thus competing for the same workers as Cordasco. The label of padrone was not automatically applied to all recruiters, but to those that failed to generate an aura of public respectability.

This suspicion of migrant recruitment easily spread to any kind of institution that facilitated migration beneath and beyond the control of national laws, including immigrant banks, notary publics, and remittance agencies. State and federal investigations in the United States at the turn of the century consistently attacked the excessive influence of immigrant bankers as "unauthorized concerns, privately owned, irresponsibly managed, and seldom subject to any efficient supervision or examination."[72] They denounced the men who ran these institutions as anything from irresponsible to outright swindlers. They were especially disturbed by the mixing of occupations they believed should be separate, with saloonkeepers and grocers also acting as bankers, transportation agents, and post offices. They saw it as an unregulated space that isolated migrants from society and perpetuated their ties with the home country at the expense of Americanization.[73]

The involvement of all sorts of charitable and uncharitable associations emphasizes that migration is never an unregulated activity. Regulation was not just the imposition of state obstacles against the free flow of human mobility. The very idea of what constituted free migration was a product of favoring certain institutions and practices over others. Over the course of the nineteenth century, most migrant networks and institutions other than the nuclear family and large transportation companies were depicted as the enemies of order and freedom. The ideal immigrant was to be extracted from these networks and reconstituted as an individual with free choice and subjected to well-monitored institutions. He was also to be an assimilable migrant, an object of police regulation and social policy defined by the nation rather than by localities and particularistic affiliations. Under these conditions, migrant networks rarely appeared in official archives except as smugglers, crimps, exploiters, unscrupulous brokers, "slave" traders, padrones, and a variety of other unsavory and criminalized terms.

All migrant groups were accused of these vices at some point, but few as regularly as Asians. For many Western bureaucrats, the very word "Oriental" or "Chinese" was sufficient to encapsulate all of the undesirable qualities of migrants. The exclusion of Asian migrants to white settler nations after the 1850s was fought out in the context of rising laissez-faire ideals. The ultimate solutions to justify and administer border controls would play a key role in making the distinction between free and illegitimate migration into legal reality. Along the way, the struggle between bureaucrats and migrant networks would be recast as a struggle between West and East, yellow and white, the civilized and uncivilized, and the geographical spaces of freedom and oppression.

Part II

Imagining Borders

"The doorkeeper deceived the man," said K.

"Don't be too hasty," said the priest, "don't take over someone else's opinion without testing it. I have told you the story in the very words of the scriptures. There's no mention of deception in it."

"But clear enough," said K., "The doorkeeper gave the message of salvation to the man only when it could no longer help him."

"He was not asked the question any earlier," said the priest. . . . "The story contains two important statements made by the doorkeeper about admission to the Law, one at the beginning, the other at the end. The first statement is: that he cannot admit the man at the moment, and the other is: that this door was intended only for the man. If there were a contradiction between the two, you would be right and the doorkeeper would have deceived the man. But there is no contradiction. The first statement, on the contrary, even implies the second. One could almost say that in suggesting to the man the possibility of future admittance the doorkeeper is exceeding his duty. At that time his apparent duty is only to refuse admittance and indeed many commentators are surprised that the suggestion should be made at all, since the doorkeeper appears to be a precisian with a stern regard for duty."   —Kafka, *The Trial*

5

Experiments in Border Control, 1852–1887

Beginning in the 1850s, white settlers around the Pacific worked to keep Chinese at the margins of their communities, if not entirely excluded. They sometimes discriminated against resident Chinese through the venerable methods of special licenses, taxes, and residential segregation. They also tried to limit the entry of Chinese through quarantines, head taxes, bonding, and passenger-per-ship limits based on passenger laws of the early nineteenth century, although the low passenger limits and exclusive focus on ships from China left little doubt that the main goal was restriction of Chinese rather than health or vagrancy control per se. Struggles over these laws generated debates around the Pacific over the relationship of local, state, national, and colonial laws, imperial interests, international treaties, and the demands of international intercourse. Parties and legislatures rooted in local popular politics were more willing to infringe on rights of Asians than were the elites and elite institutions who focused on international relations and protection of property. Objections from this latter group, based in international obligations, laissez-faire ideology, and jurisdictional struggles ultimately led to the repeal of many early laws.

In the 1880s a new wave of laws focused on stopping immigration rather than discriminating against Chinese already within the borders. By 1885, Anglophone communities around the Pacific were enclosed behind an anti-Chinese barrier. The failures of these new laws were as spectacular as the public outcry that had led to their implementation in the first place. The borders remained highly porous and subject to innumerable unresolved questions. How could the identity and status of an individual from a foreign sovereignty be defined and verified? How should documents issued by foreign governments be evaluated, and could they be rejected? Who could be punished for breaking the laws, and how could sanctions be implemented? How could officials inspect every individual who may cross the border of enormous landmasses? Did a prohibition of entry include a denial of the right of transit, trade, or access to procedural rights in general? Enforcement officials, local populaces, migrants, brokers, lawyers, politicians, courts, and diplomats from London to Beijing all claimed a say in the resolution of these questions. Their efforts were fueled by sensationalized media accounts both of the continued menace of Chinese penetrating the borders and of respectable migrants suffering injustice at the hands of corrupt and incompetent border officials. In the words of U.S. Supreme Court Justice Stephen Field, enforcement "was attended with great embarrassment."[1]

The U.S. Chinese exclusion law of 1882 took the innovative step of directly excluding the entry of Chinese laborers altogether rather than couching the regulation in terms of sanitation and taxation. But it was no easier to enforce than the earlier laws. In *Low Yam Choy*, one of the first court cases to arise from this law, California Circuit Judge Ogden Hoffman described the controversy that surrounded it:

> It is well known that the law under consideration encountered widespread and vehement opposition. It was attacked as the servile echo of the clamors of the sand lot; as fraught with danger to our commercial relations with China; as inconsistent with our national policy; as obstructing the spread of Christianity, and as violative not only of the treaty, but of the inherent rights of man. It was defended as absolutely indispensable to the preservation of our social and political systems, and even to our safety. Nothing would more gratify the enemies of the bill than that in its practical operation it should be found to be unreasonable, unjust and oppressive. . . . I am satisfied that the friends of this law do it the best service by giving to it a reasonable and just construction, conformable to its spirit and intent and the solemn pledges of the treaty, and not one calculated to bring it into odium and disrepute.[2]

A "reasonable and just construction" remained elusive. Most judges were no friends of Chinese immigration, but Hoffman's final decision was just one of many decisions around the world from the 1850s to early 1880s that privileged free movement, individual rights, and adherence to procedure over what Hoffman himself called the "evil" of an undesirable immigration that bore with great severity against "our civilization."[3] By the end of the century, however, the enormous legal, political, and administrative effort put into enforcing these laws would gradually shift the momentum in favor of borders, thus establishing the basic principles and practices of border control as an integral part of modern, liberal polities.

Chinese Exclusion Ideology

Anti-Asian racism around the Pacific was charged with a spirit of egalitarian self-government and a mistrust of big capital and elite institutions. Although particular formulations could assume infinite nuances, the general framework and vocabulary varied remarkably little around the Pacific.[4] Racist imagination was the foundation of anti-Chinese sentiment. But this racism was given concrete political shape through the conviction that self-governing societies should determine their own membership and a fear that unconstrained capital would degrade the status of the working man. These beliefs were transformed into anti-Chinese convictions through accusations that Chinese refused to assimilate, were inculcated with a totalitarian culture that was incompatible with free societies, and were willing to work for low wages and send the money home rather than settle and become invested in local working conditions. In short, Chinese played into the hands of capitalist interests that wanted to dominate and degrade the living standards of the working man rather than build an egalitarian, self-governing community. Depictions of Chinese as dirty, enslaved, heathen, servile and cunning added an emotional dimension to these accusations.

Anti-Asian sentiment drew on a long anglophone tradition of extolling the community and its common values as a bedrock of democracy and self-rule. In eighteenth-century Europe, the tensions between migration and the existence of stable, self-governing communities was generally expressed through concerns about uncontrolled exit. Early U.S. politicians, intent on populating their country, wrote eloquent defenses of the right of free exit. But they were equally eloquent in transforming the arguments against free exit into concerns about the sociopolitical effects of unregulated entry. For example, in an essay explaining the absolute right of free exit and the economic desirability of immigrants for the United States, Benjamin Franklin sounded a note of caution and offered a list of concerns about free entry that established the talking points of restrictionists for the next two centuries: migrants were a potential welfare burden, brought incompatible political traditions, refused to learn English and assimilate, and would overwhelm white Anglo-Saxon culture and undermine political stability.[5] Similarly, in his *Notes on Virginia* of 1782, Thomas Jefferson opposed the active importation of foreign laborers as a threat to the social harmony necessary for a self-governing society. He explained that the government of the United States was based on the freest principles of the English constitution:

> To these nothing can be more opposed than the maxims of absolute monarchies. Yet from such we are to expect the greatest number of emigrants. They will bring with them the principles of the governments they leave, imbibed in their early youth; or, if able to throw them off, it will be in exchange for an unbounded licentiousness, passing, as is usual, from one extreme to another. It would be a miracle were they to stop precisely at the point of temperate liberty. These principles, with their language, they will transmit to their children. In proportion to their numbers, they will share with us the legislation. They will infuse into it their spirit, warp and bias its directions, and render it a heterogeneous, incoherent, distracted mass.[6]

By the middle of the nineteenth century, anti-Chinese agitators supplemented these communitarian arguments with a critique of big capital. Asian immigration was unfair competition imported by those who would degrade the conditions of labor. Willing to live on a handful of rice a day and reside in the most unsanitary of conditions, Chinese undermined the dignity of the working man and created an unequal, caste-based society. Publicity about the "coolie trade" only cemented the identification of Chinese as bound and servile labor, whether in the service of European capitalists or of other Chinese.

Capitalist entrepreneurs and liberal elites from areas with little Chinese immigration responded with appeals to the universality of individual rights, the moral and economic virtues of free intercourse, and the utility of Chinese labor for frontier development. They characterized anti-Asian proponents as ignorant demagogues driven by irrational insecurities and unable to understand the larger picture of modern progress and national honor. As Chester Holcombe, missionary, businessman, and former secretary of the U.S. legation in China, wrote in 1904, "We have treated Chinese immigrants—never more than a handful when compared with our population—as though we were in a frenzy of fear of them. We have forsaken our wits in this question, abandoned all self-control, and belittled our manhood by treating each incoming Chinaman as though he were the embodiment of some huge and hideous power which, once landed upon our shores, could not be dealt with or kept within bounds."[7]

Anti-Asian activists easily rebuffed these insinuations. In a 1905 article accusing pro-Chinese propagandists of being "sordid profit mongers," U.S. labor leader Samuel Gompers explained that "We make no pretense that the exclusion of Chinese can be defended upon a high ideal. . . . Self-preservation has always been regarded as the first law of nature."[8] By this time the voices of men like Holcombe were drowned out by those of men like Gompers, and arguments in favor of Chinese immigration had withered in the face of anti-Chinese attitudes. Indeed, pro-Chinese activists had only rarely challenged the emotionally potent depictions of Chinese as a servile and degraded race of heathens. And as Asians gradually left the service of plantations and railways, capitalists often proved more than willing to impose harsh vagrancy and registration laws on their subsequent activities as small businessmen and craftsmen. The idea that the anglophone constitutional tradition should guarantee individual rights regardless of race still persisted among a few politicians and writers but was increasingly qualified by conditions and rationalizations, and even directly challenged by assertions that the admission of Chinese would inevitably produce antagonisms that, whether justifiable or not, would inevitably result in institutionalized racial divisions that would undermine democratic practices. Thus it was better to just keep them out in the first place. To this end, the institutions created to enforce the popular anti-Asian laws were given unprecedented powers to ignore democratic procedures as the only means of resolving the multiple enforcement difficulties.[9] Thus, the protection of egalitarian communities ultimately depended on "despotic" institutions much like those that these progressive democracies claimed to abhor. But, as we shall see in subsequent chapters, procedural technicalities and international pressures ultimately proved to be checks that preserved some vestiges of individual rights and free intercourse against the demands of popular legislation.

Taxes and Tonnage

Early attempts to restrict Chinese immigration were not especially innovative, generally adapting long-standing techniques of regulating movement toward discriminatory ends. Quarantine laws were sometimes used at the last minute to keep a particular batch of Chinese from landing. More systematic controls included taxes, licenses, and passenger laws that limited numbers of migrants by ship tonnage, generally holding shipmasters liable for bringing inadmissible migrants. Few of these laws were highly effective. Discriminatory taxes and employment laws were also consistently blocked and repealed, both on constitutional bases and because of treaties that guaranteed rights of free intercourse. Laws that restricted access to naturalization and the franchise were most successful. The basic idea that communities had the right to limit political membership as they wished was much less controversial than the idea that self-governing communities could curtail legal equality to aliens and Asians. The issues at stake with immigration laws were harder to pin down, caught as they were at the interstice between individual rights, treaty rights, community policing, and jurisdictional borders, but they ultimately proved more durable than other discriminatory laws.

The gold-mining frontiers of California and Australia enacted the earliest anti-Chinese laws (Table 5.1). In what was perhaps the most successful (from the point of view of restrictionists) of all these early laws, California placed a tax on all foreign miners in 1852. The supposedly equal application of the tax to all foreigners forestalled constitutional challenges, although in practice 90 percent of the revenue was paid by Chinese, amounting to up to a quarter of state revenue until 1870.[10] Less successful laws were passed in 1855 on both sides of the Pacific. California imposed an immigration tax of fifty dollars on all passengers "incompetent to become citizens," and the Australian colony of Victoria created a "protector of Chinese" and restricted Chinese to segregated camps, later charging an annual residence fee. Victoria also charged a head tax of ten British pounds on each Chinese arrival and restricted them to one per ten tons, limits that were considerably more restrictive than the one per two tons in the Hong Kong passenger act and the two per five tons in the U.S. and British passenger acts, all passed that same year.[11] The California immigration law was soon deemed unconstitutional by the state supreme court, in deference to the 1847 U.S. Supreme Court decision in the *Passenger Cases*. The Victorian law was soon circumvented by more than fourteen thousand Chinese who landed at Guichen Bay in nearby South Australia, and walked the five hundred kilometers to the Victorian gold fields. The back door was closed when South Australia agreed to enact a similar tonnage law of its own in 1857, followed by New South Wales in 1861.[12]

London objected to several of the Australian laws, especially after signing the Treaty of Beijing in 1860 that gave Chinese freedom to travel abroad and enter into engagements with British subjects. In 1861 the colonial secretary, Lord Newcastle, admitted to the governor of New South Wales that Her

TABLE 5.1 Chinese Immigration Laws around the Pacific, 1852–1888

	Place	Legal Provisions	Fate of Law
1852	California	Tax on foreign miners	Voided by Civil Rights Act, 1870
		Shipmasters required to post $500 bond to land unnaturalizable passengers	Struck down by California Supreme Court, 1872
1855	California	$50 capitation tax $450 penalty for landing migrants ineligible for citizenship	Struck down by California Supreme Court, 1857
	Victoria	Segregated camps	Repealed 1859
	Victoria	£10 landing tax and 1 Chinese passenger per 10 tons of ship tonnage	Repealed 1865
1857	Victoria	Residence tax	Repealed 1862
1857	South Australia	£10 and 1 per 10 tons	Repealed 1861
1858	California	Bar entry of Mongolian race	Struck down by California Supreme Court, 1862
1859	Victoria	£4 overland entry tax	Repealed 1865
1861	New South Wales	£10 and 1 per 10 tons	Repealed 1867
1862	California	Monthly head tax "to discourage the immigration of Chinese"	Struck down by California Supreme Court, 1862
	United States	U.S. citizens banned from participation in "coolie trade"	
1870	California	Ban on importation of prostitutes and cool	Amended 1874
	United States	Asians prohibited from naturalizing	Repealed 1943
1874	California	Certain immigrants require bonds	Unconstitutional
	British Columbia	Chinese disenfranchised	Repealed 1947
1875	United States	Exclusion of felons, prostitutes, and Asian labor under contract	Superseded 1882 and 1891
1877	Queensland	£10 and 1 per 10 tons	Amended 1884
1878	British Columbia	Quarterly tax	Held Unconstitutional 1878
1879	United States	15 Chinese per vessel	Vetoed 1879
1881	New South Wales	£10 and 1 per 100 tons	Amended 1888

(Continued)

TABLE 5.1 (*Continued*)

	Place	Legal Provisions	Fate of Law
	New Zealand	£10 and 1 per 10 tons	Repealed 1921
	South Australia	£10 and 1 per 10 tons	Amended 1888
	Victoria	£10 and 1 per 100 tons	Amended 1888
1882	United States	Chinese laborers excluded	Repealed 1943
1883	Hawaii	Quota of 2400 Chinese per year and passport for returns	Amended 1884
1884	British Columbia	Entry prohibited and registration	Disallowed 1884
	Hawaii	25 Chinese per ship	Repealed 1888
	Queensland	£30 and 1 per 50 tons	Amended 1890
	United States	Exclusion law strengthened	Amended 1888
1885	British Columbia	Entry prohibited	Disallowed 1885
	Canada	$50 and 1 per 50 tons	Amended 1901
	Hawaii	Laborers may not return	Amended 1893
1886	Western Australia	£10 and 1 per 50 tons	Amended 1889
1887	Hawaii	New regulation of return passports	Amended 1890
	Tasmania	£10 and 1 per 100 tons	Amended 1889
1888	Australia	Colonies agree to limitation of 1 per 500 tons	Repealed 1901–02
	Hawaii	Exclusion of all Chinese	Amended 1890
	United States	Scott Act prohibiting return of laborers	Repealed 1894

Note: This table does not include many discriminatory laws enacted in the 1870s and 1880s that targeted activities other than mobility.

Majesty's Government "cannot shut her eyes to the exceptional nature of Chinese immigration and the moral evil which accompanies it." But he objected to resorting to discriminatory taxes and prohibiting naturalization as "unnecessary and impolitic." Tonnage limitations were preferable because, "If the right to obstruct Chinese immigration be conceded, it is perhaps better that the obstruction should be directed to prevent the arrival of the immigrants than to discourage or harass them after they arrive." In addition to wanting to preserve treaty guarantees, London also held a slightly more cosmopolitan view of race relations within the empire. A Chinese presence in Australia was not objectionable in and of itself, but because of the particular nature of the migration, which Lord Newcastle associated with the coolie trade. He suggested that inducements for Chinese women could mitigate the "moral evil" of Chinese immigration. The naturalization of Chinese was also desirable because those who chose to stay were the most intelligent and "most disposed to adopt the Christian religion and habits." Such inducements would divest restrictive immigration laws of the imputation that they were "dictated by jealousy of the Chinese on the part of those with whom the Chinese might enter into competition with as laborers or producers."[13] With the end of the gold rush and corresponding decline of Chinese immigration, the colonies gave in to pressure from London, and most of the discriminatory laws were repealed by 1867, which London found to be "very satisfactory."[14]

Californians were a bit more imaginative in devising ways to discriminate against Chinese. From the 1850s to the 1870s, laws were passed that banned the entry of all "Mongolians," required a monthly "police tax," banned queues and carrying poles on public sidewalks, imposed licenses on laundries that did not use horses, required a certain amount of cubic air space in sleeping residences, prohibited the importation of Asian prostitutes and coolies, prohibited the employment of Chinese in corporations chartered under California law, and required all Chinese to reside outside of incorporated towns. Nearly all of these laws were overturned by local or federal courts as unconstitutional, some because they were discriminatory and others for interfering with treaties and federal control of commerce. It became increasingly clear that any successful legislation would have to be enacted at the federal level. California senators in Washington ultimately pushed through the Page Law of 1875, prohibiting the entry of convicted felons, prostitutes, and Asian contract laborers. With the latter two exclusions enforced almost entirely in California, this law was a transition from old-style regulations protecting local communities against moral evils and burdens, into the new realm of centralized control defined in terms of race and occupation.

Regional Politics of Immigration

Anti-Chinese agitation receded across the Pacific in the laissez-faire atmosphere of the 1860s that coincided with low Chinese migration rates. But the completion of labor-hungry railway projects, economic slowdowns, and a resurgence of Chinese migration helped revive anti-Asian agitation in the

1870s, which reached a peak in the 1880s as worker movements in North America and Australia looked to each other for inspiration.[15] Despite the common origins and linkages, the specific political structure of each locale affected the form and timing of restrictive legislation. National governments in distant capitals were more likely to cater to the needs of big business and international intercourse. Popular state and city governments on the frontier were more concerned with protecting the rights of white laborers and shaping their nascent communities, while powerful planter interests in the frontier regions of Queensland, Western Australia, Natal, and Hawaii often delayed the rise of anti-Asian legislation.[16] In the United States and Canada, central governments first resisted local legislation against Chinese but ultimately enforced anti-Chinese immigration laws at a national level. In Australia, anti-Chinese legislation was deeply rooted in most colonial governments, and the desire for coordinated exclusion laws was an important impetus for federation and increased autonomy from London. Whether through imposition, consolidation, or separation, the space of the nation became congruent with the space of exclusion and self-government.

Anti-Chinese legislation easily found a foothold in the southeastern Australian colonies of New South Wales, Victoria, and South Australia where Chinese immigration was a colony-wide issue. Colonists were especially concerned to overcome the stigma of their convict origins, generally depicting the Chinese as virtual slaves in contrast to the egalitarian mateship achieved by white settlers.[17] By the 1870s, local colonial politics was saturated with such sentiments. London was distant, and its arguments about diplomatic necessity and equality before law paled before the perceived immediacy of the Chinese threat. Queensland and Western Australia were more dominated by planters and resisted the first waves of anti-Chinese restriction. But when its gold fields began to attract high numbers of free Chinese immigration and members of the legislature began to read reports from the 1876 California inquiry into Chinese immigration, Queensland was the first colony to reinstitute the ten-pound and one-per-ten tonnage restrictions in 1877.[18]

Chinese arrivals across Australia increased in the late 1870s, and officials feared that Hong Kong was deporting its criminals to the colonies. In 1880 New South Wales Premier Henry Parkes sent a circular to the Australian colonial governments warning that pending anti-Chinese legislation in the United States and other countries would drive Chinese to Australia, and that Chinese are "for the most part bound to some unknown authority and are not really free." He asked the governments' opinions on the idea of an intercolonial conference to design uniform legislation to counter this threat.[19] Knowledge that Western Australia had just passed a law encouraging the immigration of Chinese contract labor led to a hurried conference in January 1881 and a petition to the colonial secretary in London recommending that he not oppose uniform Australian legislation against Chinese, insisting that "the action of the Government of West Australia [not yet a self-governing colony but under more direct control from London] cannot be regarded as other than opposed to the common interest in the social advancement of these colonies."[20] As a result of the conference, New South Wales, Victoria, and New Zealand enacted new laws over the next year requiring Chinese arrivals to pay a ten-pound poll tax and limiting them to one per one hundred tons. They also threatened Western Australia with the cessation of all communication if it did not repeal its Chinese labor laws. Western Australia bowed to the pressure and enacted its own restrictions in 1886, followed by Tasmania in 1887. London expressed only mild objections in the face of this coordinated sentiment, while the colonies conceded Colonial Office demands to exempt British subjects of Chinese descent from the limitations.

British Columbia was much less successful at translating its anti-Chinese sentiment into legislation. The Canadian provinces had already been unified under the North America Act of 1867. When British Columbia joined in 1871, it was just one of many provinces represented in far-away Ottawa, where proponents of free trade and big business were more likely to listen to London on the issue of migration, and the governor general (appointed by London) could recommend disallowance of provincial laws. This power was rarely used, with the major exception of laws passed in western provinces that discriminated against Asians and interfered with interprovincial railway construction.[21] Bills proposing special Chinese taxes had already failed in the British Columbia legislature in 1864 and 1872, although Chinese were successfully disenfranchised in 1875. With the arrival of more settlers, a Chinese residence tax was passed in 1878 but disallowed in Ottawa because of its discriminatory aspects that went against treaty commitments. British Columbians in the House of Commons began to agitate for Britain to work with the United States to revise their treaties with China.[22] The Canadian government responded that "It would be an unprecedented Act on the part of the Dominion and at variance with the policy of other nations to pass a Law, to prevent the immigration of people from any portion of the world."[23]

In 1884 Liu Ruifen, the Chinese minister in London, objected to a new British Columbian law that denied entry to Chinese, compelled them to register, and prohibited their ownership of Crown lands. By the time of his protests the Supreme Court of Canada had already determined that the laws were beyond the authority of the provinces and the governor general had disallowed them. Minister of Justice J.A. Campbell explained that although the North America Act said that each province may make its own laws in relation to agriculture and immigration, this was only an authority to promote rather than restrict migration. "A law which prevents the people of any country from coming into a province cannot be said to be of a local or private nature. On the contrary, it is one involving Dominion and possibly Imperial interests."[24]

The legislature in British Columbia had passed the laws expecting disallowance but hoping that they might compel Ottawa to take the province's grievances more seriously.[25] Encouraged by a note from London informing the governor general that the Colonial Office had declined to interfere in the Australian laws of 1881 on the grounds that they were a matter of internal legislation, Parliament did indeed dispatch a royal commission to investigate conditions in British Columbia and California in 1884. Hopeful, British Columbia passed a new law against Chinese immigration in February 1885, but it was once again disallowed. Referring to U.S. Supreme Court decisions, the minister of justice insisted that provincial immigration laws interfered with the right of the Dominion Parliament to regulate commerce.[26] This decision, however, was not meant to be obstructionist, but to pave the way to dominion-wide legislation. With major railway construction nearly complete, Parliament passed a law in April requiring a fifty-dollar poll tax and limiting Chinese to one per fifty tons with the exception of tourists, merchants, diplomats, students, and Canadian residents. The choice of a poll tax rather than a U.S.-style exclusion law was partly shaped by the royal commission's visit to the United States, where it found that court costs arising from the multiple challenges to exclusion probably equaled all the money collected by the Australian head tax.[27]

Even the Kingdom of Hawai'i began to restrict Chinese immigration in 1883, although the planter-dominated economy and close personal relations of the monarchy with both Chinese and planters created a highly uneven history of legislation. The government had encouraged the recruitment of Chinese after the signing of a trade reciprocity treaty with the United States in 1875 that promised a booming market for Hawaiian sugar. At the same time, growing numbers of white settlers from California brought their anti-Chinese attitudes with them, persuading native Hawaiians that Chinese merchants and artisans were pushing them out of a livelihood. A series of increasingly strict immigration laws were passed from 1883 to 1887, in which a quota of twenty-five Chinese per boat was gradually reduced to no Chinese at all except those holding return passports issued by the Hawaiian government.[28] The planters made up the slack by recruiting Japanese (and later Filipino, Portuguese, and Puerto Rican) laborers.

The government also worked with proplanter officials to design new laws that could keep the social worlds of the plantations and broader population entirely separate. In 1889 the ministers of the interior, foreign affairs, and finance presented a petition that started out in progressive exclusionist tones:

> It is a self-evident proposition that there can be no representative popular government where the population is composed of a few rich men and a large number of alien, ignorant, non-voters. An oligarchy is the inevitable government of such a population, with a strong probability that the islands would pass under the control of some foreign nation. An intelligent middle class is essential to every country which proposes to have free government.[29]

In response to people who argued that Chinese have as much right to enter the islands as anybody, they added that, "A man may be a man but that alone does not given him all the rights in Hawai'i, or any other country, that other men may have, unless by treaty with the nation to which he belongs such rights are secured." The planters' need for Chinese labor, however, could not be ignored. The petition proposed a new series of laws that were enacted in the 1890s to establish yearly quotas of Chinese migrants to be dispatched directly to plantations that requested them, with provisions for their return to China after the expiration of their contracts. A constitutional amendment of 1892 also forbade Chinese from engaging in trade or artisanal occupations. The supervision was effective enough that Hong Kong even agreed to relax its restrictions against the emigration of contract labor to Hawai'i under the belief that laborers' "freedom" was well-protected there.[30]

The Angell Treaty

Like Ottawa, Washington, DC, was far away from the centers of anti-Chinese agitation on the Pacific Coast, and like London, it was the capital of an independent nation that dealt directly with other states. Politicians there were often caught up in abolitionist idealism and not always sympathetic to the anti-Chinese cause. The Fourteenth Amendment of 1868 prohibited any state from making legislation that deprived "any person" of life, liberty, property, or equal protection of the laws. The Civil Rights Enforcement Act of 1870 specified that it was illegal to impose discriminatory taxes, licenses, punishments, and immigration taxes on "any person within the jurisdiction" of the United States.[31] But by the late 1870s, western states were increasingly important swing states in highly contested national elections. Neither party could expect western votes if it was not sufficiently committed to stopping Chinese immigration.[32] Politicians in Washington had to balance their international and idealistic obligations with the democratic pressures to support Chinese exclusion.

The most pertinent of these obligations was the 1868 Burlingame treaty of friendship and commerce with China that guaranteed "the inherent and inalienable right of man to change his home and allegiance, and also the mutual advantage of the free migration and emigration of their citizens and subjects respectively from the one country to the other for purposes of curiosity, trade, or as permanent residents." Explaining the treaty in the *New York Times*, Secretary of State William Seward expressed his understanding of the necessary unity of all intercourse:

> The free emigration of the Chinese to the American [continent] is the essential element of that trade and commerce. Chinese emigration to the American continent will tend to increase the wealth and strength of all Western nations; while at the same time, the removal of the surplus population of China will tend much to take away the obstructions which now impeded the introduction into China of art, science . . . religion.[33]

Anti-Chinese activists, on the other hand, went so far as to consider the migration clause of the Burlingame treaty to be "treasonous," an attitude that increasingly pitted electoral politics against the concerns of the State Department and other executive branches. After the election of 1878, one of the first achievements of the new Congress was to pass a bill that limited Chinese immigration to fifteen per vessel. President Hayes vetoed the bill with the explanation that the honor of the nation depended on upholding treaties. But he did suggest that, "the simple provisions of the Burlingame treaty may need to be replaced by more careful methods."[34] A new treaty was the answer. Earlier that year, the minister to China, George Seward (nephew of William), had told Secretary of State William Evarts that if the United States were to disavow the "inherent and inalienable right of man to change his home and allegiance," it should at least be done in an honorable way through discussion with China.[35] In February 1879 Evarts, fueled by the essay on Chinese slavery and translations from Chinese law codes forwarded by Consul Bailey in Shanghai, began to prepare the way for a new treaty by suggesting to the recently established Chinese Embassy that China had already failed to uphold the provisions of free emigration. He quoted section 35 of the Chinese penal code to Associate Chinese Minister Yung Wing that "All persons renouncing their country and allegiance, or devising means thereof, shall be beheaded." Yung replied that this had nothing to do with emigration but with treason and rebellion.[36] But the Zongli Yamen did agree to negotiate a new treaty, in part hoping to concede emigration restrictions for other political objectives.

As suggested by Evarts's easy conflation of emigration with a change of allegiance, the treaty was characterized by the ambiguities of applying old understandings to the new processes of modern migration. It allowed for the exclusion of laborers but the free movement of merchants, students, and officials; however, it failed to define any of these categories clearly. These labels and the negotiations that produced them would remain an object of debate for over a quarter of a century. The U.S. delegation, led by James Angell, opened the negotiations with the tactics used by Evarts, comparing limitations on the movement of foreigners within China against the complete freedom of movement enjoyed by Chinese within the United States. The delegation also insisted that the Burlingame provisions applied only to immigrants who wished to "change their home and allegiance." Trotting out the image of the Chinese sojourner, the U.S. negotiators contrasted him to the exile who was an object of protection in international law, insisting that a Chinese immigrant seeking only a temporary residence in the United States did not deserve the privileges that treaty stipulations guaranteed for those who sought permanent residence. "All other immigrants come to the US with the express purpose of changing their allegiance, with their wives and children, to be in the course of a generation completely incorporated into the country of their adoption."[37]

The Chinese response was somewhat more up-to-date with actual practices of migration as opposed to their representation in international law, albeit in the vein of debates over indentured migrants, which were the greatest Chinese concern. The Chinese delegation insisted that Chinese who traveled to the United States were not kidnapped, coerced, or under contract but "have flown thither as free as wild geese fly." It also argued that Chinese had established "a hundred lines of enterprise" in California and that their inexpensive labor had been of benefit to all U.S. citizens. But now, because of the influence of "rabble," "violent men," and the "Irish Party," the United States wanted to restrict the Chinese.[38] The U.S. commissioners objected that the U.S. government had the "right to appreciate for itself the motives of its own policy."[39] The Chinese did not press the issue because they tended to agree that a limitation on migration was the best way to reduce anti-Chinese agitation—indeed, that was the logic of their own restrictions on foreign mobility within China.

The U.S. delegation retreated from its attempt to define "immigrants" and proposed a ban on all Chinese entries other those for "teaching, trade, travel, study, and curiosity hereinbefore referred to and authorized and provided for in existing treaties." The Chinese objected that this would be impractical because the "separation of this class from the mass of subjects of China in this manner is not in strict accord with the spirit of our treaties," but this issue was never specifically resolved.[40] The Chinese also pointed out the confusion in the Angell Commission language that alternated between requests to regulate, limit, suspend, and prohibit Chinese immigration. They insisted that prohibition went against existing treaties, and they would only agree to a temporary suspension of laborers to California rather than to the entire nation. This suspension should be enforced only at Chinese ports and not applied to Chinese who might arrive from places other than China. The United States agreed to a temporary limitation but insisted on the need for controls to take place at U.S. ports. Not only did most migrants depart from Hong Kong rather than China, but "If undertaken by China it would necessitate complicated regulations; the appointment of special officers at each port to enforce them, and, failure to enforce the rules on the part of the local officers would raise questions between the two governments."[41]

The final treaty, signed in November, allowed for the suspension of Chinese immigration to all of the United States. The commission recommended that language providing that Chinese subjects would be allowed to "proceed to the United States as teachers, servants, merchants or for curiosity" should be borrowed by Congress for its own legislation, although it admitted that the category of laborers remained undefined.[42] The Chinese had insisted that the term "laborers" should not include artisans, but no mention was ever made in the negotiations of professionals, manufacturers, office workers, family members, or others who fell in the cracks between laborers and merchants or teachers. The way was now paved for a new immigration law. President Arthur vetoed the first bill of April 4, 1882, as "undemocratic and hostile to the spirit of our institutions" and against the "good faith" of the Angell negotiations. He specifically objected to the twenty-year time period as far beyond a "temporary" limitation, to the exclusion of "skilled laborers," and to the registration of Chinese residents. He also objected to the issuance of passports to nonlaborers allowed to travel freely, explaining that such provisions were dying out in Europe, and that, "A wide experience has shown how futile such precautions are, and how easily passports may be borrowed, exchanged, or even forged by persons interested to do so."[43] A new version of the law without the registration and with a ten-year limit was finally passed in May 1882.

Categorical Confusion

Enacting immigration laws was one thing; enforcing them was another. The first U.S. exclusion law was an ineffective and contentious instrument. Most of Arthur's fears about international and domestic difficulties came to pass, while Chinese entries did not decline significantly in the first six years of enforcement. At least 18,275 Chinese departed Hong Kong for the United States in 1888 alone, a number exceeded only in the early gold rush and three immediate pre-exclusion years. As late as 1898, New York Chinese Inspector J. Thomas Scharf asserted that the experience of the exclusion laws "proved that restrictive legislation did not restrict."[44]

Attempts to enforce the law were immediately challenged in U.S. courts, where the basic categories of admissible and prohibited migrants left many judges deeply perplexed. It was far from obvious how to categorize preachers, naval officers, wives of merchants, opera singers, bookkeepers, acrobats, cooks, landowners, and factory owners within the less than all-encompassing categories of laborer, merchant, teacher, student, and traveler. For example, in 1882 store manager and laundry owner Lee Yik claimed entry as a merchant despite the fact that he did not have a section 6 certificate, the document issued by the Chinese government that testified to his exempt status (the "passports" Arthur had referred to, known as section 4 certificates before new legislation in 1884 moved this provision to section 6). Oregon Circuit Court Justice Green readily agreed with earlier decisions in California that, given the congressional desire not to override treaty guarantees, the certificate was not a necessary license for entry but "a gratuitous grant of a piece of evidence" provided only "for the benefit and security of the privileged classes." Much more perplexing for Green was whether Lee Yik actually belonged to the privileged classes. He argued that a laborer was not merely a person who uses physical strength but a contextualized product of social relations in modern industrial society,

> one of those two great classes in society which seem to be coming continually in opposition to one another on the question of wages. Our amendatory treaty with China concerning immigration, and the insertion of the word "laborer" therein, arose from the relation, which the importation of Chinese bears to wages, and from the effect it produces or is liable to produce on those Americans who work for wages. A laborer, in the sense of this statute and this treaty, is one that hires himself out or is hired out to do physical toil. Physical toil is essential in the definition. So also is a contract, express or implied, to submit for wages the person who is to do the toil to him for whom it is to be done. . . . Toil itself, as a commodity, cannot be disposed of without an at least temporary or qualified disposition of the toiler. For he is, so to speak, the package in which it is bound up, the vessel from which it is to be poured. That situation of parties which in the law is known as the relation of master and servant must obtain or there is no laborer. He is not a laborer who works with his hands in his own business; but he is one who is hired out or hires himself out to do that in another's business.[45]

Green decided that since Lee Yik had only engaged in the mental labor of managing a store, he should be allowed to come and go of his own free will. Similarly, Judge Matthew Deady decided that an actor was not a laborer because the purpose of exclusion act was to reduce competition with U.S. labor, and an actor "seems as far removed from such competition as it is possible for a person to be."[46] Both avoided the question of how an official in China could certify the class of a Chinese emigrant when this would only be fully realized in the context of U.S. social relations.

In 1883, however, Judge Hoffman refused to admit a seventeen-year-old boy who held a share in his family's cigar factory and had come to help manage it. Hoffman argued that to label somebody a merchant just because he had a small share in a business would open the door to all kinds of nonmerchants. He was very unhappy with his decision, however, and recommended that it be appealed to the Supreme Court for a more definitive ruling. He later commented,

I don't know if a boy of seventeen can be said to be anything. If he is anything he is probably a merchant. He is certainly not a laborer in the general sense, but so far as appears he is to go into an old established mercantile firm. . . . Perhaps [the] suggestion may have some force where he appears to be a member of a resident family that he ought to be al-lowed to come, because he is not a laborer as yet though he may not be a merchant either.[47]

Problems of categorization were similar around the world. By 1909, when making recommendations for new Chinese legislation in Canada, the chief controller of immigration resisted including a specific definition of merchant. Referring to the many problems generated by impractical definitions in U.S. legislation, he argued that "we are endeavoring to define that which it is im-possible and which has been the subject of controversy in the English courts upon many occasions during the past century."[48] The problem was even more perplexing because of the "peculiarities" of the Chinese commercial com-munity. "The gradations between a 'merchant' and our accepted meaning of the term, to those performing a menial occupation, are so gradual and indefinite."[49]

Women and children also slipped through the categories. For the first two years of U.S. exclusion, women were allowed to join their husbands. Af-ter a revision of exclusion in 1884, the Treasury Department demanded that women must obtain a section 6 certificate on the basis of their own qualifica-tions. In the words of Circuit Court Justice Field, "The fiction of the law as to the unity of the two spouses does not apply under the restriction act. As a distinct person she must be regarded."[50] Lawyers for Chinese merchants com-plained in a petition to President Arthur, "What certificate could the Chinese government issue to the wife? A certificate that she is a woman? That is not necessary, as it is a self-evident fact."[51] Matthew Deady reversed the ruling in 1889. Referring to provisions that allowed a merchant to bring his servants, he argued that it would be absurd to think that the exclusion of his family had ever been contemplated in the exclusion laws. "The reason why the [family members] are not expressly mentioned, as entitled to such admission, is found in the fact that the domicile of the wife and children is that of the husband and father. . . . the company of the one, and the care and custody of the other, are his by natural right; he ought not to be deprived of either, unless the intention of Congress to do so is clear and unmistakable."[52] The status of women and children was now dependent on the status of the husband, and the family supplemented the individual as a main object of migration control. Deady grounded his decision in an idea of "natural right," but this decision and other attempts to define immigrant categories were rarely grounded in any sort of common understanding or universal reason. They were the products of political and legal struggles between those who wanted to privilege rights of intercourse and those who advocated community self-protection.

Evasion and Punishment

Even when there was relatively broad agreement on the meaning of the law (as in Australia after 1888), implementation remained difficult. Around the Pacific, laws were stymied by smuggling, false documents, lack of effective sanctions, difficulties of policing borders, dispersion of authority, bribery, erratic enforcement, and conflicts of jurisdiction. Migration documents quickly became a valuable commodity on both sides of the Pacific. Counterfeit and altered documents emerged almost as soon as the originals were issued, while genuine documents were sold and used long after the original holder had died or returned to China for good.[53] This was facilitated by the fact that agents had a hard time telling Chinese apart. Physical descriptions were vague and unsystematic characterizations, such as "pleasant features," "well-known here," "full face," and "flat nose."[54] Even photographs and thumbprints could be hard to distinguish.[55]

In Australia, a traffic in false and genuine naturalization certificates quickly helped immigration numbers reach pre-1881 levels. The number of Chinese with naturalization certificates who entered Victoria rose from 317 in 1882 to 1178 in 1885, which exceeded the number of total entries in any year since 1855 and amounted to about half of the certificates ever issued.[56] This number was reduced only when the Sydney collector began to strictly interpret the provision that allowed him to deny entry until he was "completely satisfied" with a naturalization document.[57] In Canada, officials confiscated 121 forged certificates of leave by 1892, and the minister of trade and commerce complained that they were "openly made an object of trade in the principal Ports of China and at Hong Kong."[58] In the United States, fake companies with inflated partnerships were established precisely to allow members to qualify as merchants. One such partnership in 1916 allowed individuals to register as partners for an investment of two hundred dollars. Members were required to pay thirty-five dollars to the partnership each time they needed testimony to obtain a merchant return certificate for themselves or to bring family members. If a member did not want to bring his own family members, he was free to sell his name to a friend.[59]

Mechanisms to regulate the issuing and verification of certificates lagged far behind. An 1885 investigation by O. L. Spaulding found grave mistakes in the early administration of exclusion at San Francisco. Customs agents had been quickly overwhelmed by the work of measuring applicants, filling forms, writing duplicates, and filing. A lack of accountability created opportunities for bribes and sloppy work. Some merchants deposited photos in the customs house to facilitate their return after trips abroad, but Spaulding doubted their usefulness in making distinctions between people with similar appearances.[60] Customs houses in different ports each followed their own procedures, some flatly refusing to follow procedures and enforce rules that were followed elsewhere.[61] In 1887 many customs houses still made no record of certificates they had issued. Chinese took advantage of this by applying for certificates at several ports or merely stealing unissued certificates from the offices and selling them to new migrants.[62]

Sanctions were hard to impose. Legislation imposed most of the penalties on shippers, including fines and the costs of repatriation. Australian officials even tried to make captains pay the poll tax for Chinese seamen who deserted ship at port.[63] These sanctions were ultimately of little value no matter how much they were strengthened in subsequent legislative amendments. Shipping companies were among the first to complain of new laws and suggest that they would drive the Chinese trade into the arms of competitors from other nations. Cash penalties were rarely enforceable except in rare cases where negligence could be demonstrated, and any costs borne in returning rejected migrants were easily recovered in increased ticket prices. Officials realized that ship captains could not make the final determination on the validity of official documents and only expected them to make sure that migrants carried at least some document (a problem for migrants who had a valid claim of entry but no document). The chief controller in Canada noted in 1892 that "It is manifestly not in the interest of the steamers to enquire too closely into the validity of the certificates presented"[64]

In Canada and Australia, it was also unclear if migrants themselves could be punished by deportation if they came in excess of tonnage limitations, especially if they were willing to pay the landing tax. The collector at Sydney worried that not allowing the payment of the head tax would just encourage migrants to jump ship, and he concluded in 1886 that "the tonnage clause is inoperative."[65] The chief controller in Canada admitted excess passengers even if they had attempted to use a false certificate because he believed that most had been deceived by brokers who promised them that all their papers were in order. In these cases, deportation "would in most cases amount to absolute ruin to innocent parties who have struggled to get together sufficient money to land them in Canada, and . . . paid that sum in good faith for that purpose."[66] He also noted that most of the forgeries had been produced in Hong Kong. It was unclear whether this could be prosecuted under either Hong Kong or Canadian law, since the documents did not break any Hong Kong laws and the actual work was not done in Canada.

Frustrated with their own system, Canadian customs officials studied U.S. methods in the 1890s and then reformed their system by abolishing all existing certificates and establishing better systems of accountability and cross-referencing for the new ones, stored only in government offices and not allowed into the hands of the Chinese themselves. But the United States hardly provided an effective model. In 1900 officials in both countries still complained about how difficult it was to enforce the laws because of conflicting regulations and decisions, unclear definitions, and the difficulty of getting people outside of the system to conform to bureaucratic procedures. Even attempts to clean up the laws through systematization and specification of procedure could make the entire process more mysterious and unwieldy. For example, many missionaries produced documents that attested to the status of Chinese students, but customs officers complained that "it is so very hard to obtain any document that is worded so as to qualify the applicant according to the act as very few of the missionaries or teachers seem to grasp at what is wanted."[67]

Border Complications

The organizational difficulties of controlling migration at the ports was matched by the lack of infrastructure to patrol land borders. Special Agent Herbert Beecher wrote in 1887 that the U.S. exclusion law was "created without practical knowledge of what was required of it. A law created apparently more for California, with no thought or knowledge of its workings in Washington Territory, situated as we are, so closely to British Columbia, commanding as it does such natural advantages of evasion of the Restriction Act."[68] Suddenly, trails in the Northwest that wound back and forth across the border

with Canada, Chinese who wintered on the Alaska coast between summer
stints in backwoods Canada, and Chinese gardeners in northern Mexico who
routinely crossed the border to sell produce in the United States all became
problems.[69] Customs officials had always dealt with the smuggling of tariffed
goods, but that could be adequately controlled by stations along major transportation routes where most shippers paid tariff costs for the sake of using
port infrastructures. As Special Agent O.L. Spaulding explained, "Chinamen who think and act for themselves can still more easily be smuggled or
smuggle themselves into the country."[70] Moreover, no leakage was acceptable
with Chinese. Each one had to be individually inspected and identified.

Customs agents noted that thousands of Chinese passed through San
Francisco in transit to Mexico each year in the 1880s, even though only about
four or five thousand Chinese were resident in Mexico. They claimed that
many had crossed the border back into the United States, while others had
just abandoned the train or been replaced by a substitute. The Treasury Department tried multiple methods of forestalling this: requiring bonds from
transit passengers, sending guards to accompany them, and abolishing transit
privileges altogether. Surveillance methods failed to stop the evasion, and the
abolishment had to be repealed because of protests from China about the
infringement on rights of free movement.[71] Meanwhile, the expansion of railway lines throughout Canada and Mexico and of tramp steamer lines across
all the borders and within the Caribbean helped smuggling routes to increase
much faster than the mechanisms of surveillance and interdiction.[72]

Attempts to control cross-border mobility were complicated by the need
for international cooperation. The U.S. Customs Department established
Chinese agents in Victoria and Vancouver in the late 1880s to inspect arriving Chinese, but this could not stop substitutions on the subsequent journey
to the U.S. border. In October 1890 Congress passed a resolution to begin
negotiations with Canada and Mexico to help stop laborers from entering the
United States.[73] Lord Salisbury promised to look into this issue, but Mexico
was more recalcitrant. Secretary of State James Blaine asked the U.S. ambassador to communicate to Mexican officials that Her Brittanic Majesty "can not
have failed to perceive the grave embarrassments attending the application of
diverse legislation to Chinese persons entering the ports of two neighboring
countries," but that Mexico had "failed to perceive" these embarrassments.[74]
The Mexican ambassador in Washington responded that the Mexican constitution guaranteed every man the right to enter and leave the republic and
travel through its territory without passport or letter of safe conduct.[75] No ar-

rangement was ever made with Mexico despite sporadic negotiations over the next twenty years. The U.S. consul general in Canada also responded in 1892 that "the Government of the Dominion does not charge itself with the duty of enforcing measures of restriction adopted by a foreign government with regard to access to its territories by persons of other nationalities."[76] Ultimately, Canadian railways were more amenable than the government. Fearing that land borders would be closed, they agreed in 1894 to carry Chinese to the border on bond, and the Canadian government allowed U.S. officials to board the trains for inspections.[77]

Deportation "to the country from whence he came" was also a sticky international problem. After 1885 Chinese attempting to travel from Canada to the United States destroyed their head tax certificates so that Canada would refuse to take them back without payment of a new head tax. U.S. officials soon gave up trying to deport Chinese in that direction.[78] Entries into Canada rose dramatically after the strengthening of the U.S. exclusion laws in 1888. Canadian officials admitted that Chinese entered Canada primarily to smuggle across the border, joking that "We get the cash and you get the Chinamen."[79] Chinese caught on the Mexican border would merely claim to be Mexican residents. After being returned to Mexico, they would try again in a couple of days.[80] The Treasury Department attempted to resolve problems on both borders in 1891 by requiring deportations to China and insisting that the burden of proof was on the deportees to show that they were the subject of a power other than China. One consequence of this decision, other than the enormous expense of deportation to China, was that some Chinese purposely courted deportation as a free trip home.[81] As late as 1910, U.S. officials complained that Canadian railways carrying Chinese on bond allowed the Chinese to pay the five-hundred-dollar Canadian head tax if they were rejected at the U.S. border, after which they could easily cross the border surreptitiously. They demanded that the railways deport the rejected Chinese back to China, but the Canadian government responded that these Chinese had fulfilled the law and the railways had no liability.[82]

Conflicting Authorities

International and domestic jurisdictional struggles also hampered enforcement. These conflicts were most intense in the United States, where the exclusion law was most complex and authority to enforce it most widely dispersed.

Responsibility for administering the law was divided between uncoordinated customs collectors at various ports, state and federal courts charged with interpreting the laws and hearing appeals, and Chinese officials required to issue section 6 certificates to exempt classes. Subsequent legislation required U.S. consuls to apply visas to section 6 certificates (1884) and internal revenue agents to issue registration certificates (1892). Nobody involved at any stage of enforcement escaped criticism from the press, higher officials, and each other. Attempts to resolve the difficulties only plunged officials into a morass of details and technicalities.

Differences in procedure and interpretation between the Customs Bureau and the courts were the most intractable sources of tension. Immigration agents placed the burden of proof on Chinese to prove their admissibility. But migrants were allowed to appeal adverse decisions to the federal courts, where the doctrine of innocent until proven guilty placed the burden of proof on the government. Thus, in the courts, a Chinese was a U.S. citizen, merchant, previous resident, or whatever he or she claimed to be until government officials could produce incontrovertible evidence to the contrary. Such evidence was generally impossible to obtain, and Chinese detained at the ports quickly learned to take advantage of habeas corpus. From 1882 to 1891, 7,080 writs of habeas corpus were presented in California, with more than 85 percent of those held gaining their liberty.[83] Chinese arrested in the interior and sentenced to deportation were also often discharged by the courts because of the inability of the government to collect irrefutable proof of their illegal entry.[84]

Conflict of authority extended into China. At first, the division of labor between China and the United States seemed simple. In 1882 Consul John Moseby in Hong Kong wrote on behalf of trans-Pacific shipping companies to Minister John Young in Beijing, asking him to inquire about provisions that the Chinese government had made for local officials to issue certificates to the exempt classes.[85] Moseby also suggested that the new law superseded the law of 1862 that required him to inspect U.S. vessels to make sure no migrants were being transported against their will, hoping that monitoring emigration would no longer be one of his responsibilities.[86] Secretary of State Frederick Frelinghuysen confirmed that the act conferred no duties or powers on consular officers, and that the issuance of section 6 certificates was purely a matter for the Chinese government to determine. He explained that the U.S. government "knows nothing of the functions, nor, indeed, officially, of the existence of local authorities in Chinese ports."[87] Minister Young further asserted that he did not want to bring the issue up to Chinese officials because it was a potentially sensitive "minor question" that might draw attention away from the "grave issue" of the treaty rights of foreigners in Chinese ports.[88]

China did issue certificates until early 1883. Its regulations were based on those designed to supervise contract emigration, requiring emigrants to report to local authorities along with a trustworthy person to stand security and guarantee that they had sufficient passage money and were departing freely and voluntarily.[89] The Canton superintendent of trade issued 1,141 section 6 certificates in 1883. California courts refused to contest them because they could not be conclusively rebutted, and the Treasury Department felt compelled to accept the certificates as prima facie evidence, despite serious reservations that the bearers were really merchants.[90] The San Francisco customs house complained that the only way to disprove the section 6 claims was "the chance of some contradictory statement being made by the interested parties themselves in reply to such questions as may be addressed to them regarding their place of residence and character of business."[91] The California press quickly raised a ruckus. Collector E. L. Sullivan complained that he was torn between popular media pressure to reject all of the certificates and pressure from the courts and the Chinese consul to admit them.[92] A substantial resolution to the problem was deferred when the Chinese government decided to issue no more certificates after November 10.[93]

Nothing in the law stipulated who had the right to issue return certificates for laborers residing in the United States. In June 1882 Secretary Frelinghuysen told Secretary of the Treasury Charles Folger that it would be a good idea to have the Chinese consulate assist in issuing the certificates.[94] Folger passed this recommendation on to Collector Sullivan, who objected that "the public is keenly alive to the operation of this law, and a political question of considerable import could be easily evolved out of any apparent neglect of this office to strictly enforce the law or any appearance that this office is dominated by the Chinese consul-general or the 'Six Companies."[95] Sullivan believed that the Chinese consul did not want to help facilitate movement, but usurp the right to monitor and control it.[96] He ultimately agreed to accept consular certificates as identity documents but not make them a requirement as hoped by the consul general.

The Chinese consulate in San Francisco also issued certificates for resident merchants who wanted to return to China. This was not required by law but was a matter of convenience for reentry. The consulate complained when the customs house began to issue certificates on its own initiative in early 1884.

The collector explained that he had never issued merchant certificates, but only return laborer certificates regardless of the status of the applicant, saying that only "the consul-general, being Chinese, knows how to discriminate the different characters among the Chinese residents."[97] Secretary Folger decided that the Chinese consular certificates for merchants should be accepted as issued under the authority of the Chinese government. Referring to a decision by Judge Green that these certificates were only prima facie evidence, Folger said the Customs House could also issue its own certificates for the sake of convenience, as could U.S. consuls in countries where no Chinese official was resident. But the diffusion of authority and accountability also meant that the collector was not required to admit Chinese solely on the basis of this certificate, a decision that would annoy both Chinese officials and U.S. consuls when the certificates and visas they issued were rejected.[98]

The amended exclusion law of 1884 required a consular visa on any section 6 certificate, making it a necessary but not sufficient document for entry. It remained unclear if the certificates themselves could be issued only by officials in China. San Francisco collector Hagar objected to accepting certificates issued by U.S. and Chinese consuls and insisted that all Chinese must return to China to obtain a certificate. He pointed out that mob violence was possible if evasions were to continue, so instead of relaxing the laws, "the Government should use every endeavor to see them faithfully enforced."[99] His superiors and the courts disagreed and compelled him to accept U.S. consular certificates from places with no resident Chinese official.[100] But Consul Moseby in Hong Kong objected to the Treasury Department circular of December 4, 1884, that authorized customs agents to accept certificates issued by U.S. consuls, saying that the Treasury Department had no right to impose extra duties on him.[101] Other consuls refused to issue certificates for fear that customs officials would reject them. The U.S. consul in Victoria, British Columbia, felt "that it would be the part of prudence for me to avoid any possible discredit of the Consular Seal by declining to grant certificates to Chinese applying to enter San Francisco at present."[102]

The amended law also strengthened penalties and deportation in cases of falsification and substitution. Chinese Minister Zheng Zaoru complained that crossing the borders of the United States was not a crime, and that penalties were in violation of the treaties, insisting that "No where else on the face of the earth can there be found an enactment of this kind."[103] The U.S. government was not highly responsive, but in 1886 Secretary of State Thomas Bayard confessed to Zheng that the section 6 statute "is obscure and defective. . . .

although intended to execute the treaty in respect to the free entrance of the exempted classes, [it] prescribes a formality which renders its exemption practically impossible in certain cases."[104] He pointed to a bill before Congress that would restrict Chinese by tonnage, with no need to make distinctions between merchants and laborers. That bill never passed.

Such was the state of the enforcement of Chinese immigration laws in the 1880s—chaotic and contested. By 1904, Portland Chinese Inspector J. H. Barbour described the exclusion laws as, "a succession of patches, so to speak, which, layer by layer, act by act, treaty by treaty, regulation by regulation, have been laid upon the roof of our social structure. Notwithstanding all this repair the roof still leaks, and it is, moreover, an unsightly affair."[105] This patching reflected the many domestic and international challenges to enforcement and would set the standards for the development of subsequent laws around the world. One of the first steps would be the unambivalent assertion that migration control was a unilateral sovereign prerogative, thus excluding the interference of Chinese officials. Subsequent reforms would gradually restrict the interference of courts, public pressure, and lawyers. Defining the extent of government authority and restricting the intervention of all those who fell outside of that authority would make it possible to clarify the basic definitions of migrant categories and better compel migrants to conform to those definitions.

6

Civilization and Borders, 1885–1895

By the 1870s, migrants had been transformed from objects of commerce into humans. This transformation was at least partly grounded in beliefs about the inalienable rights of individuals. But almost as soon as migrants became human, the source of rights was taken from their persons and relocated in the nation. At the outset, this relocation was driven by the expanding ideas of intercourse and the need of centralized national powers to better manage that intercourse. But as those national powers continued to expand, they quickly eclipsed the needs of intercourse that had once nurtured them. By the twentieth century, courts and politicians of white settler nations around the world no longer referred to treaty rights and intercourse in discussing migration. They instead promoted ideas about the unilateral sovereign prerogative of migration control, disguising their newness under assertions of traditional peoplehood and the universal right of self-protection. National consolidation, nurtured by intercourse, had matured and struck out on its own.

The formative events of this transformation were the revived attempts to control Chinese migration to the white settler nations in the 1880s. An increased focus on national border control characterized these new laws. But the treatment of Chinese after entry was the spark that caused a major international crisis over Chinese migration from 1885 to 1888. The fallout from this crisis generated the first unambiguous assertions of the unilateral right of systematic immigration control by any nation claiming to be founded on liberal principles. U.S. judges and diplomats took the lead in this new formulation. Unlike politicians in the British colonies, U.S. diplomats could not hide behind the convoluted structures of empire. They had to consider their actions in the context of relations with Chinese and, later, Japanese officials. In doing so, they formulated the principles of migration control that would shape a postimperial international order. A key aspect of these principles was the separation of the right of entry from alien rights, and the switch from intercourse to international comity between nations as the source of international order. In this way, borders and nations replaced the human bodies of migrants as the place where migrant rights began and ended.

The principles of modern migration control were critically shaped by the simultaneous need to defend extraterritoriality in Asia. Demands for extraterritorial protection in Asia were grounded in the "universal" rights of intercourse and protection and included continued pressures for Asia to open its interiors to trade and travel. These demands were hard to reconcile with the simultaneous imposition of exclusion. Thus, rather than focusing on the act of intercourse itself, U.S. diplomats focused on the existence of "civilized" institutions that provided equal access to law as the basic requirement for the very existence of free interaction. In contrast to the abstractions of natural rights and intercourse, these institutions offered the concrete rights and protections that made interaction possible. But these rights began and ended at the borders. The maintenance of free institutions even depended on the borders being properly policed against threats, the creation of a security state.[1]

Extraterritoriality

Modern extraterritorial treaties were first signed between European powers and the Ottoman Empire in 1830, China in 1843, Siam in 1855, and Japan in 1858. The precise meanings of these treaties were not firmly established until later in the century, and they contained many variations between them, but in general they unilaterally exempted Europeans from local jurisdictions and placed them under the jurisdiction of their own officials or mixed tribunals. Many also included provisions to station a permanent ambassador in the capital, set tariff rates, and establish treaty ports where foreigners could reside freely and own property. By the 1880s, similar treaties were in force around the world from Madagascar to Tonga.

Antecedents to modern extraterritorial treaties can be traced to long-standing practices across Afro-Eurasia of multiple legal jurisdictions under a single sovereign, including diplomats and foreign merchant communities allowed to govern themselves under their own laws. This jurisdictional autonomy was generally understood not as an infringement on sovereignty, but as a privilege granted by a local ruler in accordance with the norms of interstate relations (although the details of those norms were constantly disputed). They were also a way for states to maintain order at minimal expense, although local sovereigns usually reserved the right to try and punish serious crimes, such as murder. Any failure of foreign residents to maintain order among themselves could also be punished by criminal sanctions or retribution against their home states.[2]

The extraterritorial treaties of the nineteenth century came to carry different meanings from these earlier practices. While Asians may have understood them as variations of earlier practices, Europeans were more likely to see them in terms of asymmetric concessions. As much as any of the particular provisions, the very conditions of their establishment after wars or threats of war set the terms of inequality. No longer did extraterritorial rights and "capitulations" (a term used in the Ottoman Empire) expire with the death of a particular ruler. All rights and privileges were to be interpreted only in terms of the treaties themselves, which, by the second half of the century, meant that they were to be interpreted in terms of European diplomatic and legal norms. Most importantly, in the modern international system, where complete political and legal control over territory and population was increasingly considered a fundamental characteristic of a sovereign state, the existence of extraterritorial treaties was de facto evidence that a state was unqualified for inclusion in the "family of nations."

Extraterritoriality was the Janus face of self-government. For the very reasons that a people capable of self-rule were justified in policing the boundaries of their own community, they could not be expected to subject themselves to the rule of an Asian "despotism." Free people ruled and judged themselves. In contrast, it was believed that Asian law was applied unequally, inconsistently, and subject to the arbitrary whims of a despot or tyrannical bureaucracy. Asian judicial systems subjected petitioners and defendants to torture, uncertain rights, unsystematic decisions, and weak property protections. In short, Asian governments were incapable of maintaining the institutions of self-rule that guaranteed free intercourse.

It is not clear that Asian rulers immediately understood these new treaties as "unequal." In the immediate years after signing the first treaties, officials in China and Japan interpreted them in line with local legal and diplomatic practices and seemed more concerned with restricting the scope of treaty ports, limiting access to the interior, and blocking permanent embassies than with tariff autonomy and foreign legal jurisdiction. These latter two issues entailed the least significant break from existing practice, although they would later be universally condemned as the greatest indicators of inequality. Both China and Japan were somewhat lax in their early enforcement of treaties.

This was a major cause of the Arrow War in China, which led to the signing of the Treaties of Tianjin in 1858 and of Beijing in 1860. These treaties opened China to missionary activities, provided for permanent missions in Beijing, clarified the right of all foreigners to travel in the interior with passports issued by their own consuls, and required the Chinese government to indemnify any injuries experienced by foreigners in the interior.

With the Treaty of Tianjin, the humiliation and inequality implied by these treaties became clear to officials and elites across Asia. Learning from China and the much more limited extraterritorial treaties signed by Siam, Japanese diplomats negotiated treaties after 1858 that avoided opening up the interior to foreign travelers and the opium trade, but still conceded the right of permanent missions in the capital. But even as they grew more resentful of the treaties, Chinese and Japanese officials worked hard to enforce their provisions to the letter. Adherence to the treaties was necessary to forestall new military incursions. Legalistic interpretation in accordance with international law could also be used to minimize the demands of Westerners, especially by interpreting the treaties as the maximum expression of possible privileges rather than as a minimum definition of foreign rights. In the long run, treaty diplomacy and the attempt to create legal and trade institutions that could help repeal the treaties were compulsory indoctrination in the new international system.[3]

International Law in Asia

International law had a contradictory role in the creation of the new international system in Asia. Diplomats from Europe posted to Asia were versed in international law treatises and used them to guide their own actions, persuade others, and establish the norms by which Asians were expected to behave. Asians themselves soon learned the utility of framing their diplomacy in the terms of international law. But even as Asians were expected to uphold its standards, the law itself claimed that it did not apply to Asia. The idea of a "family of nations" was fundamental to the positivist methodology of the nineteenth century because it defined a region of dense interactions that could ultimately be transformed from custom and usage into law. Over the course of the nineteenth century, Christianity gave way to "civilization" as the key definition of membership. Either way, Asians were excluded from the space where law was believed to reside. But the universalizing pretensions of "civilization" created a loophole for Asian states to win small diplomatic victories and, ultimately, for Japan to be included in the "family of nations" at the turn of the century.[4]

Eighteenth-century natural law theorists had assumed their ideas were universal, even if they paid little practical attention to the world beyond Europe. For example, in 1764 Christian Wolff defined a "civilized" nation as one with usages that "conform to the standard of reason and politeness."[5] Because of the great attention given to training in morals and statecraft, the Chinese "from the most ancient times have been prominent among the more civilized nations and are so to-day, yet it happens that few, nay, almost none of them have made advances in metaphysics or physics, much less have they acquired the fame of Europeans in mathematics."[6] By the turn of the nineteenth century, however, the easy use of Chinese and Ottoman examples had become a thing of the past. International law increasingly limited its jurisdiction to Christian nations. Sometimes this entailed a recognition that other parts of the world may have their own law, but over the course of the century this was increasingly expressed as a hierarchical distinction between nations that did and did not adhere to universal and scientific principles. For example, the original 1836 version of Wheaton's *Elements of International Law* remarked only that the civilized Christian law of Europe was "one thing; and that which governs the intercourse of the Mohammedan nations of the East with each other, and with Christians, is another and a very different thing."[7] By the time of Lawrence's 1857 edition, this was replaced by a longer passage defining international law as "those rules of conduct which reason deduces, as consonant to justice, from the nature of the society, existing among independent nations." These rules were gradually expanding across the world, compelling China and other nations of Asia to abandon their "inveterate anti-commercial and anti-social principles."[8]

Common explanations of extraterritoriality also changed from a method of preserving Christian law to a method of preserving justice. Woolsey captured both sides of the transition in 1860 when writing of Asia that "laws and useages there are quite unlike those of Christendom, and in the natural suspicion of Christian states, justice will not be administered by the native courts."[9] By the end of the century, a hierarchy from "savage" peoples with no recognizable state to "barbarian" nations with imperfect institutions to "civilized" nations was increasingly common in international law. The specific contents of each category remained vague. The very diversity of states and relationships between states made it impossible to systematically apply these categories to existing treaties and evidence.[10] But the rubric of civilization was a powerful rhetorical tool, synthesizing the ideas that international law was both universal and unique to European civilization.

Asians also read international law. Wheaton's *Elements of International Law* was translated into Chinese and Japanese in the early 1860s under the guidance of U.S. missionary W.A.P. Martin, soon followed by Woolsey's *Introduction to International Law*. Many returned overseas students from Japan also wrote their own summaries of international law. The responses were varied. Many Chinese and Japanese officials rejected it as an attempt to impose foreign law, or as a superficial mask for the extension of European power. But diplomats in both countries also found it a useful tool in dealing with foreign diplomats. Some Asians were even attracted to international law on its own terms, especially in its pretensions to be a vehicle of universal peace. The broad vision of nations acting out of a sense of comity resonated with Chinese traditions of sagely rulership in which moral harmony was grounded in reciprocal obligations. The focus on diplomatic etiquette in earlier works like Vattel also resonated with a sagely emphasis on proper ritual. Many Japanese commentators were confused by the mix of natural and positivistic law in more contemporary volumes like Wheaton, especially when the translations were poor. But some Chinese were able to map them onto a neo-Confucian distinction between *xingfa* (methods of rule according to essence or human nature) and *gongfa* (methods of rule according to immediate demands of public order). Using both of these methods, a wise ruler could adapt laws to the current situation in ways that were based on firm moral principle.[11]

Ultimately, Chinese and Japanese grew bitter as they perceived that Western powers had no intention of living up to the ideals of international law when dealing with Asian nations. They believed that strong nations did not wish to be bound by international law even as weak nations were compelled to uphold it to the letter if they were to survive. But even as they grew cynical (perhaps because they grew cynical), Japanese made very effective use of international law. Japan had signed a reciprocal extraterritorial treaty with China in 1871 that depended more on traditional Qing legal terminology than on recent translations of international law terminology.[12] But in 1876 they signed a unilateral extraterritorial treaty with Korea based on international principles, followed by a new unilateral treaty with China in 1895 in the wake of military victory. After Japan's 1894 agreement with England to repeal its extraterritorial treaties in 1899 and its military victories against Russia in 1905, many European diplomats and lawyers believed that Japan had earned admission into the family of civilized nations and readily acceded to its colonial jurisdiction over "uncivilized" Korea. This change in attitude was largely an acknowledgement of military power, but Japan had been careful to prosecute its wars with meticulous adherence to the laws of war and then publish books about this achievement that included admiring prefaces by prominent international lawyers.[13]

To accommodate Japan, the idea of "civilization" was formally shorn of its European roots and framed in universal terms—terms that would obscure the crucial role of violence in gaining inclusion. Oppenheim pioneered the listing of explicit standards of civilization and conditions for incorporation into the family of nations. His three conditions were that a nation must engage in constant intercourse with other nations in a civilized manner must agree to be bound by international law, and that the existing family of nations must consent to its reception through inclusion in international conventions. More generally, the standards of civilization included respect for basic rights of dignity and property; freedom of commerce and religion; a centralized state that could maintain responsibilities of domestic policing, self-defense, and international obligations; and courts and laws that could ensure the enforcement of norms that were consistent with international law.[14]

The creation of formal standards built on international law's own historical representation of itself as something that gradually expanded from local European origins to encompass the world, not entirely without injustice, but with generally benevolent effect. In practice, however, the construction of difference had been fundamental to defining the jurisdiction of international law since at least the beginning of the nineteenth century. The standards of civilization amounted to a reformulation of difference away from the idea of Christian law to one that could reinforce inequalities across the borders of the family of nations even as it emphasized the idea of equality between nations. As the sovereign state became more fundamental to international law, lawyers increasingly between distinguished nations that had true sovereignty and those that did not.[15] A sovereignty without the kinds of institutions enumerated by Oppenheim was not true sovereignty.

As late as 1860, Woolsey had asked if it was legitimate to punish by force of arms a nation that refused intercourse. He answered that "Perhaps we may, if we get a just occasion of war with them; but not because they take a position which though disastrous for the interests of mankind, is yet an exercise of sovereignty."[16] Since the 1830s, however, the wars and threats that "opened" the Asian nations were often based on the flimsiest of "just occasions." By the end of the century, lawyers argued that civilized states were not bound to uphold international law in dealing with uncivilized states. If they did, it was only out of a sense of honor and their own interests rather than through expectations of reciprocity or respect for the imperfect sovereignty of uncivilized states. Nonetheless, members of the family of nations continued to produce treaties and other evidence of "consent" to document their unequal encounters. And uncivilized nations were expected to adhere to the treaties as if they were binding contracts between equal nations and were condemned for barbaric incomprehension and obstinacy when they refused to uphold the provisions. Moreover, the terms of the treaties made it difficult to exercise the sovereign control that was necessary to build "civilized" institutions in the first place, transforming assumptions about differences of state capacity into reality.

The confluence of civilizational distinctions and positivist methods can help explain Lassa Oppenheim's statement, quoted in chapter 4, that "no State actually does exclude foreigners altogether." He went on to elaborate that "Of course, if a State excluded all subjects of one State only, this would constitute an unfriendly act, against which retorsion would be admissible; but it cannot be denied that a State is competent to do this, although in practice such wholesale exclusion will never happen."[17] This passage remained in editions of *International Law* until 1935 in the face of well-known examples of Asian and African exclusions around the world. Oppenheim did not directly address this discrepancy, but an explanation appeared in the immediately subsequent discussion of extraterritoriality as an exception to the principle that aliens should be subject to local laws. This exception was grounded in the fact that Asian nations are "in consequence of their deficient civilisation, only for some parts members of the Family of Nations."[18] For much the same reasons, the exclusion of Chinese could be seen as irrelevant to general principles about migration control.

The logic of positivism led to acceptance of existing inequalities even among writers who, like Assistant Solicitor for the U.S. State Department Edwin Borchard, writing in 1915, were critical of extraterritorial treaties and avoided the framework of "civilization." Averse to "philosophical discussion" and a devotee of "common practice," Borchard had to admit that extraterritoriality was an existing practice. Its very existence led to de facto assumptions about the capacity of Asian states. In a discussion of government liability for mob violence against foreigners, Borchard maintained that governments that exerted due diligence to suppress the violence could not be held liable. But in "normally disturbed states" like China, indemnities were still collected despite evidence of due diligence, to the extent that China was "held liable practically as a guarantor of the security of foreigners."[19] With tautological logic he explained that, "By the fact that weak governments like China, Morocco and others in the Far and Near East are held to a high degree of responsibility for injuries due to mob violence, it may be concluded that a fundamental condition of non-liability of the government is a stable political organization normally adequate to prevent such outbreaks."[20] The failure to exert due diligence was an established fact even before the outbreak occurred, an a priori effect of international inequality.

The Rock Springs Massacre

The issue of indemnification for the death of twenty-eight Chinese in 1885 at the hands of a mob in Rock Springs, Wyoming, inspired nearly a decade of international and domestic debate in China and the United States over the alien rights and the legality of controlling international migration.[21] This was not the first incident of mob violence against the Chinese in the United States, but it became a focal point for bitterness that had been brewing in China since the 1860s over the indemnification and treatment of foreigners in China. The discussions ultimately led to a formal statement of the U.S. policy of nonindemnification and of migrants' lack of rights at the border. It also resulted in a distinction of migration and alien protection as two separate issues, a necessary condition to transform the border into a place where rights began and ended. All of these debates were entangled in the attempt to distinguish civilized from uncivilized states, with results that continued to shape migration control far beyond the context of their creation.

For years, foreign merchants in China had loudly attacked limitations on interior movement as an example of arbitrary despotism at work. But when foreigners suffered violence or property loss in the Chinese interior, their cases were usually rapidly resolved through diplomatic intervention and cash indemnities from the Chinese government. From the Chinese perspective, extraterritoriality and the exemption of foreigners from local courts made it dangerous and impractical to allow the free movement of foreigners beyond treaty ports. If free movement were allowed, the investigation and indemnification of every incident of property loss would strain the resources of any government. Passports were necessary to track and give special protection to the foreigners who did travel the interior. The Zongli Yamen occasionally offered to allow free movement to all foreigners without passports if they agreed to abide by Chinese laws, but such offers were routinely rejected.[22]

U.S. diplomats in China had a clear understanding of the relation between extraterritorial protection and the control of movement. In 1874, when U.S. Consul De Lano in Fuzhou complained that international reciprocity demanded that missionaries in China should have the same freedom of movement and residence in the interior that Chinese had in the United States, Minister Avery explained that this basic inequality was actually a function of the superiority of U.S. institutions and a crucial part of U.S.-China relations:

> That, as you say, "our people *should* have the same rights as to residence and the holding of property in the interior as are enjoyed by Chinese subjects in the United States," is a sound proposition in equity, but will not stand as a guide to official action in the interpretation and enforcement of treaty provisions. As a matter of fact, Chinese in the United States enjoy many important privileges which are not secured to them by treaty, which inure to them only by virtue of the tolerant and liberal character of our institutions and people, and which neither our minister nor consuls would be upheld by our Government in demanding as rights for Americans in China, on the ground of reciprocal obligation, without such a revision of existing treaties as would include all such privileges expressly.[23]

The free institutions of the United States also meant that Chinese could not petition the government for special protection or indemnities. In 1880, in response to Associate Minister Yung Wing's request for special protection for Chinese against the growing threat of violence on the West Coast, Secretary of State Evarts responded that existing treaties gave Chinese no more rights to special protection than American citizens could receive in the United States.[24] After a riot in Denver later that year in which over fifty thousand dollars worth of Chinese property was destroyed, Evarts further explained to Minister Chen Lanbin the constitutional basis of U.S. unwillingness to indemnify Chinese losses:

> The powers of the direct intervention on the part of this Government are limited by the Constitution of the United States. Under the limitation of that instrument, the Government of the Federal Union cannot interfere in regard to the administration or execution of the municipal laws of a State of the Union except under circumstances expressly provided for in the Constitution. . . . Whatever remedies may be afforded to the citizens

of Colorado, are equally open to the Chinese residents of Denver. This is all that the principles of international law and the usages of national comity demand.[25]

Chen pointed out that the Angell treaty stipulated that the United States would exert all of its power to protect the Chinese in the United States. As international treaties were the supreme law of the land according to the Constitution, the Denver riot should be considered an international incident rather than merely a matter of internal administration. The federal government should take more responsibility because the government of Denver had not done all that was possible to suppress the mob, bring the perpetrators to justice, and indemnify the victims.[26] He dropped the issue, however, after the Denver government agreed to pay reparations.

The Rock Springs Massacre of September 2, 1885, was an even more grievous event that gained wide publicity in China. All of the perpetrators, including local officials, were acquitted in a trial of their peers. In protest to Secretary of State Thomas Bayard, Minister Zheng Zaoru acknowledged that the United States was not bound by international law to pay an indemnity but insisted that the "usages of international comity" demanded it. He suggested that China's willingness to restrict emigration in the Angell treaty for the sake of the welfare of the western states should be met with an increased obligation on the part of the United States to protect Chinese residents in those states. He concluded his note with an extensive appendix of all the indemnities paid by China, down to the reimbursement of seventy-three dollars stolen from a U.S. citizen. "It cannot be believed that . . . the United States has required of China that which it would not, in the language of Secretary Fish, expect of a European or American state under the rules of the equitable code which regulated the intercourse of civilized nations."[27]

In his message to Congress in December, President Grover Cleveland admitted the need to maintain good faith toward China after the "palpable and discreditable failure of the authorities of Wyoming Territory to bring to justice the guilty parties or to assure to the sufferers an impartial forum in which to seek and obtain compensation." He also explained that "Race prejudice is the chief factor in originating these disturbances, and it exists in a large part of our domain, jeopardizing our domestic peace and the good relationship we strive to maintain with China." But he concluded from this fact that the answer was to stop the entry of Chinese rather than change racial sentiments.

"The admitted right of a Government to prevent an influx of elements hostile to its internal peace and security may not be questioned, even where there is no treaty stipulation on the subject."[28]

In response to Zheng's argument that the indemnification of U.S. citizens in China created reciprocal obligations to the United States, Cleveland felt it necessary to "deny, most emphatically, the conclusions he seeks to draw as to the existence of such a liability, and the right of the Chinese government to insist upon it."[29] Secretary Bayard further explained to Zheng that, "Under the respective system and nature of the two Governments [the treaties] could not have been made reciprocal, nor were they intended to be so. . . . the privileges and immunities of Chinese subjects now within the jurisdiction of the United States are vastly greater than ever were or are extended to American citizens [in China]."[30] Bayard explained that despite being a federal territory and "a rude commencement of a community on the outposts of civilization . . . [where] organization of police and judiciary is inchoate and imperfect," Wyoming had an organic law that granted local self-government, and "local authority applied to and affects all inhabitants alike."[31] Chinese who went there voluntarily assumed the same risk as American citizens in doing so. To indemnify them would give them more recourse and rights than an American citizen. He concluded that

> I should fail in my duty as representing the well-founded principles upon which rests the relation of this government to its citizens. . . . and to those who are permitted to come and go freely within its jurisdiction, did I not deny emphatically all liability to indemnify individuals, of whatever race or country, for loss growing out of violations of our public law, and declare with equal emphasis that just and ample opportunity is given to all who suffer wrong and seek reparation through the channels of justice.[32]

In an 1891 article in the magazine *The Forum*, Bayard further elaborated on the point that the nature of U.S. institutions obviated the need for reparations. More than just a matter of international comity, the refusal to grant the Chinese indemnity claims was nothing less than the preservation of the principles of self-government and states' rights. "The claim now put forward, if allowed, would usurp judicial functions by the executive and legislative branches, and would substitute a government of will for a government of law."[33] To overrule the decisions of a local court would "confuse and destroy the essential boundary between executive and judicial powers" and facilitate a "dangerous tendency in our institutions toward centralization and consolidation of power."[34] Bayard did not directly address the counterexample of why American citizens could not forgo indemnities and assume the same risks as Chinese subjects before the law in China. Indeed, what better example of the difficulties caused by foreign indemnity demands than the experience of extraterritoriality in China? But this was a condition that China had brought upon itself by having no public law that gave "just and ample opportunity" to all. Bayard was not merely claiming sovereign jurisdiction, but stipulating the conditions under which that jurisdiction should and should not be internationally recognized.

In February 1887 Congress grudgingly granted an indemnity for the Rock Springs massacre with, in the words of President Cleveland, "the distinct understanding that such action is in no wise to be held as a precedent, is wholly gratuitous, and is resorted to in a spirit of pure generosity toward those who are otherwise helpless."[35] Local officials also became more aware of the international ramifications of actions within their jurisdiction, as in November 1886 when the governor of Washington asked for federal troops to help suppress anti-Chinese riots. But the right of the Chinese government to demand such preventative actions was firmly denied.

The Supreme Court confirmed the unilateral nature of migrant protection in its March 7 decision on *Baldwin v. Franks.*[36] After local whites had chased Chinese residents out of towns in California and Oregon, counsel for the Chinese appealed to the Civil Rights Acts of 1871 and 1875 that had made it a crime to conspire to deprive others of their rights to equal protection. This provision had already been declared unconstitutional in 1883 because it legislated private conduct, which was properly under state and not federal jurisdiction. But the Chinese counsel argued that this situation was different because the Chinese were not citizens and the federal government had to make good on its solemn treaty promise to grant Chinese "all rights, privileges, immunities and exemptions." To delegate the protection of Chinese to states was absurd because states never signed treaties. The circuit courts of Oregon and California agreed with these arguments, but only in order to receive a more definitive opinion from the U.S. Supreme Court. The higher court chose to avoid the main issue. It recognized that the federal government could pass laws to punish those who impinged on treaty rights, but the Civil Rights Act of 1871 did not legislate that power because it was already declared unconstitutional and not sufficiently separable in its construction. In short, the Court recognized the central powers that must come with intercourse but confirmed that they could only be enforced through domestic politics and not automatically demanded by foreigners, at least not in the United States.

Self-restriction

Rock Springs led to over three years of heated debate among Chinese officials. The terms of the debate were framed by Zheng Zaoru's memorial to the emperor on January 20, 1886, suggesting that China should voluntarily restrict emigration. It was a plan designed both to mitigate embarrassing international incidents and to extend closer control over Chinese subjects abroad. Zheng explained that the central government of the United States was incapable of preventing the outbursts of the common people who were lawless and violent and had a jealous hatred of Chinese. "The laws of this country are too lenient. Local officials do not have the power to enforce them among the common people, and the central government does not have the power to enforce them among the local officials." Unlike the passports issued for travel in the interior of China, laborer-return certificates issued by the U.S. government provided no protection to the traveler. Moreover, U.S. officials were unable to stop Chinese who entered with false certificates or snuck in over the border, allowing all kinds of disreputable people to enter and stir up trouble. Large numbers of people like this would only increase resentment among the Americans, which would soon translate into hatred of Chinese merchants and more humiliating incidents. Zheng referred to the successful halt of section 6 certificates in 1883 as evidence of the effectiveness of Chinese self-restriction in comparison to U.S. attempts. Further self-restriction would also show that China was better able to uphold treaties and protect its subjects than the United States was.

> If we want to avoid another disaster, we have to stop the problem at the source. If we want to stop the problem at the source, China must restrict emigration itself. . . . This plan is not intended to help the Americans mistreat us, but to save Chinese from misfortune. The United States is unable to stop the undesirable type of Chinese from coming, so we must stop them from leaving. This may appear to be throwing out the treaty, so we must show that the United States is to blame for being unable to protect the Chinese, explain how Chinese have repeatedly suffered shameful injuries and have been unable to achieve compensation. Then

the self-restriction plan will be famous. . . . It will cause the United States to examine itself and stop implementing restrictive laws in order to avoid the ridicule of the nations of the world.[37]

Zheng concluded with a proposal that section 6 certificates be issued once again under a more rigorous system, and that Chinese consuls abroad regulate the issuance of return certificates.

In most respects, Zheng's proposal agreed with the logic of Cleveland and Bayard. The presence of Chinese in a racist country was a source of disorder that should be stopped at the root. The United States was not obligated by international law or treaty to pay an indemnity, but not to do so was a shameful breach of comity. The only disagreement was on whether the U.S. government should be characterized as rule of law or as an instrument of mob impulse. Chen Lanbin, now a minister at the Zongli Yamen, supported Zheng's proposal, as did literati essayists Zheng Guanying and Jiang Tongyin.[38]

Zhang Yinhuan was appointed the new minister to the United States in early 1886 with authority to negotiate a new migration treaty. Before departure he consulted with the powerful official Zhang Zhidong in Guangdong, who had been following events in the United States through telegrams from Chinese residents there and his close relations with the Tung Wah Hospital in Hong Kong. The two Zhangs saw a new self-restriction treaty with the United States as part of a much broader plan to protect and assure the loyalty of Chinese overseas.[39] They sent a joint memorial to the emperor on March 30 suggesting the establishment of more consuls abroad and the dispatch of an inspection tour to learn more about conditions overseas.[40] Zhang Zhidong followed up with a memorial that enumerated the difficulties experienced by Chinese in the United States. He described the anger of Chinese in Guangdong and the gossip among foreigners that China was unable to protect its subjects overseas. He concluded that "The U.S. has so many lawless mobs that U.S. officials find it hard not to protect [mobs rather than Chinese]. If the Court does not remonstrate strongly, the U.S. officials will just let things develop on their own."[41]

On August 3, 1886, Zhang Yinhuan and the Zongli Yamen submitted identical treaty drafts to the State Department and to Minister Charles Denby in Beijing. In the drafts, China proposed to stop the departure of Chinese laborers to the United States, including the return of current residents unless they had property or family there. That same day the Zongli Yamen also asked the British minister to request the Hong Kong government to stop ships from carrying Chinese laborers to U.S. ports, noting earlier assistance in stopping migration to Cuba and Peru. In the meantime, the Tung Wah board agreed to discourage travel to the United States as much as possible.[42]

Negotiations dragged. Zhang Yinhuan gradually relented to demands that the power to regulate migrants be left in U.S. hands. As he phrased it in a report to the Zongli Yamen, rather than an agreement for self-restriction, "the two countries hope to mutually establish regulations that are friendly and respectful, and do not subject either country to the power of the other."[43] Zhang then shifted his focus to the protection of Chinese in the United States. In March 1887, twelve days after the *Baldwin* decision, he left a note at the State Department suggesting that the new treaty could stipulate the enactment of federal legislation to guarantee the safety of Chinese in the United States. Secretary Bayard refused to put such a clause in the treaty. The protection of aliens was to be a domestic matter, entirely separate from the issue of migration. Special protection was appropriate in the context of Chinese institutions, but in the United States it was a "call on us to revolutionize our institutions."[44] Zhang responded that protection for foreigners in China went much beyond treaty stipulations. "If reciprocal stipulations were not required of the United States [in earlier treaties] it was because China had confidence in the good faith of its friend and believed that its system of government and laws was sufficient to secure protection to the Chinese who should come into its territory."[45] Unfortunately, recent events had broken that faith and required the stipulations to be made explicit. But Bayard would only agree to give Chinese the same protection accorded to citizens of all most-favored nations. They finally signed a treaty on March 12, 1888, that confirmed most existing U.S. exclusion laws. Its main innovation was to require laborers to have property or family in the United States in order to return after a visit to China. Both ratifications, however, would be a long time in coming.

1888

The Chinese ratification was delayed by a wave of anti-Chinese events in Australia (see table 6.1 for chronological details).[46] Despite the restrictions of 1881, Chinese migration to Australia had continued to grow, accompanied by renewed public polemics. Worries about Chinese political intentions also added a new dimension to Australian fears. In early 1887 a widely reprinted article by Zeng Jize (Marquis Tseng), former minister to Britain, announced that China was awakening from its long slumber with the intention of revising the unequal treaties and better protecting its subjects overseas.[47] In April the inspection commission recommended by the two Zhangs in the previous year wound up its year-long voyage of the South Seas with a visit of Chinese warships to Australia. Australian officials and media treated the visitors well but speculated openly on whether China would have increasingly aggressive intentions.

At the first conference of colonial representatives in London that same month, the Australian colonies encouraged the Foreign Office to negotiate a restrictive migration treaty with China. But it was not long before the Chinese inspection commission reported to Beijing on the discriminatory laws and taxes already enforced in Australia. Instead of beginning treaty negotiations, the British Foreign Office sent a circular to the Australian governments on December 12 asking them to respond to complaints forwarded by Chinese Minister Liu Ruifen.[48] But Australian tempers were already riled and unified against London's dilatory attitudes. In November New South Wales Premier Henry Parkes had sent a circular to the Australian colonial governments asking their opinions on the further restriction of Chinese immigration. He stated his own opinion clearly, that an excess of Chinese immigration would allow pernicious class distinctions to grow up in the colonies, and he held it "to be a question of policy of the first magnitude to cement society together in Australia by the same principles of faith and jurisprudence, the same influences of language and learning, and the same national habits of daily life."[49] Even more quickly than in 1881, the colonies reached a consensus that stricter measures were necessary. In the meantime, Parkes and Duncan Gillies, the premier of Victoria, learned of the treaty signed between the United States and China. It convinced them that local legislation was not sufficient to deal with a matter that was inherently international, and Parkes grew increasingly critical of London's failure to protect the interests of the colonies.[50] As the responses to London from other colonial governments finally trickled in, each insisted on the right of a nation to protect its own territories and requested that London sign a treaty with China to this end.[51] Parkes's own March 31 telegram to the Colonial Secretary was even less conciliatory, insisting that if London found it a conflict of interest to offer the protection sought by the colonies, "the Australian Parliaments must act from the force of public opinion in devising measures to defend the colonies."[52]

On April 27 the *Afghan* arrived at Hobson's Bay, Victoria, Australia, with 268 Chinese onboard. Officials did not allow them to disembark, claiming that the documents of returning residents were false and that new immigrants

TABLE 6.1 Events of 1885–89

Date	Event
September 2, 1885	Rock Springs Massacre
January 20, 1886	Minister Zheng Zaoru memorializes on self-restriction.
March 2	U.S. presidential address on Rock Springs indemnity.
March 30	Zhang Yinhuan and Zhang Zhidong memorialize on protection of Chinese overseas.
August 3	China proposes "self-restriction" migration treaty to U.S.
April–May 1887	Chinese Commissioners visit Australia.
	Australia recommends treaty at London colonial conference.
November 8	New South Wales Premier Harry Parkes sends circular to Australian colonies asking opinions on Chinese.
December 12	Minister Liu Ruifen complains of discrimination in Australia.
January 23, 1888	British Colonial Office inquires about discriminatory laws in Australia.
March 12	U.S. and China sign migration treaty.
March 31	Australian premiers demand that London negotiate treaty with China.
April 27	*Afghan* arrives in Victoria.
May 5	*Afghan* arrives in Sydney.
May 7	U.S. Senate ratifies treaty with amendments to restrict returning laborers.
May 16	Chinese minister in London protests treatment of Chinese on *Afghan*.
May 17	New South Wales Supreme Court allows Chinese on *Afghan* with exemption certificates and who pay poll tax to land.
June 6	Final passengers landed from *Afghan*.
June 12–13	Intercolonial Conference in Sydney results in proposal for uniform Chinese restrictions at 1 per 500 tons and petitions London to sign migration treaty with China.
June 26	British Minister Walsham proposes treaty to China, based on U.S. model.

TABLE 6.1 (*Continued*)

Date	Event
July 11	New South Wales passes 1 per 500 ton Chinese restriction.
July 20	Zhang Zhidong and others memorialize against ratifying U.S. treaty.
July 25	Zongli Yamen informs U.S. minister that it cannot yet ratify treaty.
August 27	Chinese present counterproposal to British, based on 1 per 300 tonnage restrictions.
September 1	*Times* of London reports incorrectly that China has rejected U.S. treaty.
September 3	Scott Bill proposed in U.S. Congress to prohibit all returning laborers.
September 6	U.S. Minister Denby cables that ratification delayed.
September 13	U.S. passes exclusion act based on treaty.
September 14	Australian colonies informed of proposed British treaty with China.
September 17	Zongli Yamen officials visit Minister Denby to object to treaty amendments.
September 18	Scott Act passes Congress prohibiting return of Chinese laborers.
September 21	China formally refuses to ratify treaty with U.S.
October 1	President Cleveland signs Scott Act.
December 8	South Australia enacts 1 per 500 ton Chinese restriction.
December 22	Victoria enacts 1 per 500 ton Chinese restriction.
May 13, 1889	Scott Act confirmed by U.S. Supreme Court in *Chae Chan Ping*.

thus exceeded the 1 per 100 tons restriction. The ship sailed to Sydney, where it was joined by the *Tsinan, Guthrie,* and *Menmuir.* Under intense popular pressure, officials refused to allow any of the combined 580 Chinese passengers to land even if they carried naturalization papers or were willing to pay the poll tax. Lawyers for the Chinese submitted a writ of habeas corpus to the supreme courts of each colony. In lengthy opinions, the judges in New

South Wales differed on whether a nation had the right to exclude subjects of a friendly nation or to abrogate its own laws in refusing admission to migrants willing to pay the tax. They agreed unanimously, however, that exclusion was a prerogative of the queen that had not been delegated to the colony, and they ordered that the Chinese be allowed to disembark. Most also emphasized the need to treat all individuals equally under British law, whether aliens or not.[53] The supreme justices of Victoria were a bit less sure of themselves in considering the habeas corpus petition of Chung Cheong Toy, engaging in elaborate interpretations of the Constitution Act of Australia to determine the extent of self-government and delegation of the royal prerogative. Two judges decided that the colony did have the right to exclude anybody it wanted, but they were in the minority.[54]

Customs official in Sydney still refused to allow some passengers to disembark if they were believed to have false documents. Harry Parkes, the premier of New South Wales, supported them and proclaimed to the judges, "I cast to the wind your permits of exemption, I care nothing about your cobweb of technical law; I am obeying a law far superior to any law which issued these permits, namely, the law of the preservation of society in New South Wales."[55] The chief justice demanded that all Chinese be allowed to disembark if they paid the poll tax, reminding customs officials that "The law is clear that a man illegally deprived of his liberty is justified in taking life if it is only by that means that he can obtain his liberty. Killing, under such circumstances, is not murder, but is justifiable homicide."[56] Under such a threat, the Chinese were finally allowed to land, followed by a special act of Parliament to exempt customs officials from any possible punishment.

Despite the judicial setback, this was a defining moment of Australian identity and political consolidation in the face of London and Asia. Parkes gave a series of incendiary anti-Chinese speeches that would be quoted throughout the Pacific for the next quarter of a century. He directly linked the exclusion of Chinese with the consolidation of Australian unity in the face of unreasonable imperial demands. "Neither for Her Majesty's ships of war, nor for Her Majesty's representative on the spot, nor for the Secretary of State for the Colonies, do we intend to turn aside from our purpose, which is to terminate the landing of Chinese on these shores forever."[57] In a slightly less confrontational mode, he embellished a statement by Queensland Colonial Secretary Samuel Griffith and insisted that he "did not want to see any race here who were not entitled to all immunities, privileges and rights of citizenship—of equal marriage, equal salvation, with the best and truest of any of the races here already."[58]

Another intercolonial conference was rapidly organized to develop uniform laws and present a uniform front to London. It met in Sydney on June 12 and 13, and the premiers agreed to forbid movement between colonies and establish a limit of 1 per 500 tons with no exceptions other than diplomats and seamen. They also petitioned London to establish an exclusion treaty with China. The Colonial Office balked and proposed that Australia should exclude foreign laborers in general rather than discriminate against Chinese, but the Foreign Office agreed to prepare a treaty, which Minister John Walsham presented to the Zongli Yamen on June 26. Thinking that the Chinese would be more willing to follow the precedent of the U.S. treaty, the drafters asked for the exclusion of laborers and admission of specific exempt classes rather than tonnage restrictions. In the meantime, New South Wales amended its Chinese immigration law according to the guidelines stipulated by the conference, followed by South Australia and Victoria later that year, Western Australia in 1889, and Queensland in 1890.[59]

The U.S. Senate had finally ratified the treaty with China on May 7, with amendments making it more difficult for resident Chinese to return. Chinese officials, watching the events in Australia, now had second thoughts. Zhang Zhidong and the Zongli Yamen had received numerous petitions from Chinese around the world that criticized the proposed treaties and excoriated Zhang Yinhuan for designing it.[60] Merchants in San Francisco, Sydney, Hong Kong, and Canton attached their names to a pamphlet, "Preliminary Discussion of Commerce" (*Shangwu chuyan*), which reached many Chinese officials. It complained that the exclusion of laborers would hurt the interests of merchants abroad and remittances to coastal areas would be halted, leading to a bad economy, unemployment, and increased disorder. The population of China was too large, and its people needed to emigrate and colonize, as did the peoples of European countries. The recognition of this need was a matter of international comity, "To facilitate commerce, common people should be able to go there and come here, if we allow them to come they should allow us to go. According to international law, this is a universal principle and it is against basic reason [*li*] for a country to break it."[61] The pamphlet added that U.S. restrictions singled out Chinese and when other countries heard of it they would want similar treaties themselves, thus further isolating Chinese from participation in world affairs.

On July 20 Zhang Zhidong and several other officials sent a memorial to the emperor that repeated many of these arguments and pleaded against ratification of the U.S. treaty, especially emphasizing the detrimental effect it would have on the wealth that Chinese merchants could channel back to China.[62] On July 23 Li Hongzhang, who had previously shown little interest in migration, joined in opposition to the treaty. He pointed out that "there is no day when [the treaty] is not discussed in the foreign papers. It embodies what the English most desire, and what Chinese merchants most fear. If we ratify the U.S. treaty, England will also ask for one and it will be hard to permit one and reject the other."[63] Li developed an alternative proposal that modified his earlier mistrust of emigration in light of arguments about its potential financial benefits for China. If emigration was limited to merchants, anti-Chinese agitation would not be such a problem. He suggested that merchants most wanted to avoid U.S. style exclusion and discriminatory taxes such as the landing taxes in Australia or the recent residence and licensing taxes in the Philippines and Saigon. Tonnage quotas were thus the best solution. Following up on this, the Zongli Yamen sent a counterproposal to the Minister Waltham on August 27 that called for the removal of landing taxes and a limitation of 1 Chinese per 300 tons, not applicable to merchants.[64]

The Zongli Yamen continued to delay ratification of the U.S. treaty. The *Times* of London reported incorrectly on September 1 that the Chinese had rejected the treaty. Word of this soon reached the United States, and on September 3 the Scott Act was proposed in the Senate to stop the return of all departed laborers, including those with property and family in the United States. In the meantime, Congress asked Minister Denby to look into the delay and passed an act based on the unratified treaty. On September 17 members of the Zongli Yamen visited Minister Denby in Beijing to ask that the period of exclusion in the treaty be reduced from twenty to ten years and that Chinese consuls be allowed to issue return certificates. They explained that the delay was due to the fact that "For the first time in the history of treaties the people had protested."[65] The Scott Act passed in Congress the next day, and China formally rejected the treaty on September 21.

Ex-Secretary of State Evarts told Congress that this was the first time in the diplomatic history of the United States that the legislature had intervened with regard to a treaty pending adoption by a foreign nation, and that this had seriously affronted that nation.[66] But the people of the United States had also protested. When President Cleveland signed the bill on October 1, a headline in the *San Francisco Examiner* proclaimed, "He dare not oppose the will of the people."[67] Cleveland explained that the bill was necessary because "the mercenary greed of the parties who were trading in the labor of this class of the Chinese population was proving too strong for the just execution of the [existing] law." To have gone along with the Chinese suggestion that consuls issue return certificates would be to place the execution of the treaty beyond the control of the United States: "The admitted and paramount right and duty of every government to exclude from its borders all elements of foreign population which for any reason retard its prosperity or are detrimental to the moral and physical health of its people, must be regarded as a recognized canon of international law and intercourse."[68]

The Customs Bureau was thrilled, interpreting the disregard of international constraints as license to enforce the laws as strictly as possible. Laborers on ships in the Pacific when the Scott Act was passed were rejected on arrival in San Francisco, and the right of transshipment to Mexico was stopped. The Treasury Department granted great leeway to local officials. In response to inquiries about the kinds of documents necessary to enter the country, the assistant secretary responded, "The nature and form of such evidence rest wholly within the discretion of the collector."[69] The San Francisco collector stopped issuing return certificates to resident merchants and demanded section 6 certificates from them.[70] He argued that it was the duty of the Chinese government to issue certificates, a stance that Circuit Court Judge Lorenzo Sawyer had once overturned as "practically tantamount to an absolute refusal to permit their return."[71]

From Self-restriction to Self-control

Chinese officials were appalled by this new state of affairs. From 1888 to 1893 Chinese ministers wrote at least ten memorandums to the State Department denouncing the Scott Act. Minister Charles Denby rarely visited the Zongli Yamen without being reminded that the United States had violated its treaties.[72] But as they debated their failures and distributed blame among themselves, Chinese officials failed to develop an effective counterstrategy against unilateral exclusion. In the end they could only criticize the discriminatory aspects of U.S. laws as going against the self-proclaimed principles of a civilized nation. They also reformulated Zheng Zaoru's self-restriction plan, with increased emphasis on the need for moral self-discipline among migrants so as to create a better international image. Rather than emphasize the universal rights of intercourse, they focused on the need to overhaul national institutions and character as the way to gain status in the international system. This effectively condoned the doctrine of sovereign prerogative.

Zhang Yinhuan felt betrayed by the opposition of Zhang Zhidong and other officials to his 1888 treaty. In January 1889 he reminded the emperor that Zhang Zhidong and many Chinese merchants had originally agreed that self-restriction was the best route. Most of the problems stemmed from U.S. inability to enforce its own laws. This made U.S. officials intransigent in their demands for stricter laws and contributed to a bad reputation for Chinese that helped justify discrimination against them. Poor enforcement was also the root of Chinese protests against Zhang's treaty. Nearly all the secret societies and Chinese merchants in the United States (such as the men behind the "Preliminary Discussion of Commerce") profited from the organization of fraudulent entries and stood to lose if restriction were more effective. These private interests were the real troublemakers in both the United States and South China.[73]

In response, Zhang Zhidong raged at Zhang Yinhuan for changing Zheng Zaoru's proposal for self-restriction into one of mutual restriction.[74] He insisted that merchant protests were based on the desire for comity, not their personal interests. He also blamed Zhang Yinhuan for including protection and indemnities as part of the treaty negotiations. It was the duty of U.S. officials to protect Chinese in the United States as a matter of comity and without treaty stipulations. Zhang Yinhuan had made it appear that the Chinese were trading self-restriction for the promise of indemnification. Zhang Zhidong proposed to retaliate against the Scott Act by gathering contributions from merchants to pay back the Snake River and Rock Springs indemnities and then expelling all Americans from China. This plan was wisely ignored, but nobody had any better suggestions. Chinese officials were not willing to sign a treaty that gave unilateral rights of migration control to the United States, but they thought that the lack of a treaty was a de facto concession of those unilateral rights and would encourage other countries to similarly undermine international comity.

The Scott Act failed to bring under control fraud and smuggling into the United States. In January 1892 San Francisco Consul Li Ronghui suggested to Minister Yang Ru that the United States was finding it too costly and embarrassing to debar and deport so many Chinese and might be ready to sign a treaty of self-restriction.[75] Instead, Congress passed the Geary Act in May to register all Chinese laborers upon penalty of deportation—thus creating the undocumented alien as law-breaker. But during subsequent legal challenges to the act, the State Department told Yang Ru that it would be willing to negotiate a new treaty if Yang would encourage Chinese to register. The resulting Gresham-Yang Treaty, signed in March 1894 and quickly ratified, was similar to the one developed by Bayard and Zhang Yinhuan in 1888, with additional guarantees for transit to Mexico and a reciprocal concession allowing the Chinese to demand the registration of Americans in China.[76] Yang also conceded the State Department's insistence that the issue of protection be made separate from the issue of immigration and not included in the treaty. To a large extent, the treaty was merely a confirmation of the U.S. power to enact laws as it pleased. But Congress also repealed the Scott Act and allowed laborers with property or family to return. The State Department and extensive Chinese protest had restored a token degree of international comity.

Later that year, Yang Ru explained to the emperor that the treaty was indeed based on Zheng Zaoru's principle of self-restriction. Unlike the last six years of humiliating unilateral control by the United States, this treaty would give Chinese control over their own people and provide face (*timian*) in their dealings with the United States.[77] But, explained Yang, the treaty was only the first step in resolving the larger problem of migration. China must now turn more attention to the roots and branches of the problem. Vices and crimes such as opium, gambling, and factional violence were at the root of anti-Chinese sentiment. Proper protection of the Chinese abroad should include ridding them of these vices. Chinese officials abroad have "spent many words remonstrating with foreign officials, but few to teach their own people. . . . . If we fail to carefully guide the people the humiliating situations will continue." Yang suggested that Chinese diplomats and local Chinese associations should spread the words and edicts of the emperor and establish mutual pledges similar to the village compacts in China. This "will make workers and merchants learn to feel ashamed and mutually persuade each other [to behave well]."[78] The branches of the migration problem were the pervasiveness of migration fraud. Reforms in the identification and documentation of merchants would help to resolve this and forestall the need for the United States to enact harsh regulations. Yang said he had already taken steps in this direction by replacing Consul Tan Qian in Havana, who had freely sold section 6 certificates to unqualified laborers.

In this way, Chinese officials also began to understand both migration and comity in terms of regulating the national community rather than as a matter of treaties and intercourse. In some ways it was a return to long-standing Chinese methods of governance through the moral cultivation of the people.

But the extension of moral cultivation to those who had physically departed from the moral community was a step beyond earlier concerns with security. Moral cultivation was no longer primarily an issue of domestic order but of participation in an international system. Of course, the emigrants who were to be cultivated did not quite see it this way. They would expand their attacks on the discrimination inherent in Chinese immigration laws and against Chinese officials who blamed them for the bad treatment they received. But after the 1890s, Chinese rarely criticized the power to control immigration unilaterally at the border, only the methods of doing it.

From Intercourse to Borders

In the six years after 1888, U.S. courts and officials generated a web of legal and policy decisions to justify the Scott Act and more narrow interpretations of the laws. The Scott Act was widely understood as a breach of the Angell and Burlingame treaties, not to mention the norms of free intercourse that Western powers were trying to impose on China. The foreign press in China and Hong Kong mocked the Australian and U.S. actions as "selfish," "arbitrary," and concessions to the pressure of the mob.[79] But these decisions would ultimately become the foundational principles of unilateral immigration control. The specifics were inseparable from the need to justify extraterritoriality in China, which was itself embedded in the geopolitics of "civilization."

Before 1889, in the many Chinese cases that came before them, federal judges usually ruled in favor of Chinese and against the enactment or narrow enforcement of discriminatory laws. Circuit court judges Ogden Hoffman and Lorenzo Sawyer in California and Matthew Deady in Oregon made many of these decisions. All of these judges were opposed to unrestricted immigration, and none was a great friend of the Chinese. But neither were they great friends of the "sandlotters" and Kearnyites who they saw as behind such legislation. In the face of intense public criticism, all of them upheld the protection of property and individual freedoms, over the will of the electorate. In public speeches Deady even expanded his contempt of the popular will to "The insane rage for equality which overflowed from the volcano of the French revolution."[80] Senator William Stewart of Nevada expressed their ideals more tactfully when he explained to Congress why he had proposed some additions to the Civil Rights Enforcement Act of 1870 that were explicitly aimed at protecting the Chinese despite his opposition to Chinese immigration: "We have pledged the honor of the nation that they may come and shall be protected. For twenty years every obligation of humanity, of justice, and of common decency toward those people has been violated by a certain class of men. . . . It is as solemn a duty as can be devolved upon this Congress to see that those people are protected, to see that they have equal protection of the laws, notwithstanding that they are aliens."[81]

Of all the judges involved in Chinese cases, Stephen Field had the broadest experience and impact, having sat on the California Supreme Court from 1857 to 1863 and then on the California Circuit and U.S. Supreme Court until 1897. Field is mostly remembered as a proponent of liberty of contract and the idea of "substantive due process" that protected the natural rights of person and property against government intervention. In this vein, he frequently interpreted the Fourteenth Amendment as guaranteeing broad economic rights to individuals and corporations.[82] Although he initially grounded immigrant rights in treaties and intercourse, he gradually developed a more nuanced approach to better navigate the competing claims of sovereignty and intercourse. It was grounded in the idea that proper constitutional guarantees, rather than the subjection of domestic law to treaties, were the conditions that made international comity and exchange possible. These guarantees would mitigate the more extreme assertions of arbitrary sovereign will. They were also made possible by "civilized" institutions. As such, they stopped at the border.

Field's first Chinese opinion was a dissent from the California Supreme Court decision that the 1862 capitation tax was unconstitutional. He argued against the majority's expansive application of Marshallian intercourse over an issue that should be left to local legislative discretion.[83] Over the next decade, however, his ideas on intercourse and the limits of local legislative self-rule changed along with his experience in the federal courts and expanding friendships with big businessmen. In African American civil rights cases, many of which were concerned with political participation and the jurisdiction of private law, he remained a strong defender of state legislative powers. But in Chinese immigration and discrimination cases, often linked to both international trade and local economic rights, he repeatedly helped overturn state legislation.[84]

In 1872 Field gratuitously (given that no Chinese cases were pending) explained to a California grand jury that, "so long as our country seeks to enlarge her commerce by treaties with Asiatic countries, and to secure protection to her own citizens in those countries by pledging protection to their citizens in this country, it is the duty of the government to exert its power, its entire power if necessary, to enforce its obligations in this respect." If public policy required that Chinese should be excluded, "let the general government so provide and declare." Until then they had a perfect right to immigrate, and it was "base and cowardly" to mistreat them.[85] Field had an opportunity to act on his new ideals in 1874 when he struck down the California bonding law in a case that later would go to the U.S. Supreme Court as *Chy Lung*. In his opinion he confirmed federal power over "intercourse" and the unconstitutionality of a law that exceeded the justifiable limits of local police powers. If the immigrants posed a threat to state law, "the remedy lies in the more vigorous enforcement of the laws, not in the exclusion of the parties."[86] He dismissed earlier decisions to the contrary as no longer relevant after the end of slavery. Over the next several years he wrote many more circuit court decisions in favor of the Chinese on the grounds of Fourteenth Amendment rights and the need for reasonable constructions of immigration laws to avoid violating treaties.

Field reached the limit of his interpretations in favor of treaties in his 1884 dissent to *Chew Heong* This case considered the right of entry of a laborer who had left for Hawaii before the enactment of the exclusion laws and was unable to obtain a return certificate. Although the revised exclusion act of 1884 demanded a certificate as the only evidence for reentry, the Court decided that Congress could not have intended to exclude somebody like Chew Heong, who had a legitimate right but was unable to fulfill the documentary requirements. Field argued that this time the Court had gone too far and mangled rather than construed the act to conform to the treaty. He argued that this new law had been specifically designed to close the loopholes that had compelled the clogged California courts to land innumerable Chinese on perjured testimony.[87] A treaty was indeed the law of the land, but no more so than congressional legislation, and a treaty could be superseded by subsequent laws (as was confirmed that very same day in the *Head Money Case* decision that confirmed the power of the federal government to charge a head tax on immigrants).[88] But the bulk of Field's dissent was devoted to justifying his change of attitude on the grounds of his having recently learned that China was not living up to the reciprocal treaty provisions. "No American citizen can enjoy in China, except at certain designated ports, any valuable privileges, immunities or exemptions. He can trade at those ports, but nowhere else" (567). In contrast, Chinese could move freely in the United States and take advantage of local institutions. Nonetheless, they chose not to assimilate but to live within their own institutions and laws, many of which violated treaty descriptions of "voluntary emigration" by placing migrants in "the bond thralls of the contractor—his coolie slaves" (568).

Field followed this logic in crafting the unanimous decision for *Chae Chan Ping* in 1889. To justify the Scott Act, he asserted that the "plenary power" of a nation to exclude aliens at will was an essential attribute of sovereignty that need not be enumerated in the Constitution. The right of entry and reentry was held at the pleasure of the government and revocable at any time. "If [the nation] could not exclude aliens it would be to that extent subject to the control of another power."[89] This decision was the Janus face of laissez-faire doctrines. It was very much in line with trends to centralize power in the context of international engagements, arguing that "For local interests the several States of the Union exist, but for national purposes, embracing our relations with foreign nations, we are but one people, one nation, one power" (606). But if centralized rule was necessary to facilitate intercourse, it was also necessary to protect against the dangers of intercourse.

Chae Chan Ping was framed as the right of self-protection against foreign aggression and encroachment "whether from the foreign nation acting in its national character or from vast hordes of its people crowding in upon us" (606). But, just as Field and other judges had often prophesied as the effect of local discriminatory legislation, a landslide of new policies and opinions in the wake of *Chae Chan Ping* quickly transformed the power of self-protection against a particular perceived threat into a general norm of systematic regulation during peacetime. In June 1891 Attorney General William Miller drew on *Chae Chan Ping* to confirm the long-standing Treasury Department contention that the exclusion laws were intended to admit specifically defined exempt classes, not all Chinese except laborers. He also explained that exempted Chinese were a "privileged class" with no necessary rights and the burden of proof was on them to demonstrate that they deserved the privilege of entry.[90] The general immigration act of March 1891 that created the federal Bureau of Immigration and excluded many of the traditional undesirable types, including those likely to become public charges, also built on *Chae Chan Ping* with the stipulation that administrative decisions were final and could not be appealed to the courts. The constitutionality of this was confirmed the next January in the case of *Nishimura Ekiu*, who was rejected without appeal as liable to become a public charge.[91] Chinese, however, were not included in the general immigration act, and the Court agreed to hear the case of *Lau Ow Bew* later that month. The Court admitted Lau despite his lack of a section 6 certificate, in large part because it believed that previous domicile combined with his treaty protection as a merchant gave him rights beyond the rigid documentary requirements for excluded aliens.[92] This loophole was closed in 1894 when a rider to a general appropriations act also stopped Chinese immigration appeals to the federal courts, thus ending the habeas corpus mill.

The Geary Act, requiring Chinese laborers to register upon penalty of deportation, extended these powers far beyond what Field intended, projecting them inside the border to the heart of the nation. In the *Fong Yue Ting* decision of 1893, the Supreme Court confirmed the constitutionality of the Geary Act as the logical extension of *Chae Chan Ping*. It described the decision to expel as a "political question," rather than one of law that could be determined by the courts.[93] Field wrote an angry dissent and even wrote privately that Congress should force a reconsideration of the case and increase the size of the court to ensure a "proper" decision.[94] This did not mark a change of mind since *Chae Chan Ping* so much as the culmination of various (and often convoluted) lines of thought regarding the protection of rights against governmental power that Field had developed since the 1870s.

From 1879 to 1882, Field had spearheaded the overturning of discriminatory San Francisco laws. This work had culminated in the 1886 U.S. Supreme Court decision in *Yick Wo* that overturned the discriminatory enforcement of laundry inspections in San Francisco, arguing that Chinese merited protection not only under the treaty of 1888, but also under the Fourteenth Amendment, which applied "to all persons within the territorial jurisdiction, without regard to any differences of race, of color, or of nationality."[95] In 1880, however, Field had dissented from three decisions overturning state laws and practices that banned blacks from juries, arguing that this was an issue of political rights and private law that properly belonged to local self-government. The rest of the Court eventually came around to Field's reasoning and increasingly overturned federal civil rights legislation in favor of discriminatory state laws. Yet Field dissented from *Baldwin v. Franks* in 1887, which had apparently used Field's reasoning to deny federal protection to Chinese evicted from towns in Oregon. He argued that if the federal government had the power to sign treaties with foreign governments, it should also have the power to guarantee their enforcement rather than delegate that protection to states. In the absence of specific legislation, a treaty to protect foreigners should apply of its own force. The conspirators against Chinese rights were aware of the treaty, and "their purpose was to nullify and defeat it."[96] He argued that the

Court's decision to sanction these actions had ramifications for the treatment of all aliens, seriously undermining the nation's power to make the guarantees necessary to back treaties.

If Field seemed more concerned to guarantee the rights of Chinese than of African Americans at the federal level, this concern was increasingly grounded less in the needs of intercourse between equal nations than in the need to maintain "civilized" institutions within territorial boundaries. In his majority opinion on *in re Ross* (1891), Field upheld a juryless murder conviction made by a U.S. consul exercising his extraterritorial jurisdiction in Japan. With extensive citations from international law, Field argued that the framers of the Constitution "were fully aware of the necessity of having judicial authority exercised by our consuls in non-Christian countries if commercial intercourse was to be had with their people." They also must have known that it would have been impossible to enforce all constitutional guarantees abroad. But while "In one aspect the American accused of crimes committed in [Oriental] countries is deprived of the guarantees of the Constitution against unjust accusation and a partial trial, yet in another aspect he is a gainer, in being withdrawn from the procedure of their tribunals, often arbitrary and oppressive, and sometimes accompanied with extreme cruelty and torture."[97] Of course, as Field well knew, trial "by one's peers" was hardly a guarantee of civil rights. It was precisely the source of injustices at the root of diplomatic struggles over the U.S. ability to protect Chinese migrants, not to mention a right that he was perfectly happy to allow state legislation to exclude African Americans from enjoying. But location made all the difference. In the context of a civilized state, trial by jury was concrete evidence of self-rule, however constituted. Outside of the civilized world, it was a luxury.

These threads came together in Field's conclusion about the need for legal protections for aliens within national borders in *Fong Yue Ting*. In his dissent, Field started not from the intercourse and treaties that had framed his earlier immigration decisions, but from the idea of resident aliens. Unlike aliens at the border, residents had entered political society and could claim guarantees as a right, not a privilege. The Geary Act was aimed not against individuals who had broken existing laws, but against an entire class of people after they had entered with the consent of the nation. It set a precedent (just as *Chae Chan Ping* had) that could easily be expanded beyond a specific act of self-defense against the "obnoxious Chinese" and "exercised to-morrow against other classes and other people."[98] Field also went beyond constitutional law to situate both constitutional and plenary powers within the context of international comity between friendly nations. He criticized the use of international law in the majority opinion, arguing that the cited authors only justified the exclusion of aliens and not arbitrary expulsion against those who had been domiciled by consent. In the movement of people between friendly nations, "such consent will always be implied when not expressly withheld."[99] Field wanted to ground alien rights as a necessary legal protection against excessive state intervention rather than political privilege. In doing so, he replaced the principle of intercourse with reciprocal guarantees given by distinct, bounded nations as the main source of migrant rights. In comparing the Geary Act to the acts of despotic "Asiatic" tribunals, he rooted this comity in the civilized institutions necessary for membership in the family of nations.[100]

Much of Field's trajectory can be understood in terms of his opposition to "class legislation," whether overturning state laws that legislated against Chinese or federal laws that he believed legislated in favor of African Americans. But this cannot account for his demand in *Baldwin* that such federal legislation be enacted in favor of aliens. The needs of international comity were equally important. Similarly, justices David Brewer and Rufus Peckham, known for their equally strong if not dogmatic commitment to laissez-faire constitutionalism and "substantive due process," remained lone dissenters in the increased judicial restriction of immigrant rights through 1907. Brewer's dissents dated back to his opposition to the removal of judicial review at the border in *Nishimura Ekiu* (1892). He is perhaps most famous for his assertion in *Church of the Holy Trinity* that same year that the United States is a "Christian nation."[101] This assertion was also made in the context of an immigration case in which Brewer argued that the 1885 law prohibiting contract immigration for "services of any kind" could not possibly have been intended to keep out a Christian minister. In his later dissents on Chinese cases, he often commented that the majority decisions had condoned the creation of despotic institutions in the United States that would leave bad impressions on Chinese visitors and undermine missionary work in China.[102]

Peckham is most famous for writing the majority decision in *Lochner* (1905), which upheld freedom of contract over state labor laws.[103] That year, Oliver Wendell Holmes followed the opposite trajectory from Peckham, moving from his powerful dissent in *Lochner* to writing the majority opinion in *Ju Toy*, which removed judicial review even from citizens at the border.[104] Similarly, the "Great Dissenter" John Harlan also consistently joined with the majority in Chinese cases. He is most famous for dissenting against decisions that overturned civil rights legislation and supported segregation, opinions like *Lochner* that nullified workplace regulation, and cases that argued that the Constitution did not extend to newly conquered territories after the Spanish-American War. In all these cases, Harlan consistently showed himself to be a strong proponent of greater federal intervention for the sake of social justice. But his faith in federal justice also shaped the majority opinions he wrote for *Lem Moon Sing* (1895) and *Yamataya* (1903), which, respectively, further removed previous residents and immigrants with treaty guarantees from judicial review at the border, as well as his dissent from the *Wong Kim Ark* (1898) decision that conceded citizenship to U.S.-born Chinese.[105] As he explained to his night-school students, the nation had a duty to the African Americans it had brought to its shores, but granting citizenship to a race that was "utterly foreign to us" and here merely by the accident of birth would cause the United States to lose power over its naturalization laws. More generally, he objected to immigrants "not born and reared under the institutions of countries like England that understand what life, liberty, and property mean, but born under despotisms; who have been in the habit all of their lives of bowing to titles and powers that did not know what liberty was, and who come to this country mistaking liberty for license and license for liberty."[106] Harlan was no less committed to the Fourteenth Amendment and the providential mission of the U.S. Constitution than Field or Brewer, but these commitments could still generate differing trajectories of civil rights. Apparently, the borders and racial composition of the civil rights nation had to be more rigorously guarded than the Christian nation rooted in economic freedoms.

Legacies

Chae Chan Ping remains the precedent for denying rights at the border. But treatment of resident aliens has remained highly debated, and Field's dissent has been followed in practice more often than the majority opinion of *Fong Yue Ting*. As early as 1896, the court insisted in *Wong Wing* that a Chinese sentenced to deportation for not having a certificate could not be imprisoned at hard labor without trial by jury.[107] And at least since *Ng Fung Ho* in 1922, which gave migrants arrested in the interior who claimed citizenship the right to judicial review, the Supreme Court has slowly chipped away at administrative deportation powers (although often stymied by new legislation) and expanded the access of resident aliens to rights and services.[108] The arena of arbitrary sovereign power was to be limited to the border and carefully circumscribed powers of deportation.

In the early twentieth century, however, alien rights found their last defenders among diplomats and other executive officials concerned with international relations and the guarantees that a civilized government should provide. Charles Hyde's 1922 book on international law as interpreted by the United States duly cited *Fong Yue Ting* on the absolute sovereign power to expel. But it then went on to cite other State Department correspondence from the 1890s (none of which involved Chinese) to the extent that expulsion is an "extreme police measure" that should be effected with sufficient reason and as little injury to the safety and property of the individual as possible. From this, Hyde concluded that "Expulsion may savor of an abuse of power unless the decision to expel be founded on a *bona fide* belief as to the evil effect upon the State of the continued presence of the individual within its domain."[109]

But guarantees on the interior were made possible only by careful control of the borders. This argument could already be seen in Thomas Bayard's 1891 article in *The Forum*. Having argued that federal nonliability for indemnities was grounded in the civilized institutions of self-rule that gave equal access to aliens, Bayard went on to say that

> [If] the principles of law and the arrangements for their exercise declared by our courts to be consonant with the provisions of the Constitution and essential to the preservation of individual liberty, cannot be peaceably possessed and enjoyed by our citizens, and be acknowledged and recognized as the basis of our government, because of the presence within our borders of alien subjects . . . whose personal wrongs may not be remedied to their satisfaction or to that of their government without the impairment and disorder of our system, then the time has arrived when the unquestionable and sovereign right of the United States to determine by positive law who shall be permitted to enter our gates and who shall be excluded must be exercised.[110]

In other words, if the presence of Chinese incited violence, discriminatory laws, and embarrassing incidents, it was best to keep them out in the first place. The border was the place where constitutional rights—the foundation of civilized government in the United States—could be ignored with limited repercussions. As Assistant Secretary of Commerce and Labor Louis Post described in 1916,

> An alien who lives in the United States, no matter now long his residence here may have continued, must have a care if he goes near the Canadian or the Mexican boundary line lest he stub his toe against it and fall over to the other side. His stepping back at the place where he fell, this not being an authorized port, would constitute an unlawful entry and subject him if captured to deportation to the country whence he had originally come.[111]

To make national borders into the containers of rights, migration had to be separated from the issue of domestic protections so that particular institutions rather than intercourse per se were the foundation of international order.

By 1907, in the wake of Chinese boycotts and struggles with Japanese diplomats over immigration, presidents Theodore Roosevelt and William Taft went beyond merely asserting the existence of protections within the United States and echoed Field's earlier concerns that no legislation had ever been implemented to protect Asian treaty rights. In his inaugural speech of 1909, Taft explained that "It puts our government in a pusillanimous position to make definite engagements to protect aliens and then to excuse the failure to perform those engagements by an explanation that the duty to keep them is in states or cities, not within our control."[112] In his 1915 book on diplomatic protection, Edwin Borchard also wrote that "Constitutional arguments do not avail to excuse the non-performance of international duties, although the US has often tried."[113] Borchard went on to argue that the universal requirement of intercourse was a foundation of these international duties, echoing Oppenheim's argument that although nations had a formal right to unilaterally determine which foreign elements are considered dangerous, most nations freely granted the right of entry because not to do so was to endanger membership in the international community.

By 1915, however, Borchard's internationalist perspective on border control was somewhat extreme. But U.S. diplomats were still reluctant on to rely solely on the equally extreme position of absolute of sovereign prerogative, a position that made it difficult to defend extraterritoriality in China and maintain smooth relations with other "civilized" nations. Rather they chose a middle position such as Taft's in which sovereign prerogative must be justified by the maintenance of civilized protections. In the 1920s, however, even this relatively moderate stance would give way before Wilsonian self-determination and a reframing of migration as a matter of assimilation rather than intercourse.[114] By then, the machinery of U.S. immigration law was complex enough to distinguish categories of aliens who, by virtue of temporary "nonimmigrant" residence or the "illegality" of having evaded border controls, had not received the "consent of the nation" and could be justly subjected to discriminatory treatment and systematic expulsion. Even Hyde qualified his mild statements on expulsion with the observation that "The deportation of an alien who enters a State in violation of its immigration or exclusion laws, is merely to be regarded as incidental to their enforcement."[115] His only supporting citations were the U.S. immigration acts of 1917 and 1918, making U.S. border control the effective arbiter of who deserved protections in the interior and who did not..

7

The "Natal Formula" and the Decline
of the Imperial Subject, 1888–1913

A ddressing the collected colonial politicians at the imperial conference of
1921, British Prime Minister Lloyd George explained that

> No greater calamity could overtake the world than any further accentua-
> tion of the world's divisions upon the lines of race. The British Empire
> has done signal service to humanity in bridging those divisions in the
> past; the loyalty of the King Emperor's Asiatic peoples is the proof. To
> depart from that policy, to fail in that duty, would not only greatly in-
> crease the dangers of international war; it would divide the British Em-
> pire against itself. Our foreign policy can never arrange itself in any sense
> upon the difference of race and civilization between East and West. It
> would be fatal to the Empire.[1]

In such a gathering, this could only sound like a quaint genuflection to
imagined traditions. The reality of empire in 1921 was of internal borders fortified against the movement of Asians and Africans. For more than twenty
years, the self-governing colonies had worked to define the British Empire as
a voluntary association of autonomous states. In their minds self-government,
the bedrock of British power, was inseparable from racial segregation. The
viceroy of India Lord Curzon had already understood this principle in 1903.
Reflecting on the "imperialist" proposition that "all citizens of the Empire,
independent of colour or origin, ought to be at liberty to live and labour in all
parts of it on the same footing, unhampered by any racial disabilities or social
or economic restrictions," he could only conclude that "It postulates a development to which the British Empire has not yet attained, or may perhaps
never succeed in attaining." The main obstacle was that "The colonists, to
whose Colony has been conceded the right of self-government, argue that the

first and most necessary of the rights that he thereby acquires is that of admitting whom he pleases and excluding whom he pleases from his country."[2]

Specific legislation to limit migration, however, had to simultaneously satisfy London officials as well as colonial populations. The former wanted not only to maintain the appearance of an imperial polity that was equally benevolent to all, but to avoid offending the governments of India and Japan. Starting with the "Natal formula" of 1897, an English-language immigration test implemented by the South African colony of Natal, colonial legislatures and officials successively refined and promoted a series of laws that were nondiscriminatory on the surface yet allowed great leeway of interpretation by officials on the ground. By 1909 this had culminated in the so-called Canadian principle that gave government officials the broad discretionary power to restrict immigration on the basis of perceived economic needs. Japan and India ultimately conceded the nondiscriminatory nature of this formulation and even agreed to institute their own passport controls over potential emigrants. The logic of discrete cultural nations and border control had superseded empire as the most relevant political form for a world of mass mobility.

Imperial Center and Periphery

In the late 1880s officials in the Colonial Office were split between sympathy for the Australian desire to preserve Australia's community and contempt for the rhetoric of protectionism and belligerent populism in which that desire was expressed. The issue of migration was especially tricky because it exacerbated tensions over the proper relationship between the imperial polity and the self-governing units that made up much of the empire. Granting autonomy to Australia in the matter of migration control would look hypocritical in the face of efforts to protect British interests in China and to assure the free migration of British subjects, including Indians, into the Republic of South Africa. Yet to refuse Australia the right to control migration would kindle bitterness toward London and spark moves toward autonomy. Ultimately, the very complexity of imperial politics proved to be the best buffer against the kinds of diplomatic difficulties experienced by the United States. The need for extended communication among Australian colonies, the Colonial Office, the Foreign Office, and Beijing provided ample cause for delay and the avoidance of a clear policy. Australia was spared the embarrassment of dealing with China directly, and London could defer the issue in negotiations with

China by pointing to the grants of self-government in Australia and Canada that limited possible interference from London.[3]

In September 1888 London circulated to the Australian colonial governments a copy of China's counterproposal for an immigration treaty of 1 per 300 tons with exemptions for merchants. Most of the answers that dribbled in over the next two years simply stated that the issue was no longer relevant now that the colonies had already implemented stricter tonnage limitations without merchant exemptions.[4] The Chinese government, frustrated by the turn of events in the United States, raised no objection, and everybody was happy to let the matter drop. The case of *Chung Teong Toy* resulting from the *Afghan* incident reached the Privy Council in London on appeal in 1891. The decision (cited in *Fong Yue Ting*) briefly declared that an alien had no necessary right to enter British territory and, more to the point, did not even have the right to put forth a legal action to demand the right of entry: "Circumstances may occur in which the refusal to permit an alien to land might be such interference with international comity as would properly give rise to diplomatic remonstrance from the country of which he was a native; but it is quite another thing to assert that an alien, excluded from any part of Her Majesty's dominions by the executive government there, can maintain an action in a British court."[5]

The decision did not respond to the assertion of some judges that aliens willing to pay the poll tax could not be considered as "excluded." Nor did it touch upon the long disquisitions that had so preoccupied the Victorian judges about the meaning and very existence of the royal prerogative of exclusion or the extent of self-government in Australia. It avoided these issues by asserting that since an excluded alien cannot maintain an action in a British court, he cannot compel a decision on them. This unwillingness to confront jurisdictional tensions caused British courts and officials to move much more slowly than post–Civil War U.S. ones to develop a consistent understanding of the legal rights of migration.

This was a battle over political turf and the power to make decisions. Dominion politicians claimed that their superior on-the-ground experience and the powers of self-rule should be the foundation for all decisions that affected their interests. London bureaucrats emphasized how their empirewide vision could ultimately work for the greater benefit of all. These broad issues, however, could be rapidly lost in the technicalities of complex legal speculations. For example, in a report on the Australian situation submitted in 1888,

E. H. Parker of the Chinese consular service considered the issue in terms that recalled the ambiguous space between sovereignty and intercourse framed in international law. He claimed that common law in the metropole had already accommodated the needs of mobility: "The right of any alien to settle in British territory is, I presume, a common law right, which would yield to considerations of safety, or, at all events, to an Act of Parliament." But the applicability of these customs and laws to different parts of the empire, especially the self-governing portions, was far from clear. Even English visiting Australia had to submit to local laws that went against English tradition. Could the Chinese, on grounds of enforcing treaty rights, demand even that which Englishmen could not attain in Australia? "For Chinese to demand in Australia full English rights as enjoyed in England from the one point of view of settling, would seem to assert the principle that the treaty was above protective measures, and that Great Britain could grant more than she could reserve for herself." He then countered this with the argument that Australian sanction of Chinese immigration for many years had the effect of establishing immigration as a right. He framed this as an issue of international comity and treaty rights in China, noting that "there are many instances where foreigners in China have prescribed similar doubtful rights, which it would look unfriendly to take away." But from yet another perspective of international comity, Chinese would most likely not agree to the specific reciprocity of allowing foreigners to settle the frontiers of China.[6]

The political struggles could also be formulated in terms of free-trade ideology. Officials and politicians committed to free trade were even more vocal in the non-self-governing colonies than in London. In 1881, during debates in the Hong Kong Legislative Council over Australian requests that Hong Kong help enforce the new Australian immigration laws, F. B. Johnson said he was sure that nobody in the room was in sympathy with the "economical heresies of our Australian brethren" in their objections to Chinese labor. He compared the Australian anti-Chinese movement to hand-loom weavers who resisted the power loom, and he engaged in a long disquisition about the relation of free migration and trade and their beneficial effects for everybody. But Governor John Pope Hennessy responded that Australian attitudes had some basis because Chinese emigration reduced the attraction of Australia for British emigrants and did nothing to increase the trade in high-class goods.[7]

Perhaps most importantly, differences between London and the self-governing colonies were rooted in class. Parker approvingly recounted Australian arguments about the right of a self-governing colony to shape its own community but was contemptuous of how the Australians had put it into practice. Fair government and respectful treatment would allow the Chinese to prosper, and it was to the detriment of British status in Asia that Australia was unwilling to grant it. He dismissed the idea that Chinese were a threat to Australia, noting that "Whilst it is impossible not to see with pleasure the humbler classes of one's countrymen enjoying an easier, brighter, and less wearing life than they usually do at home, it is equally impossible not to observe with regret that they are disposed to go too far, to abuse their power and their good fortune by acting greedily and unreasonably."[8] He compared Australians unfavorably to the "calm firmness and dignified generosity" of Chinese diplomats and merchants, and he lamented that there were no educated classes in Australia "to exercise a sort of calmative imperial influence on the spot."[9] The only educated class in Australia was the capitalists, but they were the natural enemy of the working-class politics that dominated southwestern Australia and could not easily exert influence. Most British officials did not have such a high opinion of Chinese officials and migrants as Parker did, but many shared his class-based understanding of the makings of a harmonious empire.

Suzerainty and South Africa

The situation in Australia also embarrassed imperial officials because of events in the Republic of South Africa. Since 1884 London had objected to local laws that included a twenty-five-pound registration tax for Asian immigrants and the power to concentrate them in restricted residential zones. The London Convention of that year between Britain and South Africa had established a condition of "suzerainty" in which London had granted autonomy to South Africa in most issues except foreign relations. Article 14 of the convention also asserted that "All persons, other than natives, conforming themselves to the laws of the South African Republic will have full liberty, with their families, to enter, travel or reside in any part of the South African Republic," as well as rights to possess property, carry on commerce, and not be subjected to special taxes.[10] South Africa was supposedly free to enact local laws to which aliens must conform, but what if those local laws were discriminatory or aimed at regulating mobility? The line between domestic police powers and international intercourse subject to treaty was unclear.

By 1888 the Colonial Office took a position that was consistent with its attitude in Australia. It conceded that it did "not desire to insist upon any such construction of the term of the Convention as would interfere with reasonable legislation in the desired direction" (i.e., toward the restriction of Asians), although it made clear that this was only a concession and not the acknowledgment of a unilateral right to regulate Asians.[11] What constituted "reasonable legislation," however, would prove to be highly contentious for the next decade. The Colonial Office was satisfied with the "reasonableness" of a law to register and restrict the residence of Asians when South Africa explained them in terms of sanitary precautions. The India Office was less convinced and complained in 1890 that the law was implemented in a discriminatory manner. In 1893, when South Africa established new regulations to enforce the law by relocating Indian businesses as well, the Colonial Office agreed that this was a breach of the convention and the right of free trade. After two years of inconclusive discussion, the case was finally submitted to arbitration before Justice Milieus de Villiers of the Orange Free State.

Villiers argued that a literal construction of the convention was unreasonable because the contracting parties never contemplated the admission of Asians. It was especially unreasonable in the South African Republic, where inequality between white and colored people was written into the constitution. He dismissed the relevance of international law, explaining that

> Every European nation or nation of European origin has an absolute and indefeasible right to exclude alien elements which it considers to be dangerous to its development and existence. . . . There is a strong presumption against any intention on the part of the delegates of the South African Republic to surrender this right, or on the part of Great Britain to insist upon a surrender of this right, more especially in favour of foreign coloured races who are not presumed to be the subjects of international rights, since international law is not supposed to exist otherwise than between civilised European races.[12]

He pointed out other examples where "principles theoretically unreasonable have been adopted as the bases of practical legislation" to protect a nation, including antimiscegenation laws, segregated schools in the United States, and Chinese immigration laws in Australia, Canada, and the United States.[13] Villiers concluded that conditions of immigration and settlement should be subject to local laws as interpreted by competent local tribunals. A foreign government could intervene only if access to those courts was refused or a government did not enforce their judgments. In this case, Britain had the right to object that the 1893 regulations did not uphold the intent of the law, but the final determination would be in the hands of South African judges. Villiers' decision echoed U.S. policy and legal decisions in asserting that national institutions are the only relevant source of rights, but without the pretense of insisting that civilized institutions should uphold equality before the law.

Unsurprisingly, Indian residents were very unsatisfied and complained that the decision did not touch upon the primary issue of whether international commercial activity could be legitimately included under the rubric of a domestic law.[14] They were also understandably unenthusiastic about the prospect of taking their case to the South African courts. Their misgivings were confirmed by a negative decision in a subsequent test case. London, however, seemed satisfied with Villiers' decision. That this satisfaction was based more on race than on legal reasoning became apparent in November 1896, when South Africa passed a new immigration law that excluded all "aliens," including white British subjects, who were unable to support themselves. It also required all aliens to have their passports "revised" by consular agents abroad before entering South Africa. A deportation law aimed at indigent foreigners followed soon after. London appealed again to article 14 of the London Convention and insisted that South Africa had no right to expel, restrict, or impose burdensome conditions on foreigners who have conformed to the laws of the Republic. British residents of South Africa added that the laws degraded them to the same status as natives and ex-coolies in the neighboring British colony of Natal, where they were subject to registration and a pass system.[15]

South African officials replied that article 14 stipulated that those who "conformed themselves to the laws of the South African Republic" were at liberty to enter, and that this was one of those laws. The law was purely a domestic concern and applied to all aliens in a nondiscriminatory way.[16] Secretary of State C. van Boeschoten added that the London Convention must be interpreted according to the generally accepted principles of laws of nations, which hold that every state has the right to restrain foreign elements as a right of self-defense. Surely no civilized state would ever demand the right of entrance for lepers and paupers. The mere status of being a British pauper is not grounds for demanding entrance. He pointed out that England had not opposed immigration restrictions in the United States and Canada, and the passport is a common document that does not impose a burdensome condition. Rather, it helps a state to control its affairs and works for the convenience of the stranger.[17]

But after this long justification, van Boeschoten reported that the passport (but not the deportation) law had already been revoked. The government had realized that it subjected the inhabitants of neighboring states to inconveniences and decided it would be better to develop legislation through discussion with those states. He continued to deny that there was any need to consult Britain before enacting such a law, and he proposed that the issue be taken to international arbitration. Colonial Secretary Chamberlain rejected arbitration on the grounds that the London Convention was not a treaty between two equal states but a declaration by the queen in which she "accorded complete self-government to the South African Republic subject to her suzerainty."[18] The issue was ultimately decided only by Britain's military victory in the Boer War.

The Natal Formula

Events in the South African Republic made clear that most London officials had only a superficial commitment to Indian rights. But Indian demands that London live up to its claims of formal equality between imperial subjects would not go away. Even as London was demanding rights of mobility for British subjects in South Africa, those same white subjects in the neighboring colony of Natal were attempting to exclude Indian subjects. The resulting negotiations between representatives of Natal, London, and India resulted in the creation of the "Natal formula," a language test that was nondiscriminatory on the surface but allowed broad administrative discretion.

More than sixty thousand indentured Indian laborers had been imported to work on sugar plantations in Natal since 1860. To the dismay of British colonists, many Indians outlived their service and remained in the colony. In 1894 the colony sent a delegation to India to negotiate the mandatory return of all Indians who had finished their indenture. The viceroy of India, Lord Elgin, feared overpopulation in India and wanted to maintain an outflow of emigrants, but the fear that Natal would prohibit immigration altogether led him to agree to an annual three-pound tax on all free Indians who did not return. Natal also passed a law prohibiting the franchise to Indian settlers, but the Colonial Office advised the king to disallow this law, reminding him of the loyalty of the Indians. The Natal legislature changed the law in 1896 to invoke civilized qualities rather than racial discrimination, denying the franchise to people "who (not being of European origin) are Native or descendants of the male line of Natives of countries which have not hitherto possessed elective representative institutions founded on the parliamentary franchise." The government of India objected that Indians already voted in municipal elections, but it did not press the point because it felt that its main duty was to protect indentured emigrants.

Popular agitation against Indian immigration grew in Natal despite legislation. In December 1896 the *Courland* and *Naderi*, arriving with over a hundred self-paying passengers from India (including Gandhi), were met by mass anti-Indian demonstrations. Officials held the ships in quarantine outside of Durban for twenty-six days longer than required by law, despite no evidence of plague at the ports of departure. Officials finally allowed the passengers disembark on January 16, but only after mollifying public opinion by promising to immediately enact a new immigration bill against Asians.[19]

Attorney General Harry Escombe quickly drafted a bill modeled on laws recently passed in New South Wales, Tasmania, and South Australia that extended Chinese tonnage-based restrictions to include all colored migrants. But he soon learned that the governor had reserved that bill in November and the Colonial Office would likely disallow it. Chamberlain sent a telegram to the governor of Natal saying that if the cabinet had to restrict immigration, "I earnestly hope they will legislate against impecunious or ignorant immigrants, and not against race or colour."[20] Chamberlain later explained that by "ignorant" he meant those who had been induced to emigrate without sufficient knowledge of conditions abroad. But Natal had already drafted a new bill that invested immigration agents with the power to prohibit the immigration of anybody unable to write out an application in a European language. As (now premier) Escombe explained during the second reading on March 25, the bill was "founded on the American Act" of 1891 that excluded certain classes of aliens. It was also inspired by literacy tests for voting enacted in Mississippi (1890) and South Carolina (1894) and by the immigration literacy test that had just passed Congress, only to be vetoed by President Cleveland in March. Escombe explained that the Natal law went "one step further" in giving immigration agents great discretion to choose when to implement the exam and in what language.[21]

The white and Indian residents of Natal were both unenthusiastic about the proposed law. In a petition to Lord Chamberlain, the Indian community pointed to passages in the legislative debates in which the framers of the bill explicitly stated that the language test would not be applied to Europeans. They complained that an educated Indian or an Indian prince would have more rights to enter an independent state like South Africa than to enter the

British colony of Natal.[22] The white residents also complained that the law was un-British, but because of its indirectness rather than its potential for discrimination. Critics insisted that it would be impossible to guarantee enforcement of a law with such a high amount of discretion. An editorial in the *Natal Mercury* summarized, "It has been urged by those people who consider the Bill objectionable because it is not straightforward, that a Bill should be passed against Asians in particular, that we should enter upon the 'long constitutional fight.'"[23] Escombe defended the bill by arguing that "When a ship is heading against a wind, she has to tack, and by and by she accomplishes her goal. When a man meets difficulties, he fights against them, and, if he can not knock them over, he goes round them instead of breaking his head against a brick wall."[24] An assembly member responded, "Why not just call it an Asiatic Restriction Bill? They do not talk of tacking in these days of steamships, but go straight ahead."[25]

Despite the misgivings, the bill was passed on April 29, and the governor soon gave his assent. Although disturbed at the misconstrual of the idea of an "ignorant" migrant and worried about the possibilities of enforcing the law along color lines, the India Office, highly aware of Indian popular sentiment on this matter, grudgingly accepted the wording of the new legislation. It requested only that more specific recognition of the rights of domiciled Indians be written into the bill. In December the Natal immigration officer reported with satisfaction that 868 Asians had been turned back, and only 113 Indian men had been allowed to land. Most were admitted on the basis of former domicile, and only 10 had passed the language test. He made only a few technical recommendations about the need for better documentation for domiciles and visitors, and that the language test should be varied so that the answers could not be memorized.[26]

The Australian Solution

Chamberlain was pleased and promoted the "Natal formula" relentlessly around the empire. At the Inter-Colonial Conference in June 1897, he encouraged the premiers of Australia and Canada to adopt similar legislation. He sympathized with the need to stop an "influx of people alien in civilization, alien in religion, alien in customs, whose influx, moreover, would most seriously interfere with the legitimate rights of the existing labour population." But he also warned that any bill that might provoke "ill-feeling, discontent and irritation, would be most unpalatable to the feeling, not only of her

Majesty, but of all of her people." Any restriction must bear in mind the traditions of the empire that refused distinctions on the basis of race or color:

> What I venture to think you have to deal with is the character of the im-
> migration. It is not because a man is of a different colour from ourselves
> that he is necessarily an undesirable immigrant, but it is because he is
> dirty, or he is immoral, or he is a pauper, or he has some other objection
> which can be defined in an Act of Parliament. . . . I hope, therefore, that
> during your visit, it may be possible for us to arrange a form of words
> which will avoid hurting the feelings of any of Her Majesty's subjects,
> while at the same time it would amply protect the Australian Colonies
> against any invasion of the class to which they would justly object.[27]

In dominions around the Pacific, Japan rather than India compelled the
need for discretion. The 1894 Anglo-Japanese Treaty of Friendship and Commerce had guaranteed free intercourse with Japan. It did not apply to the
self-governing dominions unless they voluntarily chose to adhere within
two years. None of the dominions except Natal showed any interest in the
offer because Japan had made it clear that it would consider any immigration restrictions that did not apply equally to all foreigners to be a breach
of the treaty.[28] But the "Natal formula" offered a way out. In a letter to the
governor general of Canada, Chamberlain explained that "It is not the practical exclusion of Japanese to which the Government of the Mikado objects,
but their exclusion *nominatim*, which specifically stamps the whole nation
as undesirable persons."[29] To the premier of Western Australia, he wrote that
"no nations would have the right to object to legislation which is of universal
application."[30] Minister Kato Takakiro in London confirmed that "The point
which had caused a painful feeling in Japan was not that the operation of the
prohibition would be such as to exclude a certain number of Japanese from
immigrating to Australasia, but that Japan should be spoken of in formal documents . . . as if the Japanese were on the same level of morality and civilization as Chinese and other less advanced populations of Asia."[31]

Western Australia passed a European language test in December 1897, followed over the next two years by New South Wales, South Australia, Tasmania, New Zealand, and British Columbia in 1900, and the Cape Colony in
1902.[32] The British Seaman's Union even adopted a dictation test for aliens in
1908.[33] A fifty-word dictation test in a European language was one of the first
laws to be enacted after Australian federation in 1901, soon followed by the

repeal of most provincial legislation. Many Australians thought this was one of the most important steps in creating an egalitarian and democratic "White Australia." As Deputy Prime Minister Alfred Deakin famously asserted, "No motive power operated more universally on this continent . . . and certainly no motive power operated more powerfully in dissolving the technical and arbitrary political divisions which previously separated us than did the desire that we should be one people and remain one people without the admixture of other races."[34]

This first version of the Australian dictation test ran into some obstacles.[35] Legal challenges were launched within Australia by Chinese and shipowners who often won small victories on technical grounds, such as a supreme court decision that the dictation test was invalidated with the addition or subtraction of even one word from the prescribed fifty. Japanese diplomats also complained to the Foreign Office and Australian government that only European languages were allowed. Minister Hayashi Tadasu in London referred to the Australian parliamentary debates in which officials made it clear that they fully intended to test only Asian immigrants and in languages that they would not understand. The Colonial Office responded that disallowance would only result in a more explicitly insulting law, and Hayashi withdrew formal acceptance of the "Natal formula" in early 1902.[36]

Australia and New Zealand amended their laws in 1905 to allow a dictation test in "any prescribed language" (i.e., Swahili, Basque, Nahuatl, or any other language that the immigration officer felt confident the migrant did not know) and to demand mandatory penalties from shippers for bringing proscribed migrants. The change was made both to satisfy Japan with less Eurocentric languages and because thirty-two Asians had passed the dictation test in a European language. Japan acquiesced to the new formulation, probably because it had already made an arrangement by 1904, based on an 1897 agreement with Queensland after it adhered to the Anglo-Japanese treaty, whereby a limited number of merchants and students carrying Japanese passports could enter for renewable one-year periods. Each passport would receive a visa from a British consul, whose only duty was to "satisfy himself that the holder of the document is the person to whom it is issued."[37] A similar agreement was made with India in 1904 and with the governor of Hong Kong in 1905 after he had complained of discrimination against British subjects, although this latter arrangement was made on the condition that only a select few of the leading Chinese would be made aware of it.[38]

The law served its purposes wonderfully. The Chinese population in Australia declined from 32,717 in 1901 to 14,349 in 1933, one of the most dramatic declines in the world. The beauty was that it hardly had to be enforced because once it became clear that nobody could pass the test, few people made the attempt. The enormous discretion written into law made it nearly impossible to challenge the enforcement on legal grounds. Only well-established residents and people who held a Certificate of Exemption were allowed to enter. Exemptions were granted on an individual basis, mostly to students and, less commonly, to the families of "well-recommended" Chinese residents. Immigration officials continued to have problems with stowaways and false naturalization certificates and suffered from embarrassing publicity when they refused to allow family members of resident Asians to enter. But for the most part, fewer attempts to enter led to fewer scandals, fewer court cases, and fewer diplomatic incidents than in the United States.[39] As historian Harley McNair observed in 1924, echoing the earlier words of Thomas Bayard, "The greatest guaranty of protection for the Chinese in Australia is the fact that since 1901 their nationals have been practically excluded from entering the country."[40]

Uniformity of immigration laws was also a major theme at the South African Customs Union Conference of 1903. Natal Immigration Officer Harry Smith, now less satisfied with the working of the Natal law than before, proposed several amendments that included the adoption of an Australian-style dictation test, albeit one that still retained the specification of a European language. These suggestions were made into law in Natal and Southern Rhodesia that year. Japan showed no great concern over these distant colonies, but the viceroy of India complained in 1907 of the need for a "less invidious test." Chamberlain defended the test on the grounds that it helped create uniformity in legislation across the entire region, making less cause for invidious legislation within specific colonies.[41]

In the Transvaal, British authorities wanted to conciliate their conquered Boer subjects and found that the potent mix of self-government and immigration restriction was an ideal means of doing so. They reimplemented Boer laws that London had once objected to in the 1890s, and they enforced them more effectively than the Boers ever had, under the supervision of a newly created Asiatic Department. The department compiled a booklet that brought together all of the anti-Asiatic laws in one place and, according to Gandhi, helped the British to realize that the laws "were neither adequately severe nor systematic."[42] The India Office complained of the irony (to put it mildly) of the British now enforcing Boer laws that had caused so much trouble. In response, Assistant Colonial Secretary Lionel Curtis explained that the registration laws were necessary because the only honorable course of action for the British was to stop the flood of Indian immigrants until responsible government was returned to the locals:

> The Imperial Government undertook, and rightly undertook, to administer the country in accordance with the wishes of the people of the country themselves. . . . [If it used its powers] to give effect to the policy in respect of Asiatics which it had urged upon the late Republican Government, it would violate obligations, no less sacred, imposed upon it through unforeseen circumstances towards the European inhabitants of the Colony.[43]

The Transvaal eventually enacted a European language immigration test in September 1906, along with a law requiring registration of all Indians. The latter law was the so-called black act that spurred Gandhi's satyagraha movement. An Indian delegation immediately traveled to London to try to convince Colonial Secretary Lord Elgin to disallow the measure. Elgin agreed to disallow it but then immediately turned around and hastened the granting of self-government to the Transvaal in January 1907. The registration act and an Australian-style immigration act were among the first laws passed by the new legislature in March. When Southern Rhodesia amended its immigration laws in 1908 to more closely resemble the Transvaal act, the attorney general wrote that Southern Rhodesia was "now joining the last link in that chain which must form the cordon around the white people of South Africa. The strength of that chain was its weakest link and if they failed in their duty they were leaving a breaking point in that chain."[44]

Canada Between Empires

Canada never succumbed to the pressure to adopt a language test, despite repeated attempts in British Columbia. In part, this was because the laissez-faire orientation of the cabinet in Ottawa inclined it to take the commercial treaty with Japan very seriously, but also because Canada had to take the laws and policies of the United States into account. As an alternative to the Australian solution, Canada helped pioneer two new forms of restriction: secret agreements for self-regulation with Japan, and legislation that authorized Canadian officials to issue orders to stop certain types of immigration for economic reasons. This latter technique, sometimes referred to in imperial correspondence as the "Canadian Principle," would be an influential model for much subsequent immigration legislation around the world.[45]

Of twenty-two provincial laws disallowed by the federal government from 1878 to 1922, eight were aimed at immigration legislation in British Columbia, and many others were aimed at discriminatory employment laws.[46] The Chinese head tax of 1885 had put Asian immigration issues on the back burner for awhile. But by 1899 British Columbians complained that the head tax was ineffective in reducing Chinese migration and that Japanese were also coming in great numbers. Prime Minister Wilfrid Laurier explained that discriminatory employment and immigration laws appeared hypocritical in the context of Ottawa's attempts to establish free trade and grant steamship subsidies to Asia. He also noted, referring to the Anglo-Japanese treaty, that "We should be prepared and ready for every sacrifice which our Imperial connection may demand at our hands. If we take the glory and advantages we must also take the duties and be ready for them and abide by them."[47]

British Columbians were not impressed, especially given their knowledge of Chamberlain's promotion of the Natal Act. In 1900 the British Columbia legislature passed its own Natal act. To a large extent the law was only a symbolic gesture. British Columbians knew it would be disallowed, but they insisted on the necessity of passing it as a matter of demanding "provincial rights." Even in the few months that it was enforced, it served little practical purpose. The British Columbian courts determined that the act was not applicable to the Chinese because of existing federation restrictions. And in June the Japanese government had already stopped issuing exit passports for laborers to Canada and the United States. The Japanese minister to Canada later explained that it was "not desirous of forcing their people into British Columbia against the wish of the province."[48] But the law had the symbolic effect of expressing British Columbian frustration with national policies and of inspiring Japanese objections to tests only in a European language.[49] The law was disallowed in September 1901, at the last moment that it was legally possible to do so. British Columbia passed six more immigration restriction laws by 1909, many of which were also disallowed only at the last moment. Ottawa and British Columbia were at a stalemate.

In the meantime, a new Canadian immigration policy was emerging out of the nexus of cabinet members desirous to import immigrant labor, the growing electoral power of labor, and U.S. pressures. In 1897 the government finally bowed to labor pressures to restrict contract labor after the United States expanded its contract law to include immigrants from Canada. This same law also prohibited employment of Japanese and Chinese on public works. In 1901 Canada allowed U.S. public health and immigration officials to be stationed at Canadian ports to ensure that immigrants in transit to the United States could pass the immigration laws. Fearful of being stuck with the U.S. rejects, the Canadian government soon passed its own general immigration laws in 1902, 1906, and 1910 that were modeled on U.S. laws. But rather than specify excluded categories in legislation, Canadian laws were designed to respond more flexibly to labor needs by giving the governor general power to proclaim and repeal exclusion categories through administrative decree.[50]

Ottawa also raised the Chinese head tax to one hundred dollars in 1902 and to five hundred dollars in 1903. Zhang Deyi, the Chinese minister in London, complained that Australia and Canada had changed their laws in response to Japanese complaints but would not listen to Chinese complaints. The Foreign Office answered that the colonies were under no treaty obligations to China, and that it looked odd for China to ask other nations to stop excluding Chinese while it agreed to exclusion in the United States. It also noted that the Canadian government needed to respond to U.S. complaints that Chinese were smuggling in through Canada. Zhang responded that international comity required that migration should be free unless international agreements, such as China's treaties with the United States, stipulated otherwise. His objections got nowhere.[51]

Canada proved more willing to defer to Japanese complaints, but this was contingent on Japan's ability and willingness to control its own emigration. This willingness was rooted in the fact that broad segments of the Japanese public and officialdom shared with white settler nations a commitment to the idea of sovereign power over immigration control and the racial integrity of nations, a commitment often expressed in terms of anti-Chinese attitudes. But such attitudes were more likely to be framed in terms of how to build a respected nation state than in assertions of self-government and the rights of a free people. Although laissez-faire ideals of free intercourse were widely discussed in Japan in the 1860s, they never had a strong hold. By the 1870s, any embrace of self-government and domestic freedoms was usually justified as a means of making the nation strong rather than as ends in themselves.[52] Japanese immigration laws accordingly provided for strong administrative powers and discretion. As early as 1874, an imperial ordinance charged local officials with the duty to prohibit movement of vagrants, beggars, people with contagious diseases, corrupt morals, and "those who may act against the interests of the Empire or are suspected of furthering the interests of an enemy nation." Public debates in Japan were over the extent of exclusion rather than the need for it, and rarely worried about means of enforcement.

The abolition of extraterritorial treaties in 1899 was preceded by extensive public debate about whether Chinese, who no longer had extraterritorial privileges in Japan, should also be allowed to move freely in the interior along with Westerners. Much of the debate rehashed the same negative stereotypes and concerns over cheap labor and the power of capital that had circulated around the Pacific for nearly half a century. But the Japanese debates added two distinct issues: concerns that Chinese exclusion would undermine attempts to gain rights of mobility for Japanese migrants around the world, and the idea that Japanese should make common cause with Chinese as part of a greater Asian civilization that could resist Western incursions.[53] In an extraordinary session on July 10, one week before extraterritoriality was repealed, the Imperial Cabinet decided that only Chinese merchants and industrialists would be allowed to reside in the interior. Accordingly, imperial rescript 352 of July 27 decreed that "laborers without special permission from government authorities" would not be permitted to live or work outside of the former extraterritorial settlements. A supplemental ordinance clarified that the rescript was "concerned primarily with the maintenance of discipline over Chinese workers, since they are not only apt to vitiate public morals, but are also likely to enter into conflict with Japanese workers through competition, thereby causing disorder to industry and society and ultimately disturbing public peace and order." Many Japanese and Chinese residents in Japan praised the rescript as a victory of Asian brotherhood because of its restrictions based on occupation rather than race, despite the fact that the actual categories of exclusion and admission were much the same as in the United States.[54]

Given their commitment to discriminatory immigration control, Japanese officials were careful to express their protests against discriminatory treatment abroad in terms of treaty clauses and claims to be a civilized nation rather than as a universal principle of equity. In 1899 Japan avoided potential conflict by limiting the number of exit passports to countries with latent anti-Japanese attitudes. But after its 1905 victory in the Russo-Japanese War, Japan was increasingly recognized as a "civilized" nation and colonizer in its own right. Britain established a formal alliance with Japan, and Canada signed on to the Anglo-Japanese commerce treaty, based on a promise from the Japanese consul general that Japan would continue to restrict emigration. In the wake of these events, Japan began to loosen its emigration controls to North America and make stronger demands for nondiscriminatory treatment.

The rise in Japanese migration to North America after 1905 stoked anti-Japanese activities up and down the Pacific Coast, where residents were less impressed by Japan's "civilized" status than fearful of its military and political intentions. Japanese migration to Canada rose from nearly nothing in 1904 to more than seven thousand in the fiscal year ending June 1908. The Japanese government explained that the consul general had no authority to promise continued restriction, and that free migration was protected under the treaty. Migration to the United States also boomed, with more than thirty thousand Japanese entering the United States and Hawaii in 1907, double the previous year. Tensions exploded into an international issue with the enactment of a California law in 1906 that required segregated Japanese schools. They were further inflamed by increased movement from Hawaii to North America that was beyond the control of the Japanese government, and the suspicion that Japanese boarding-house owners and even non-Japanese companies were actively recruiting new migrants. The U.S. general immigration law of February 1907 empowered the president to refuse entry to migrants carrying passports designated for any country or territory other than the mainland United States, and San Francisco stopped issuing licenses to Japanese employment agencies in July 1907.[55] In Canada, an investigation by Deputy Minister of Labor Mackenzie King in October found that the Japanese consul in Vancouver had even formed the Canadian Nippon Supply Company to help make links between Japanese labor and Canadian employers.[56] Such discoveries reinforced the belief that unchecked capital was conspiring to encourage an "unnatural" migration of induced laborers.[57]

A boom in Indian migration happened at this same time. Fearing that Japanese immigration would be restricted, the Canadian Pacific Railway had begun promoting migration from India. The trickle of Indian immigration developed into a stream of over two thousand a year in 1907 and 1908, some of it moving on to the United States. Chinese migration problems also continued to capture the public imagination. The Chinese boycott of 1905–06 against U.S. immigration laws had gained wide publicity, if limited practical results. The Vancouver customs house was also wracked by fraud and corruption scandals surrounding Chinese immigration in these years.[58]

All of these events encouraged local anti-Asian organizations to consolidate into an Asiatic Exclusion League with members on both sides of the border. Violence against Japanese and Indians spread up and down the coast. Rioters chased Indians from the Washington town of Bellingham on September 5, 1907. On September 7 the Asiatic Exclusion League organized a parade in Vancouver. Lieutenant Governor James Dunsmuir of British Columbia, believed by many to want to import Japanese laborers to work in his mines, had just withheld consent to the new immigration law. Activists gave inspirational speeches about the valiant actions in Bellingham and burned Dunsmuir's effigy. The parade soon turned into a riot in which Asians suffered extensive property loss. Politicians in both Ottawa and Washington, DC, were convinced of the necessity of tougher restrictions on Japanese and Indian immigration, if only to maintain public order. The people had spoken again.

In October, Canada sent Minister of Labour Rodolphe Lemieux to Japan to follow up on a 1903 suggestion from Japanese Consul General Nossé Tatsumoro to negotiate a secret restriction agreement. The United States had been engaged in such negotiations since February 1907, when Japan had proposed to restrict emigration to the United States if the California school law was rescinded. Secretary of War William Taft was even sent to Japan in September, but negotiations went nowhere because the United States wanted a formal treaty like that with China. Japanese officials—who had watched the Chinese anti-American boycott intently—preferred a secret agreement so that the Japanese public would be unaware of any concessions and the international image of formal equality could be maintained. On arriving in Japan, Lemieux rebuffed overtures from the U.S. minister to make common cause in their negotiations. The main sticking points in the Canadian negotiations were precise numbers and the Japanese desire to place its own immigration officers abroad to inspect passports (arguing that a breach of passport conditions was a violation of Japanese rather than Canadian law).[59] By early January 1908, both the United States and Canada concluded secret agreements in which Japan would limit the number of passports for each country.[60]

Skeptics in both North American countries were wary. They feared that this agreement would undermine sovereign control of migration, and that secrecy would make it impossible to enforce. As opposition leader Robert Borden argued in the House of Commons, "Canada has handed over to Japan that control of immigration which Canada herself ought to exercise; the regulations governing immigration in future are to be Japanese regulations; the control and policy are to be Japanese, and in case of difficulty our remedy, and our only remedy outside of the abrogation of this treaty, is by appeal to the Japanese government from time to time."[61] The legislature of

British Columbia acted on these suspicions by continuing to pass provincial immigration acts in 1908 and 1909, both of which were disallowed within a month.[62]

Even U.S. President Theodore Roosevelt continued to speak belligerently of Japan. During three visits by Mackenzie King in January 1908, followed by a visit from four members of Parliament, Roosevelt declaimed at length on the need for a united white front against Japan and his plans to send the U.S. fleet to the Pacific. Asked if the Monroe Doctrine would be applied to the Pacific Coast, he replied, "Yes, and to Australia as well—if it doesn't I'll make it apply."[63] King reported that Roosevelt wanted "some kind of Convention between the English-speaking peoples, whereby in regard to this question, it would be understood on all sides that the Asiatic peoples were not to come to the English speaking countries to settle, and that our people were not to go there."[64] Canadian officials declined the offer, preferring to uphold the Anglo-Japanese alliance and maintain autonomy from a U.S.-dominated pact.[65] Canadian members of the Asiatic Exclusion League even decided not to send delegates to a convention of exclusion leagues in Seattle in 1908 so as not to "involve Western Canada in California's war with Japan."[66] Migration control remained a national issue.

In the end, faith in Japan's willingness to enforce the agreement was not misplaced. Early difficulties were soon ironed out, and Japan apologized that it had not yet imposed sufficient control over local officials who issued passports.[67] By the end of 1908, migration had decreased to levels that pleased nearly everybody, and Japan regularly forwarded emigration statistics to U.S. and Canadian officials. A Canadian order in council of 1908 (exercising powers in the general immigration law of 1906) also stopped Japanese migration from Hawaii by requiring that all immigrants travel to Canada on a direct voyage from their home nation.

This success led Canadian officials to authorize Mackenzie King to attempt to negotiate a similar agreement with China at the end of 1908. Chinese officials were initially uninterested, speaking of the sufficiency of existing regulations to protect contract laborers. They grew more interested when King told them of the Lemieux agreement and the possibility of revoking the discriminatory poll tax.[68] Canada and China began to negotiate possible numbers of migrants, but the Waiwubu (Foreign Office) continued to vacillate in its commitment to a formal agreement. In the meantime, a riot in Peru in May 1909 led to a protocol in which China agreed to prohibit the departure of all "emigrants," defined as migrants looking for work. China also made an arrangement with Australia in 1912, based on earlier arrangements with Japan and India, in which merchants and other travelers with passports would not be subject to the dictation test.[69] In 1911 the Waiwubu asked provincial officials across China to comment on the possibility of self-restriction of migration to Canada. All the officials supported the idea because sovereignty over the mobility of Chinese subjects and national reputation were at stake. Some also emphasized that enforcement should be rigorous, with strict punishments for migrants who were deported or gave false representations.[70]

But these hopes came to nothing. The Peruvian protocol had established a system of self-restriction in which nonemigrants would apply to the local Chamber of Commerce in China to be issued a passport for visa by the Peruvian consul in Hong Kong—a procedure that, as we shall see, already had a record of proven failure with the United States. Migration to Peru soon reached pre-1909 levels. In 1914 the Peruvian government denounced the protocol and the 1875 Treaty of Friendship and Commerce with the argument that "All civilized nations can exercise (as an attribute of their sovereignty) to fix the conditions in which foreigners, whether immigrants or not, are admitted to the national territory, and in some countries, like the United States, these are very strict."[71] That same year, China proposed a self-restriction agreement to Canada, but the negotiations went nowhere.[72] Australia also canceled its agreement in 1920 after only forty merchants had entered on Chinese passports. China had failed to demonstrate its ability to conform to the standards of civilized nations.

Japan's success, on the other hand, helped to preserve the international reputation of Japan as a country that could maintain its agreements. A proponent of the international management of migration, Paul Peirce, later observed that the amicable adjustment of Japanese immigration problems "must be accounted a triumph of international coöperation."[73] More backhanded praise came from former secretary of state Elihu Root, who explained in 1910 that many countries had achieved a common recognition of the difference between "ordinary travel and residence upon individual initiative to which the usual conventions relating to reciprocal rights of travel and residence relate," and the kinds of mass migrations of unassimilable people that "may virtually take possession of considerable portions of the territory of another country to the practical exclusion of its own citizens." He noted, "After many years of discussion China has come to recognize the existence of such a distinction in respect of Chinese emigration to North America. Japan has recognized it from the first, and there has never been any question between the Governments of Japan and the United States upon that subject."[74] Japan continued to arrange "gentleman's agreements" with countries such as Cuba in 1929 and even South Africa in 1930, the latter earning Japanese the title of "honorary whites."[75] But the international honor gained by avoiding discriminatory laws came at the expense of admitting the legitimacy of such laws in the first place.

The Canadian Principle

The order in council that required a direct voyage set a precedent for Canadian migration control that would soon be refined in attempts to stop Indian migration and would ultimately endure longer than the Japanese agreements.[76] As early as 1905, Canadian officials were writing reports and cabling London to explain how the climatic and employment conditions in Canada were unsuitable for Indian laborers. In March 1908 King visited London to convince the Colonial and India offices to discuss the need for migration restrictions in Canada. Referring to the shiploads of Japanese brought from Hawaii, he warned of unscrupulous private entrepreneurs and "that one was unable to say what purpose it might not serve to have a shipload of Indians dumped down in Vancouver with a view to creating disturbances in that city."[77] The secretary of state for India wrote to the viceroy suggesting a passport system similar to that established by Japan. The viceroy objected that such a scheme was opposed to the freedom of movement embodied in the Indian Emigration Act of 1883 and warned that strong public resentment would be engendered by such controls. He did promise to "take steps to warn intending emigrants that their landing in Canada is likely to arouse strong popular feeling."[78]

The continuous voyage order effectively restricted Indian migrants because of the lack of direct lines between India and Canada. A requirement that migrants also carry two hundred dollars was added later, and then reworded in 1909 to state that immigrants "may" be prohibited, so that the "absurd" necessity to enforce it against white immigrants could be avoided. Officials originally justified the continuous voyage provision in terms of convenience of deportation on the same ship on which the immigrant arrived. The renewed order of 1909, however, offered a much more straightforward explanation aimed at those who would claim the right of free movement throughout the empire:

It has always been understood that in the maintenance of Imperial interests such policy rested on the principle that each part of the Empire
should be governed in the best interests of the people of that part, and
that where self-government is established the views of the people, as expressed in legislation, should be considered as the best evidence of what
constitutes Imperial interests in that part of the Empire.[79]

The general immigration law of 1910 reduced the need for indirect restrictions
by empowering the governor general to order the exclusion of immigrants
"Belonging to any race deemed unsuited to the climate or requirements of
Canada, or of immigrants of any specified class, occupation or character." For
the next several years, orders in council repeatedly forbade direct immigration
to British Columbia due to "overcrowded conditions of the labour market." In
1914 Chinese were brought under the purview of the general immigration
laws so that the orders could apply to them, cutting Chinese entries by over
70 percent over the next four years.[80]

The carefully nondiscriminatory wording allowed the Canadian government to inform the governments of Japan and India that restrictions were
not for "racial reasons, but wholly on account of considerations which are
economic."[81] Growing fears of sedition among overseas Indians also made the
Indian government more sympathetic to restrictive laws.[82] An embarrassing
event in the spring of 1914, in which 376 Indian passengers on a ship chartered by a private Indian businessman were detained on board for two months
and deported back to India, also caused many officials to rethink their opposition to passports. The government of India conceded that circumstances now
compelled a "stricter definition of membership in the British empire" that
did not necessarily carry the right of free entry into all parts of the Empire.
"It will no longer be held that every measure of exclusion of Asiatics from territories forming part of the Empire is necessarily and *ipso facto* an injustice
to Indians."[83] But resistance from Indians themselves, stoked by Gandhi's satyagraha movement in the Transvaal, still caused officials to waver. In a 1915
memorandum, the India Office asserted:

The Emperor of Japan can take measures of this kind because of the very
peculiar moral authority that he exercises over his subjects, and, even so,
Japanese policy in this matter extends to all Japanese subjects. But the Indian Government believe, from their experience in similar controversies,

that if they were to prohibit Indians from proceeding to Canada they would be attacked for denying to the particular class of British subjects that is under their own guardianship advantages within the Empire open to other British subjects.[84]

As with Japan, an agreement between equals was preferable to a limitation imposed by coercion. India was much more willing to restrict emigration after it was promised higher status within the empire in recognition of its service in World War One. Indian representatives were admitted to the Imperial Conference for the first time in 1917, where they proposed to issue passports for travel to the self-governing colonies only to businessmen, travelers, and family members, on the conditions that those colonies would reciprocally require passports for travel to India. Despite some misgivings, the dominions went along with the proposal. The Canadian minister of immigration and colonization expressed the sentiments of the collected representatives when he explained that with this arrangement, "It would be clearly recognized that the exclusion . . . was not motivated by prejudices of race, but was the outcome of different economic conditions."[85]

By this time, however, it was largely a symbolic gesture. Immigration controls based on broad administrative discretion in the receiving country were firmly established across the empire. In 1911 the new Union of South Africa began to consider a comprehensive new immigration law that could replace the "Natal formula," which was increasingly attacked by Indians and also by whites who objected to the concentration of arbitrary powers that could be used to exclude Europeans as well as Indians. After two years of protracted negotiation, the framers believed they had found the solution in the "Canadian principle" of a board of appeal that stopped access to the courts while still providing some checks on administrative discretion (a technique that Canada had learned from the United States) and adding the clause, "Any person or class of persons deemed by the Minister on economic grounds or on account of standard or habits of life to be unsuited to the requirements of the Union or any particular Province thereof."[86] Even Gandhi agreed with the framers' assertion that "this method of prescribing what persons shall be prohibited immigrants, without actually naming particular races in the law, is preferable to the Australian method."[87] At the first meeting of the board of appeals after the passage of the law, the chair simply read an order from General Jan Smuts declaring, "every Asiatic person to be undesirable on economic grounds."[88] New Zealand enacted similar legislation in 1920, adding a clause that required all non-British applicants to apply for admission by mail before arrival.[89] For its part, India ended up banning the emigration of unskilled labor altogether in 1922 except to countries specifically authorized by orders in council, a law that has generally been given a positive twist as the end of the coolie trade and unfree migration.

Even U.S. officials were impressed by Canadian methods, a 1910 report on Canadian immigration law calling them "admirably adapted to carrying out the immigration policy of the Dominion."[90] The long-standing U.S. practice of defining admission standards in formal legislation made it impossible to fully emulate the Canadian principle, but officials found creative ways to expand their discretion. In 1910 the U.S. consul in Calcutta began to deny visas without explanation, and immigration agents in the United States excluded the entry of Indians on a variety of discretionary premises. The immigration inspector in Seattle excluded Muhammadans because they were inherently polygamists, whether married or not. Much more effective, however, was liberal use of the "liable to become a public charge" clause to exclude Indians deemed constitutionally unfit for the North American climate and those who would not find a job because of racial antagonism. In 1912 shipping companies even agreed not to sell tickets to Indian laborers.[91] The public charge clause was later used to great effect by consuls to deny visas to Jews and other European emigrants in the 1930s.

U.S. officials also played an important role in redefining immigration restrictions as an economic issue. During his 1907 tour of the Pacific Coast, Secretary of Commerce and Labor Oscar Straus described recent riots as purely economic in origin as a way to distance himself from anti-Asian rhetoric while placating its demands. Secretary of State William Jennings Bryan crafted these arguments into eloquent form when he denied to the Japanese minister that the 1913 California law prohibiting landownership to "aliens ineligible to citizenship" was racially discriminatory. He argued that even though economic struggles appeared to take place along racial lines,

It does so not because of racial antagonism but because of the circumstance that the traditions and habits of different races have developed or diminished competitive efficiency. The contest is economic; the racial difference is a mere mark or incident of the economic struggle. All nations recognize this fact, and it is for this reason that each nation is permitted to determine who shall and who shall not be permitted to settle in its dominions and become a part of the body politic, to the end that it may preserve internal peace and avoid the contentions which are so likely to disturb the harmony of international relations.[92]

By the middle of the century, the economic interests of the nation would become not only a globally accepted justification of all forms of migration control, but a foundation for the very understanding of migration and regulation.

Decline of the Imperial Subject

Lord Chamberlain had hoped to use the Inter-Colonial Conference of 1897 as a format to promote a united empire, or at least a stronger federation. By the next meeting in 1902, it was already clear that the colonial politicians were more likely to have their way. Although open to common defense arrangements and willing to at least discuss trade preferences, they refused to entertain the possibility of any modification to their immigration and naturalization policies. Those with more imperialist goals found it hard to press the subject, both because they believed the power of self-government to be the foundation of British glory and because racism and civilizational differences had justified imperial conquest in the first place. By 1907, conference rhetoric had shifted to an understanding of the empire as, at most, a voluntary union of self-governing peoples that respected the autonomy of the other members.[93] This loose conceptualization helped bring the contentious Boers and French Canadians into the fold. By 1917, General Smuts could proclaim how pleased he was to belong to an empire "founded on principles which appeal to the highest political ideals of mankind . . . principles of freedom and equality."[94] He made clear that this had been made possible on the foundation of migration control. "I have always felt sure, that once the white community in South Africa were rid of the fear that they were going to be flooded by unlimited immigration from India, all the other questions would be considered subsidiary and would become easily and perfectly soluble."[95]

The category of imperial subject had proven inadequate to the task of regulating free migration in the modern world. Territorial nations defined by race, borders, and citizenship were much more appropriate. But proponents of empire made one more attempt in the decade before World War I to fortify the white portions of the empire under the idea of an "imperial citizen." The outlines of imperial citizenship remained vague, but it was broadly conceived as a means to unite the self-governing portions of the empire through uniform policies on naturalization and political rights. In a paper on "The Imperial Problem of Asiatic Immigration," read to the Royal Society of Arts in 1908, journalist Richard Jebb explicitly linked the attraction of imperial citizenship to the recent struggles over the Indians in the Transvaal. He argued that the purpose of imperial citizenship was not political amalgamation, but a form of association for the "promotion and protection of nation-states." Imperial unity came precisely through the power of the empire to help protect the autonomy of its parts. London's grant of self-government to the Transvaal was the perfect example of how this could encourage a stronger attachment to the empire. "It follows that Imperial citizenship cannot confer any rights inconsistent with it, *e.g.*, the right of any citizen to settle in any State where his presence would be injurious to its national civilization."[96]

But even this conception of imperial citizenship ran into trouble when fleshed out in detail. *United Empire*, the journal of the Royal Colonial Institute, sponsored a discussion of imperial and British citizenship in 1911. Most participants agreed that under existing conditions, a "British citizen" had no practical meaning across the empire because franchises were not transferable between dominions, and not all subjects were free to move. Nor was free mobility and the transfer of franchise desirable because people that obtained rights in one dominion or colony may be objectionable in another. International lawyer John Westlake argued that citizenship could only be locally relevant as a category that implied political rights. Internationally, "there is no universal agreement as to the conditions or tests which determine to what State sovereignty each individual shall be subject."[97] From the practical international perspective of diplomatic relations, citizenship was little different from subjecthood in that it served to link the individual to a sovereign political power but provided no necessary rights or privileges abroad other than those that the sovereign could negotiate or extend.

Australian Chief Justice S. W. Griffith also emphasized that even within the empire, political rights, citizenship, and migration laws were entirely the concern of local governments. The Immigration Act of Natal had established the right to legislate on the subject and had put British nationals on same footing as aliens as far as entry was concerned. British nationality had an international value in that it could be used to claim protection against foreign powers. It could also be taken as a necessary condition to enjoy rights within the empire, but not a sufficient condition to confer political rights within all parts of empire. Other respondents noted the emotional resonance of citizenship in an empire that valued self-governance. But this very resonance only served to buttress distinctions within the empire between peoples thought capable and incapable of self-government. Ex-governor of New South Wales Walter Hely-Hutchinson even argued that it was unwise to even bring up a discussion of citizenship because it would only draw attention to the disabilities of certain subjects by telling them "You are not a British citizen, you are only a subject."[98]

In summing up the discussion, E. B. Sargent said he had come to the understanding that "The chief advantages of being a British subject are experienced in foreign lands. In regard to many private rights, he is not much better off in his own country than is the actual alien."[99] Referring specifically to the objections of Hely-Hutchinson, he remained committed to keeping the term "citizen" because of its lineage that went back to traditions of municipal self-government and because it extended the promise of equality. He conceded, however, that under current conditions, full imperial citizenship was impossible. The ideal of citizenship was only realistic within the parts of a federation of self-governing dominions. But, he predicted, an empire defined only by issues of mutual defense, trade privileges, and allegiance to a crown would ultimately decay,

> That the United Kingdom should have charge of the common affairs of the Empire and that each Self-governing Dominion should have charge of its own affairs—what could be more plausible and what more unsound than this? The direct consequence is that the individual affairs become more numerous and more important and the common affairs dwindle away. Canada has barely escaped a continental fiscal policy; Australia is pre-occupied with the white man's future in the Southern Seas; South Africa, perplexed by her own native problem, has obtained the sanction of the Imperial Parliament to a constitutional distinction as to race which must henceforward accentuate the difficulties of the Imperial Executive in regard to Indian and Crown Colony administration. . . . If we welcome to our minds thoughts of Canadian and Australian citizenship which do not grow out of, and remain organic parts of, our common citizenship, will not defense and allegiance go the way of all other common affairs?[100]

Race and the ideal of self-government had worked together to make the national community more attractive than empire as a form of political membership in a modern world of free migration—both in their ability to consolidate states and provinces, as in the United States and Australia, and in their ability to break apart larger, self-avowedly multiracial and multijurisdictional entities.

Other Empires

Racial discrimination, in and of itself, did not create a world of emigration control at national borders. Race was equally significant in the making of other empires—including the non-self-governing portions of the British Empire—where attitudes toward mobility control were quite different. It was the potent mix of race and self-rule that built a world of border control. Despite repeated attempts at reform, the Dutch Indies and French Indochina implemented a byzantine web of discriminatory taxes, registrations, administrative decrees, headman arrangements, and pluralistic legal systems that reeked of the premodern regulation of aliens.[101] In parts of the British Empire without self-government, attitudes toward migration that were a mix of laissez-faire and obsession with indenture persisted until the 1920s. Control and distinctions were enforced through plantations, property laws, master-servant laws, and distinct jurisdictions for certain legal issues, such as inheritance. In Korea, Japan enacted an emigrant protection law in 1906 to prohibit the private organization of emigration. Ostensibly designed to protect emigrants from exploitation as indentured labor, it functioned to stop emigration altogether and limit competition with Japanese workers in Hawaii.[102] Exit control would continue through the twentieth century as a common aspect of migration control, albeit one that would increasingly become a defining difference between the "free" and the "unfree" worlds.

Migration policy in the U.S. empire was more a harbinger of things to come. In 1898 Chinese exclusion was applied to the newly occupied territories of the Philippines, Puerto Rico, Cuba, and Hawaii almost by reflex. Extensive debate ensued over the necessity of exclusion in the new possessions. Many people objected that conditions on the islands were different from those on the mainland, and that Chinese should be recruited for the sake of economic development. For the Philippines, this debate ultimately revolved how best to prepare the natives in self-rule. Some argued that Chinese would provide a model of hard work and commercial diligence. But the argument ultimately prevailed that "Philippines for the Filipinos" could be best attained by keeping the Chinese out, and appropriate legislation was passed in 1904.[103] As the chair of the Senate Committee on Immigration explained, it was "better to postpone the commercial and industrial development of the islands for a time and to preserve these islands for the Filipino people themselves and not threaten them with what we understand they had the greatest apprehension, that the islands should be immediately thrown open to the exploiter and speculator."[104]

The logic of tutorship created a U.S. empire that was meant to break apart into its components almost from the very beginning. In addition to excluding Chinese from the colonies and territories, the United States also maintained its own exclusion laws against Chinese migration from the colonies to the mainland. Stopping the movement of Filipino nationals into the United States was also one of the main motivations behind granting Philippines independence in 1934.[105] The logic of self-rule that had contributed to the disintegration of the British Empire was now imposed from the top down in an empire that made no pretenses of unity in the first place. Self-rule had once been a justification of migration restrictions. Now immigration controls were imposed around people not yet thought capable of self-government. The mere fact of sovereignty, or of potential sovereignty, was now sufficient to justify border control. Border control had even become a precondition of sovereignty.

Part III

Enforcing Borders

[The doorman] is conscious of the importance of his office, for he says: "I am powerful"; he is respectful to his superiors, for he says: "I am only the lowest doorkeeper"; he is not garrulous, for during all these years he puts only what are called "impersonal questions"; he is not to be bribed, for he says in accepting a gift: "I take this only to keep you from feeling that you have left something undone"; where his duty is concerned he is to be moved neither by pity nor rage, for we are told that the man "wearied the doorkeeper with his importunity"; and finally even his external appearance hints at a pedantic character. Could one imagine a more faithful doorkeeper? Yet the doorkeeper has other elements in his character which are likely to advantage anyone seeking admittance. Take the statements he makes about his power and the power of the other doorkeepers and their dreadful aspect which even he cannot bear to see—I hold that these statements may be true enough, but that the way in which he brings them out shows that his perceptions are confused by simpleness of mind and conceit. The commentators note in this connection: "The right perception of any matter and a misunderstanding of the same matter do not wholly exclude each other." One must at any rate assume that such simpleness and conceit, however sparingly manifest, are likely to weaken his defense of the door; they are breaches in the character of the doorkeeper. To this must be added that the doorkeeper seems to be a friendly creature by nature, he is by no means always on his official dignity. In the very first moments he allows himself the jest of inviting the man to enter in spite of the strictly maintained veto against entry; then he does not, for instance, send the man away, but gives him, as we are told, a stool and lets him sit down beside the door. The patience with which he endures the man's appeals during so many years, the brief conversations, the acceptance of the gifts, the politeness with which he allows the man to curse loudly in his presence the fate for which he himself is responsible—all this lets us deduce certain feelings of pity. Not every doorkeeper would have acted thus. . . . Some push this mode of interpretation even further and hold that these words express a kind of friendly admiration, though not without a hint of condescension.   —Kafka, *The Trial*

8

Experiments in Remote Control, 1897–1905

To imagine and proclaim the principles of border control was difficult enough. To enforce those borders was an even greater challenge. In 1906 Commissioner General of Immigration Frank Sargent tried to justify his rigorous enforcement of the Chinese exclusion laws to Congress:

> The Chinese exclusion laws [are] among the most difficult on the statute books to enforce. This condition arose from three causes: First . . . there was a divided responsibility, due to the disconnected official agencies through which the laws were administered, and it was not possible to effect the organization and systematization necessary for even a reasonably thorough enforcement of the laws; second, a certain element of the citizenship of this country has never believed in the exclusion policy, being actuated either by strictly interested motives or by the missionary spirit, and the persons forming that element are never willing to assist, and are often ready and glad to oppose the enforcement of the law; third, the laws relate to a people who, according to all recognized authorities, are deficient in the sense of the moral obligation of an oath, and who in their political views hold caste in higher esteem than law, and are 'clannish' to the highest degree.[1]

The Bureau of Immigration had worked diligently both to define and to resolve these three problems over the previous eight years. It was especially challenging because U.S. immigration agents had only a portion of the discretionary power enjoyed by their counterparts in the British Empire. Excluded categories were written directly into legislation for all to interpret and challenge. And challenge they did, as well as mock, ignore, and manipulate for personal profit. The actual enforcement of border control was forged at this nexus of pressures from diplomats, lawyers, politicians, the press, and migrants around the world. The negotiations and compromises that accompanied enforcement, however, were ultimately the vehicle by which the principles of unilateral border control were made into a reality. Even those who challenged the laws became participants in the enormous edifice they had helped to construct.

Centralization and standardization of information were the bedrock of migration reform. Given the transnational nature of migration, this control could not be limited to within the borders of the United States. But the identification of people outside U.S. jurisdiction was especially challenging. Many consuls, if willing to identify migrants at all, resorted to collaboration with private entrepreneurs. The State Department, despite its objections to the diplomatic embarrassments of migration control, was increasingly brought in to exercise "remote control" over migrants and its own consuls. Officials in China also had to be disciplined in the production of appropriate documents and identifications. The resulting procedures would become a standard for migration control and identification around the world. Their creation, however, came through trial and error, more reactive than proactive in meeting the contradictory pressures to enforce both discrimination and equal access to law, to be both more restrictive and more humane. This chapter will focus on the many difficulties of enforcing migration reform, especially as an international problem, and the next chapter will analyze the solutions.[2]

Fixing the Categories, Ordering the Files

In 1898 power to enforce the Chinese exclusion laws was still dreadfully scattered and uncoordinated. Responsibility for the general immigration laws was shifted from individual states to the Treasury Department in 1888 and consolidated under the Bureau of Immigration in 1891. But responsibility for Chinese exclusion remained with the Bureau of Customs until 1900. Customs collectors were mostly patronage appointees and largely left to devise their own procedures. Chinese rejected at one port could try again at another, often with good results. Registration certificates required by the Geary Act of 1892 were issued by internal revenue collectors who stored the records in offices scattered around the nation. Section 6 certificates were issued by officials in China, Hong Kong, and myriad foreign nations around the world. These were stamped with a visa by U.S. consuls whose main duties entailed the facilitation of smooth international intercourse and who were often critical of exclusion laws. Even Treasury Department officials in Washington often prioritized international relations and overturned the sometimes ill-conceived attempts at more rigorous enforcement devised by the collector in San Francisco.

A series of open and undercover investigations from 1897 to 1900 found sloppy administration, demoralized and corrupt officials, and the pervasive influence of Chinese smuggling rings and their lawyers. Special investigator J. Thomas Scharf summarized in 1898:

> Owing to the loose interpretation of the laws by sympathetic U.S. Commissioners, and the radical diversity of opinion between the judges of the Federal Courts, the crafty practices and fraudulent devices of the Mongolians themselves, the ready aid of well-paid allies on the border line, perjured witnesses, and the oath-breaking and bribe-taking public officials, the exclusion laws have become more honored in the breach than in the observance. With several years' experience in attempting to enforce this supreme law of the land, our faith in effective legislation upon this subject is much impaired. Laws deemed apparently faultless have proven but legislative makeshifts. They do not meet the evil, but rather aggravate it by offering opportunities for their evasion through perjury, chicanery, and frauds.[3]

Similarly, in the words of a Chinese broker as reported by special investigator Oscar Greenhalge (who turned out to be collaborating with smugglers himself), "Any Government officer would fail in enforcing the law, for the law is too lenient with the Chinamen. In the hands of a skillful lawyer, and a packed jury, or a Commissioner who will 'lean' towards the Chinese, a Chinaman is bound to escape. The Americans don't know how to make the Chinese obey the laws."[4] The demoralization was only exacerbated by public criticism that alternately blamed the Customs Bureau for being too harsh, too ineffective, too rigidly bureaucratic, and too unpredictable.

By his own request, former grand master of the Knights of Labor Terence Powderly was appointed commissioner general of immigration in July 1897. He embodied all of the extremes of the nineteenth-century anti-Chinese movement: fiercely egalitarian, prolabor, mistrustful of capital, and deeply racist. He also had a progressive devotion to the government management and protection of deserving migrants, explaining that "if a government is 'for the people' it must be paternalistic."[5] He devoted much of his tenure to the investigation of malfeasance and maltreatment of immigrants at Ellis Island. His larger ambitions included a nationwide system of information collection on labor conditions that would be distributed to consulates throughout Europe to connect immigrants to jobs. He abhorred the punitive nature of immigration laws, explaining that immigrants "are driven from the other side of the Atlantic to this side; and then they are turned loose where the corporation drives them. They are driven into the hospital and driven out again and then they are deported. We take great pains in hunting up a man to deport him. . . . I would rather see the per diem expended in hunting for a job for the man so he won't have to be sent back."[6]

But not all immigrants deserved this kind of solicitousness. He also supported laws that encouraged the selection of "desirable" immigrants. He expressed his regulatory ambitions in verse:

America's claim to the world's leadership
May lose in its strength, it may weaken and slip,
If we give all our time, to those we reject
And pay little heed to the kind we select.
Don't you see that the man who comes here selects us,
And that is what causes our worries and fuss;
Our selection of aliens should begin over sea,
And not when they enter this land of the free.[7]

Asians were among those who should be peremptorily rejected. Powderly was critical of the exclusion laws as they existed, but he felt they should be enforced as rigorously as possible so long as they were on the books. He called the union of customs and the Chinese Bureau "unnatural" because of its mixed mandate of facilitating trade and keeping people out, and he helped transfer authority to the Bureau of Immigration in 1900.[8] He worked closely with James Dunn, who had begun a rigorous system of enforcement upon his appointment as collector of customs in San Francisco in 1899. Dunn traveled around the nation, giving advice to Chinese agents and other government officials.[9]

But whatever their reformist zeal, neither Powderly nor Dunn had the political acumen to survive the "friction" engendered by their reforms. Powderly's Ellis Island investigations generated great animosity that led to his dismissal on corruption charges in 1902. Dunn was a victim of charges by lawyers and the press that accused him of using "nimbleness in the art of vituperation . . . to continue the infliction of injustice upon offending Chinese, to insult gentlemen applying at the Bureau on business, and to reap petty vengeance upon attorneys."[10] He was transferred to St. Louis in 1903. That same year, however, the Bureau of Immigration was transferred to the Department of Commerce and Labor, and Powderly and Dunn's reforms were continued with even greater skill by Commissioner General Frank Sargent, former grand master of the Brotherhood of Locomotive Firemen, and by the San Francisco Commissioner of Immigration Hart Hyatt North, a progressive bureaucrat who had been appointed in 1898.

Powderly, Dunn, North, and Sargent established rigorous and systematic interviews at the ports (described in detail in chapter 10), more thorough investigations to verify Chinese claims, and more thorough and standardized reporting by agents on the ground. They constructed extensive cross-referenced files and improved channels of communication around the nation. Chinese registration records formerly held by internal revenue agents and duplicate copies of other documentation now being produced in increasingly large quantities were centralized in Washington for arrangement into "systematic order." Documents in the possession of Chinese were cross-checked with centrally filed documents each time a migrant petitioned the bureau. The use of photography and the Bertillon system of physical measurement to identify laborers were expanded. Immigration officers were encouraged to learn legal procedures and assist public attorneys in aggressively pursuing Chinese cases in the courts. Opportunities for bribery and outside intervention were reduced by excluding lawyers from hearings, fixing fees for commissioners who heard Chinese cases, and regulating the issue of deportation warrants by local officials.[11] Supreme Court decisions in *Sing Tuck* (1904), *Ju Toy* (1905), and *Chin Yow* (1908) capped the twenty-year legal fight to stop appeals to the courts by making administrative decisions final in immigration cases at the border, even for migrants claiming U.S. citizenship.[12]

Organizational reforms were accompanied by the clarification of formal regulations and categories. The Treasury Department began this process in 1899 by publishing a collection of treaties, departmental decisions, court decisions, and correspondence titled "Digest of the Chinese-Exclusion Laws and Decisions." These were classified and indexed for republication in 1902.[13] An entirely new digest in 1903 transformed these decisions into a list of numbered and categorized rules. Thus, claimed Sargent, it "became possible to issue definite and detailed instructions intended to meet every possible contingency, and to lay down, so far as possible, an exact rule of procedure."[14]

The rules sought to clarify unresolved problems in fundamental categories of exclusion. These included the questions of whether exclusion applied only to laborers or to all Chinese except the specifically enumerated exempt classes, what qualified one to be considered a student or merchant, and whether a Chinese could change status after admission without being subject to deportation. The bureau generally opted for the most restrictive possible definitions. For example, students had to be able to support themselves and to study topics in the higher branches of learning that could not be studied in China. Issues surrounding change of status were more challenging and never entirely clarified, although the general rule of thumb was that a Chinese must maintain his or her status for at least a year, after which merchants and their families could become laborers by virtue of circumstances beyond their control.[15]

On the question of who was excluded, the bureau gained strength from Attorney General John Griggs's 1898 opinion (echoing Miller's 1891 opinion) that the "true theory" of exclusion was that only the specified exempt classes could be admitted. Chinese Minister Wu Tingfang complained that Griggs's decision went against treaties and that it was absurd not to include people of high status like bankers, scholars, and philosophers. Griggs answered that the courts should be allowed to make the final decision, but Wu, aware of trends to defer to administrative decisions and congressional legislation in immigration matters, wanted to avoid this option. He argued that treaty rights could not be arbitrarily determined by the courts of only one party to the treaty: "However much the courts may feel bound to follow the legislation of Congress, I apprehend you will not contend that adverse legislation or the judgment of a domestic tribunal can release a Government from its solemn treaty obligations."[16] The practical consequence of Wu's attitude was that China relinquished one of the last remaining channels to challenge regulations. Subsequent complaints about the restrictiveness of exempt category definitions fell on deaf ears. Frustrated, the Chinese refused to renew the Gresham-Yang Treaty of 1894 when its ten-year renewal period came due, hoping unsuccessfully to fall back on the more expansive rights of the Angell Treaty.[17]

Frank Sargent's personal charisma topped off these reforms. He earned the support of his superiors and reversed the demoralization of his subordinates while simultaneously binding them to a more rigorous routine. He made a point of visiting immigration stations around the country and establishing personal relations with local agents "as a stimulus to their efforts and a source of enlightenment to the Bureau."[18] Even a prickly fellow like Dunn felt he could confide in Sargent during his 1902 visit to San Francisco:

When considering in retrospect your visit at this port, I sometimes fear I wearied you with the recital of details, but there was so much to be told, and I find that so many things were left unsaid, that I hope I may be pardoned, in view of the fact that it has never before been possible to show my superior officer the conditions as they exist, and to have definite personal advice and assistance where it has been so greatly needed. I shall take advantage of your invitation to write you frequently and fully, depending on you to call me down if I err in this regard. All of my officers express the same feeling of gratification over your visit, and the encouragement they feel on account thereof. . . . We can and will accomplish more hereafter with your kindly support and encouragement.[19]

Dunn concluded his letter with a request for Sargent's photo and autograph. Inspector Bechtel in Honolulu also wrote to Sargent a year later. Despite a payroll that was three months late, he still asserted:

We wish you to understand chief, that although many leagues of land and a vast waste of ocean intervenes between this little office and the great Bureau in Washington over which you preside, yet we feel as near to you, and all that concerns you personally and the welfare of the service, as though we were nearer to the main office. We have a full sense, moreover, of your personal interest in us, of your proven friendship for us, and solicitude for all we do. With that feeling you have our earnest and conscientious desire to perform our responsible duties in such a manner as will reflect credit upon the Bureau and upon ourselves as men, and as officers of the Immigration Service.[20]

In 1906, Sargent could look back and claim:

There had never been such a complete and satisfactory enforcement of those laws before as was accomplished . . . up to about the first of June, 1905. By a system of close supervision over the officers in charge of districts and at ports of entry, calling them strictly to account for any, the least, dereliction of duty by themselves or their subordinates, and pointing out to them the proper methods of performing their duties, making investigations, and carrying out the various details connected with the enforcement of the law, the existing conditions were raised to a point bordering on the ideal.[21]

Sputtering Beginnings of Remote Control

One problem that remained unresolved in 1905 was the issuance and visa of section 6 certificates. Sargent mistrusted both Chinese officials and consuls abroad, recommending that either immigration officers be stationed in China or the procedure for identifying exempts be changed through new legislation.[22] Consular and diplomatic officials were equally scornful of the Bureau of Immigration. They thought immigration agents were crude and uneducated, wielding the exclusion law like a bludgeon, and that the law itself established absurd categories and excessive restrictions that worked against harmonious relations with China. An "exclusion" policy was particularly embarrassing in the face of the "Open Door" policy of free trade in China promoted by the State Department after 1899. Even Sargent conceded that "even though the consul is an officer of the highest integrity . . . his position is one of difficulty and embarrassment when it comes to deciding between the importance of these several duties laid upon him by the law."[23]

The State Department was also caught up in its own spirit of reform, albeit at a much slower pace than the Bureau of Immigration. Consular reform meant routinization, civil service exams, and closer surveillance over employees. Many reforms were spurred by allegations of consular corruption in Chinese migration issues. A 1903 congressional investigation of consulates in East Asia, driven largely by allegations of malfeasance in the issuing of Chinese visas, played a key role in getting the Consular Reform Bill passed in 1906.[24] This investigation also spurred a greater willingness to cooperate with the Bureau of Immigration to develop techniques for the "remote control" of migration.

China was the only place where U.S. consuls were required to issue immigration visas at the turn of the century. Proposals for consuls to inspect migrants before departure had been floated since at least 1832, when Consul Frederich List in Germany proposed that potential emigrants obtain testimonials about their criminal records for certifications by U.S. consuls.[25] Suggestions to expand consular involvement in migration became increasingly common after the 1880s. As journalist Broughton Brandenburg explained in 1904 after masquerading as an Italian emigrant partly to investigate the evasion of contract laws, "Only in the home town can the truth be learned and the proper discrimination made. Any other plan is fallacious."[26] Brandenburg proposed an itinerant immigration board under the supervision of the consul that granted visas in the villages. But few such proposals were adopted outside of China before 1917, other than the stationing of public health officers in a few countries (most of whom were recalled). Even the Immigration Restriction League opposed them, arguing consuls would be too unsupervised and depend on corrupt native clerks.[27] The Dillingham commission, which made an extensive investigation into all aspects of European immigration from 1907 to 1911, reported that consular inspections would add little to procedures currently used by foreign governments and steamship companies. It also worried about the international complications of enforcing U.S. laws abroad, especially in countries that did not want to encourage migration.[28]

U.S. consuls in Hong Kong, on the other hand, had enforced migration laws since 1862 when they assured that all passengers on departing U.S. ships departed voluntarily. They also enforced the Page Law against the immigration of prostitutes and Asian contract laborers from 1875 to 1882. They generally found these duties to be peripheral and even inimical to their primary responsibilities of protecting and promoting trade. When the first Chinese exclusion law of 1882 came into force, the State Department insisted that consuls had no authority to investigate the truth of passports or certificates issued by a foreign government. Thus in 1885 Consul Moseby in Hong Kong (who also depended primarily on surety bonds issued by the Tung Wah hospital to guarantee that a woman was not a prostitute) certified all section 6 documents issued by the local justice of the peace without even seeing the individuals to whom the documents referred. He insisted that he could only attest to the official character of that official and could not second-guess the contents of the document.[29] The Treasury Department insisted that consuls should check the accuracy of the certificates, but Minister Denby complained that this was "practically impossible of execution. . . . I do not see how a consul at a port can ever satisfy his conscience as to the truth of the facts that he must certify to officially on his own knowledge or on proof made before him."[30] Moseby's successor, Consul Robert Withers, added that genuine and false return certificates were bought and sold in Hong Kong and he had no power to stop it or to verify that certificates were in the hands of the rightful owners, especially as the sale of certificates was not even an offense under the laws of the colony.[31]

Issues surrounding section 6 certificates dwindled after 1888 in the face of a new determination to enforce the laws unilaterally from the United States. The government of Hong Kong continued to issue a few hundred every year to be given a perfunctory visa by U.S. consuls, the fate of which would be determined at U.S. ports. Both the consuls and the Hong Kong registrar general had come to appreciate the small but steady income this provided.[32] The Chinese government, committed to its program of self-restriction, was much less generous. In 1889 the Canton *hoppo* (superintendent of trade) refused the U.S. consul's request to issue certificates to three merchants, saying that authorization to issue such certificates had been revoked in 1883 at the request of the Chinese minister in Washington.[33] In March 1890 Minister Denby wrote to Secretary of State Blaine that he was reluctant to approach the Zongli Yamen on the issue of obtaining a section 6 certificate for a student because of recent tensions over the Scott Act and Denby's assumption that "Taking into consideration the peculiar language of China, its form of government, its immense population, the general ignorance of foreign law and customs, the requirements of the statute are almost impossible of performance."[34] After consultation with the secretary of the treasury, Blaine responded that the Shanghai *daotai* (circuit intendant who was concurrently superintendent of trade) could issue the certificate. The daotai set up a procedure that required the customs commissioner (an office manned by foreigners) to issue the original certificate and a wealthy sponsor to guarantee the applicant before the daotai would give his seal. Twenty-eight certificates were issued under these regulations by July 1891. Several were rejected at San Francisco, and accusations of consular corruption appeared in California newspapers and through official channels. After several rounds of recrimination, the basic problem turned out to be that the U.S. collector placed no faith in any certificate issued by the Chinese government. Consul J. A. Leonard in Shanghai responded that he was convinced of the thoroughness of examinations by Chinese officials and that he had no right, in any case, to openly contradict the documents they produced. He defended his own honor with the assertion that he had virtually no contact with the individual applicants and thus no opportunity to be bribed. As in 1883, the problem was resolved by a Chinese decision to stop issuing certificates.[35]

The issue would not die. In response to an 1896 inquiry from the Pacific Mail Steamship Company about authorizing an official in Canton to issue section 6 certificates, Denby reported that only four had been issued in China since 1883 (it appears he was referring only to those issued by the Zongli Yamen) and the Zongli Yamen was upset that they had been rejected in San Francisco. Minister Yang Ru consulted with the Treasury Department about acceptable documents and procedures and then proposed a system whereby a local daotai or superintendent of customs would make a preliminary investigation and issue a certificate. The applicant would then go to the local viceroy or prefect, as appropriate, who would sign the certificate after further investigation and pass the applicant on to the consul for a visa. Information about the bearer of the passport would also be forwarded to the Chinese consul or minister at his destination. These arrangements were put into place in Canton in September 1896 and in Fujian Province in April 1897.[36]

Translating Categories

Almost as soon as the new Chinese procedures were in place, newspapers and immigration officials in the United States accused consuls and local officials in China and Hong Kong of issuing certificates indiscriminately. Following up on a Treasury Department request for investigation, the State Department asked consuls to explain their methods of certification and required them to issue reports of visas issued for each departing ship—the first time that South China consuls had to report on routine work of any kind. The State Department also retreated from its earlier stance that identity documents produced by foreign governments could not be questioned, reassuring consuls that they were justified in refusing visas to candidates that did not seem satisfactory.[37] Attorney General Griggs's "true theory" increased pressure for consuls to make a positive identification of occupation rather than merely ascertain that they were not laborers.[38]

Although not accompanied by a formal statement of policy, this new attitude toward identity documents signaled a significant transformation in their usage. What had once been primarily a token of official responsibility for the bearer was now expected to accurately identify the status, occupation, and physical identity of a specific person to the satisfaction of a foreign government. The methods of identification, however, remained uncertain. It was very difficult to make these bureaucratically defined categories correspond to actual people in China. The Bureau of Immigration rarely acknowledged the difficulties and was happy to interpret the categories in any way that made admission more difficult. State Department officials were more troubled by the difficulties and contemptuous of absurd bureau categories and procedures. And the consuls were bitter that the final decision still rested with customs officers who could overturn their certification.

Consul Rounsevelle Wildman in Hong Kong responded to State Department inquiries and accusations of laxity by criticizing Bureau of Immigration definitions as unrealistic, expecting that merchants wear "silken robes." He described Hong Kong as a "vast warehouse" with 65 to 85 percent of the residents engaged in some kind of merchandising. The partners in these businesses were proprietors, workers, and laborers all in one, and nothing in the law stopped them from picking fruit once they arrived in California. He insisted that the registrar general issued certificates only to men who had been positively identified by district watchmen and required dubious cases to post an additional $500 bond. He added that even though he had no authority in law to deny a certificate issued by the registrar general he still checked each applicant carefully for the "marks of the coolie," which consisted primarily of shabby clothes and calluses on the shoulder from carrying poles and sedan chairs. Despite his defense of the registrar general, Wildman still claimed to deny over half of all visa applicants on the basis of this examination.[39] In a similar vein, Vice-Consul Hubbard Smith in Canton mocked the Treasury Department requirement that students be of "adult age." He wondered if this meant the legal age of majority in the United States, which was twenty-one, or in Chinese civil law, which was fourteen.[40]

Minister Denby published an extensive ridicule of the exempt categories in *The Forum* in 1902. By this time students had been redefined as those intending to pursue a branch of higher learning that could not be studied at home. Denby quipped that despite a centuries-long tradition of scholarship in China, "All China's knowledge of students had never taught her the real meaning of the word."[41] He also cited the new definition of "teacher" as

One who, for not less than two years next preceding his application for entry into the United States, has been continuously engaged in giving instruction in the higher branches of education, and who proves to the satisfaction of the appropriate Treasury officer that he is qualified to teach such higher branches, and has completed arrangements to teach in a recognized institution of learning in the United States, and intends to pursue no other occupation than teaching while in the United States.

In response, Denby remarked,

The examination of the teacher would be something like that of the colored applicant for a vote in the South who is required to expound the Constitution to an Election Board—it would hardly ever be satisfactory. . . . [In China, the teacher] belongs to the class of literati, but is among those who cannot get an official appointment. From the literati cometh the doctors, the *yamen* runners, and the teachers. If China knew anything at all she knew what a teacher was; but diplomatically speaking it is evident that she knew nothing. In the above definition we have clearly got the advantage of the heathen Chinee.[42]

Denby concluded that it was impossible for a consul to determine the true occupation of a section 6 applicant from the interior of China, and that such identification was necessarily lodged in the hands of Chinese officials. An attack on the integrity of those officials was beside the point. The problem lay in the U.S. regulations because "In no country would it be right to undertake to carry out a system of exclusion by putting all the machinery of its execution in the hands of foreign officials, whose interests might be directly opposed to the purposes in view."[43]

Chinese joined in the critique and proposed their own definitions of exempt categories. In 1906 the viceroy at Canton insisted that a student meant somebody who had passed the Chinese imperial exams.[44] That same year the U.S. consul general in Canton told Collector Henry McCoy in Manila that the decision to admit actors to the Philippines

is affording amusement to the Canton officials as well as Cantonese gentry, literati and merchants who watch with such keen interest every move of the American Government tending to modification of the provisions of the present Exclusion act. In the eyes of the Chinese, actors and barbers are the lowest in the scale of their civilization and are ineligible to take the civil examinations open to the other subjects of the Empire. . . . They express amazement at our willingness to admit Chinese actors, and at the same time exclude Chinese managers, cashiers, accountants, clerks, salesmen, buyers, bookkeepers, storekeepers, apprentices, agents, physicians, etc.[45]

The opinions of Chinese migrants themselves are hard to obtain given that their mobility was dependent on public demonstration of their adherence to official definitions. But at least one Chinese in Chicago, an individual named

Kong Sing, found the investigation to be ridiculous. When asked about the mercantile status of his relative Kong Gong, he reflected on the absurdity of the question itself:

Q: Did Kong Gong ever work in the store for one year continuously and engage in no other labor during that year?

A: Now, suppose I ask you what time you come to the office and what time you close, you cannot answer. When he worked in the store he worked in the store, and when he worked outside he worked outside.

Q: What did he do when he worked outside?

A: Now suppose I asked you this; you are working in the office, now you do Government work, but when you go home you do your own work. Now, how can I answer that question?

Q: You, then, can not state that Kong Gong was ever for one year at one time in your store continuously, all his time devoted to its business?

A: A Chinaman is employed at a time for one year or two years as white people are. Of course, when he is in the store a year he is in the store a year. When he is in the store two years he is in the store two years and . . .

Q: Can you answer that question yes or no?

A: Yes, for if I say no how can he be a merchant?[46]

Kong Sing may have made his point, but Kong Gong failed to attain merchant papers because of it.

Turf, Profit, and Blame

Debates over identification procedures also revolved around the more prosaic issues of jurisdictional turf and profit. When Consul Edward Bedloe arrived in Canton in early 1898, he circumvented Chinese officials by issuing section 6 certificates on his own initiative. In response to the hoppo's objections, Bedloe explained that the current system of issuing certificates through multiple Chinese officials caused delays of six to seven months and hindered commerce. To the State Department he also accused Chinese officials of issuing certificates wantonly, only interested in collecting the large fees. If the department wanted to counter criticisms from San Francisco, it is "of paramount importance that the Hoppo or other Chinese official authorized to grant permission to Chinese subjects to depart from China shall *not* decide as to who shall *enter the United States*; the corruption of Chinese officials being notorious."[47] When the State Department and Zongli Yamen both insisted that the hoppo must issue certificates, Bedloe encouraged the hoppo to propose to the Zongli Yamen that only the hoppo need issue the certificate without getting the viceroy or county-level officials involved. The Zongli Yamen briefly permitted this new plan until Viceroy Tan Zhonglin explained that even though the hoppo could start an investigation, his jurisdiction over trade was not sufficient to provide final certification, and that procedures should be uniform around the country.[48]

In the meantime, Bedloe had made an arrangement with the hoppo's secretary (with the hoppo's knowledge, claimed Bedloe's interpreter) that both Bedloe and the hoppo's office would accept initial applications for certificates. The application would then be passed to the other office for completion, from where the applicant would go to the viceroy for his signature and then back to the consul for the final visa. The original office of application would pass $50 of the fee on to the second office and be allowed to keep whatever else it could get from the applicant, up to a maximum of $90. After most of the applicants chose to approach the hoppo first, Bedloe broke the arrangement. At about this time, the hoppo asked the Zongli Yamen to request the U.S. minister to tell the consul to maintain proper procedure and stop issuing his own certificates. The hoppo claimed that embarrassing rejections at San Francisco could be avoided only if he was able to do a proper investigation.[49] On his part, Bedloe got the approval of Minister Denby to communicate directly with collector Jackson in San Francisco and share documentation. Citing the new difficulties of enforcing the "true theory" of exclusion, Bedloe arranged for section 6 certificates issued by the Chinese government to be accompanied by a certificate that he issued and sent under separate cover. This new procedure almost guaranteed admission and caused a rush in Canton to obtain Bedloe's certificates, which he issued at $180 each, and $165 for friends. The consular interpreter later claimed that so many were issued and resold that "A regular quotation of the market price was reported every day in Hong Kong and Canton."[50]

An investigation by Shanghai Consul John Goodnow (who would himself become an object of investigation in 1903) resulted in Bedloe's suspension, restoration of the original procedure, and reduction of the visa fee to one dollar.[51] The State Department was much more disturbed by Bedloe's use of his office to enrich himself and to engage in private negotiations with Chinese officials than by failures to appropriately identify the Chinese. But the department still left consuls to their own devices in developing procedures. It engaged in erratic surveillance of immigration practices over the next five years, generally in response to specific complaints.[52] Consuls in Hong Kong emerged from these investigations with their reputations largely intact, adeptly diverting the blame to others. Wildman used the tried and true technique of blaming the inherently corrupt Chinese and asserting that certificates with his visa "have been as nearly honest as it is possible for Europeans to make it when dealing with Chinese."[53] During a scandal in 1904, Consul Edward Bragg aimed his blame on the exclusion laws themselves for undermining treaties and delegating final decisions to rigid and prejudiced immigration agents who were "selected from a class who may be well qualified for good constables under the public eye and within the control of the courts, but whom no one would think of entrusting, at the remote points where they are on duty without the constraint of well regulated society, even determining Treaty rights, with a judgement, so protected by the semblance of law, as to be substantially final."[54] Despite Bragg's characterization, the Bureau of Immigration was actually more successful than the State Department in disciplining its employees. The State Department found it difficult to exert control over its own officials in distant lands and was reluctant to infringe on the jurisdictions of foreign countries. Chinese brokers flourished in the gaps between these jurisdictions.

The Commerce Protection Bureaus

Correspondence between Chinese and American officials referred to immigration documents as if only government officials processed them. But private entrepreneurs were involved in nearly every aspect of migration in China. The line between corrupt collaboration and honest official activity was not yet drawn in issues of migrant identification, and these entrepreneurs flourished as businessmen, semi-official organizations, and even officials and consuls themselves. Like the Bureau of Immigration and the State Department, the Chinese government was also engaged in administrative reform at the turn of the century. But Chinese attempts to reform their system of migrant identification relied heavily on official collaboration with private organizations rather than the suppression of that collaboration.[55] The resulting overlap of private and official interests led only to recriminations, abuses, and a series of corruption investigations that were simultaneous with the State Department inquiries. Each government tried to pin the blame on errant individuals within its own administration. But the Chinese reliance on private enforcement helped the U.S. investigations additionally to blame all of Chinese officialdom and society as congenitally corrupt.

As seen in its willingness to sign the Gresham-Yang Treaty, the Chinese government had developed a growing interest in the protection and regulation of overseas migration other than contract labor since 1893. That year Minister Xue Fucheng in London wrote his famous memorial calling for Beijing to better protect its subjects abroad by dispatching consuls, issuing passports, and spreading information about Chinese laws and official attitudes. In its memorial endorsing Xue's proposal, the Zongli Yamen also commented on the importance of protecting returned migrants. "No matter how long [overseas Chinese] have lived abroad or if they are married and have kids, they should all be allowed to obtain passports from diplomatic officials abroad and return home. Their livelihood and occupations should be governed under the same laws as people in China, and if they continue to do business abroad they should not be subjected to extortionate demands like before, and offenders should be punished according to law."[56]

The Qing government formally repealed its anti-emigration laws in September 1893 and stated its intention to protect overseas migrants. Other than a few exhortations and a failed attempt to issue passports to returning emigrants by the Chinese consul in Singapore, this new policy generated few practical changes before 1899.[57] That year, in response to migration difficulties caused by the U.S. occupation and imposition of exclusion in Manila, several local gentry (*shendong*) in Amoy gained the cooperation of Viceroy Xu Yingkui to establish a gentry-run organization called the Baoshangju (Commerce Protection Bureau).[58] Xu obtained an imperial edict permitting its activities, which included the protection of returned overseas merchants from the exploitation of port officials and hoodlums, and the provision of documentation required to enter Manila. The success of the Baoshangju soon led to an imperial edict for the establishment of similar organizations in other emigrant ports. In addition to the duties undertaken by the Amoy Baoshangju, these bureaus were to contact with Chinese consuls and emigrant associations abroad to help repatriate emigrants who had been kidnapped or deceived.[59] In 1900 Canton Viceroy De Shou reported that the local Baoshangju would support itself through the contributions of migrants. It would also take up the additional duties of prohibiting women and children to board ships without its passports, and of sending blank passports to leading Chinese associations around the Pacific for use by returning migrants. Upon return to Canton, the document would be presented to the Baoshangju so that it could better monitor abuses, collect fees, and distribute benefits. De Shou also recommended that the director of the Baoshangju be granted official rank.[60] In 1900 the Amoy daotai even asked the U.S. consul to cooperate with the Baoshangju to promote the use of passports and registration by returned migrants so that the government could use fees to protect foreign trade in the interior.[61]

An edict of March 23, 1903, reaffirmed the imperial commitment to extending sympathy to Chinese abroad and protecting them from extortion upon their return as a means to promote commerce, loyalty, and investment. This confirmation was part of a broader project of creating chambers of commerce and permitting greater involvement of merchant gentry in local governance.[62] The need for a new edict specifically protecting migration, however, reflected the fact that extortion had only adapted in conjunction with the new structures of surveillance. Responding to complaints from overseas merchants, the newly formed Board of Agriculture and Commerce investigated the Amoy Baoshangju in 1903. The investigators concluded that the gentry who had established the original bureau had turned the management over to hooligans and disreputable types. It now charged exorbitant fees for travel documents to Manila that were often ineffective, extorted fees from returning migrants, did not hold general elections, wasted money, and provided no useful services.[63]

The investigators reorganized the bureau as the Shangzhengju (Commercial Administration Bureau) but left the same shadowy characters in charge. Board of Commerce official Wang Qingmu was dispatched for a new investigation in 1905. He consulted with local merchant-gentry who told him of the effectiveness the Baoshangju five years earlier. Wang was fully aware of the checkered history of the Baoshangju but wanted to find a way to simultaneously support Qing policies to promote commercial organization, attract and protect the investments of overseas merchants, and support local "self-rule" organizations as a critical aspect of reform. After careful reflection, he decided that the best way to attain all of these goals was to reorganize the Shangzhengju into a Chamber of Commerce (Shangwu Zongju) under the leadership of the original founders of the Baoshangju.[64] The fate of the Chamber was no better than that of the earlier organizations, having essentially restored power from one faction of brokers to another. When the Chamber became a leader in the anti-American boycott of 1905, Minister William Rockhill took a firm stance against it by insisting to the Zongli Yamen that it was the responsibility of Chinese officials and not a merchant organization to investigate claims made on passports.[65]

The responsibility of protecting overseas merchants was also extended to Chinese consuls abroad, again resulting in conflict and corruption. By 1902 Chinese in Manila, San Francisco, and Honolulu had accused local consuls of a variety of offenses ranging from misuse of relief funds and extortion to sexual immorality.[66] Like the U.S. consuls in China, many Chinese consuls had very close relations with the business community. In Manila father and son Carlos and Engracio Palanca (Chen Qianshan and Chen Gang) each briefly served as consuls in 1899 and 1900 and had organized a system of registration and passport fees in conjunction with the Baoshangju. They were prominent local merchants, and Carlos had previously been gobernadorcillo de los Sangleyes (governor of the Chinese) under the Spanish. They were widely accused of supporting factional interests during their tenure, and both were dismissed from their position under U.S. pressure. But they also succeeded in having the Zongli Yamen dismiss Consul Li Rongyao in 1900, a Cantonese who likely had ties with an opposing faction. Engracio Palanca would retain his semi-official involvement in migration, later becoming one of the gentry who convinced Wang Qingmu to reorganize the Baoshangju in 1905 and playing a prominent role in the boycott.[67]

Honolulu Consul Yang Weibin was appointed directly from China, but local Chinese still criticized him for using his office for personal gain and political retribution. They accused him of increasing the price of certifying documents for migrants planning a trip to China and demanding registration of all Chinese in Hawaii as a way to monitor their loyalty (the reformist Emperor Protection Society led by exiles Kang Youwei and Liang Qichao had gained many adherents in Hawaii). Minister Wu Tingfang dispatched his charge d'affaires Shen Tong to investigate the San Francisco and Honolulu consuls in 1902.[68] Shen exonerated them by blaming the attacks on political subversives, but both were still removed from their positions on the pretext of their having embarrassed the government in the eyes of foreigners and failing to develop harmonious relations with migrant elites. As Shen explained, the task now "is to give moderate and discriminating guidance to the confused common people, to gain anew the trust of those who have been victimized and alienated, and extend love and protection that produces sincere feelings of mutual trust. This will make it easy for people to change their feelings, to listen and not be confused, so that heterodoxy will disappear of its own accord."[69] He also made more practical suggestions about limiting fees and canceling the registrations. But he did not propose a systemic disentanglement of merchant organizations, consular duties, and immigration matters, even praising the extent to which the United Chinese Society in Honolulu had handled immigration matters in the past.

Private Identification

The U.S. State Department did not promote the use of private organizations to identify and monitor migrants. But it was unsure how to respond when entrepreneurs found ways to insert themselves. In 1903, Charles Richardson and a group of lawyers and customs brokers based in Amoy and Manila formed "a partnership for the procuring, from the proper authorities in the district of Amoy, China, certificates for Chinese merchants and exempt classes, which will enable them to proceed to the Philippine Islands and apply for admission."[70] They offered Chinese who used their certificates a money-back guarantee that they would be admitted to Manila. They claimed that the Amoy daotai (who later said he knew nothing of Richardson) agreed to issue certificates for a fee of $45 only to applicants who were forwarded by the partnership or by missionaries. As Richardson told William Taft, who had been asked to investigate him in during his visit to the Philippines that November, "this has been considered a legal business since the exclusion act of 1881 [sic]."[71] He explained that the daotai, consul, and Manila collector were still free to refuse any certificates that they put forward. Any coaching that they gave to applicants was no different from what law firms and missionaries had long been doing.

Vice-Consul Carl Johnson was somewhat uneasy about the arrangements. He resented the pressure from Richardson to visa all applicants, although it remained unclear whether he ever accepted any money beyond the nominal official fees. When Richardson tried to expand his operation to Canton, he found it much easier to deal with Consul-General Robert McWade. Richardson then threatened Johnson:

> I have discussed these questions of vise thoroughly with Mr. McWade, and you are quite too particular, and without cause. You cannot set up an arbitrary ruling from your own judgment. The law says you must investigate, but the only investigation you can do is to have a set of questions to ask the men, and if his testimony is correct you are bound to vise. In

fact, the Canton C. G. told me that if the hoppo sent him a dispatch with a certificate and the man answered the questions set forth in the passport that he would always vise. He said it was a matter of treaty right, and for trade and other interests he would not refuse. . . . I will have the taotai write you an official dispatch covering each certificate, and, if the party is turned down, will have the taotai ask for a reason. On your answer I will have him protest, and, armed with the protest and data, I will appeal to the consul-general at Canton.[72]

Despite the favorable beginnings with McWade, Chinese brokers in Canton ultimately proved too competitive. In Richardson's words, "The Cantonese are so damned smart and know what their rights are so well that it presents many difficulties over Amoy."[73] The hoppo would not agree to collaborate with Richardson, and competition drove prices for certificates down from $250 to $125. McWade also felt compelled to visa certificates presented by competitors, "so long as parties answer correctly," in order to "maintain good relations so inside trade relations will not be hampered."[74] McWade and Richardson tried several schemes to undercut their competitors. McWade hung a placard in Chinese in the consulate listing the official fees and asking to be notified of any broker who charged more so that he could proceed against him.[75] He and Richardson also had the consular clerk fill in certificates presented by competitors incorrectly so that they would be rejected at Manila, but they found that the certificates had been corrected by the time they arrived in the Philippines. They also drew upon the example of technical rules used in San Francisco to encourage the Manila collector to require the Chinese and English versions of section 6 certificates to be exactly the same. They even suggested that the State Department require fingerprints rather than photographs because "five out of every ten Chinamen look alike."[76] None of these schemes succeeded in undermining the competition. Richardson and McWade soon fell out with each other, and McWade began to persecute Richardson for using his name as a front for Chinese to transport goods into the interior under the foreigners' tax exemption.

Officials in Manila and Washington were very uncomfortable with these activities but could find no ground for prosecution. McWade was dismissed from his post after the 1903 consular investigation on charges of drunkenness, employing a clerk convicted of larceny, illegal fees, extending protection to noncitizen Chinese, interfering with the Chinese government, and, ironically, conspiring against American citizen Charles Richardson. Inappropriate methods of identification was not among the charges.[77] Vice-Consul Johnson resigned of his own accord, and the consulate was destroyed by fire so that no evidence could be accumulated to make charges against him.[78] Richardson was never formally charged. His confederates John Miller and J. V. Ballantine were found not guilty in a Manila court in early 1904. The attorney general's office reported that the coaching of applicants seemed like an intent to defraud, but nobody could prove that any money was given to Chinese or U.S. officials. Even if an exchange of money was discovered, it could still be explained as fees for the investigation, which was a matter of departmental discipline rather than law.[79]

Richardson, McWade, and Engracio Palanca all had reputations as noted philanthropists and upstanding citizens. To judge their activities as corrupt is to enforce a perspective from hindsight, after the government had asserted a monopoly over the right to identify migrants and drawn a firm distinction against private interests. At the time, many (but not all) of these men had strong local reputations, often built precisely on their skills in managing the multiple jurisdictions presented by migration and extraterritoriality on the South China coast.[80] Men who engaged in these activities but survived investigations with their reputations intact are hard to identify because their very success in remaining respectable depended on their skill in redirecting accusations. The play of accusation and counter-accusation in these investigations was the very site where legitimate and illegitimate relationships, institutions and procedures were defined. As we shall see, the U.S. government ultimately gained the upper hand in clarifying jurisdictions, suppressing private organizations, and monopolizing the power to identify. This was an important step in establishing government control of the border as the main site of migration regulation. The attempts of the Chinese government, on the other hand, to develop regulatory institutions in formal collaboration with merchants would ultimately lead to their losing credibility and initiative in matters of identification.

9

The American Formula, 1905–1913

In late 1903 Consul McWade in Canton described the procedure by which he granted visas to section 6 applicants. A potential migrant would tell his village elders that he wanted to go to the United States. They would draw up a document testifying that he had been a merchant for three years with capital of at least five thousand Mexican dollars and introduce him to a banker who would post a bond guaranteeing the truth of the certificate. The migrant and the banker would then visit the hoppo's office, where a clerk would investigate his business and the validity of the bond and fill out an unsigned section 6 certificate for him. The banker would then accompany the migrant to see McWade, who would interrogate, fingerprint, and strip the migrant to check his health and search for "signs of the 'coolie' class." If satisfied, McWade would send him back to the hoppo with a note that he had been "passed by me." The hoppo would then ascertain that the individual was not involved in revolutionary activities, take a hundred-dollar application fee, and sign the certificate. McWade would then accept another bond for five hundred dollars to be turned over to charity if the statements were false and would stamp a visa on the certificate. McWade insisted that he only accepted applicants introduced by two bankers who were well-known to him.[1]

McWade allowed Chinese networks to identify merchants for him. He felt no reason to hide this procedure. How else were identities produced if not through social relationships? What better way to guarantee an identity than by staking one's wealth and getting the recommendations of well-established men? McWade was not reprimanded for this procedure, but an official corruption investigation revealed the extent to which his migration activities were entwined with other offenses. From the perspective of Washington officials, as long as the identification of migrants was rooted in Chinese social and business networks, the financial and diplomatic integrity of the consular office was in peril. But how else could the identities of people over whom the U.S. government had no power be documented? And how could local identities be translated into the terms of immigration regulations?

Solutions to these problems were compelled by consular scandals and the 1905 anti-American boycott in China. The Bureau of Immigration reforms became the model for State Department reform. Originally designed to keep Chinese out, these reforms were now put in the service of accountability and predictability. The ability to point to specific procedures was an effective defense against outside criticism and constructed a firm line between legitimate official identification procedures and corrupt private interests. Cross-referencing, monthly reports in triplicate, and carefully defined categories built a structure of surveillance over both the Chinese migrants and the officials who dealt with them. To be properly identified, migrants had to be torn out of their social networks and evaluated as individuals placed face to face with a government agent, free from the meddling of brokers and middlemen. The true identity of a migrant could only be known directly through his body and bearing, his mode of speaking, his expression, the condition of his hands, his gait, all the way down to the amount of dirt under his fingernails and calluses on his feet. These signs were then translated into standardized immigration categories through the collection and production of extensive documentation. Uniformity of decisions was now the goal, using the procedures of bureaucratic decision making to give meaning and order to the impressions of the agent on the ground. A new identity was created for the migrant and fixed in a matrix of cross-referenced files, forcing the migrant to constantly reproduce himself in the terms of those files. In the case of any discrepancy, the files were right and the migrant wrong.

Proceduralization obscured the political and racist origins of Chinese exclusion and recast it as the impartial administration of law. Migration brokers and networks were stigmatized as unscrupulous smugglers, hustlers, and commercially "interested" parties. The same people whom McWade had once treated as the guarantors of identity were demonized as incorrigibly corrupt and unreliable. This easily expanded into blaming the Chinese themselves by depicting brokerage activities as the natural result of "clannish" Chinese society and corrupt Chinese officials. In Frank Sargent's words, "No matter how trustworthy and honorable a Chinese merchant or laborer may be in the conduct of his daily business, he seems to have no compunction whatever in practicing deceit concerning matters in which the Government is interested."[2] Thus the very process of transforming migration control into a technical problem also cast it as a contest of cultures, the natural result of a rationalized administration coming up against the impenetrable schemes of an uncivilized people. If Chinese ran afoul of the law, it was only a result of their own immorality and failure to be self-willed individuals who submitted themselves to the rule of law. The very organization of Chinese migration was essentially illegalized.

Boycott and Presidential Intervention

Complaints against the new exclusion reforms accumulated rapidly after the turn of the century. Several high-profile cases received extensive media publicity in the U.S. and Chinese press: Chinese delegates to the 1904 St. Louis World's Fair were subject to excessive restraints; several diplomatic officials were harassed, one resulting in suicide; two students sponsored by missionaries to study at Oberlin College were delayed for a year and a half; and the Chinatowns of New York and Boston were subject to raids and mass arrests in 1902 and 1903. Chinese and their sympathizers, such as the businessmen of the Asiatic Association, openly attacked the Bureau of Immigration in pamphlets, newspaper articles, and petitions to U.S. and Chinese officials. This groundswell encouraged the Chinese government to denounce the Gresham-Yang Treaty in early 1904 before it came up for renewal in December and demand that a more equitable treaty be negotiated. Negotiations dragged. In the meantime an appropriations bill passed in April 1904 containing riders that forbade noncitizen Chinese who resided in the insular possessions from traveling to the mainland, extended exclusion indefinitely, and clarified that domestic legislation could not be altered by treaty stipulations.[3]

Retaliatory boycotts against U.S. goods had been proposed in the Chinese press around the world since at least 1903. On May 10, 1905, the Shanghai Chamber of Commerce resolved that unless certain reforms in the exclusion law and treaties were made, a boycott against American goods would begin on July 20. The boycott lasted until the beginning of 1906 but was unsuccessful in prompting new legislation or treaties. It did, however, generate significant shifts in the administration of the law. President Theodore Roosevelt and most members of his cabinet grew nervous thinking about how a boycott could affect strategic interests in China and the Pacific. They pressured immigration officials for a more relaxed enforcement of the law. As early as May 19, Sargent issued a circular telling immigration agents to give all possible consideration to exempts so as to prevent just cause for complaint: "To state my desire in a few words, it is that the administration of the law shall, just as far as a proper enforcement of its terms and existing circumstances will permit, be stripped of all harshness of word or action."[4]

By the middle of June, Roosevelt and other cabinet members demanded more than just courtesy: entirely new regulations that were "sufficiently drastic to prevent the continuance of the very oppressive conduct of many of our officials."[5] Sargent and Secretary of Commerce and Labor Victor Metcalf resisted, insisting that the complaints were only a symptom of efficient enforcement. Sargent later explained that any harshness or inconvenience caused by enforcement was the result, "not of the injustice or inhumanity of the officers, but of the failure of the Chinese themselves to comply with the provisions of the law."[6] Roosevelt prevailed, and on June 24 the Department of Commerce and Labor issued a circular that stated, "The purpose of the Chinese exclusion laws is to prevent the immigration of Chinese laborers and not to restrict the freedom of movement of Chinese. . . . Any harshness in the administration of the Chinese exclusion laws will not for one moment be tolerated, and any discourtesy shown Chinese persons . . . by any of the officials of this Department will be cause for immediate dismissal of the offender from the service."[7]

The State Department issued a similar circular on June 26. In his address to Congress in December, President Roosevelt emphasized the need to revise the laws and treaties pertaining to exclusion and shift more of the examinations to China before departure. A bill was even presented to Congress the next January, jointly written by the Asiatic Association and State Department, that would have made all section 6 certificates with proper visas irrefutable at U.S. ports of entry and reversed the "true theory" by admitting all Chinese except laborers.[8]

The June circular listed no specific reforms, but by February 5, 1906, the Bureau of Immigration issued new regulations that included broader definitions of students and other exempt categories, lengthened the time for appeal, specified kinds of evidence that could be presented, allowed attorneys and the Chinese consul to examine and copy testimony, and allowed resident merchants to take out certificates that would facilitate their return. In addition, Bertillon measurements were stopped, plans for a census and new registration were canceled, and an investigation of immigration agents was to start later that month. Metcalf was transferred to the Navy Department in December and replaced by the much more pro-Asian and pro-immigrant Oscar Straus.[9] The Department of Commerce and Labor increasingly sustained appeals from adverse immigration decisions. It especially insisted that for Chinese who had lived in the country for several years, doubts should be resolved in their favor.[10] In 1907 Straus (with the Japanese also in mind) explained the new attitude:

> The real purpose of the government's policy is to exclude a particular and well-defined class, leaving other classes of Chinese . . . as free to come and go as the citizens or subjects of any other nation. As the laws are framed, however, it would appear that the purpose was rigidly to exclude persons of the Chinese race in general and to admit only such persons of the race as fall within certain expressly stated exemptions—as if, in other words, exclusion was the rule and admission the exception. I regard this feature of the present laws as unnecessary and fraught with irritating consequences. It is needless to point out that discriminations on account of race, color, previous condition or religion are alike opposed to the principles of the republic and to the spirit of its institutions.[11]

Similar phrases would soon be repeated all down the chain of command, confirming the rights of certain Chinese to travel without harassment. Uniformity in public relations became as important as uniform bureaucratic practice. Even though framed as the unilateral generosity of American principles, the boycott and diplomatic and public pressure had mitigated the insistence on sovereign prerogative in migration control, if only to a very limited extent.

On the Defensive

Sargent presented an extensive defense of his policies to Congress in 1906. He blamed any actual harshness on Chinese who did not understand or evaded the law and consular officials who did not administer it properly. He insisted that "The majority of complaints which have been made . . . have been of a general character, and it has been impossible to obtain from the complainants a citation of any specific instances upon which such general complaints were supposed to be based. Matters of this kind of course permit of only a general and comprehensive denial, springing from a knowledge of the Bureau's own policy and efforts toward an efficient but just administration of the laws."[12] This was a strategy that the Bureau would use to great effect in coming years: moving the grounds of contention to the realm of specific procedure where few people had the ability to challenge the Bureau in its knowledge of on-the-ground practice in the context of complex legal requirements. Sargent went on to respond to twenty-four specific charges by showing that the subjects had been given more lenient treatment than required by the letter of the law, that erroneous initial decisions were reversed on appeal, that officers in the wrong had been corrected, that the law itself was written in such a way as to require actions that appeared harsh, or that the initial charges had been frivolous. He blamed the negative image of the bureau on a sensationalistic press and the influence of missionaries and capitalists who wanted to bring cheap labor to the South and "who repeat their charges with such frequent repetition as may serve to invest falsehood with a semblance of truth."[13] He dismissed such criticism out of hand, as "so little governed by patriotic respect for lawful authority as seemingly to justify these free thinkers . . . in making or applauding active resistance to the laws and its executive officers."[14]

The attorney general decided that Sargent had successfully defended himself, and he was spared any official reprimand.[15] But the bureau was still compelled to relent in its practice of enforcing the letter of the law as strictly as possible. Victor Safford, chief medical examiner at Ellis Island, claimed that after June 1905, Sargent was "brutally pushed aside so far as even an opportunity to express an official opinion in matters affecting the administration of the law was concerned." He claimed that immigration officers grew increasingly demoralized when Sargent and others overturned their decisions, and that Sargent himself grew despondent and ill, leading to his death in 1908.[16] While Safford's account is doubtless overdramatized, a change in enforcement style is apparent in the day-to-day records of Chinese investigations. The machinery of the reforms was maintained, but now largely used in the service of predictability. The interviews became much more formulaic, field investigations declined, and fewer applicants were denied. The discretion of immigration agents was subsumed under procedure and paper trails.

In Philadelphia, for example, the quality of investigation into claims of property and debt to qualify for laborer return certificates had been extremely low in 1899 before the reforms.[17] Officers did little more than collect affidavits. By 1903 the officers made extensive inquiries into all applications, collected corroborating testimony, and traveled personally to estimate the value of various laundries. In 1904 they started a filing card system and received systematic reports on the disposition of cases in New York. Agents repeatedly contested Chinese self-estimates of the value of their property and debts and checked to see if the property and debts still existed when they returned. They would reject Chinese applications on the basis of a hesitating manner during the interview, for seeming to recite their answers, or for seeming either too thrifty or too wealthy to borrow money for the claimed debt.[18] Favorable decisions were reported in a way that drew attention to the extensive investigation: "As will be seen by a comparison of the sworn statements of the witnesses, the facts stated by the applicant are fully corroborated, in every instance, and it therefore appears that the necessary qualifications of claims of unascertained and unsettled debts are complied with and that the applicant is entitled to readmission."[19]

In the second half of 1905, after the departmental orders for courtesy, the summaries of positive investigations were laced with cynicism: "The testimony of the applicant and the witnesses agrees in nearly every particular, and although the debts in this, as in many other cases of like nature, seem improbable . . . the statements of the applicant have all been verbally corroborated by the witnesses."[20] Applications for return certificates rose in October, and investigations became increasingly minimal and formulaic. By 1906, investigators around the country had developed a number of routine formulations, such as "I consider that the usual showing has been made in this character of cases," or "In the absence of means to discredit their statements I am constrained to commend the applicant to the favorable consideration," and most commonly, "Statements regarding loan are in accord."[21]

The main concern of many officers by this time was to assure that files were uniform and systematic. As the Philadelphia commissioner of immigration advised the new commissioner in Baltimore in 1906, "It is my earnest desire to have all investigations, conducted by the various Inspectors of the District, in as nearly a uniform manner as possible, and that said investigations be thorough and complete, so that after the report has been concurred in by this office and transmitted to the proper port of entry, it will be accepted as final by the Officer in Charge at that port, and not be returned for further information."[22] Knowledge was increasingly located in files and prepared testimony rather than the experience of agents on the ground. Such facts had to be generated through a predictable method that allowed for ready cross-filing and sharing of information.

Remote Control Established

The State Department was especially embarrassed by the boycott of 1905 because of its own commitment to the Open Door policy in China. Like the Bureau of Immigration, it responded with bureaucratic systematization as a way to avoid criticism. In contrast to the Bureau of Immigration, however, the routinization of consular procedure meant greater rigor in immigration matters rather than restraint of zealous officials. The clarification of official and private realms in the regulation of migration was an indispensable aspect of this routinization. The responsibilities of consuls were made clear and separate from the activities of private brokers, and the admissibility of migrants was to be determined only in terms of the official definitions of identity.

In its circular of June 26, 1905, the State Department repeated the warnings against harsh enforcement from the Bureau of Immigration circular two days earlier. After remarking on recklessness by both Chinese officials and U.S. consuls in producing certificates, it added:

> The purpose of this government is to make these visaed certificates of such real value that it is safe to accept them here in the United States. This will result in doing away with most of the causes of complaint that have arisen. . . . But in order that this plan may be carried out it is absolutely necessary that the diplomatic and consular officers, instead of treating their work in visaing these certificates as perfunctory, shall understand that this is one of their most important functions. They must not issue any such certificates unless they are certain that the person to whom it is issued is entitled to it and they will be held to a most rigid accountability for the manner in which they perform this duty.[23]

In November the State Department asked its consuls in China to describe their visa procedures in detail and brought them up to date on Bureau of Immigration regulations. The State Department digested the consuls' responses into a set of instructions on March 26, 1907, that explicitly laid out the duties of the consuls in the issuance of section 6 certificates.[24] The very act of inquiring about existing practices had already led the consuls to be more careful in their procedures. They passed copies of the regulations on to Chinese officials and increasingly requested specific instructions from the department on how to interpret Bureau of Immigration rules.[25]

Continuing events and the initiative of local consuls made Amoy particularly important in the formulation of new procedures, including the discipline of Chinese officials to conform to U.S. reforms. As early as May 1905, Consul George Anderson described stricter measures he had undertaken to exclude Manila lawyers from the section 6 process, explaining that, "In view of the more or less extensive reputation Consulates hereabouts have had for looseness in such matters in the past, I am especially anxious to have these matters placed upon a strictly legal basis, known of all men."[26] In October he asked that section 6 certificates with his visa be considered definitive in Manila, so as to avoid the embarrassment and inconvenience of rejection. He noted that the Chinese "resent being given papers which seem to entitle them to admission and then to be refused admission after reaching American shores."[27] In March 1906 Vice Consul Stuart Lupton obtained an order of twenty-five bamboo lashes from the local mixed court for two migration brokers who had attempted to bribe his interpreter, reporting that "It is hoped that by this measure we will be able to get rid of the evil which seems to obtain in the Orient."[28] In April Lupton told the daotai that no more certificates would be accepted that had been issued through the Amoy Chamber of Commerce (although the Chamber of Commerce continued to require that local emigrant boarding houses only accept migrants with papers that it had stamped or issued).[29]

Events surrounding the Bo An Surety Company were key in the formulation of the 1907 departmental instructions. In November 1906 Amoy Vice Consul Rea Hanna reported that Consul Samuel Gracey in Fuzhou (the capital of Fujian province) was granting visas to section 6 certificates that Hanna had earlier rejected. Hanna claimed that these applicants were trained and represented by a surety company, the ultimate object of which was "extortion and bribery."[30] A month later, Hung Chao Hsun walked through the front door of the Amoy consulate, showed Hanna a copy of the Bo An regulations, and proposed to establish a similar company in Amoy. Hung told Hanna that Bo An founder Li Cheng had approached the tartar general of Fuzhou in late 1905 with a petition that stated, "We understand that the number of people entering [Manila] increases each year, and it is a pity that some persons not having any craft also devised means to enter that port and they have often committed crimes, etc. This is a disgrace to our nation. For this reason, the Government of Manila has begun to exclude Chinese of the inferior class. It is understood that our Government is to blame for allowing them to go instead of strictly cautioning them."[31]

As a way to assure that U.S. regulations concerning migration to Manila did not grow even stricter and further hinder legitimate travelers, Li had offered to form the Bo An Company to guarantee that all section 6 certificates were issued only to men with good reputation and reliable recommendations. The Fuzhou superintendent of customs said the proposal was a "convenient arrangement designed to discover unworthy classes" and promised to consider no applications not accompanied by a Bo An representative. The tartar general forwarded the proposal to Consul Gracey, who suggested a few changes in the regulations to standardize fees, make the company more responsible for false claims, and make it clear that the company guarantee was not conclusive and that migrants would still be subject to investigation by U.S. officials. The company had rewritten its by-laws accordingly, and Chinese officials all the way to Beijing were now in the process of approving the proposed arrangements.[32]

Hanna's immediate reaction was to tell Hung that his plan was impractical because it was impossible to monitor the status of migrants after they arrived in the Philippines, that brokers were an unnecessary expense for the migrants, and that "any company, whose life depends on the number of Chinese it may be able to introduce to the Philippine Islands, and whose avowed purpose is such introduction, can only be viewed with suspicion by this Consulate."[33] As he learned of the attitude of the local Chinese officials, however, Hanna doubted his original position and decided that the procedures they used were not his concern so long as he was allowed to engage in his own independent examinations. Indeed, the custom of having merchants put up guarantees for potential emigrants as a way to assure their loyal behavior was a long-standing practice on the southeast coast.[34] The consuls could also understand these arrangements as part of the civilizing process. As Consul Gracey later wrote in justification of his actions, "China in its waking up was taking on many foreign things, and as Guarantee Companies had proven to be very good in America I believed they might not be all bad in China."[35]

Hanna's superiors were surer of themselves. Minister Rockhill immediately wrote to the Waiwubu to say that his having learned that a Chinese official had delegated the proper investigation of section 6 certificates to a commercial organization "destroys the confidence of my Government in the reliability of the statements made in the certificates granted by the said Viceroy. Suspicion is cast upon all such certificates, and this may work hardship to persons properly qualified to enter the United States." He went on to assert "that the motives of the company are wholly mercenary, that it is altogether untrustworthy, and that it ought to be suppressed."[36] The company stopped business in January 1907, although section 6 papers with its chop continued to appear in Manila for months.

In March the State Department praised Hanna for his "repressive attitude (towards) promoters seeking to establish a company designed to intervene in and make money out of the issuance of section six certificates."[37] It also criticized Gracey for allowing bonds to take the place of "scrupulous investigation," reminding him that bonding is a "useless if not objectionable practice."[38] Gracey was chastened and said, "I have now most thoroughly changed my mind, and believe [Bo An's] chief purpose to be 'graft,' and its regulations only fine spun theories."[39] He continued, however, to defend his techniques of investigation as more appropriate to Chinese mentality than the rude and direct questions demanded by Manila customs officers:

> We, of the West, have been taught to believe that the more direct a question is, the easier it is to comprehend and answer, but this is not in accord with the mental operation of most Chinese. He never goes in a straight line in anything. He never gives at first what he intends to have regarded as his final answer, there must be several other questions and much discussion. . . . Under Western bluntness, directness, positiveness, and suspicious tone, he becomes embarrassed and impossible, and only answers to his own hurt. He can't help it, and we think he is prevaricating.[40]

He added that the practice in Manila of testing merchants by having them do calculations with pencil and paper was also absurd for men who relied only on an abacus.

The State Department instructions of March 26, however, were more interested in systemic procedures than cultural sensitivity. The instructions affirmed that applications accompanied by any middlemen or "interested parties" should be treated with suspicion, and that the responsibility for investigation "can be shifted neither by confidence in the authorities issuing the certificates, who may or may not be thorough in their investigations or undeceived in their findings, nor by a delegation of the work of investigation to a subordinate."[41] The instructions went on to carefully define merchants, students, and travelers in the narrow senses preferred by the Bureau of Immigration. They also described a standard report form for each investigation and ordered that multiple copies be shared with ports in China and the United States.

A Failed Crackdown

The obsession with files and procedures was not only an urge to extend the embrace of the state. It was encouraged by almost everybody who took an interest in the exclusion laws. Both critics and supporters of the exclusion laws promoted the need for predictable methods, formal categories, and due process. Supreme Court decisions in *Ju Toy* and *Chin Yow* had made the failure to follow due procedure the only cause for judicial intervention into Bureau of Immigration decisions. For the State Department, procedure was to be the foundation of institutional discipline, limiting interference by unscrupulous parties and establishing harmonious relationships with other departments and nations. Similarly, the San Francisco commissioner of immigration in 1915 saw it as a tool of public relations, arguing that "the Immigration Service is judged by what people think of it on the outside," and that censure by courts for lack of due process generated a bad image and encouraged interference by attorneys.[42] Partisans of more rigorous enforcement within the bureau saw rigorous procedure as a tool to control the borders and a way to counteract the whims of departmental secretaries in Washington who were beholden to special interests and the mass media. But even politicians appreciated careful procedure so that they could point to rigorous enforcement of the laws as an example of good government. Lawyers and brokers appreciated predictable procedures because they could use their knowledge of them to guarantee successful results to their clients. Even anti-exclusion activists such as Max Kohler saw procedure as the antidote to racism and discriminatory enforcement. In Kohler's words, "proper classification, and not race discrimination, ought to underlie legislation."[43] All of these perspectives worked together to transform a new attempt at rigorous exclusion into the entrenchment of an institutional structure with a life of its own.

In the middle of 1908, after the Japanese crisis had subsided, Sargent began to resume more rigorous enforcement, but with greater attention to public relations and more subtle use of procedure. He began with deportations. Arrests and deportations had decreased by two-thirds since 1905. Sargent now encouraged arrests of the most flagrant cases, but with the caveat that "All inspectors must be very careful not to take any action that could justly be criticized as persecutory in character, or attempt any systematic canvas of the Chinese in any particular locality."[44] Immigration officials were to represent the impartial rule of law applied to individual cases.

After Sargent's death in 1908, Acting Commissioner General Frank Larned refined Sargent's policy with an even more specific suggestion to start out by arresting recent immigrants rather than those who had had time to develop friends and connections,

It is believed . . . that a discreet and very gradually readopted exercise of the power of arrest can be made to effectually discourage the smuggling of Chinese under the present existing belief that once they reach the interior they are safe from molestation, and at the same time will avoid a situation in which the rather uncertain public opinion regarding the arrest of Chinese can be tested and accentuated by not giving prominence to the exercise of arresting power through exercising it against well-known and well-connected persons of the Chinese race.[45]

Sargent's successor Daniel Keefe pursued this policy even more aggressively. At the same time, Keefe loudly affirmed his commitment to the official line of courtesy, fair treatment, and the idea that the current exclusion laws were "unduly harsh at points where rigidity does no good."[46] He streamlined the Chinese regulations in 1910 and claimed that the new procedures were "made as broad and liberal as possible under the law, and have been reduced to simpler terms than any rules heretofore issued."[47] He even repeated Secretary Straus's complaint that special discrimination against Chinese was the root of enforcement difficulties:

The invidious distinctions . . . now so apparent on comparing the treatment of necessity meted out to Chinese with the treatment accorded to aliens of other nationalities, in my judgment would not exist but for the fact that the subject of Chinese immigration is distinguished from all other immigration by being dealt with in a separate code of laws. . . . Essentially the entire question involved in the admission or exclusion of Chinese is not a distinct and independent matter of legislative regulation, but in reality is merely a part of the larger problem of immigration."[48]

To act on this assertion, he planned to have the Chinese section "merge into the main [annual] report," and even drafted a general immigration law that included the Chinese and would allow for the repeal of the exclusion laws (although it continued to mention Chinese by name for special restrictions).[49]

The practical effect of the revised regulations was to further concentrate power in the hands of immigration agents and to require more extensive documentation of migrants. Brokers and lawyers were increasingly excluded from hearings. No Chinese could even leave the country without going through a Bureau of Immigration pre-investigation that would prepare them for reentry. Keefe further proposed a reregistration of all Chinese as a way to replace the existing hodge-podge of identification documents and firmly establish the status of resident Chinese. This plan was never put into action, although the bureau continued to discuss it for nearly a decade.[50] Keefe also presided over the opening of Angel Island in 1909. Almost from its inception, Angel Island was the most notorious symbol of the humiliation of Chinese exclusion, its isolation in San Francisco Bay making it a physical metaphor of Chinese marginalization.[51] But Keefe justified Angel Island in the same way that he justified all of his reforms, as part of the general attempt to "frame our laws and treaties to make admission the rule and exclusion the exception."[52] Increased documentation would make entry smooth and reliable for qualified migrants, and the exclusion of lawyers and tricksters from the island would remove the necessity of tiresome investigations. Admission would be the rule because the "undeserving" would no longer even make an attempt.

Debarments at the border, deportations, and the proportion of arrests that resulted in deportations rose briefly from 1909 to 1911 (see fig. 9.1). By 1912 Keefe bragged about the effectiveness of his efforts, "so handled that the Chinese have become satisfied that it is useless to bring any applications unless they are backed up by convincing proof."[53] Under these conditions, officers once again felt encouraged to deny borderline applications and start clearing out some of the uncontrolled identity documents. In February 1911 Inspector Harry Brown in Honolulu rejected the application of Yong Guan Pai on the basis of what he considered to be one of many false Hawaiian birth certificates:

> I am so morally certain that an attempt is being made to use "Hawaiian birth" as a means of defeating the exclusion acts that the case is submitted for decision, not on the testimony, but on the circumstances which I recite and hope the Bureau may see its way clear to stand back of me and approve my finding, and thus assist me in frustrating a scheme which I am reasonably sure proposes to unload a number of Chinese laborers into this Territory under the guise of Hawaiian birth.[54]

By this time, however, the crackdown had already reached its limits. Keefe upheld the exclusion of Yong Guan Pai, but the acting secretary of commerce and labor overruled Keefe and upheld the appeal. The secretary was reluctant to challenge a document issued by another department and was highly sensitive to public opinion. Using the reasoning of the courts rather than

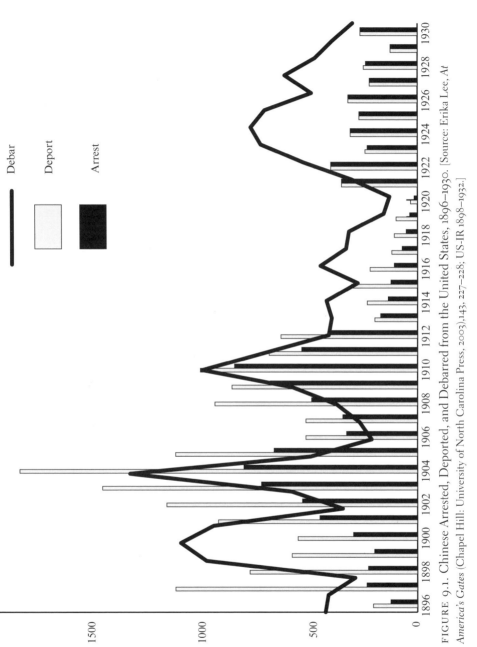

FIGURE 9.1. Chinese Arrested, Deported, and Debarred from the United States, 1896–1930. [Source: Erika Lee, *At America's Gates* (Chapel Hill: University of North Carolina Press, 2003),143, 227–228; US-IR 1898–1932.]

administrators, he agreed that the birth certificate was probably fraudulent but that that could not be definitively proven for this individual case. He insisted that the only way to break down such a case was through cross-examination in which the immigrant was made to contradict his own testimony—despite Brown's protestation that it was impossible for a legitimate Chinese immigrant to remember so many details after such a long time and that "if there is some little variance [in the testimony] it would tend to show more reliability than in a case where every detail checks perfectly."[55]

This disagreement was just one incident in a longer struggle between Keefe and his superiors over the proper enforcement of the exclusion and general immigration laws. In addition to being sensitive to public opinion and rising interdepartmental tensions, Secretary of Commerce and Labor Charles Nagel also believed that a liberal attitude at the departmental level was necessary to counteract the zeal of officials on the ground.[56] The experience of the 1905 boycott had also helped Chinese develop skills and resources in mobilizing the media and public opinion. By 1910 officials and newspapers in China and the United States were swamped with petitions and accusations of harshness and corruption, and another boycott was being threatened in China. The consul general in Hong Kong and Keefe blamed much of this publicity on brokers and commission houses that stood to lose money if migration slowed down.[57] But the critics also included sources that were not so easily dismissed, including the San Francisco Chamber of Commerce, Self-Government Society of Canton, and British newspapers in China and Hong Kong.[58] By the middle of the summer, Keefe's crackdown had become a trans-Pacific debacle of accusation and counteraccusation, what the Hong Kong consul called "a carnival of publicity, extortion, recrimination, and bitterness."[59] Public accusations caused consuls and immigration officers to resume their bitter mutual criticisms, and even well-established immigration officers in San Francisco began to accuse each other of corruption and collaboration with Chinese smugglers.[60]

Despite his adherence to the official line of equitable treatment, Keefe's efforts were mostly directed at keeping immigrants out and reducing fraud. The efforts of Keefe and Nagel converged, however, in their devotion to formal procedure. Nagel often sustained appeals on the grounds that the record was too incomplete to justify exclusion. Keefe also instructed officers to make their decisions on the basis of testimony alone and to avoid making decisions on the basis of subjective criteria such as the perceived level of "Americanization" or on how well-known the applicant was. All decisions had to be a matter of record, based on routinized internal procedures that were free from unpredictable interventions. But this also meant that each decision could be challenged by those who understood procedure and the bases of decision making. Ultimately, the emphasis on procedure helped to institutionalize practices that went beyond the control of any of single official or government department.

By the end of Keefe's tenure in 1913, debarments and deportations had declined to some of the lowest rates ever. The reforms of 1898 to 1905 and 1908 to 1911 had failed to sustain their high levels of rejection, although they did have other long-term effects. The rising proportion of arrests resulting in deportations was one concrete result of adherence to procedure and the influence of Chinese exclusion on the writing of more effective deportation clauses in general immigration laws. In turn, the inclusion of Chinese into the general immigration laws in 1921 helped generate more effective deportations of Chinese and a spike in debarments. Bad publicity and friction with the courts were also reduced, and agents were increasingly unwilling to challenge the documentation of other departments lest the patterns of regulation be disrupted. The system once created by bureaucrats now defined the limits of bureaucratic action.

Man to Man Without the Middleman

In China, consular reforms attained nothing near the level of centralization achieved by the Bureau of Immigration. After 1907 consular officials made several attempts to improve filing systems, facilitate communication, institute uniform procedures, and establish direct investigations of individual claims in the Chinese interior. Most of these efforts proved difficult to maintain over the long run in the face of other consular duties.[61] But lasting procedural reforms were achieved in the methods of investigation, as consuls grew increasingly convinced of the necessity to precisely identify each migrant. No longer did consuls respect the opinions and assistance of brokers, Chinese officials, and middlemen. Rather than depend on Chinese society to produce candidates for migration, they relied on strictly defined legal categories and the direct encounter with individual applicants. A person was no longer a teacher, student, or merchant because of who he knew but because of how he conformed to administrative definitions. The qualities of an "exempt" person were found on his body, in his bearing, and in the documents he possessed. The possible interpretations of these qualities, however, were determined by standardized definitions and formulaic paperwork. The brokers were never suppressed but were successfully marginalized as an unavoidable evil and convenient scapegoat to divert accusations of malfeasance.

The consuls tried to retain a space of discretion and insisted that the heart of the examination was in the direct encounter between government agent and applicant. As Hong Kong Vice-Consul Leighton Hope wrote in 1918, "So very much depends on the personal equation in these cases that the opinion of the examining officer is entitled to the utmost consideration."[62] The 1907 instructions stopped short of specifying the exact questions and kinds of evidence to be considered in an investigation. Officials even rebuked consuls if they felt their investigations were becoming too formulaic or they were sharing too much information about the procedure with Chinese. This was "to provide elasticity in the enforcement of difficult legislation" and to make sure that Chinese could not prepare too carefully for the examination ahead of time.[63] But that personal equation was now one of evaluating the extent to which an applicant presented an image demanded by formal categories rather than relationships generated through social connections. The characteristics of a member of the "exempt classes" were defined beforehand, and each individual was then analyzed to see if he possessed these qualities.

Whereas the consuls had once mocked the applicability of Bureau of Immigration categories in China, they now claimed to be able to read the signs of the "exempt classes" directly on their bodies, as an aspect of their very being. In 1909 Consul Amos Wilder in Hong Kong explained the skills necessary to uncover "coolies" who posed as merchants. He examined their ability to read and write cursive script, their teeth, sunburn, dialect, "alertness," and control over the tone of their voices, arguing that these qualities can "betoken a good mode of life and substantial connections." He refused to allow Chinese to fill in applications at home where they might be coached. Out of 60 to 80 applications a week, he claimed to accept only 70 to 140 a year now that he had perfected his techniques of observation.[64] Only through the intimate encounter of applicant and examining agent could true identity be detected and the applicant categorized as a "genuine" merchant, a "bona fide" student, or a coolie. The construction of abstract legal categories made it possible to identify an individual's status without relying on the evaluation of brokers, friends, and social relations. These categories specified particular qualities that were the possessions of individuals but could be clearly perceived only when that individual was observed in isolation from the deceptive claims of interested parties. The main exception to this was relationships created by the nuclear family. The admission of nearly all noncitizen women and children was dependent on the establishment of a relationship as the spouse or child of a resident of the exempt classes. And even that relationship was determined through testimony given in the United States rather than in China or based on Chinese documents.

The emphasis on the personal encounter went hand in hand with the demonization of middlemen. The proper determination of each case was only possible through direct, unmediated observation. Whereas bondsmen and personal recommendations had once been the best guarantee of a visa, they were now the best assurance of failure. An applicant had to be torn out of his social networks and judged on his "own" merits. Government agents argued that lawyers, brokers, and promoters of all kinds extorted unnecessary fees from ignorant migrants for useless services. These interlopers sullied the reputation of U.S. representatives by claiming their fees were necessary to bribe the consul, and they were "the first to cry 'boycott' when they find their business is being hurt."[65] Officials blamed corruption and commercialism not only for the perpetuation of fraud but also for instigating the migration of undesirable individuals who would otherwise have happily stayed at home.[66] True students and merchants would migrate of their own volition.

The mistrust of middlemen extended beyond Chinese to include lawyers and other brokers of all nationalities and occupations. The Bureau of Immigration could only limit the participation of lawyers at immigration hearings to a passive role. Consuls abroad could exclude them altogether from immigration interviews but could never stop their own clerks from collaborating with brokers and lawyers. Consuls were also in constant conflict with U.S. missionaries and teachers who tried to recruit students for study in the United States. Secretary of Commerce and Labor Nagel identified the grounds of conflict in 1912, when he explained that official policy was to encourage students, but not when the policy "is availed of selfishly by persons whose object is merely to gain a commercial profit and who in order to effectuate their purposes adopt plans having in view the promotion and encouragement of immigration upon a mere pretext of an intent on the part of the aliens to study."[67]

Consuls and immigration agents made life difficult even for Caroline Ober, a professor of Spanish at the University of Washington and charitable activist whose "high-minded" goals were attested by letters from senators and university professors. After the 1911 republican revolution in China, Ober worked with the commissioners of foreign affairs and education in Canton to set up examinations to select students to study modern subjects in the United States.

Consuls in China refused to grant visas to many of these students, claiming that Ober was profiting from the interactions and that the commissioner of education was not authorized to make section 6 investigations. Immigration inspectors in the state of Washington also accused Ober of sending the students to substandard schools and inflicting "gross injustices" on the Chinese boys.[68] Inspector Barbour in Portland, Oregon, further explained that the test of a student "is not necessarily his mental equipment and his avowed intent," but rather his adherence to procedural definitions: "The bonafide student or merchant—the one of honest purpose and intent—who applies for credentials is generally easily identified. Such a student is backed by the Government or by a well-to-do resident of this country or, and this infrequently, by some member of a well-known and prosperous firm in China. The Chinese student contemplated and defined by our laws and regulations cannot in the nature of things spring from a village pinched by want."[69]

U.S. officials routinely suspected nearly all the institutions and individuals involved in migration of "commercialism" and "interested actions." Belief in the corruption of Chinese officials in immigration matters was accepted without question. As the Hong Kong Consul George Anderson wrote in 1914, "It has been found by years of experience by many officers and with all forms of government in China that Chinese investigation of such cases cannot be relied on in the least."[70] In 1919 he simply stated that the Chinese system of signing certificates was "a system of extortion."[71] No Chinese contribution to the procedure was to be taken at face value except the physical necessity of an official Chinese signature on the final document. Hong Kong colonial officials, who had less interest than the Chinese government in guaranteeing the identity of their Chinese subjects, had already avoided such stigma by conceding to U.S. consuls the responsibility to conduct the entire investigation for section 6 certificates in 1909, with the registrar general only adding a signature as a matter of form.[72] New migrant identities were to be lodged in the receiving state.

The Officer as Object of Control

Proceduralization also helped officials in Washington, DC, better control their own agents and discourage fraternization with the objects of regulation. However much inspectors may have spoken about the "personal equation" in evaluating a case, the bottom line was the official's ability to fit that case into the web of standardized forms and cross-referenced files. Both officials and immigrants were extracted from the clutches of brokers and Chinese social relations and reinserted into new networks of bureaucratic surveillance. Identities were to be generated internally.

When posted to Angel Island in 1917, Inspector John Sawyer noted in his personal diary that "What has impressed me most is the remarkable system that has been developed to protect the Government against its own officials." Officers and clerks were constantly rotated between cases and unable to form an overall view of any particular case. He wrote that Special Investigator John Densmore had just filed a report on the recent corruption scandal on the island and advised new inspectors "particularly not to work to get denials, nor to show lengthy examinations, also not to follow up cases after they leave our hands to learn if law sector or Commissioners or Bureau reverses us, also to render decisions without fear of what others might think of us."[73] Proper procedure, not inferences, evaluations, or the implications of a particular conclusion, was to be the only guide to a decision. The burden of sifting through individuals was entrusted to the system rather than to individual officers.

Washington officials also discouraged socialization with Chinese. To be sure, few immigration agents willingly associated with any but a select few Chinese. But often the best smugglers and hustlers were precisely the "respectable" Chinese who spoke the best English, wore tailored suits, contributed to charity, and fraternized with officials. Charlie Sam of El Paso was just such a Chinese. Inspector Clifford Perkins later recalled how Sam joked with officers about how many Chinese he had smuggled. On the night before his final return to China, Sam invited Perkins over for whiskey and cigars and confessed many of the schemes he had worked against the immigration officials. They then "parted with many good wishes for our unknown futures."[74] Similarly, Inspector Lorenzo Plummer of Chicago wrote to Indianapolis lawyer Cass Connoway about the impending marriage of Ching Gum Shing: "I am sure that in the very near future we will hear the blast of trumpets, and invitations to various banquets will be forthcoming, and chop-suey and Chinese cock-tail will be served with a lavish hand. I notified the gentleman last night by letter that he owes to you a very great deal, and I am sure that you and I, with our friend, [Inspector] Ward [Thomson] will meet around the banquet table where we will drink to the health of Ching and his new bride."[75]

This kind of fraternization was increasingly frowned upon. Plummer was criticized for a lack of thoroughness in his investigations and ultimately transferred to Montana over his strenuous objections.[76] His successor, Howard

Ebey, established a very different tone for the office, writing to Chinese who had left him Christmas presents in 1911 that, "while I appreciate the friendly spirit in which these gifts are tendered, I regret to say that under the rules of the service, I am not allowed to receive presents."[77] Even agents with better reputations than Plummer had to change their practices. In 1905 Chief Inspector Richard Halsey in Honolulu said he resolved doubtful cases by consulting Chinese of high profile who show "a fine spirit of earnestness, sincerity and honesty."[78] By 1913 he reassured the commissioner general that "the assurances of prominent citizens or aliens or attorneys that a case is good are not considered; the law and the testimony alone are conclusive."[79]

The reliance on law and testimony had made it possible to generate identities without relying on middlemen other than for some formulaic written affidavits. In a 1922 report promoting greater uniformity, preservation of records, and more comprehensive instructions among consulates in China, John Sawyer (now posted at the Shanghai consulate) argued that as the immigration agent's information of this sort increases, he "no longer feels helpless in the hands of steerers of fraudulent immigration but finds that he is largely master of the situation."[80] Similarly, in China by the 1920s, ambitious young vice-consuls charged with visa duties no longer bragged of their wide social contacts and ability to understand the Chinese mentality as Consul Gracey had once done. The new breed of consuls curried favor by showing off their ability to manage complex filing and identification systems, such as Vice-Consul Perry Jester of Hong Kong who listed fifty-four improvements he had made in the section 6 record keeping and developed a method of classifying Chinese facial features.[81]

Not all officers made these changes willingly. At a conference of immigration inspectors held in San Francisco in 1915 (which was dominated by Chinese issues because they still accounted for the bulk of the paperwork and set precedents for the overall work of the Bureau of Immigration), they complained of attempts to impose stricter discipline. The bureau law officer opened and closed the conference with speeches on the importance of uniformity and high standards of fairness in immigration work. "There never has been in the history of this country so much power vested outside of the courts as is put in the hands of the Immigration officers and we have to watch ourselves very carefully."[82] He gave numerous examples demonstrating how adherence to due process made it difficult for courts and lawyers to interfere and sully the image of the department.

The assembled inspectors did not all agree. Agents from the Mexican border were especially critical of calls for more paperwork, complaining that "Thousands of pages of records of testimony taken by boards of special inquiry have never been referred to and probably never will be," and that "the greater the number of requirements under the rule, the greater the opportunity to attack the proceedings for the lack of their observance."[83] Even James Dunn, who had created much of this system in San Francisco, complained of the excessive time spent collecting voluminous records for Chinese laborer return certificates, "wherein there is no possible means of contesting or disproving the palpably fraudulent claims."[84]

Inspector Barbour of Portland responded with a spirited defense of bureau requirements, insisting that individual agents should understand their place in the larger scheme of things: "We may think that our heads are pretty high above the ground and that we see a great deal of territory, but we don't see it all. The Bureau is way up above all of us. They may write letters which we will laugh and hoot at but I find in the majority of cases they are always right in the end. So trust the common sense of the Bureau always and exercise your own common sense and I do not think that any of us will go far astray and I think we will bring about the unity that we all desire."[85]

Immigration procedures had taken on a life of their own, existing beyond the agency of any single office or official. Some inspectors even started to see themselves less as enforcers than as a kind of service provider whose job was to assist Chinese applicants to negotiate confusing procedures. In 1911 Inspector Ebey in Chicago explained that "I am not in favor of subjecting a departing Chinese laborer to a minute examination in reference to the indebtedness on which his claim is based, when he is the holder of a genuine certificate of residence."[86] In 1924 John Sawyer simply wrote in his diary that "I have always found great joy in a real and unusual social service in handling Oriental immigration problems."[87] The regulations were treated as an irrevocable given, an instrument of abstract law rather than of the will of any particular group or individual.

According to Law

In 1920 Anthony Caminetti, another commissioner general of immigration with venerable anti-Asian credentials, reported that "The annual immigration from China has not changed materially during more than a quarter of a century and it long ago responded to the policy of exclusion."[88] Chinese matters had already dwindled from more than thirty pages in the annual reports of the 1900s to less than four or five pages. Chinese exclusion was no longer a crisis but business as usual. On the other hand, Caminetti devoted much of his term to the potential crisis of Indian immigration. The discretionary use of the "public charge" clause was a temporary solution, but Caminetti was not satisfied until the achievement of formal legislation in 1917 prohibiting immigration from an Asiatic "barred zone" (not applied to Chinese or Japanese).[89] Higher officials like Caminetti were increasingly adherents of the idea that transparent procedure was the most effective means to deflect criticism and accommodate multiple contradictory interests.

Caminetti's satisfaction appears somewhat odd given that the conditions of Chinese immigration in 1920 were much the same as those that had appeared to be a crisis in the late 1890s. Chinese admissions still averaged over six thousand a year. The immigration service was no less dishonest and demoralized, as an investigation into massive corruption at Angel Island had confirmed in 1915.[90] Attempts to place Bureau of Immigration officers at consulates in China had only generated more jurisdictional struggles between departments and complaints about the "unbearable situation" of having to place faith in the acts of officials from another department.[91] And smuggling was rampant. A crackdown at one border area only pushed smuggling to another. When agents patrolled the rail lines the smugglers used boats, and when agents patrolled the coasts the smugglers used autos.[92] None of these conditions was on the verge of improving. By 1924 Chinese admissions had doubled, stowaways became a larger problem, the two departments remained contemptuous of each other, and at least two more massive corruption schemes were uncovered in Honolulu and Canton.[93]

But Caminetti could ground his satisfaction on the fact that bad publicity had receded and the daily production of paperwork had become routinized and relatively predictable. Departmental instructions to boards of inquiry dealing with Chinese cases told them to ascertain facts only, to give aliens full opportunity to present his evidence, to avoid leading and trick questions, and to establish discrepancies beyond any possibility of reasonable refutation.[94] These techniques helped deflect legal challenges and other complaints. Before 1907, public accusations often prompted embarrassing official and nonofficial investigations. As early as 1905, however, Bureau of Immigration officials had learned to diffuse criticisms by demanding reference to specific cases rather than to the broader principles of exclusion, thus shifting the discussion into the impartial application of law and technical procedures that nobody but bureau officials could master.[95] As the Canton consul told petitioners from the Self-Government Society who were threatening a boycott in 1910, "If the Chinese did not comply with the regulations and were rejected on that account . . . they could blame no one but themselves."[96]

Other officials cloaked themselves in procedure more tactfully. In response to a 1924 complaint from the Six Companies about shabby treatment of first-class passengers and the "harassing, unfair and prolix examinations of all Chinese witnesses,"[97] the San Francisco commissioner of immigration responded that

> This allegation is general and permits of no specific answer and our response therefore must be general in character. Our endeavors have ever been to handle this and all other classes of travelers in a courteous and expeditious manner, consistent with the facilities available, complications involved and a proper observance of the laws, regulations and instructions of the Bureau and Department. Under these conditions we feel that the foregoing allegation can be considered as finding support only in the law itself, held by most Chinese to be offensive, and disregard of which in its enforcement would appear to be the sole solution, unless the law is repealed.[98]

Similarly, in 1926 a committee of white San Francisco merchants questioned the necessity of intensive interviews and incarceration at Angel Island, even if enforced with all courtesy. They were treated to a tour of the island and a demonstration of the procedures. The merchants conceded that "The Bureau of Investigation has to be technical. . . . When they have not done so they have found themselves open to attack and . . . they naturally are on the alert to strictly follow the laws and rulings."[99] But most complaints were not dealt with at such length. Instead, officials just responded with terse notes making bland assertions that the case had been "dealt with as the law requires," sometimes enclosing a copy of the rules and regulations for good measure (as they did for the former president of the Chinese Republic, Sun Yat-sen, in 1915).[100]

The most persistent Chinese complaints usually came from students from northern China who traveled without brokers and were unfamiliar with the procedures. They especially resented the humiliation of the medical exam.[101] This was the easiest complaint to deal with because the officials could just point to laws that required immigrants from all nations to undergo similar exams (although in practice the actual form of the exam was different and likelihood of debarment was higher for Chinese).[102] Most other Chinese immigrants were well entrenched in a dense networks of files and surveillance and had learned to live with them. They were still bitter about the law, but their criticisms were muted and no longer became international incidents. As we shall see in the next chapter, many even had a personal interest in the maintenance of stable identities and predictable files as a way to facilitate their own movement and that of their real or alleged families, and even to earn money.

Even if a specific allegation proved to be true, it could be treated as an aberration by an official who was not conscientious rather than as an incidence of the failure of the system as a whole. In this way, procedure served the interests of higher officials much less than lower. In 1925 the San Francisco immigration office produced a massively documented report on Chinese fraud. It concluded that the rigor of existing methods compelled even legitimate applicants to resort to fraud and that "The present system is not conducive to the welfare of the government nor in fact to the interests of the bona fide applicant, and by gradual steps it has gotten more and more into a rut which becomes deeper and narrower as time goes on, making it more difficult and expensive for the government to detect the fraud and easier for the perpetration and success of irregular practices."[103] Secretary of Labor Walter Husband expressed his appreciation of all of this hard work but rejected all of the suggestions for improved enforcement on the grounds of difficulties they presented "from an administrative standpoint." He explained, "While it is known that, as a general proposition, the Chinese falsify by continually claiming all boys and no girls, yet it is quite impossible to apply this knowledge specifically and to state in a given case that they cannot be all boys and no girls. While such knowledge is used indirectly in determining cases, it cannot be made a matter of record in a given case."[104]

Higher officials claimed that their possession of the big picture provided the proper understanding of appropriate adjustments. From their perspective, only a systematic and predictable system could manage the many contending forces that came together in immigration cases. Fully aware of statistical arguments and anecdotes that demonstrated the pervasiveness of fraud and bitter feelings, department officials chose to interpret the big picture in terms of a broader distribution of justice that transcended specific complaints. As Commissioner General Keefe had argued in 1911, "The law is far-reaching in its ultimate effects and its close application and proper enforcement may mean progress and its lax enforcement retrogression to many American communities, indeed to the Nation. Nowhere else is there a better illustration of the axiom that the individual must often suffer that the community may benefit; that there must be temporary individual inconvenience in favor of the general permanent convenience."[105] Of course, Keefe was talking about inconveniencing migrants for the sake of the national community, not Husband's concern for the enforcement of justice among individual migrants. But in both cases, a broader justice was best achieved by adherence to rule of law as embodied in procedure.

China as a Lawless Space

The construction of migration procedure as rule of law also defined people and activities that were outside the law. Officials increasingly understood middlemen and social networks in terms of rogue individuals who took advantage of unfortunate legal loopholes. This was essentially a struggle of territorial officialdom against geographically dispersed institutions and social networks over the power to generate identities and organize movement. But U.S. officials preferred to frame this struggle as one against the decadent moral atmosphere of China and the corrupt nature of the Chinese themselves. In this way, U.S. officials diverted attention away from the limitations of centralized state power to control mobile people and refocused attention on the alleged Chinese inability to adhere to "civilized" standards of law and personal conduct. Power and the rule of law were mapped in geographical terms that were congruent with national membership and the broader categories of East and West.

U.S. immigration officials often justified rigorous procedures as protecting simple peasants from the unscrupulous brokers, pettifogging lawyers, and immoral clerks who preyed on the ignorance of common farmers, goaded them into false claims, and devised cunning tricks to exasperate and deceive worthy but harried officials. This narrative could have been cribbed from any number of Chinese bureaucratic documents over the previous eight hundred years.[106] The Chinese and U.S. governments actually had a common interest in framing migration control as a state concern, suppressing uncontrolled private intermediaries, and generating internationally acceptable identity documents. China perhaps had even greater interest because the possibility of being taken seriously as a member of the family of nations was dependent on its ability to complete these tasks. Chinese diplomats in the late nineteenth century had tried to project failures of regulation onto unscrupulous brokers and shabby U.S. enforcement. By the early twentieth century, however, as excessive U.S. rigor had become the main cause of complaint, accusations of laxity and corruption were increasingly restricted to the Chinese.

The construction of Chinese as congenital foes of honest immigration law took two complementary forms. On one hand, the images of inscrutable Chinese networks and self-serving brokers were embedded in a broader depiction of an entire people seeped in schemes and lies, unable to understand the nature of an oath, and who would "testify against the law of nature itself."[107] But many Chinese migrants were also depicted as the dupes of the brokers. Their shortcoming was not immorality but ignorance. Both threads came together in John Densmore's comments after his investigations into Angel Island corruption: "It is not felt that the Chinese sense any right and wrong element in this system of bribery, in order to secure favorable action. They regard a bribe in the same light that a merchant procures war-risk insurance in sending goods on a ship through perilous waters . . . no such feeling actuates the Chinese 'go-betweens' or inspectors—with them it is pure graft."[108]

This perspective was often elaborated to demonstrate that Chinese were not genuine migrants who traveled on their own finances and of their own volition. A State Department memorandum of 1911 explained how the clan system and family networks had made it possible to emigrate with little or no money, with the result that migrants were dependent on brokers and unable to control their own destiny.[109] Even Chinese came to accept these interpretations. For example, in 1913 immigration interpreter Dea complained that migrants who tried to enter on false papers were turned back even though they had "committed no crime," while the people who sold them the papers were never prosecuted.[110] While critical of the actual enforcement of the law, he accepted its justifications.

Whether as unscrupulous brokers or ignorant peasants, the relentless commercialism of the Chinese was at the root of their corruption. As one immigration inspector reported after an inspection of emigrant villages in the Chinese interior, "It seems impossible to find a case which has its origin in the village or town which is free from the taint of commercialism."[111] Regardless of any commitment to free trade, immigration bureaucrats held no doubt that identity documents should not be subject to market forces. Any financial transaction related to migration documents immediately gave rise to suspicion of fraud. Even when not under an indenture system, Chinese migration was still inherently unnatural and unfree, trapped in a dense culture of profit and exploitation.

This criticism can appear somewhat ironic given that U.S. citizens were often inordinately proud of their entrepreneurial spirit, and the protection of free trade was a keystone of U.S. diplomacy in China. But this was a venerable characterization of Asians, with a pedigree that went back at least to the establishment of the indenture trade. It was easily appropriated to explain contemporary difficulties in migration enforcement by blaming Chinese who did not understand the proper moral boundaries between private and public, commerce and government. In Keefe's words, Chinese migrants were seeped in "Transactions which, from the point of view of our statutes, are illegal and nefarious, but which, from the Chinaman's point of view, are a matter of ordinary everyday business."[112] The average Chinese migrant could still be held up as a victim in need of the protection of civilized law even as he or she was not exempted from the broader taint of unbridled commercialism that characterized all Chinese. Rigorous migration laws were necessary to protect both the United States and the innocent dupes against this unbounded and immoral commercialism.

10

Files and Fraud

In 1908 Secretary of Commerce and Labor Oscar Straus called the exclusion laws "cumbersome, exasperating, expensive and relatively inefficient."[1] In 1911 Commissioner General Keefe claimed that they "fail to exclude those clearly within their inhibitions."[2] Why did immigration officials persist with this frustrating bureaucratic structure that had apparently failed in its purpose? Bureaucratic inertia is an easy but misleading explanation, unless it is understood not as torpor but as active management by zealous officials striving to absorb and deflect multiple challenges through the creation of predictability and order. But even these officials (and their self-criticisms) are ultimately constrained by the institutional trajectories and standards that they created.

Failure was to be found not so much in the limitation of migration but in the processes of identification that consumed so much bureaucratic energy. Exclusion did reduce the actual number of immigrants but could have excluded even more through other methods, such as the Australian dictation test. But U.S. officials at all levels were deeply committed to the intensive investigation of each individual, justifying the procedures as the search for "truth" about the identity and rights of each applicant. It was precisely in this ambitious task of sifting through migrants one by one to determine the status of each, however, that the procedures were thought to fail most decisively. By the 1910s immigration agents routinely estimated that 70–90 percent of Chinese immigrants gained entry on the basis of fraudulent claims.[3] By the 1910s fraud was most extensive in the realm of citizenship claims, precisely the emotionally charged inner sanctum of political membership that officials would have been expected to guard most zealously. Agents even admitted that the complex machinery, exhaustive investigations, and extensive files designed to establish "true" claims actually helped to create, systematize, and facilitate fraud. Either these procedures served a purpose other than that of ascertaining of truth and rights, or they asserted a greater "truth" than that which was to be found in the specifics of individual cases.

We should search for the "truth" of identities created at the border not in substantive claims and results but in the very methods of investigation. Truth resided in the cross-referenced files rather than in the individual bodies that each inspector purported to examine. It was located in the impartial formulation and application of laws, in the construction of borders as the proper site of regulation, in the categories of identification, in the recognition of people properly allowed to move, and, perhaps most importantly, in the power of the U.S. officials to be the mediators of truth. In short, migration procedures were less an investigation into how things actually were than an assertion of how things *should* be. To create and fix a new identity was much more important than to discover or confirm a preexisting one. In all subsequent interactions with the government, migrants had to reproduce themselves in the terms of the files, thus gradually investing their new identities with political reality.[4]

In 1903 Frank Sargent worried that Chinese exclusion would degenerate into "merely an idle ceremony enacted at our seaports."[5] His reforms were intended to halt this perceived degeneration and create a rationally instrumental procedure. But the "idle ceremonies" themselves were actually complex acts of hegemony. Sargent's reforms expanded these idle encounters into carefully orchestrated and meaningful rituals that wielded and distributed massive symbolic power. This power was experienced as greater truths about world order and the insecure place of Chinese in that order. Whatever status the Chinese brought to these ceremonies, they came out as merchants, laborers, students, family members, and citizens. They also came out marked as inherently suspicious outsiders, as somehow incapable of adhering to rule of law on their own initiative, as not yet autonomous individuals who could be fully a part of international society. The very epithet of "idle ceremony" that was used to discredit previous procedures was part of the process of hegemony. Modern industrial societies are littered with the ghosts of rituals now deemed little more than empty ceremonies, remnants of a superstitious past. But this process of discrediting old rituals as empty form and remnants of tradition is a necessary aspect of instituting new ones in their place.[6] For Sargent, it was a proclamation that the reformed procedures were the bulwark of rationality and rule of law that protected the very order of things against all that was corrupt and uncivilized.

Ceremonies of Admission

Many aspects of the procedures instituted under Sargent corresponded with common descriptions of ritual.[7] They were standardized and repetitive. They took place in special locations, set off from the events of everyday life. A smooth encounter depended on proper behavior and adherence to form. Language and channels of communication were highly formalized. Unfamiliar utterances were neither expected nor desired. The result of any encounter was highly predictable if participants were properly prepared and performed their roles in a consistent manner. But complete knowledge of the details and proper preparation was mysterious and esoteric information, accessible only to a few experienced lawyers, brokers, and administrators. The participants may have had very different interpretations of the acts and symbols, or no interpretation at all. More important was that the procedure was executed properly, in correct sequence, with the correct paraphernalia, with the proper words in the proper places, and with every document filed in its proper place according to the proper technicalities. Answers to questions were not found outside the process, but within the procedure and files themselves. In this way, distinctions were confirmed and status assigned. The complexities of social life were rearranged into concrete specifics that were the practical reflections of universal truths. If those earthly reflections often seemed contradictory and absurd, this was only due to our imperfect and self-centered understandings. A properly performed procedure harmonized participants into that greater universal order despite their incomprehension.

What do we gain by understanding these encounters as rituals? To a large extent, the immigration procedures can be understood by reference to the very material workings of technologies of surveillance that tore migrants out of social networks and reconstituted them within a new network of power made up of individuals defined and set in relation to each other within a matrix of standardized qualities. Indeed, this kind of Foucauldian perspective has driven much of my analysis so far. But an emphasis on technologies of surveillance generally works best as a kind of long-term socialization, which cannot account for the existence and persistence of alternate consciousnesses. It also cannot account for relatively brief and infrequent encounters such as those at the border that, despite their brevity, leave a large impact on individual and public imaginations. These encounters are a moment of transition, less significant for the enduring surveillance than for investing a moment of passage with meaning. These passages take place at the borders of nations and colonies. Foucauldian analyses usually take these borders for granted, remaining within the same containers that have been defined by the institutions that they critique. This is understandable because actual institutions and common discursive frameworks can quickly become diffuse and hard to identify beyond those borders. But ritual studies can help us to focus on the border. They share with Foucauldian analyses an emphasis on bodily dispositions, institutions, and discursive frameworks. But a ritual perspective can also frame those brief border encounters as orchestrated events that redefined the messy experiences of everyday life in terms of a greater universal truth of an international order that was not articulated but experienced through due process and civilized institutions. It was at the borders that the international system of national containers was transformed from vague and indeterminate concepts into experienced truths.

Many studies have already analyzed secular activities in terms of ritual, from habits of personal interaction and consumption, to labor negotiations, sports events, and government pomp.[8] This broad application potentially makes the concept of ritual so diffuse as to be meaningless as an analytic tool. Many critics have argued that ritual analysis should be reserved for activities that are clearly set off from everyday life or characterized by an attempt to form a relationship with the sacred and unseen.[9] To be sure, it would be hard to argue that any participant in these migration procedures saw himself or herself as engaged in anything other than a mundane, secular activity. But what could be more characteristic of new forms of power in the specific historical context of the turn of the last century than to define themselves as grounded in the universal truths of secular rationality and science? In the words of Pierre Bourdieu, "Symbolic power is that invisible power which can be exercised only with the complicity of those who do not want to know that they are subject to it or even that they themselves exercise it."[10]

Many (but by no means all) attempts to analyze secular ceremonies suffer from simple understandings of ritual as means to facilitate social bonding, generate communal feeling, or display state power.[11] They rarely analyze the mechanisms by which this is achieved other than through vague references to the creation and manipulation of communal emotion. But not all ceremonies produce a sense of solidarity or harmony. Hierarchy, distinction, transformation, and the ordering of mundane relationships and authority are also enacted through strategic ritualized activity. Most importantly, a powerful ceremony engages people emotionally, socially, and physically in a structured relationship. These relationships are embedded in a larger truth that simultaneously transcends, reflects, and promises to bring significance to the sullied arrangements of everyday human society. Rituals can create and confirm the status of imperfect institutions and individuals, but only by constructing the framework within which that imperfection is judged in the first place. Along the way, an effective ritual can order and harmonize (but not necessarily equalize and homogenize) social relations, cultures, and ideologies that appear to be in tension in daily life, embedding them into the fabric of a larger cosmic order. Participants are not convinced of the truth of the social or cosmic order embodied by the ritual because that truth is never explicitly enunciated. Instead, they experience that truth. In the words of Catherine Bell,

> People generate a ritualized environment that acts to shift the very status and nature of the problems into terms that are endlessly retranslated in strings of deferred schemes. The multiplication and orchestration of such schemes do not produce a resolution; rather, they afford a translation of immediate concerns into the dominant terms of the ritual. The orchestration of schemes implies a resolution without ever defining one. . . . In seeing itself as responding to an environment, ritualization interprets its own schemes as impressed upon the actors from a more authoritative source, usually from well beyond the immediate human community itself.[12]

In this sense, exclusion procedure also did more than just use proper classification to create the identities of Chinese immigrants. It asserted a vision of properly ordered global social relationships, a vision that was inseparable from the routine encounters, failures, and contradictions inherent in its enforcement. A broad order of nations and intercourse, of law and civilization, and of simultaneous equality and hierarchy between individuals and nations was given concrete form in oppositions such as fraudulent vs. genuine, corruption vs. rule of law, unscrupulous brokers vs. respectable merchants, illegitimate social networks vs. government authority, and Asiatic vs. white and American/Australian.

Flexible Citizenship

Like all rituals, border procedures claimed to embody and reflect timeless truths. But, like all rituals, they were actually products of a specific history.

The most elaborate U.S. border procedures were built on a set of events surrounding Chinese citizenship claims. Chinese had entered as U.S.-born citizens at least since the Scott act barred returning laborers in 1888.[13] The appeal of citizenship as a mode of entry expanded after the appropriations act of 1894 made Customs Department decisions final for Chinese aliens because citizens could still appeal their cases to the much more favorable environment of the federal courts. In hearings before the department, proof was on the Chinese to demonstrate their right of entry. The courts, working with the assumption of innocent until proven guilty, assumed that the migrant was who he claimed unless the government could prove otherwise. The department rarely had access to conclusive proof that the applicant was *not* born in the United States or that he was *not* the foreign born son of a citizen. The Treasury Department attempted to block this appeal to outside powers with the argument that excluded Asians who were ineligible for naturalization could not become citizens by birth. But the Supreme Court confirmed their citizenship in *Wong Kim Ark* (1898), and the evaluation of citizenship claims soon grew into the main work of the Chinese Division.

Chinese migrants and their lawyers readily exploited this gap between the administrative and judicial branches. The border between the northeastern United States and Canada offered an especially capacious gap. After 1896 over a thousand Chinese crossed the Canadian border into New York and New England each year, only to be quickly arrested by immigration officials. At the Bureau of Immigration hearings they refused to answer any questions other than their names and were sentenced to deportation. Lawyers would then submit a writ of habeas corpus to the courts claiming that the migrant was a U.S.-born citizen. At the court hearing, witnesses appeared who claimed to be his father or uncle or to have known him as a babe in arms in San Francisco. Bureau officials could produce no conclusive evidence to the contrary, and the lack of original testimony from the bureau hearing removed the chances of getting caught in a contradiction. Judges were compelled to release the Chinese on the basis of their citizenship claims. Any remaining difficulties were resolved by well-placed bribes and strategic advice and mistranslations from Chinese interpreters.

Migration brokers and lawyers quickly learned which judges would readily discharge Chinese with a minimum of fuss, whether through humanitarian sentiments, amenability to bribery, or strict adherence to the letter of the law. The first and most notorious of these judges was Felix McGettrick in St. Albans, Vermont, who discharged over a thousand Chinese from 1895 to

July 1897. McGettrick printed up hundreds of forms that said the applicant was brought before him at such and such a date, and "it was adjudged by me that said [name] had the lawful right to be and remain in the United States and was accordingly discharged." Later investigators claimed he did not even see many of the applicants himself before signing these papers, and he admitted that he kept no records of his discharges.[14] Other judges continued these practices after McGettrick retired.[15] From 1900 to 1906, more than five thousand citizenship cases were appealed to New York district courts.[16] In the words of the U.S. attorney-general's office, "nine out of ten of these cases do not amount to the dignity of a farce."[17]

Other "safe districts" emerged along the gulf coast and at districts in the interior where Chinese came up on deportation cases. Some judges berated the immigration officials for their infringement on the rights of freeborn citizens. Others, like Judge Wing of Cleveland, insisted that the burden of proof was on the government even to establish that the accused were Chinese because they may well have been Koreans.[18] Immigration officials felt that bringing a case before such judges was wasted effort that would only result in embarrassment and the creation of false citizens.[19] As explained by Marcus Braun at the Mexican border in 1909,

> The highly technical rules governing the admission of evidence before tribunals make it many times almost impossible to secure convictions, aye, far worse, many Chinamen who were smuggled into the country during the night at some convenient place, have had and have the audacity to present themselves the next morning at the office of our Chinese inspector in charge, with an affidavit, made by someone in some interior city of the United States, in which affidavit it usually is stated that so and so is a merchant or laundryman, residing for the last ten or fifteen years.[20]

The Bureau of Immigration struggled against these loopholes in the courts. The *Sing Tuck* (1904) and *Ju Toy* (1905) decisions meant that the only Chinese who could routinely appeal to the courts were citizens arrested for deportation more than a mile from the border. Otherwise, the court could not intervene in substantive matters but only in cases where due process had not been followed. The bureau helped enforce these decisions by limiting the number of ports where Chinese were allowed to enter and strengthening their arrangements with the Canadian Pacific railway to carry Chinese to the

United States only by bond. Access to equality before law had become completely dependent on territory, even for citizens.[21]

These efforts were too late. Thousands of Chinese had already been admitted as citizens, and they began to bring in their foreign-born children as citizens. By the 1920s the Bureau of Immigration frequently asserted that if all the Chinese who claimed birth in San Francisco were actually born there, it would mean five hundred to eight hundred male children for every Chinese woman who had lived in San Francisco before the 1906 fire.[22] Thousands of discharge certificates remained in circulation and could be transferred from person to person with a relatively easy substitution of photos (although some certificates carried no photos at all). The status of the bearers of these certificates was still vague. The certificates generally said little more than that the holder "was not guilty of said charge; that he had a lawful right to be and remain within the United States," and they rarely included a positive confirmation of citizenship.[23] But the immigration officials were loath to challenge the decisions of U.S. commissioners and generally accepted that, in the absence of evidence to the contrary, the certificates were valid evidence to enable a Chinese to reenter the country or bring over family members. After the fire of 1906 destroyed all the birth records for San Francisco, the immigration agents could only ask for corroborating evidence of birth in the form of oral testimony. Marcus Braun concluded that this helped make discharge certificates "incontestable" and "considered by the smuggling craft a far better and safer document than a *bona fide* Chinese certificate of residence."[24]

The web of surveillance also left a gap in the interior, where Chinese citizens could appeal to the courts. Immigration officials occasionally received anonymous letters tipping them off to undocumented Chinese. They would find the accused immigrants exactly where the letter indicated, arrest them, try them, and sentence them to deportation. They would then appeal and be discharged as citizens.[25] The bureau made fewer and fewer arrests under the exclusion laws after 1910 (see fig. 9.1) because, "In the end, inability to prove they were illegal entrants made citizens out of them."[26]

Chinese citizens began to bring over their alleged family members, especially foreign-born sons who could be admitted as citizens before they reached their majority. On trips to China, migrants with citizen or merchant papers generally claimed to have fathered at least one son. From 1923 to 1931 (exclusive of 1924), 8,251 returning citizens claimed 21,808 sons and 1,741 daughters.[27] Fathers claiming to have eight or more sons and no daughters were not uncommon. Their nonexistent sons were known as "slots" and

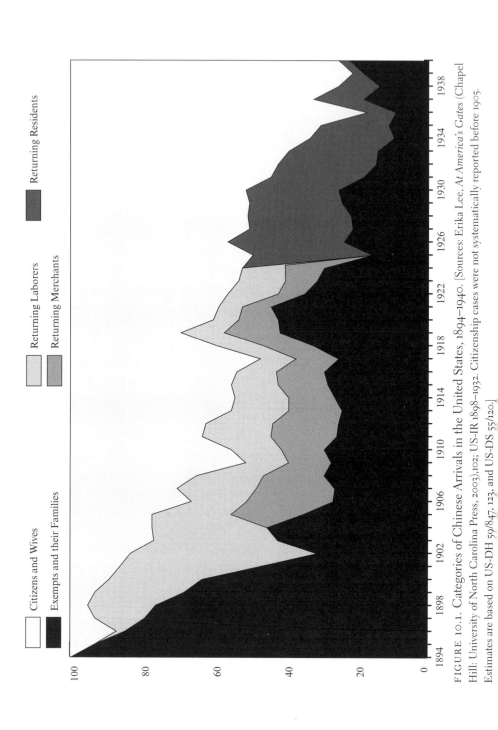

FIGURE 10.1. Categories of Chinese Arrivals in the United States, 1894–1940. [Sources: Erika Lee, *At America's Gates* (Chapel Hill: University of North Carolina Press, 2003),102; US-IR 1898–1932. Citizenship cases were not systematically reported before 1905. Estimates are based on US-DH 59/847, 123, and US-DS 55/120.]

Citizens and Wives

Exempts and their Families

Returning Laborers

Returning Merchants

Returning Residents

could be sold, exchanged, and even transferred along with dowries to young men who wished to work in the United States.[28] These "derivative" citizens increased rapidly from 148 cases in 1911 to 3,220 in 1930.[29] Citizenship claims as a whole rose to nearly 80 percent of all cases at the border, especially after the general immigration law of 1924 made it more difficult to enter as a merchant (see fig. 10.1).

The Web of Cross-referenced Files

The Bureau of Immigration responded to these rapidly expanding families with extensive interviews of each applicant and alleged family members. These interviews could last well over a week, during which Chinese remained incarcerated at Angel Island or other immigration stations.[30] Officials constructed a battery of detailed questions from migrants and their relatives about family members and life experience. For those claiming entry on the basis of native-born citizenship, these questions included the streets and major events in American cities of previous residence. For derivative citizenship, the questions focused on physical environment and events in China, including the layout of the applicant's home village; the numbers of windows, doors, and animals in the house; landscape features; nearby villages; and gifts given during visits from other family members. These testimonies were stored and compared against the testimony of newly arriving Chinese. Discrepancies between testimonies were taken as evidence that the migrant was not who he or she claimed to be. The effectiveness of this system depended on an extensive system of cross-referenced files and rapid communication between Washington, ports of entry, immigration offices within the United States, and consulates abroad.

The Chinese were up to the challenge. As Inspector M. J. Griffith wrote on his arrival in Chicago in 1896, "The most striking fact which has impressed itself upon me . . . is that the Chinamen are fully informed in advance, concerning each case, before my investigations are begun."[31] The very systematization of testimonies made it easy to fabricate a case. Each slot came with extensive coaching papers based on previous interviews, with answers to up to six hundred possible questions and diagrams of sometimes nonexistent villages. Many were appended to contracts that required the migrant to pay half of the migration fee up front and half after successful entry. They also required the holder to appear as a witness in the hearings of alleged "brothers" and "parents" and stipulated payment for each appearance. Even people migrating to join genuine families used coaching books on the assumption that they could never remember so many details on their own. Specialists made a living by writing coaching papers and running classes in Hong Kong, Mexico, and the United States to train the applicants in memorization, the streets and events of major U.S. cities, how to behave in the interviews, how to explain mistakes, how to conveniently forget the answer to questions for which they had not been coached, what clothes to wear and gestures to make in order to be recognized by witnesses during a lineup, and proper behavior in front of the examiner.[32] If difficulties arose, brokers would sneak additional information to the migrant's holding cell at Angel Island or other port, sometimes camouflaged by insertion within a peanut shell, banana, or other food item.[33] The following is typical of the advice written into coaching papers.

> Give answers only to the questions asked: do not say any more than a question requires. . . . If an inspector or interpreter talks loudly to show anger, do not be afraid, but be composed and answer the question in an easy manner according to the demand of the occasion. . . . Any question the inspector might ask you regarding matters that occur when you were small, just say that your mother told you or she never told you. . . . When you forget any statements that appear in the statement papers, you should say that you forgot instead of answering those questions at random. When the same question is asked three or four times, there must be something wrong about your answer, and you must think clearly before you answer.[34]

In short, migrants were expected to project a specific, ritualized demeanor, focused on concrete details and the avoidance of extraneous material and interpretation.

The migrants and their agents generated a parallel archive alongside the Bureau of Immigration archive. The very systematization of bureau files helped migrants evade control. After a migrant was released, brokers would go over the interview questions and note any new questions or changed answers. Migrants were instructed to send mail and money to false relatives in China to produce yet more documentary evidence of relationships to future migrants. Some Chinese even requested a pre-investigation of their status just for the purpose of establishing a record.[35] These practices worked in conjunction with the surreptitious alteration of government archives to make it better correspond to the parallel Chinese archive. In 1917 special investigators at

Angel Island reported that officials and lawyers had rewritten testimony on the number of sons, fabricated pre-investigation papers for people who had never been in the United States or had died, replaced photos by bleaching and soaking new photos in tea to make them look old, and destroyed relevant testimony to create a "cleaned record."[36] On the other extreme, some Chinese altered themselves through means ranging from learning new dialects to scarring their faces so as to better correspond to archived photos.[37]

Chinese migrants and exclusion administrators embraced each other in a web of surveillance and evasion that perpetuated the very fraud that the regulations were designed to prevent. Immigration agents were perfectly aware of this fact and often disagreed over the value of these files. As early as 1899, Special Agent Power criticized San Francisco reforms that included the collection of more testimony: "Surely this cumbersome system with its retinue of employees, with all the attendant delay, circumlocution, and expense, cannot be considered an improvement upon the former method, where a Deputy Collector saw the applicant, heard his story and promptly decided and passed upon every case where no reasonable ground existed for denial of right to land."[38] Collector Dunn defended his system with the assertion that "There can be no better proof of the strictness of our investigation than the fact that a majority of cases of all classes are now represented by attorneys and brokers, fully twice as many as in the past."[39] Immigration procedure had become the realm of specialists in obscure knowledge.

Dunn would soon come to regret the involvement of brokers, just as many other agents would come to resent the embrace of the cross-referenced files. For example, in 1904 Inspector Halsey of Honolulu had written to Frank Sargent with enthusiasm for the new system of extensive interviews in attaining their goal of learning the truth about each applicant. He reported that "respectable" local Chinese had told him that "in every genuine case of relationship the Chinese people *know* their family history perfectly, as well as other intimate things connected with their business and movements from place to place, and could not possibly disagree upon any of the question usually asked them by inspectors. When the contrary is the case the assumption is perfectly warranted that the case is not a genuine one and that the testimony is trumped up."[40] By 1911 Halsey had changed his mind, insisting that "if there was some little variance it would tend to show more reliability than in a case where every detail checks perfectly."[41] He also explained that only way to "avoid collusion" among Chinese was to stop the practice of collecting more testimony than was absolutely necessary. "If testimony is taken here touching the family in China and a line on that testimony is then made known in China, it will open a way to much fraud and make it an easy matter to cover up an assumed relationship."[42]

Many inspectors thought that coaching and the obviousness of "correct" answers in standardized interviews made them useless as an investigatory tool.[43] They frequently asserted that it was more likely for a fraudulent candidate to gain entry than a genuine one who had not been coached.[44] In the words of the Amoy Consul Julian Arnold in 1909, the result was that "Cross-examining these applicants only results in putting a premium on dishonesty."[45] Consul Anderson in Hong Kong even admitted that more than 75 percent of the visas he issued were probably fraudulent. He had given the applicants a break because he believed that most of them were probably merchants in the interior who had created false identities as Hong Kong merchants because of the difficulty of obtaining officially acceptable evidence and witnesses from the interior.[46]

Proper procedure ultimately trumped content and the qualms of inspectors. Investigators felt compelled to grant certificates to applicants who gave standardized and uncontradicted testimony, even if their senses and discretion told them that the applicant was of the "coolie class," or not a "genuine citizen" because of his lack of English knowledge and American mannerisms. Many even influenced the testimony so as to create a case that fit into the forms. Some investigators asked stenographers to record only answers that were relevant to the question, prompted applicants to rephrase answers to better fit with previous testimony, and called back witnesses to inform them of discrepant statements and allow them to reconcile the contradiction.[47]

Those who questioned the standardized files fought a losing battle. Some consuls and inspectors continued to insist on the value of impressions gained through the face-to-face encounter, but such impressions were useful only if they could be translated into documentable qualities By the 1920s, files had become the primary method of generating knowledge about Chinese migrants. At many offices, this knowledge was embedded in standardized interview and report forms. Forms used in San Francisco in 1925 included questions to guide the interpretation of personal impressions in the context of testimony, framed so as to imply that personal impressions should be used as a way to resolve discrepancies rather than as a basis for rejection: "Does testimony disclose any discrepancy on essential points of case? Do you believe relationship exists? If not, is your adverse opinion based upon the discrepancies in testimony? If your opinion is adverse to relationship claims made, would it be otherwise if you disregarded the discrepancies in testimony?"[48] Forms used by U.S. immigration agents in Montreal in the 1930s openly promoted the collaboration between Chinese and inspectors in producing a systematic archive, reminding inspectors that "Witness should be advised that his statements in reply to these questions will be used should he testify at any future time as to the relationship claimed to exist between an applicant for admission and a Chinese resident of the U.S."[49]

Alternative procedures were increasingly difficult to imagine. Even officials who continued to be disturbed by the tight relationship of files and fraud could imagine improvements only in terms of more testimony and better filing techniques. For example, in 1934 Vice-Consul Donald Dunham in Hong Kong wrote an extensive report that included a thorough summary of the techniques of evasion:

> In determining relationships the most satisfactory method of investigation has been the examination and cross-examination of the applicants. The elements of conflict are collusion between the aliens' close relatives, efforts of immigration brokers, and coaching by schools in Hong Kong designed especially to prepare Chinese for the questions they are likely to be asked on examination by the consular officer abroad and by the immigration authorities in the United States. The first two difficulties can be overcome by minute interrogation but the schools are painstaking in their tutoring and the smallest detail rarely escapes them. Any new turn in phraseology of the questions is reported by aliens to the schools, incorporated in their drilling, and is brought to light within an astonishingly short time in the testimony of subsequent applicants.[50]

Dunham went on to add that that with a limited number of possible questions they would inevitably become formulaic. He was clearly aware that the very systematization of information made it easier for false facts to be consistently reproduced. But all he could recommend was more files, more testimony, more systematization, and more cooperation with the Bureau of Immigration in accumulating and cross-referencing that testimony. "The effectiveness of the consular examination depends in a measure on the completeness of the transcripts."[51] His solution was a perpetuation of the very conditions that produced the problem in the first place. Migrants and bureaucrats alike were subsumed in the embrace of the cross-referenced files they had created.

The Identity Market

It is far from clear what Chinese thought of these encounters, given that they were understandably disinclined to make public statements that challenged the officially proclaimed principles of border control. But Chinese understanding must surely be interpreted at least partly in the context of a market-based morality of trust and responsibility. Nearly every aspect of Chinese migration could be and often was commoditized. This commoditization included not only cash advances and labor contracts, but also false papers. Medical inspections, visas, witnesses who would claim to be your uncles and brothers, paper families, and old ladies who knew you as a baby in San Francisco could all be bought, sold, and exchanged around the Pacific. In the middle of nineteenth century, labor recruiters, remittance bankers, import-export houses, shipping agents, and a wide range of other businessmen dominated profits from the control of migration. Many of them were considered as respectable elites in Hong Kong, Singapore, and other cities around the world. The surveillance of indentured migration and secret societies helped stigmatize many of these activities, and with the rise of border controls even the most respectable men involved in the recruiting, financing, and provisioning of migrants came under suspicion as potential smugglers. But increased regulation only created new opportunities for profit, and entrepreneurs remained attracted to the business.

In scattered statements, these entrepreneurs have evaluated their action in terms of the market-based virtues of reputation and trust rather than the official morality of accurate identification. The honesty of a smuggling contract or migration document lay in whether its promise was fulfilled, not in what an official thought of it. In an 1898 letter to his partners arranging the entry of several migrants under false papers, broker Soo Hoo Fong wrote disparagingly of the "selfish" practices of their competitors: "They seem to ignore all the demands of equity—unbridled in their payments or their ordinary expending. Those who are bent on deceiving each other will in the end spoil the whole business, each blaming the other, and no profit saved to anybody."[52] Immigration inspectors also occasionally came upon migrants who were surprised when their false papers did not secure them admission, more disturbed about the breach of trust by the man who sold them the paper than by the opinion of the inspector. For example, in 1908 several migrants holding false Hawaiian birth certificates were indignant at not being permitted to land at Honolulu. One of them testified that he had no hesitation in buying the paper and "felt that when I reached here, I would be landed immediately."[53] Another one even asked the inspector for advice on how to get his money back from the man who had guaranteed his landing.[54]

When Chinese inspectors confronted Moy Lee Yuen of Chicago in 1904 with the possibility of two distinct systems of morality, Moy refused to privilege one over the other. After telling the inspector that he was born in China, Moy had to explain that he had previously told the Chinese interpreter that he was born in the United States, "on account of the instructions with the paper I bought." The inspector continued,

Q: Which time are you lying?
A: I only told what the man told me. I didn't lie. The other man lied.
Q: Are you telling now what somebody told you to tell?
A: I am telling the truth now.
Q: How are we going to know which time you are telling the truth?
A: I told the truth both times.[55]

Such statements could be interpreted in terms of the official line of cynical brokers and their ignorant dupes. But movement across multiple jurisdictions offered plenty of reasons for brokers and migrants to believe that their activities were not necessarily illegitimate. For example, late-nineteenth-century Hong Kong had no laws to prosecute the creation of documents that could be seen as fake outside the colony, and U.S. consuls had no means to stop counterfeiting operations of which they had full knowledge. Hong Kong courts even upheld some lawsuits demanding repayment on unfulfilled smuggling contracts, although they later reversed this opinion for activities in which the offending parties were aware that they were violating the laws of a friendly nation.[56]

The very process of increased inspection and individualization of migrants made official depictions of a pervasive commercial mentality into a self-fulfilling prophecy. The linking of migration rights to particular individuals by virtue of family, citizenship, and occupation, as well successful crackdowns on large smuggling rings by the 1910s, meant that migration opportunities were increasingly dispersed among migrants of all classes. More and more migrants had a personal stake in the accumulation and sale of migration opportunities to the United States. The possession of a good paper with multiple slots was a strong personal investment. Not only could it guarantee personal reentry, but it could also promise future income when sold to alleged business partners or family members. These opportunities could be used on behalf of the migrants' own relatives, sold on the market, or even included in dowry packages. Immigration agents across the United States confiscated hundreds of Chinese letters that carefully shared information about the cost, availability, and efficacy of smuggling routes, false and genuine papers.[57] All migrants began to have an interest in the perpetuation and predictability of the existing regime.

This interest could even be found in the editorials in politicized newspapers that, before 1905, had openly opposed the exclusion laws. For example, revolutionary activist Yong Got was stopped from entering Honolulu in 1911 because somebody had informed the Bureau of Immigration that his Hawaiian birth certificate was false. The *New China News* (*Xin Zhongguo ribao*) in Honolulu—a newspaper run by constitutional reformers who were opposed to the revolutionaries, and credited with having first proposed the anti-American boycott in 1903—criticized the hypocritical use of U.S. citizenship by a man who was deeply involved in Chinese politics and complained that immigration officials would now be more suspicious of all Hawaiian birth certificates.[58] In response, an editorial in the revolutionary newspaper *Liberty News* (*Ziyou ribao*) titled "Emperor Protection Society Acts as Loyal Official to the American Government" accused the reformers of betraying Yong to immigration officials, being traitors against China, and sullying the good reputation of the Chinese in Hawaii. Although the title framed the issue as one of collaboration with oppressive officials, the editorial ultimately emphasized that the reformers had undermined the law-abiding public image of local Chinese:

> The American government's treating the Hawaiian born so well is a result of the Hawaiian overseas Chinese having created these conditions for themselves. The natives born in San Francisco all know about the special privileges of the Hawaiian born, and want the same privileges. Why can't they get them? Because of the big smuggling industry. The people involved in it attack each other daily. If it is not A attacking the legitimacy of B's certificate, then B is attacking the witnesses for A's certificate. . . . We Chinese have caused the laws to be stringently enforced.[59]

This argument put the reformers on the defensive, claiming that they would never have voluntarily called attention to Yong's status.[60] Regardless of what the newspaper editors actually thought about Yong Got's certificate, their agreement to remain silent about institutions, identities, and social relations that compete with border control categories helped to expand the legitimacy of those latter categories at the expense of the former.

The Migrant as Bureaucratic Subject

However migrants and agents on the ground actually understood the meaning and efficacy of border encounters, all had to submit to its procedures and categories. Their varied interpretations were subservient to the successful completion of a common procedure. Even though Chinese won innumerable individual battles over identification and admission, the procedure itself ultimately set the rules of the game.

In a pamphlet teaching Chinese applicants how to pass their visa examinations, Zeng Cangling, a clerk at the Amoy consulate in the 1920s and 1930s, offered some insight into the significance of these "cumbersome, exasperating, expensive and relatively inefficient" procedures. The pamphlet described the interview process step by step—how to fill forms, what to say, what to wear, how to behave, and how to be ready for trick questions like "How many times have you worn shoes and socks like this in your life?" He admitted that the process was never entirely predictable but insisted that every candidate who followed his guidelines would receive a visa. He also denied common perceptions that bribes were necessary or that decision were based on an arbitrary whim of the consul. He insisted that despite their "crafty methods," all the consuls were ultimately honest and impartial. He explained that "Even though [the consuls'] personalities are not the same, they are all one in maintaining their country's directives. All the consuls can humiliate Chinese and call it the exercise of competence."[61] An anonymous poem carved in the detention barracks at Angel Island offered a similar insight about U.S. immigration agents, "Even while they are tyrannical, they still claim to be humanitarian (*ren dao*)."[62]

Immigration procedure embodied two contradictory aims bound together as one well-ordered package. On one hand, the exclusion laws were an exercise in coercion, a demonstration that the U.S. government could obstruct the desires of individual Chinese, probe them, measure them, evaluate them, label them, humiliate them, detain them in dirty sheds, treat them like criminals, and re-create their identities in terms of bureaucratic categories. On the other hand, procedure and administrative expansion were presented as a vehicle of justice, rule of law, fair play, and modern efficiency. Immigration encounters were long and humiliating procedures, but they were also an orderly and impersonal procedure based on clear regulations and scientific inquiry applied equally to all migrants. Those who encountered problems had only themselves to blame because of their inability to fulfill impartial legal standards. These contradictory drives—unchecked force and the rule of law—were unified as one in the implementation of exclusion.

This combination of coercion and civilizing rule of law was expressed in terms of other, often contradictory macro categories. The exclusion laws divided the world politically between sovereign nations and socially between races. At the same time, they defined certain individuals in terms of wealth, education, and occupations, which gave them the right to cross those boundaries because they promoted the general well-being of mankind. They monopolized the power to define and determine those identities yet claimed that the truth of those identities was written onto the bodies and histories of the migrants themselves. They were openly discriminatory in character while simultaneously justifying rigorous procedures with the argument that civilized justice demanded that *all* peoples should be treated equally regardless of differences.

These contradictions coexisted perfectly fine in practice. In fact, practical work was even predicated on these contradictions inasmuch as it was framed as the necessary methods to effectively deal with a complex situation. Chinese continued to complain that "The practice with the immigration officials is to regard every Chinese applicant for admission as a cheat, a liar, a rogue and a criminal."[63] But this was merely to state the obvious: that Chinese were being marked as a disreputable category. The trick was to sustain this impression while simultaneously asserting that all Chinese received equal treatment under law. This equal treatment was made concrete by tearing migrants out of their social networks and imposing new identities in terms of legal categories. One academic observer in the 1930s remarked that not all Chinese are crooks and complained that "the immigration officials' lack of individualized treatment of honorable people makes them suffer injustice and hardship."[64] But it was precisely the individualized treatment that made the process so difficult. The great effort necessary to dislodge Chinese from their social networks and treat them as individual cases was necessary for their reinsertion into the broader categories of laborer, merchant, student, or other "honorable" person.

However ineffective these procedures may have been for the categorization of existing social relations between the Chinese—of describing how things *were*—they were extremely effective in describing how things *should* be. They asserted a geopolitical order that ranged from individuals to occupations to nations to races. Migrants were given a chance to obtain rights by adhering to these categories. Any failure was attributable to the migrant rather than to the categories themselves. It was the migrants who schemed to take advantage of and circumvent the equal application of law, or were the victims of illegitimate and exploitative brokers. It was the migrants who lived in premodern social relations and could not understand how to conform to the demands of a rationally formulated institution. The constant expression of hegemony was inseparable from the constant production of precisely that fraud and corruption against which legitimate hegemony was defined in the first place. Every time a migrant complained that the law was not enforced impartially rather than challenge the very foundations of the law, he just reinforced the fundamental principles of that law and the institutions designed to enforce it. Truth was lodged in the procedure itself, not in the migrants.

Rites of Marginalization

The ordeal of Chinese at U.S. ports resembled a rite of passage, the ceremonialized crossing of a boundary into a new identity.[65] It was a passage from one nation into the next or, perhaps more appropriately, from uncivilized to civilized. But it was an incomplete rite. The migrants ended up not reincorporated but stigmatized, marked as outsiders by virtue of both their Chineseness and the suspicious circumstances of their entry. They had entered the territory of a civilized state, but their personal state was not yet transformed.

Rites of passage are usually separated into three stages: separation from an old identity embedded in a social structure; a period of liminality and unstructured community; and reintegration into a new identity. The first two are apparent in Chinese immigration procedures. Events in the journey over, such as the fumigation of clothes and luggage, boarding the steamer in Hong Kong, the memorization and then tossing overboard of coaching papers at the sight of land, or the ferry ride across the water to Angel Island all mark separation from old social roles. The time spent in incarceration during the interview procedure and subjection to invasive medical examinations was a period of transitional "liminality." The migrants were isolated from the social world, often for weeks. Social distinctions of clothes, food, and lodging were reduced or abolished. It was a period of invisibility, unfamiliarity, and the suspension of normal social relationships and responsibilities. The migrants were left only to ponder the fabrication of their new identities. Some Chinese found their incarceration to be a period of relaxation and game playing, reflecting the common depiction of liminality as a period of creative playfulness and intense social bonding in which a new social identity can be constructed. But for most Chinese this was a grim liminality, clearly shaped by the structured weight of the state. As expressed in poems they carved on the walls of Angel Island, they grew depressed, angry and suspicious of their fellow inmates and humiliated by their own weakness and that of their nation.[66] They rethought their identity through these emotions, asking what it meant to be Chinese in this new world. As one migrant who had never expected that his papers would be challenged recounted,

> The first day I entered the immigration bureau [i.e. the detention barracks] all I saw was the slight movement of heads, and pair after pair of hopeless eyes looking at me. I couldn't help but be startled. They mostly had disheveled hair, wore pajamas and slippers. To look at them, they looked like criminals who had committed some grave crime. . . . Later, after I had lived in the Bureau for a long time, my hair was also disheveled, the few pieces of clothes I had brought from Hong Kong were worn out, and when I looked in the mirror while washing my face, I found I had also become a 'criminal.'[67]

Previous residents and those with section 6 certificates (i.e., migrants with better claims to belong to a transnationally mobile global elite) passed through this process more quickly and experienced a less intensive version of this transition. Family members of exempt classes and first-time claimants of citizenship—referred to as "raw" citizens in official documents—experienced the brunt of this process.

The period of incarceration was not followed by any significant rites of reincorporation. One Chinese interpreter did argue that admission entailed some recognition of transformed administrative status, stating that "we might have come under fraudulent papers but we got in here legally."[68] They also possessed new names, new families, new villages in China, new citizenship, and the chance to create a new home in the United States. But none of these possessions implied incorporation into U.S. society. Their social lives were still shaped by their old families, villages, and the networks from which they had been separated during the ordeal. Only now the networks that had brought them to the United States were marginalized as sources of fraud and disreputable practices that existed in the interstices between legitimate national communities. Their old families were made invisible as the men joined "bachelor" enclaves and feared that even other Chinese would use knowledge of their true families to blackmail them. The experience had marked the migrants as suspicious, illegitimate, and fraudulent, leaving them with the skeleton of a social identity.[69] The raw citizens were not cooked.

Incorporation into the Universal Order

The ultimate effect of these encounters was not to exterminate movement and replace it by boundaries and static categories of race and nation. It was to establish hegemony over movement, and define legitimacy and hierarchy on the world stage in terms of race, class, nations, particular kinds of institutions, and particular kinds of procedures. Over time, whether through constant exposure to public discourse, disciplinary institutions, or ritualized performances, Asians have gradually been drawn into—and drawn themselves into—the fundamental principles asserted in the ceremonies of admission. The new names grew increasingly real as they were repeated in public and written into property deeds, tax returns, and school registration forms. Especially with locally born generations, the distinction between the original and assumed names and implications of a "sojourning" life was attached to Chinese were badges of shame, distinguishing them from the true "immigrants" that made up the nation.[70] The immigration files themselves have taken on a new life, as the descendants of immigrants mine them to discover their family history. But even as these files recount a history of shame, they are also interpreted as evidence of the immigrant struggle against adversity, helping families finally to incorporate themselves into the narrative of American identity and power.

In the 1950s a "confessions" project offered Chinese a preliminary forum to clear their identities and fix their immigration status. But rather than an opportunity to recover their old identities or be more fully integrated into the nation, the confessions worked to reaffirm lingering marginality. A confession required migrants to voluntarily reveal their secrets to the government, to bare their past sins and place themselves at the mercy of the state. The format was determined by the files, as each confessor had to re-create previous testimony both as proof that the amnesty was being granted to the proper persons and to help track down the remaining paper relatives and pull them into the reformed files. The families were generally forgiven (unless they confessed to communist sympathies), but this process still reconfirmed the original stigma of an incomplete passage. Identities outside the files remained suspect, as even confessors were often unable to sponsor their true relatives on the grounds that, without any prior record of their existence, there was no evidence of a genuine relationship.[71]

Over time, Chinese themselves came to complete the integration, in part by reinterpreting the files and procedures as evidence of their struggle as free immigrants against discrimination and class legislation. For example, during an interview in the 1970s, Mr. Dea reinterpreted the Angel Island experience, saying that at the time most migrants just endured the ordeal and hoped it would be over soon. "But looking back now at how the United Sates treated Chinese and Asian immigrants, we can see how unequal and unfair the treatment was."[72] The letters to home and poems carved on the walls were also complained of unequal treatment, but they often blamed it on corrupt officers, exploitative brokers, or the weakness of China. Now, discrimination and the failure of institutions to live up to civilized ideals of equality before law are the main culprits. In many cases, the struggles of Asian migrants and minorities have come to embody the virtues promised by U.S. institutions better than the institutions themselves. In the words of Gary Okihiro, "In their struggles for equality, these groups have helped preserve and advance the principles and ideals of democracy and have thereby made America a freer place for all."[73] It is a story of "belief in the human spirit, of certitude in human agency, of an abiding faith in the individual, however mean, and in the power of human will however fragile."[74] Such narratives reinforce the very principles upon which the United States makes its claims to both universality and exceptional power. Despite unfortunate deviations, U.S. borders are still the container of these ideals and institutions that can guide the individual struggle for freedom and equality.

More subdued accounts have explained how judges and administrators made decisions that went against their immediate desire to exclude Chinese because they were "captives of law," constrained by an overriding commitment to the letter and spirit of national institutions and impelled by the natural determination of Chinese to obtain these rights.[75] The failures of migration law are explained by practices that did not accord to social justice or the "social reality" of immigrant identities. The legacy of those failures has created a body of law that is "a maverick, a wild card . . . radically insulated and divergent from fundamental norms of constitutional right, administrative procedure, and judicial role that animate the rest of our legal system."[76] This is the power of ritual, to cut through all the contradictions, technicalities, arbitrary evaluations, prejudice, and bad legislation and convince us that the force of justice, law, and social reality is still made manifest. Deep within all the chaos and inequities of human affairs, a greater truth and purer justice does exist and will ultimately liberate us. And that greater truth is to be found in the very institutions that generated inequity and fraud in the first place.

Part IV

Disseminating Borders

At the end [the doorkeeper] says regarding the entrance to the Law: "I am now going to shut it," but at the beginning of story we are told that the door leading into the Law always stands open, and if it always stands open, that is to say at all times, without reference to the life or death of the man, then the doorkeeper cannot close it. There is some difference of opinion about the motive behind the doorkeeper's statement, whether he said he was going to close the door merely for the sake of giving an answer, or to emphasize his devotion to duty, or to bring the man into a state of grief and regret in his last moments. But there is no lack of agreement that the doorkeeper will not be able to shut the door. Many profess to find that he is subordinate to the man even in knowledge, toward the end, at least, for the man sees the radiance that issues from the door of the Law while the doorkeeper in his official position must stand with his back to the door.   —Kafka, *The Trial*

11

Moralizing Regulation

It is one thing to describe how migration control was standardized and enforced at a single border. But how did these principles take root across the world? This question can be answered in different ways. The next chapter will look at the diffusion of legal and institutional templates for border control after 1907. But that diffusion could not have been possible if the cultural and social ground had not been prepared to accept the basic legitimacy of border control. That is the subject of this chapter. Much of this groundwork came as part of the rise of nationalisms and understandings of the nation as a social organism that must be protected and nurtured. But struggles over migration control also compelled participants to be more specific about the legal and administrative constitution of a nation in relation to other nations and human mobility. If all nations and peoples want to exercise self-determination, under what circumstances is this compatible with the self-determination of individuals and other peoples?

The act of resistance against objectionable migration policies was key to the internalization of the principles of migration control. Not only did protest movements engage broad emotional and physical participation, but they also generated extensive debates over what precisely was objectionable and acceptable about migration policies. In the Chinese anti-American boycott of 1905, protest against U.S. migration laws expanded into a formative moment of nationalist mobilization. Ultimately, the very sentiments of national self-determination that inspired the boycott made it difficult to formulate an effective critique of U.S. plenary power doctrines. Boycotters finally focused only on the discriminatory aspects of U.S. laws, but with a growing resignation that equal treatment at the borders would be achieved only after China had become a strong nation with international prestige.

Popular resistance was also a vehicle of physical and moral discipline, ceremonial drama, and emotional intensity. The international order of sovereign peoples was not just understood but experienced. No movement perfected these techniques better than Mohandas Gandhi's satyagraha movement against anti-Asian legislation in South Africa from 1906 to 1914. Gandhi developed a powerful practice of resistance in which personal moral and physical discipline, national honor, sovereign integrity, and expert legal nuances all came together in one highly moralized, intensely spiritualized package. The lesson inscribed through this practice was not so different from that argued by Stephen Field and Thomas Bayard, that discrimination is acceptable at borders but not within the body of a nation.

Self-discipline and the Nation

The Chinese anti-American boycott of 1905 was path breaking in both its national and international scope and awareness.[1] Boycotts and commercial shutdowns had long been familiar forms of local resistance to specific grievances in China. As early as 1893, the Shanghai newspaper *Hubao* proposed that a boycott of American goods would be preferable to Zhang Zhidong's suggestion to chase all Americans out of China as a way to protest the Geary Act.[2] But the likelihood of a popular boycott that was national in scale, international in its goals, and focused on issues beyond the immediate interests of the majority of boycotters was still small. The growing nationalist agitation at the turn of the century, especially in Shanghai and among Chinese overseas, provided the ideological and organizational framework for a more broadly based movement. The enormous momentum of that movement, in turn, helped consolidate an emotionally charged blend of traditional statecraft and modern nationalist thought that largely confirmed the geopolitical order of borders, civilizational standards, self-rule, and unilateral prerogatives over human mobility that was defined by the exclusion laws.

Despite the expanding background of nationalist activity, the uncontrolled scale of mass mobilization for the boycott surprised nearly everybody, including the leading nationalist agitators. The revolutionaries associated with Sun Yat-sen were disinterested in the boycott during its early weeks, thinking that it diverted attention from the more pressing need of expelling the Manchus. In any case, Kang Youwei and Liang Qichao were much more influential among Chinese abroad and in treaty ports in the years from their exile in 1898 until 1905. They preached a message of constitutional reform centered on the creation of modern institutions under the auspices of the emperor that had little enthusiasm for unsupervised mass mobilization. Even in his relatively radical turn-of-the-century assertions that the nation must be grounded in the participation of the people, Liang Qichao conceived of popular inclusion in terms not much different from the forms of personal self-discipline that Minister Yang Ru had proposed a decade earlier. National power and prestige came through education and self-discipline, not by catering to personal desires for freer mobility. It was also firmly class-based and grounded in ideas about the proper comportment of a civilized people.

In the first years of his exile, Liang traveled through Europe, North America, Japan, Hawaii, and Australia. In each place, he visited Chinese communities to give speeches, collect money for his cause, establish proreform newspapers, and organize branches of the reform party. By 1899 he had already collaborated with the Chinese merchants of Japan to write a petition that objected to any potential exclusion of Chinese but admitted that "his country would not entertain any umbrage against Japan if she thought it expedient to impose some restriction upon the immigration of the labouring classes."[3] He also toured and admired not only the democratic institutions of the countries he visited, but also the iron and steel landscape of trains, towers, factories, and ports. In contrast, he grew steadily less impressed by the Chinese that he met, and increasingly convinced that Chinese people must reform their own behavior if they were to develop modern institutions and gain international acceptance.[4]

During his visit to Australia in 1901, Liang was caught up in the celebrations of federation and the birth of "White Australia." He admired the Australians for their ability to unite for the sake of self-rule and autonomy. The racist origins of Australian federation were regrettable, but not his main object of interest. The festivities instead inspired Liang to write an article, "On Tracing the Sources of China's Weakness" (based on speeches to local Chinese), that compared Chinese unfavorably with Australians. He insisted that the Chinese state was sick in body and spirit, organized on a principle of slavery. The Chinese people were unpatriotic, selfish, slavish, mendacious, timid, and passive. They had yet to learn to assert mastery over the state and treat each other as equals. In contrast, Westerners were taught to govern themselves (*zizhi qishen*, literally "self-govern their bodies") from childhood. Even the local Chinese papers were caught up in the enthusiasm of federation, pointing out how disunity and imperial repression in China compared unfavorably with the leniency of a British imperial policy that permitted this kind of egalitarian republicanism.[5]

In his memoirs of travels through the United States in 1902–1903, Liang expanded his list of negative Chinese qualities to include a lack of noble ambitions, authoritarianism, and tendencies to litter, to talk all at once without listening to each other, and to walk like scattered ducks rather than in groups.[6] He summarized:

> It is not only that my countrymen do not have the ability for self-government of the nation. They also can not rule their towns, their homes, or their bodies. This is the case to the extent that what they walk on can not be called a road, what they live in can not be called a room, and what they lie on can not be called a cot. . . . I also think that my countrymen do not have the ability to speak in a way that can be called speech, stand in a way that can be called standing, or walk in a way that can be called walking. This must be carefully managed. The character of the people is the root of the country's strength and weakness.[7]

Liang did praise Chinese he met abroad for their love of home (the root of patriotism), their unwillingness to assimilate (the spirit that promotes national independence), and their patient, laborious, and trustworthy characters (which helps build commerce).[8] But his experiences among Chinese overseas increasingly convinced him that the people themselves were more a problem than a solution to China's troubles and poor international status. Not surprisingly, Liang considered immigration to be a crucial problem in the formation of national character and was undecided about the desirability of non-Teutonic immigration for the United States.[9]

Even as Liang grew more conservative and elitist after 1902, members of the political reform movement he had fostered took the lead in objecting to discriminatory immigration laws.[10] Liang rode with the flow. In 1903 he published an article criticizing the White Australia policy as against the tide of world history because it did not affirm the fundamental principle of the equality of mankind.[11] In 1904 he added an appendix to his U.S. travelogue called "Notes on the Chinese Exclusion Act." Rather than criticizing the Chinese character, he argued that anti-Chinese charges were also true for laborers from southern Europe and that discriminatory labor practices were the true cause of low Chinese living standards in the United States. The roots of discrimination could be found in the international weakness of China and the ways in which U.S. politicians catered to the prejudices of the "Worker's Party."[12] But the movement itself would go much further than Liang in its willingness to embrace mass activism. The education of a national people would come not through discipline and restraint, but through the outspoken expression of national sentiment and outrage. The exclusion laws were more than just a consequence of weakness. They were a source of national and personal humiliation, a clarion call for retaliation through national unity—at least until more practical diplomatic and administrative solutions were proposed and dampened the enthusiasm.

Anti-American Boycott of 1905

The Chinese boycott was perhaps the first mass movement to protest migration laws as a matter of national honor. But it ultimately foundered in its inability to formulate practical goals. Perceptions of class differences were one source of tension. Some participants wanted the laws abolished altogether, while others aimed only to mitigate the harassment of exempt classes while conceding the legitimacy and desirability of excluding uncultured laborers. But a few participants began to wonder how a national movement could impact foreign legislation. The very act of protest was driven by the same goal of national self-determination against foreign incursions that had justified exclusionary laws in the first place. Protesters debated whether the right to control migration lay in international treaties or national law, and whether this was an issue that should properly be resolved through mass protest or negotiations by diplomats who could perceive the broader picture of national and international interests. Unwilling to embrace arguments grounded in treaty rights and free intercourse—the very arguments that had justified extraterritoriality—boycotters were unable to formulate a substantial critique of sovereign autonomy over borders. Ultimately, the boycotters found themselves able to protest only the discriminatory aspects of U.S. immigration law and not the basic principles. And even then protests could be grounded only in vague terms of moral justice that carried little institutional necessity. In a world where civilized government meant self-rule and the practice of self-rule was inseparable from calls for exclusion, the responsibility for discrimination was laid equally on the prejudices of white nations and the weakness of China.

By 1903 Chinese all around the Pacific were publicly demanding equitable treatment in national migration laws. This was especially the case in the United States, where Sargent's reforms were making exclusion ever more rigorous. In San Francisco, the Chinese Six Companies and other merchant associations produced widely circulated petitions to the U.S. government that complained of harsh enforcement. They also wrote to the Chinese government demanding that it negotiate a new treaty when the 1894 Gresham-Yang migration treaty came up for renewal the next year. On the other hand, Chen Jiyan's 1903 article in the Honolulu reformer paper *New China News* contended that diplomacy and good intentions could not be trusted. Often cited as the first open call to boycott, Chen insisted that the Chinese people must take matters into their own hands: "Today's world is a world of power, a world of competition, and a world of predominance of the superior and the subordination of the inferior. . . . Appeal to reason alone is by no means enough to persuade people. . . . What is the way to abolish the treaty then? It is a boycott."[13]

The Chinese government did renounce the treaty in 1904, but Congress unilaterally enacted the exclusion laws for an indefinite period, and Sargent's reforms continued to intensify. Negotiations for a new treaty stalled, and many Chinese grew suspicious of the commitment of the Chinese government to this cause. On May 10, 1905, the Shanghai Chamber of Commerce announced a boycott of American goods to begin on July 20 if a more favorable immigration treaty was not signed. Few Chinese ever migrated to the United States (or to anywhere) from Shanghai, and it was clear that the boycott was generated as much by concerns over national honor as by the concrete concerns of the migrants. But it quickly spread beyond Shanghai. Associations and individuals up and down the China coast and around the world sent telegrams of support. Activists produced endless pamphlets, novels, pictures, performances, speeches, and other educational materials and carried them around the globe from rural China to South Africa.[14] The scale of organization and grass-roots participation startled both Chinese and American officials.

Despite the enthusiasm, the concrete goals of the boycott remained muddled. Sympathetic observers complained of rambling speeches, sensationalized stories of abuse, and hyperbolic expressions of outrage that failed to address complicated matters of treaties and regulations.[15] But any attempt to talk in concrete rather than emotional terms quickly generated tension rather than unity. Only the more radical students challenged the basic right of the United States to exclude laborers and called for a complete abrogation of the exclusion "treaties." Merchants and people more familiar with the laws focused on the harassment of the exempt classes. San Francisco newspaper editor Ng Poon Chew expressed this attitude succinctly: "Chinese laborers of all classes have been excluded from the United States by mutual agreement, and the Chinese themselves are not now asking for any change in this arrangement, but they do ask for as fair treatment as other nationalities receive in relation to the exempt classes."[16] Claimants to exempt status saw themselves as cosmopolitan businessmen and students, the representatives of a new, modernizing China whose rights to move around the world with others of their class were guaranteed by international treaty. They distinguished themselves from uneducated and uncultured "coolies" and did not question the right of a sovereign nation to exclude "undesirable" classes even if they did question the precise definitions of those classes.

As early as May 20 the *New China News* suggested that the aims of the boycott could be achieved through a series of administrative reforms in the United States. Although the editorial placed much of the blame on Department of Commerce and Labor officials who were political appointees from the "labor party," many of its suggestions read as if they could have been written by Frank Sargent. It argued that China did not want to remove the restrictions against laborers, but that the Bureau of Immigration needed better regulations to distinguish exempts and laborers and coordinate the many aspects of administration. Administrative centralization was also a priority, "The task now is to make the purpose of the Department of Commerce and Labor and the other departments to correspond, and to stop this irrational and chaotic adding of laws on top of laws. Any country with a modicum of face would resolutely not agree to continue with these arrangements with the United States." The humiliating aspect of exclusion lay not in the laws themselves, but in the means of enforcement. "If officials at the ports of China made their investigations more conscientiously their status could be ascertained and Chinese could avoid interrogations, troubles, spending money, and wasting time at the U.S. border and still failing to obtain entry, all of which humiliates them and the country."[17] In other words, as the bureau itself had realized, if everything was done according to law and procedure, there would be little cause for complaint.

A group of Hong Kong merchants generated one of the few statements of explicit demands on December 9. Most of their recommendations were similar to those that Minister Liang Cheng was using as the basis of his treaty negotiations: acceptance of section 6 certificates at U.S. ports without question, registration of Chinese laborers only if also applied to all other immigrant laborers, participation of Chinese doctors in medical exams, free admission

Chinese laborers into Hawaii and the Philippines, an end to harassment of exempt classes, and renunciation of specific exempt classes (i.e., the "true theory" of exclusion) in favor of the exclusion only of laborers as defined in the *Oxford English Dictionary*. They also wanted all changes in regulations to be approved by the Chinese government. The viceroy of Guangdong, Cen Chunxuan, endorsed this proposal, and similar demands were included in a letter from Kang Youwei to President Roosevelt in January.[18]

Demands such as these were doomed from the beginning. They were trapped between U.S. officials who could see them as nothing but an infringement on U.S. autonomy, and more radical Chinese who insisted that anything short of entire abrogation failed to address the root offense of discriminating against Chinese in the first place. This latter group repudiated the demands as a capitulation by merchants who were fearful of losing their trade. This break highlighted the fundamental confusion in the formulation of the issues. The relationship between a popular nationalist movement and international relations was far from clear. The fact that most boycott propaganda focused on the exclusion "treaty" rather than on U.S. legislation highlights some of the conceptual problems. Many boycotters saw the honor of China as entangled in the establishment and enforcement of equitable international agreements. Few boycotters grappled with the previous twenty years of U.S. legal and political decisions that had unilaterally removed migration from the realm of international concerns. Indeed, awareness of these developments would have introduced even more uncertainty to a movement that was largely driven by the desire to protect its own sovereignty against foreign penetration and humiliation.

Masses and Experts

Confusion over the relationship of a popular boycott and international relations was a reflection the more fundamental tensions between self-government and free mobility that lie at the heart of modern liberal and "civilized" society. Both historians and contemporary participants have seen the boycott as a significant step toward the ideals of popular participation and self-government in China. The fact that this boycott was aimed at a foreign nation underlines the extent to which these ideals were inseparable from concerns over international status. But when both Chinese and non-Chinese began to talk in more practical terms about the rights of citizens abroad and the means of protecting them, mass movements—both the boycott in China and anti-Asian movements in North America—quickly came to be seen as a problem rather than a solution. Both Chinese and U.S. officials increasingly emphasized the need for a more educated and disciplined populace that did not undermine the work of expert diplomats struggling to iron out the complexities of global intercourse. Even many of the boycotters who thought carefully about the practical aspects came around to thinking that the best solution was a more disciplined national populace and reformed institutions to create a China with the strength to be taken more seriously in international affairs.

Some of the tensions between ideals of international comity and national self-determination came out in the disparate assumptions that crosscut the class-based interests of the boycotters.[19] Many participants understood the boycott as a call for the United States to adhere to universal moral principle (*gongli*) rather than naked power (*qiangquan*). Kang Youwei framed it this way when he reminded Theodore Roosevelt of his promise to "bring about a change [in the exclusion laws] in the interest of justice and square dealing."[20] Kang approached the issue as primarily a matter to be solved between honorable elites to facilitate the movement of other elites. But those who (unlike Kang) advocated the complete abolition of exclusion could also appropriate the high ground of moral principle. As phrased by Shanghai novelist Wu Woyao, "If the boycott is just for the rights of a few, it is not morally correct and our conscience will never be at peace."[21] Other boycotters such as Chen Jiyan, however, understood international relations as a Darwinist struggle between peoples. For them the boycott was useful primarily as an act to unify and strengthen the Chinese nation. Moral pretenses amounted to nothing without power. Boycotters of all persuasions, however, generally concurred that a boycott was the most effective way to bring China's concern into the international limelight. As phrased in a December 1905 editorial in Liang Qichao's Tokyo-based paper *New Citizen* [*Xinmin congbao*], the boycott demonstrated the weakness of the Chinese government in comparison with the "magical power" of the Chinese people to shake the world.[22]

But when it came to searching for the source of exclusionist sentiments, it was precisely the magical power of the U.S. people that was the cause for objection. Both Chinese officials and boycotters commonly targeted the influence of workers' parties over the U.S. government. As one boycott ditty put it, "The Workingmen's Party is wooed as sluts are courted / Why is it so? Is it the way a democratic country works and civilized law dictates?"[23] Similarly, Minister Liang Cheng told Minister Rockhill in early 1906, "My country deals with and recognizes only the government of a single country, not a mass of worker parties."[24] But even as they mocked the power of the workers' parties in the United States, many boycotters demanded recognition of their own movement. They commonly insisted that treaty negotiations of direct interest to the common people should be not held in secret, and that the government must listen to the needs of the people and get their approval for any treaty. Not all boycotters, however, agreed with this stance. Some felt that the practical understanding of the treaties was complicated, and negotiations should be left to skilled diplomats. The purpose of the boycott was only to offer suggestions and make sure that the government did not sign a discriminatory treaty.[25]

Non-Chinese observers also divided over the meaning of mass politics in China. Many European papers in China at first took the side of the boycotters, seeing it as an opportunity to undermine U.S. prestige in China by noting the hypocrisy of excluding Chinese while claiming to uphold the Burlingame treaty and proclaiming an Open Door in China. Over time, however, many papers began to worry about their own future interests and to call upon the British or U.S. government to intervene directly against all movements that might hinder free trade.[26] This was the perspective of most U.S. officials. They refused to recognize the boycott as an exercise in popular government and insisted that the Chinese government's failure to suppress it was an infringement against treaty provisions that protected trading rights and the property of U.S. citizens. On August 8 Minister Rockhill threatened that if the Foreign Office did not punish the ringleaders, he would hold the Chinese government directly responsible for failing to uphold the treaties.[27] U.S. consuls went further and blamed the boycott on the instigation of Chinese officials and self-interested migration brokers, complaining that boycott organizations illegally intimidated merchants who wished to buy American goods. State Department officials in Washington tended to be a bit more restrained, rejecting proposals to demand the cashiering of local officials and censuring consuls who requested that warships be sent to Chinese ports. But they were also greatly disturbed by their lack of control over these events. In this vein, President Roosevelt acknowledged the justice of Chinese grievances even as he insisted that the boycotters needed to be taught a lesson.[28]

Chinese official responses were varied and reflected the contradictory drives both to build a stronger China based on broad participation and to carefully manage China's actions in the international sphere. One of the earliest official responses was a proclamation from the Waiwubu on June 29 (reiterated as an imperial edict on August 30) telling provincial officials that "our merchants' boycott and propaganda activities merely show the public anger against the United States policy. For fear that scoundrels might take advantage of their activities in instigating a revolt, we advise you to persuade the merchants to give up the boycott and to explain that our government is conducting the necessary negotiations now."[29] This edict set the official line of formal disapproval tempered by nonintervention and recognition of the legitimate grievances of the people. Viceroy Cen referred to this edict when refusing Consul Julius Lay's demand to suppress the boycott immediately, adding that the boycott was not an international but a domestic question. Moreover, the laws of civilized countries did not permit the prohibition of free speech, and he could not interfere with the people's right to buy what they wanted. Cen promised only to arrest anybody who used force to compel others to buy one thing or another. "This is reasonable and agrees with the custom of the various countries of the world."[30]

Most U.S. officials considered Cen to be uncooperative and obstructionist. But he actually adhered to a middle path between the opinions of other Chinese officials. The governors of Shanxi and Zhejiang went so far as to criticize the existing "treaty" as against international law. They asked the emperor to support the boycott because it had already impressed foreign powers with the power of the Chinese people, and success would help prevent future international humiliation.[31] Governor-General Yuan Shikai, on the other hand, repressed the boycott in the northern provinces almost before it had started, insisting that the United States was a valuable ally that could not be offended. Other officials further justified Yuan's actions by insisting that the court had lost control over the behavior of Chinese overseas, and that suppression had to be followed by better methods of control and education.[32]

Two of the more nuanced analyses of these issues were produced in a memorial from Beijing official Wang Buying and in an anonymous polemical novel titled *Extraordinary Speeches on the Boycott* (*Jiyue qitan*). Although very different in their origins and concerns, both authors agreed that the mass mobilization was impressive and inspiring but had caused as many problems as solutions. They also converged on a similar resolution in the idea that international problems could be solved only after China itself had grown strong and disciplined. Wang discussed the strength and limitations of mass democracy from the perspective of conditions in the United States, which he considered to be the most democratic of all countries. Although U.S. officials were constrained by their inability to ignore the selfish demands of the Workers' Party, "The power of the people is very strong, and we should fear their uniting against an enemy country." This presented a challenge both internally and internationally to China's own attempts to grow stronger. If the Chinese court failed to meet this challenge, "The people [of China] would see this as a thorn and later it would be more difficult for the Court to deal with this problem in ways that the people would not see as wanton repression of their spirit. It would make the people feel contemptuous of officials and cause a rift between the court and the people. How then could we build the country?"[33] He suggested that rather than allowing the United States to unilaterally impose exclusion, a provisional treaty with a ten-year limit would help mitigate the worst excesses and avoid causing a rift with the United States until China was strong enough to negotiate more favorable terms. The treaty should be augmented by a secret edict to local officials to convince the local Chambers of Commerce not to act rashly. The cultivation of the power of China's own people had to come slowly and orderly.

Sick Man, the protagonist of *Extraordinary Speeches*, was less convinced of the efficacy of either official or mass action but concurred in the need for a strong China. In discussing the idea that exclusion was not based on treaty but on the domestic laws of the United States (one of the few proboycott voices to focus on this distinction), he concluded that immigration laws still had international implications, especially when they discriminated against a single nation:

> Were the harsh exclusion laws promulgated to regulate the Americans or to regulate the Chinese? If they were for the Americans, then they are indeed domestic matters, and there is no reason for us to interfere. But these laws are exercised against the Chinese. Furthermore, are they promulgated against immigrants to America in general or exclusively against the Chinese? If they are against all the rest . . . then we could sit back and wait for people of other countries to complain and denounce them. But they are used exclusively against the Chinese. Since the exclusion laws discriminate only against the Chinese and not against immigrants in general, they are domestic laws with international implications.[34]

But Sick Man ultimately concluded that a boycott had a limited potential to influence the United States. The weakness of China was the root of the problem. Economic development was the only solution, both to make China powerful and to make it possible for Chinese to commit to buying only Chinese products. As with Wang Buying, Sick Man was forced to conclude that reinforcement of the domestic sphere was the only basis of participation in the international system.

In subsequent years, other essayists and journalists in China echoed Wang Buying and Sick Man. In addition to emphasizing the link between institutional reform and economic power, they also remarked on the importance of reformed institutions in creating international acceptance even in the absence of substantive power. In this vein, essayists increasingly criticized restrictions over the movement of foreigners in the interior of China as an embarrassment to the nation and evidence of the inability of the Chinese government to provide international standards of protection.[35] The very process of challenging U.S. exclusion laws had made more Chinese aware of the standards of free internal movement and equal protection under law that the United States had used to justify its own border controls. In raising this awareness, the boycott had ended up reinforcing some of the basic principles of migration control. Free intercourse and guaranteed rights were reduced to spaces within borders, and critiques against borders were limited to complaints about discrimination.

Chinese officials were not alone in their ambivalent reactions to these mass movements. With both the boycott and recent Pacific Coast disturbances against the Japanese in mind, U.S. Secretary of State Elihu Root noted in 1907 that "The practice of diplomacy has ceased to be a mystery confined to a few learned men . . . and has become a representative function answering to the opinions and the will of the multitude of citizens." Although perhaps an inevitable development, he lamented that

> the rules and customs which the experience of centuries had shown to be
> essential to the maintenance of peace and good understanding between
> nations have little weight with the new popular masters of diplomacy;
> the precedents and agreements of opinion which have carried so great a
> part of the rights and duties of nations toward each other beyond the pale
> of discussion are but little understood. The education of public opinion,
> which should lead the sovereign people in each country to understand
> the definite limitations upon national rights and the full scope and re-
> sponsibility of national duties, has only just begun.[36]

The institutions of self-government that Bayard and others had once promoted as the foundation of border control and the domestic protection of alien rights were increasingly identified with the mass politics that threatened the rights of aliens and international order. Specialized bureaucracies, expert management, and public cultivation through education were upheld as the best means to regulate the unruly interactions between nations made of and for the people.

Spiritualizing Self-regulation

As in many other fields of thought and action, Mohandas Gandhi developed one of the most compelling and highly moralized syntheses of proper personal and political comportment in relation to migration control. The Chinese boycott had become mired the tensions between sovereign self-determination, mass politics, expert knowledge, and migration control. In developing the practice of satyagraha (often glossed as "passive resistance," although Gandhi preferred to translate it as "love force" or "the firmness born of truth") to protest the discrimination against Asians in South Africa, Gandhi managed to subsume these tensions under more transcendent practices and ideals. He combined personal self-rule, disciplinary techniques, social equality, national honor, legal expertise, border control, and the search for spiritual meaning altogether into one seamless package. In resisting discriminatory legislation, he developed a highly charged moral and spiritual vindication of the role of civilized institutions in maintaining the link between individual and nation as the foundations of modern identity.

Gandhi arrived in Natal in 1893 to work as a lawyer and soon became involved in struggles to protect the rights of resident Indians against discriminatory legislation. When the British began to enforce the old Boer laws in the Transvaal after 1903, Gandhi felt that legal tactics were no longer enough and started to develop the practice and principles of satyagraha. Gandhi's most comprehensive theoretical statement, *Hind Swaraj*, was written while he was on a ship traveling from London to South Africa in 1908. His elaboration of love-force in that work is striking for its radical rejection of violence and the machinery of modern life. But this rejection was grounded in a conflation of national and individual freedom that was very modern in its conception. The very title of the book, which he translated as "Indian Home Rule," embodies the link between individual and national salvation. Gandhi explained that "real home rule is self rule or self-control." The best way to cultivate this self rule was through participation in the political activity of love-force.[37] "If we become free, India is free. And in this thought you have a definition of *swaraj*. It is *swaraj* when we learn to rule ourselves" (47).

True *swaraj* was rooted in civilization. "Civilization is that mode of conduct which points out to man the path of duty. Performance of duty and observance of morality are convertible terms. To observe morality is to attain mastery over our mind and passions. So doing, we know ourselves" (45). Gandhi's civilization cannot be mapped directly onto the standard of "civilization," but the use of a common word is not simply coincidental. Both point toward a disciplined community with institutions linked to individualized modes of being. Both also point to cultural attainments linked to particular national societies. Gandhi occasionally complained that Asian registration laws in South Africa brought educated Indians down to the level of the natives. In his 1896 pamphlet, *The Grievances of the British Indians in South Africa*, he explained that that, unlike for Indians, "There is a very good reason for requiring registration of a native in that he is yet being taught the dignity and necessity of labour."[38] And in 1906 he complained to the London *Times* that "The British Indians of the Transvaal respectfully but firmly oppose the [registration] Ordinance because it imposes wanton, uncalled for and unjust degradation upon them. It reduces them to a level lower than the Kaffirs [natives]."[39] Gandhi also accepted the major cultural and political categories of the modern world: a spiritualized, earth-bound East contrasted to a materialist, restless West; the distinctions between peoples and nations as primary sources of identity and law; and political membership as the primary issue linking the social and the personal. And, despite his criticisms of spiritually barren "modern civilization," Gandhi consistently identified his own struggles in South Africa with the rights promised by membership in the British Empire, the self-proclaimed avatar of "civilization" in the world.

The question of the responsibilities and limits of political membership was at the very heart of Gandhi's conception of satyagraha and its political goals, and it resonated well with modern concepts of self-rule. In *Hind Swaraj* he explained the process of love-force in terms that resonated with ideals of political equality, self-rule, and consent:

A petition backed by force is a petition from an equal and, when he transmits his demand in the form of a petition, it testifies to his nobility. Two kinds of force can back petitions. "We shall hurt you if you do not give this" is one kind of force; it is the force of arms. The second kind of force can be thus stated: "If you do not concede our demand, we shall be no longer your petitioners. You can govern us only so long as we remain the governed." (53)

A petition was the act of a free man, whose consent was necessary in order for governance to take place. The fashioning of one's self into a free man with the ability to participate in governance was the work of love-force and the foundation of a free political community.

But the specifics of a self-ruling political community could quickly grow complex in the context of practical struggles in the British Empire. Gandhi appealed more often to the ideals of the British Empire than to the concrete institutions of self-rule in South Africa. He often demanded rights in South Africa by virtue of his being a British subject, complaining that discriminatory Asiatic laws in the colony did not distinguish between Indians, who were British subjects, and Chinese or other Asians, who were not.[40] In justifying his participation in the British medical corps during the Boer and Zulu wars, he explained that empire was the relevant space of duty, rights, and community:

> Our existence in South Africa is only in our capacity as British subjects. In
> every memorial we have presented we have asserted our rights as such. . . .
> If we desire to win our freedom and achieve our welfare as members of
> the British Empire, here is a golden opportunity for us to do so by helping
> the British in the war by all the means at our disposal. It must largely be
> conceded that justice is on the side of the Boers. But every single subject
> of a state must not hope to enforce his private opinion in all cases. The
> authorities may not always be right, but so long as the subjects own al-
> legiance to a state, it is their clear duty generally to accommodate them-
> selves, and to accord their support, to acts of the state.[41]

As hinted in the first line of the quote above, Gandhi was aware that a self-governing South African republic would generate little foundation for Indian rights. But rather than recognizing the self-determination of local polities, he often cast doubt on the very existence of viable political communities in South Africa that could support the institutions of self-rule. For example, after a 1907 case in which the governor of Natal reprieved a black man who had been judged guilty in trial by jury, Gandhi suggested that it would be best for trial by jury to be "abolished altogether" in South Africa:

> How is it possible to get any satisfaction out of jurymen in a place like
> South Africa, where different nationalities are still in the melting pot,
> and a South African nation has yet to rise in the dim and distant future?
> We are no worshippers of the idol of equality, when there is no founda-

tion for it. . . . White people from different parts of Europe, who come to South Africa with no notion of Imperialism, cannot be expected either to think of Imperial obligations or other notions of justice and equal rights as between themselves and others whom they hold to be inferior.[42]

Of course, by this time the rhetoric of imperialism and British subjecthood already carried little practical efficacy. In line with the sentiments of the self-governing colonies, Gandhi did not emphasize the right of British subjects to free movement. Rather, he emphasized the rights and equality before law that should come with long residence within the borders of a community under British rule. After early protests against the 1897 Natal dictation test, Gandhi increasingly acknowledged the right of a nation to enact immigration laws as it wished and focused his attention against discriminatory domestic laws. He acknowledged the need for the Peace Preservation Ordinance of 1902 that blocked the entry of Indians who were not previously resident in the Transvaal, although he complained about the harshness of enforcement. The reenactment of discriminatory residence, registration, and licensing legislation after 1903 was a much more serious issue. In a 1904 editorial in his paper *Indian Opinion*, Gandhi criticized any kind of discrimination against Indian subjects within the British Empire but considered the obstacles against new migration to be much less serious than the infringement on rights of current and previous residents:

> While we may not say much against a ruthless carrying out of the law so far as new immigrants are concerned, we do feel that the Department will be going a little too far in attempting to drive away men who are already established in the Colony. It is hardly fair to hound decent people out of the Colony as if they were criminals, especially when it is known that the very Department which allowed them to enter the Colony is driving them away.[43]

In September 1906 the Transvaal passed its own version of the Natal Act requiring a language test for immigration alongside the "Black Act," which required new registration with fingerprints and authorized the deportation Indians who did not show their identification on demand. Gandhi argued that the Black Act should be the main object of protest because once it was repealed the Immigration Restriction Act "would lose the sting."[44] As he explained to the *Times* of London, "British Indians in their wildest dreams have never claimed the right of free immigration into the Transvaal. They recognize the several prejudices against any such immigration, and have therefore accepted the principle of restriction in vogue at the Cape, Natal and other British Colonies."[45] At a ceremony to burn registration certificates in August 1908, Gandhi further elaborated on the difference between the rights of residence and the rights of international movement:

> I claim that this country belongs to the British Indians just as much as it belongs to the Europeans . . . but what does that claim mean? I do not therefore, mean that it is open to us to have an unchecked influx of Asiatics into this country. No, I claim to be a colonist, I claim to have passed a fair measure of my life in this country, and if this country, the welfare of this country, demands that Asiatic immigration should not proceed unchecked, then I should be the first man to say, let that be so. If the majority of the inhabitants of this country demand that Asiatic immigration should cease—mind, I lay stress upon the term immigration—if Asiatic immigration should be under well-ordered control, then I say that I should also accept that position, but having accepted that position, I should claim that this country is just as much mine as any other colonist's, and it is in that sense that I put forward that claim on behalf of my countrymen.[46]

Physical presence was still only the first step in obtaining rights. Indians also had to earn them through their deportment as a civilized people. When he persuaded Indians to voluntarily accede to a 1905 reregistration of Indians in the Transvaal, he explained that this reaction was intended to be understood as "proof of their veracity, tact, large-mindedness, commonsense and humility . . . in the hope that new restrictions might not be imposed upon them."[47] This conciliatory attitude diminished with the Black Act of 1906, but the importance of civilized status remained. He later recalled of the act that

> I have never known legislation of this nature being directed against free men in any part of the world. I know that indentured Indians in Natal are subject to a drastic system of passes, but these poor fellows can hardly be classed as free men. . . . If we fully understand all the implications of this legislation, we shall find that India's honor is in our keeping. For the Ordinance seeks to humiliate not only ourselves but also the motherland. The humiliation consists in the degradation of innocent men.[48]

Ultimately, the perception of Indians as a free and civilized people was at stake more than the preservation of British rights or institutions of self-rule. Whatever the tension in the ways that Gandhi imagined civilization, community, and peoplehood, these were transcended by the power of satyagraha to create free individuals and communities through intense and uncowardly spiritual, physical, and political action. And this new consciousness forged by satyagraha would ultimately help refocus on rights as a consequence of belonging to a recognized self-determining nation, rather than as a consequence of imperial subjecthood or as the abstract rights of a mobile humanity.

Love Force and Law

Many of Gandhi's objections to discriminatory laws in the Transvaal resonated with Japanese and Chinese attitudes that international status must begin with discipline at home. Much of his thinking about satyagraha was suffused with a vocabulary of honor, manliness, and bravery. He even agreed that national honor could take precedence over the necessity of nonviolence: "I would rather have India resort to arms in order to defend her honour than that she should in a cowardly manner become or remain a helpless witness to her own dishonour."[49] In his practical negotiations, he also echoed Japanese demands for equality in the letter of the law even if laws were administered discriminatorily. Formal equality helped maintain the public status of Indians while protecting the right of a sovereign nation to control its own social composition. As Gandhi explained in the 1920s,

> If the anti-Indian laws did not mention the Indians by name and were not thus made expressly applicable to them alone but to all subjects, and if their enforcement had been left to the discretion of administrators . . . the object of the legislators would all the same have been achieved by such laws, and yet the laws would have been general laws. None would have felt insulted by their enactment, and when the existing bitterness was softened by time, there would be no need to modify the laws, but only a more liberal administration of the laws would have sufficed to relieve the aggrieved community.[50]

Gandhi went beyond the Japanese in developing methods of compromise and resistance that transcended formal law and restraints. Instead of emphasizing top-down state controls, Gandhi placed personal sacrifice and self-discipline at the heart of his movement. In this way, legal nuances that might be interpreted as a circuitous attempt to save face could be reinterpreted as a significant moral victory by a free and civilized people. At a mass meeting of protest shortly before the Black Act was passed, Seth Haji Habib made a solemn oath before God to resist the new laws. This generated an epiphany in Gandhi: the struggle against discriminatory laws was, first and foremost, a commitment to personal discipline, a discipline that was the foundation for community discipline. He soon spoke up:

> Every one of us must think out for himself if he has the will and the ability to pledge himself. Resolutions of this nature cannot be passed by a majority vote. Only those who take a pledge can be bound by it. . . . Every one must only search his own heart, and if the inner voice assures him that he has the requisite strength to carry him through, then only should he pledge himself and then only will his pledge bear fruit. . . . If some one asks me when and how the struggle may end, I may say that if the entire community manfully stands the test, the end will be near.[51]

The nonregistration movement was a great success. Soon the local jails were full and the satyagraha movement had gained some support among the local white population. In January 1908 the Transvaal government agreed to negotiate the repeal of the Black Act in return for Gandhi's promise that the voluntary registration of all Asians that could later be legalized under an amendment to the immigration restriction act. Many followers felt betrayed that Gandhi would make these agreements behind closed doors. When it came to the complex negotiations that shaped the practical agreements between people, even Gandhi found it hard to resist the convenience and lure of privileged negotiations between experts.

Many followers were also unconvinced about the moral and political distinction between compulsory and voluntary registration. Gandhi explained in the *Indian Opinion* that voluntary conformance was a categorically different moral act from submission:

> I am not surprised at your being unable to understand this. The law brought compulsion to bear on us to make us register; that was humiliating. So much for compulsory registration. But if we take out the same kind of register of our own free will, that will save us the dishon-

our and even show that we are magnanimous. To take an example. If, by way of service to a friend, I wash his feet or carry his bed-pan, that will strengthen our friendship, give me an inner satisfaction and win for me the good opinion of others. Another, although he dislikes such work and thinks it derogatory, may yet do the same thing either under duress or for the sake of money. We shall think him base and regard him as a slave. We shall call him mean. He will himself feel ashamed of his job. If anyone finds him engaged in that work, he will try to hide himself. He is in reality a sinner and will never feel happy in himself. The difference between voluntary and compulsory registration is much the same.[52]

As with indenture contracts, potential bondage was made free through prior, voluntary consent.

Gandhi also responded to critics who charged that the law would be enforced regardless of whether or not they volunteered, and that in going through the motions of self-registration, "what you call voluntary therefore appears to be tainted both with compulsion and self-interest." In response, Gandhi moved his argument to a spiritual level, insisting that the very act of coming together in resistance had changed the meaning of voluntary registration and even worked to the greater good of all humanity:

If we had been moved at any time by fear, we could not have held out against the Government for 16 months as we have done. Afraid of our power—the power of our truth—the Government has accepted voluntary registration. . . . In voluntary registration there is undoubtedly an element of self-interest. If a man living as a servant of God devotes himself wholly to the service of men or of all living creatures, he is also impelled by self-interest in seeking to be in the presence of God, to work for *nirvana*. We revere such a man. If there were many such in this world, we should find it in holiness, prosperity, peace, happiness and unity instead of the wickedness, suffering misery starvation and disease which we see in it today.[53]

To critics who noted that the voluntary registration still included fingerprinting, which had once been the main symbol of the humiliation under the Black Act, Gandhi responded, "We were against finger-impressions only so long as they were a body inhabited by that Satanic law," which was no longer the case now that fingerprints a voluntary choice of a newly self-conscious

Indian people.[54] He did, however, amplify his argument that educated men should not give their fingerprints:

> Educated persons and men of means and standing can be identified by the knowledge they possess and by their appearance. It is humiliating to them even to be asked to give finger-impressions. Looking at it thus, it does not appear wrong that illiterate persons who are not otherwise known should have to give finger-impressions. On the contrary these would ensure the fullest protection for them.[55]

As with the Chinese exclusion laws, international mobility and the very possibility of being a truly free man were dependent on a certain class status and the ability to surround oneself with the accoutrements of "civilization."

Not all Indians were convinced. One of the unconvinced nearly beat Gandhi to death on his way to register. But most Indians did register and have their fingerprints taken. General Smuts, however, later denied having agreed to repeal the Black Act, and many Indians again blamed Gandhi for having negotiated with the South African government without having taken the broader community into account. The satyagraha activities slowed down after 1909, and Gandhi retreated to the communal Tolstoy farm where he perfected the theoretical framework and practical behavior most appropriate to satyagraha. He experimented with forms of self-regulation that included diet, physical training, celibacy, and self sufficiency, emphasizing that strength of mind and body were necessary to engage in satyagraha. He also experimented in forms of social organization to maintain discipline among farm residents, including an insistence on an open public accounting of all money.[56]

The development of new immigration laws for the Union of South Africa from 1911 to 1913 generated a resurgence of the satyagraha movement. The issues under contention included free movement between the states of the Union, the definition of domicile, the definition of minors, the definition of legal marriages and wives, the right of educated Indians to enter South Africa freely, and the continued existence of the registration fee in Natal. Many of these issues revolved around highly technical legal distinctions and phraseologies that could be even more subtle than the distinction between coerced and voluntary registration. Gandhi the lawyer became inseparable from Gandhi the moralist. Most of the compromises ultimately written into the law amounted to a promise not to enforce the law rigorously and to allow official discretion in granting special permits to selected Indians.[57] The provisions of the South African act of 1885 that had started all the resistance remained untouched, only now reformulated in terms of the "Canadian principle" of discretionary exclusion for "economic" reasons.

Gandhi departed South Africa in 1914, satisfied that truth had at least partially prevailed. In practice, South Africa never made good on most of the discretionary promises. Gandhi's legal agreements, however, had helped move migration law out of the hands of popular self-government and into the realm of administrative expertise. But in doing so, he retained the strong moral overtones of migration control by casting the technicalities and justifications of border control as spiritualized ideals of personal identity and political belonging. He transformed participation in the enforcement of migration laws from an issue political necessity and national honor, as it was with the Japanese, into an individual moral imperative.

12

Borders Across the World, 1907–1939

In 1936 Harry Laughlin analyzed immigration laws in all the countries and colonies of the Americas for the Eugenics Record Office of the Carnegie Institution. In his report he insisted on the universal right and even necessity for each nation to control and select immigrants as a matter of domestic policy:

> Within its own territory each race must, by all mankind, be granted the right to conserve its own race integrity. The right to strive for race integrity is like the pursuit of happiness; it is one of those things which is not given by one human group to another, but it is an inherent right. An alien in a host country exists there either by virtue of his military prowess—a conqueror, or on sufferance of the host country—and not in accordance with any inherent rights either moral or legal.[1]

For Laughlin, a fragmented world of self-determining political, social, and racial units was the source and object of human rights. He went on to argue that to establish immigration regulation by treaty rather than legislation was to sign away fundamental rights associated with sovereignty. Treaties were useful only to establish convenient procedures such as passport uniformity, not to uphold standards of selectivity. He acknowledged that the international movement of travelers and temporary aliens should be encouraged as a commercial benefit and peace-making activity. But this realm of intercourse should be bracketed off behind firm legislative distinctions between citizens, travelers, and immigrants. The integrity of the social-territorial unit was the first moral priority.

According to Laughlin, this world of borders and territories could best be maintained through standardized immigration laws. His report concluded with a model immigration control law.[2] It began with an assertion that the nation had sole and sovereign authority over immigration and went on to propose clauses that made legal distinctions between visitors and immigrants; established a quota formula; set standards of selectivity based on potential for assimilability as measured by anthropometry, mental tests, and health standards; required loyalty tests; set forth clear procedures for expatriation, deportation, naturalization, issuing passports, and registering foreigners; and established appropriate institutional machinery and authority to enforce the laws. Each nation could tailor the details to fit its needs. But the very possibility of preserving national autonomy in the first place required that those details be drawn from the most advanced and scientific legislative models.

Although expressed in a vocabulary of self-determination, Laughlin was actually proposing machinery for the standardization of global norms and regulation. His proposal could be taken seriously in the 1930s because many people had come to believe that it reflected the world as it actually was—a world of inherently distinct nations searching for the best arrangements to protect their integrity against external challenges. To an extent, such people were right. The principles and machinery of sovereign border control, once developed to limit Asian participation in global intercourse, had become universalized. Border control had become a precondition rather than a result of sovereignty and self-rule. Laughlin's openly eugenicist perspective did not survive World War II, but the rest of his proposal still represents the basic possibilities in most thinking about migration (now better labeled "immigration") policy.

The diffusion of the principles and practices of migration control was a complex process. Every specific adoption and adaptation took place in distinct historical circumstances. But over the long term, imitation, diplomatic pressure, international conferences, the ease of reproducing established precedents, and adherence to what was believed to be the most advanced legal and scientific techniques all generated a broad consensus about the parameters and justifications of migration control. Even innovations, such as the U.S. quota laws of the 1920s, were framed as attempts to perfect existing mechanisms and to reconcile the principle of the international equality of all peoples with the right of a nation to determine its own population. Although not everybody agreed that the quota law actually achieved this reconciliation, this law still set the technical standards for migration control around the world. Institutions that had their origins in exceptional methods necessary to preserve the ideals of self-government from the threats of an uncivilized world had now become indispensable technologies of population management. Their adoption became a prerequisite for recognition as a self-determining state in the international system.

Policy Diffusion

The diffusion of migration laws was not merely a response to growing numbers of migrants. Many countries established restrictive laws well before the arrival of any significant migration. Their adoption had much to do with a perception of how a civilized country should define its social and political borders. Indeed, laws and techniques were repeatedly adopted as state-of-the-art methods with little evidence of their effectiveness and often with evidence to the contrary. Failed enforcement was rarely interpreted as a call to question the efficacy of the methods, and certainly not to question the basic need of border control. Rather it was interpreted as evidence of the inadequacy of the state or institution that implemented the law, or of the moral deficiency of the migrants who evaded it. Nonetheless, the adoption of immigration laws also implied an intention to develop the administrative, legal, and political structures that could enforce such laws, not only domestically but as part of an international system of acceptable documentation and categorization.

Laughlin's collection of actual migration policies across the Americas shows that they had already converged significantly in terms of formal principles and methods by the 1930s. All were formulated in terms of controls and surveillance exercised at the border. Nearly all restricted immigrants on the basis of health, criminal record, and politics (i.e., rebels, anarchists, radicals). Most also demanded that the immigrant provide himself with documents before departure, such as a passport, health certificate, police record, or letter of good conduct. Attitudes toward contract labor showed the most variation, ranging from selective encouragement to absolute prohibition. Laws in colonial possessions around the Caribbean were the most heterogeneous, often still based on nineteenth-century legislation to encourage and monitor plantation labor. Independence brought legislative homogeneity.

In most cases, formal convergence was achieved well before the arrival of significant migration flows. This was especially the case for racially based legislation. Of twenty-two independent nations in the Americas, eighteen explicitly excluded Asians despite having little or no experience with Asian migration. The remaining four—Argentina, Brazil, Chile, and Peru—had (along with Panama) the most extensive diplomatic relations with Asia and were consequently the most discrete in their methods of regulation: Brazil inserted them into larger system of nationality quotas, while Peru and Chile excluded them through administrative decrees.[3] Most of these nations banned Asians when their migration was at best a mere trickle, such as Ecuador in 1889, Guatemala in 1896, and Nicaragua and Costa Rica in 1897. They were impelled by a general perception that a civilized nation must protect itself in advance against what was, in the words of the Costa Rican law, a "noxious race."[4]

This diffusion of migration laws in the Americas does not support an understanding of policy diffusion as a functional response to common economic and structural challenges.[5] Rather the adoption of these laws must be understood as part of the spread of institutions and ideologies of population management that were necessary for international recognition as a modern nation state. In Europe during the 1920s, it is difficult to separate the role of domestic and international pressures because the rise of immigration restrictions came hand in hand with the rise of welfare states and expanded suffrage that demanded more careful distinctions between citizens and noncitizens and their eligibility for jobs and benefits. Expanding electoral politics also encouraged politicians to promote border policies believed to protect the domestic economy and wages.[6] But the appropriation of migration laws even by states in the Americas with no significant welfare institutions, immigration flows, industrial labor force, or electoral politics emphasizes the important role of global norms, power, channeled knowledge, and standardized possibilities in the diffusion of policy. Border control was no longer just a possible consequence of self-rule but a prerequisite to recognition as a self-governing state, whether democratic or not.

Even in American nations receiving significant migration, there is little evidence that the models they appropriated were the most efficacious ones. For the most part, those models were associated with powerful states such as the British Empire and the United States, where they had been forged piecemeal out of the compromises, diplomacy, and accumulated decisions of excluding Asians in the late nineteenth century. But by the 1920s, after these specific historical experiences had been written into more general migration laws, they had taken on the status of universally applicable models. At times, the United States propagated its models through direct pressure on neighboring states to coordinate migration policies or to adopt more acceptable standards for the treatment of U.S. citizens. But once these models were entrenched, it was hard to establish alternatives. The need to screen migrants before departure, furnish them with appropriate documents, and engage in the diplomacy and commerce of migration meant that many states and businesses had already adjusted to the institutional standards of migrant regulation well before they produced legislation or decrees to that effect.

At a practical level, knowledge of these models and their operation spread through networks of experts, diplomats, consultants, legal writings, and scientific thought. When searching for precedents and principles, these advisers repeatedly pointed to trans-Pacific migration laws as a key source—at least until derivative examples in which the racial divide was less explicit had been established. At a more abstract level, the incentive to adopt these models was inseparable from more general ideas and institutions that shaped the emerging international system, including those that defined modern sovereignty, scientific racism, the scope of individual rights, and the impact of immigration on national welfare and the social body. To not frame migration control in these terms was to refuse to behave as a civilized society, to reject scientific methods, and to place oneself outside of world historical progress. The very willingness to adopt standard models, even without any realistic ability to enforce them, demonstrated an intention to participate in the global order while simultaneously reinforcing the legitimacy of that order.

Beyond establishing global standards of physical and mental fitness, race, and family, the diffusion of migration laws also established individuals as the fundamental object and product of global regulation. The process of documenting, legalizing, and illegalizing migrants operated on the premise that migrants themselves carried the bulk of responsibility for their status. Regulatory agencies merely investigated and confirmed an individual's claims. This understanding helped justify the never-ending suppression of privately organized migration that did not directly collaborate in official regulation. It also produced a standardized object of regulation to exist alongside the standardized methods and principles. As argued by David Strang and John Meyer in a discussion of the global diffusion of modern institutions in general, modernity's "careful analysis of the bounded individual, the rationalized organization, and the purposive society create powerful standardizing forces. The diffusion processes involved directly oppose the internal rationalization sought by the modernizing process and presupposed its analysis. The modern actors whose uniqueness and autonomy are most celebrated are precisely those most subject to the homogenizing effects of diffusion."[7] In other words, the nearly infinite proliferation of unique individuals was not a challenge to regulatory institutions and categories, but a product. Theoretically, the proliferation of individual difference is limited only by the abstract concept of a common humanity. But it is precisely this quality of encompassing nearly infinite difference that requires special privileges and distinctions to be leveled out through equal treatment and standardized procedures. The institutions to enforce those procedures are not universal but lodged in particular nations, themselves part of an international society defined by the formal equality and standardized uniqueness of all members.

The individualization of the objects of regulation makes it possible to enforce categorical distinctions, that is, distinctions defined by standardized criteria rather than generated through social networks.[8] As individuals came to be treated as the physical bearers of difference, they could be more easily distinguished and rearranged through standardized matrices of difference. Those matrices, in turn, defined the criteria of making distinctions among individuals (physical features, health, occupation, test scores, credentials, etc.) or nations (GDP, flags, constitutional structure, cultural heritage, landscape, resources, etc.). Most of the institutions identify and categorize individuals are key parts of the infrastructure of nations themselves, doing the heavy work of establishing proper relationships with citizens, noncitizens, and the many possible gradients in between. This work is a crucial aspect of participation in the international society of nations.

Of course, the acceptable criteria of difference remain a considerable source of debate. But these debates are framed by the concepts and procedures that were established as part of the new regulatory institutions in the first place. The ideal of individualized cases subject to equal treatment is as fundamental to modern bureaucratic procedures and free-market ideologies as it is to antidiscrimination activism and egocentric demands not to be pigeonholed but to be recognized for one's unique qualities. Struggles between proponents of these different issues are over the interpretation and legitimacy of certain categories rather than over the process of categorization based on individual qualities itself. Even the most adamant opponents of racial and national labeling still promote the investment of enormous resources into translating individual experiences into categories like refugee, worker, college graduate, or Asian American. Social networks that continue to generate alternative identities grounded in relationships rather than individual qualities are either obscured behind a fog of concepts like corruption, tradition, illegality, and informality or depicted as a radical new challenge to stable and traditional identities.

The laws designed to regulate Asian migration did not entirely achieve equal treatment and individualization, intent as they were on excluding parts of the world from participation in these processes. But they established the template for later refinements that eventually superseded the most overt discriminations in the name of greater inclusion. What began as a method to carefully regulate and limit the participation of certain peoples in the family of nations thus expanded into the very structure of the international system itself.

Diffusion of Autonomy

The diffusion of migration policy was rarely a smooth process of adapting and enforcing standard models. It was more often mediated through struggle and negotiation, a mutual learning process that produced a more careful delineation of the requirements and parameters of acceptable policy. In places like Central America and the Caribbean, where U.S. pressure on domestic immigration regulation was most intense, nations often resisted those pressures. But in the long run, all paths led to more strictly enforced borders with legislation based on the U.S. models.

In addition to racially based exclusions, nations throughout the Americas also enacted immigrant medical inspections that were explicitly based on U.S. models.[9] Although U.S. officials were generally pleased to see the erection of common standards, their early enforcement often caused practical difficulties when they worked against imperatives to protect the interests of U.S. citizens abroad. But in cases arising during the 1900s that involved the refusal to admit U.S. citizens of Asian descent into Haiti, Panama, and Ecuador, U.S. officials ultimately chose to confirm the right, indeed the necessity, of a sovereign nation to control migration as it wished—within certain parameters, at least. In fact, the lesson was often aimed more at U.S. diplomatic representatives who upheld lingering ideals of free intercourse than at local governments. For example, when U.S. Consul Herman Dietrich in Guayaquil asked for advice on how to deal with Ecuador's refusal to admit U.S. citizen Wong Koon Hou in 1908, the State Department told him that the United States had no basis for objection, "provided that such exclusion is a result of a general law reasonably administered."[10] But Ambassador Charles Hartman remained unclear on this principle. When U.S. citizen Goo Kwai attempted to enter Ecuador in 1914, Hartman sent a note to the Ecuadorian Foreign Office filled with international law citations about freedom of movement and asked, "Will a person who holds a passport in due form, issued by the Secretary of State of the United States, certifying that the holder thereof is an American citizen, be admitted into the territory of Ecuador or not?"[11] The government of Ecuador and the State Department agreed that that person would not.

But the idea of "reasonable administration" offered a loophole for the exertion of U.S. objections to local laws, which could lead to greater standardization. In 1904 Haiti passed a law forbidding Syrian immigration and business ownership. Similar laws had already been passed in Costa Rica and Panama with no objection from the United States. But the persecution of Syrians in Haiti promised to be much more intense, and a relatively large proportion of them claimed U.S. citizenship. The State Department launched a formal objection on the grounds that the Haitian laws were vague and incoherent. In particular, it objected to the category of "any person styled a Syrian, or so called in popular language," and argued that this should not be applicable to Syrians with U.S. naturalization certificates. The Haitian government responded that many of the naturalization papers were false and, more to the point, that the United States excluded the Chinese regardless of their nationality.[12] The United States never formally withdrew its objections, but by 1905 the U.S. ambassador advised Syrians with U.S. citizenship to close down their businesses in case the Haitian government ever attempted to rigorously enforce its laws.

The United States did successfully pressure the Haitians into delaying enforcement of the law until 1911 but did not compel a change in the law until after taking the Haitian side in response to the threat of armed French and British intervention. When the Haitian government resumed enforcement that year, the British threatened to send gunboats to protect the interests of British subjects, and the French actually did so. In response, the United States rallied in support of the Haitian right to determine its own immigration policy. Secretary of State Huntington Wilson wrote to the British ambassador explaining the working of Asiatic exclusion laws around the Pacific and concluded that "This Government does not perceive upon what grounds it would be justified, in view of the applicable principles of international law, in disputing the right of Haiti to exclude from its territory persons classed as undesirable by its local law upon avowed considerations of economic and political necessity."[13] U.S. officials also took this opportunity to counsel Haitian officials to modify their laws in a way that would better protect foreign intercourse. Haitian politicians were moved by the threats and advice and finally agreed to permit the continued residence of Syrians who had naturalized in foreign countries before 1904—a partial if incomplete gesture toward the equal treatment of resident aliens.

Mexico also frequently came into conflict with the United States over Asian migration. But under the liberal government of Porfirio Diáz before 1911, these conflicts generally revolved over the Mexican commitment to free movement rather than attempts to exclude U.S. citizens. The United States had sent advisers, experts, and diplomats since the 1890s to encourage Mexico to better regulate the entry and exit of Chinese and other migrants who may evade U.S. laws. They suggested draft migration legislation to Mexico and proposed railway agreements like those that had been established with Canada. But Mexican officials remained unsympathetic to U.S. immigration problems.[14] Mexican officials felt that if the "Government of the United States with the greatest resources at its disposal has been unable to adopt workable means to prevent the entry of Chinese into its territory," it was not therefore the duty of Mexico to take up the slack.[15] Some officials, such as the president of the Mexican Board of Health, Eduardo Licéaga, supplemented this stance with more positive arguments in favor of free international movement. This included the liberalization of quarantine laws around the world in favor of more advanced domestic hygiene regimes to "safeguard the interests of the public health without impairing . . . the interests of the commerce and of the free communication of men."[16] A civilized state should mold the health of the immigrants, not the other way around.

But Chinese did not escape discrimination even in a pro-intercourse political atmosphere such as this. A Ministry of the Interior report in 1908 raised grave concerns about the health and morality of the Chinese. It resulted in new immigration legislation based on U.S. medical restrictions, but with a focus on contagious diseases likely to be carried by Asians. Officials in the United States were pleased, but the measure hardly helped to reduce cross-border smuggling and the Bureau of Immigration ended up closing the Mexican border to Chinese entries. The rise of revolutionary and populist Mexican governments after 1916 finally took up the torch of popular self-government, often explicitly aimed against the alliance of elite and foreign economic interests. North American business often did not fare well under these regimes, but the exclusion and expulsion of Asians (many of whom made a living by provisioning foreign mines and agriculture) was enforced with even more enthusiasm.[17] In this case, sovereign border control arose out of the very process of resisting the United States, although it replicated longstanding Pacific Coast ideals of popular self-rule pitted against the twin threats of Asians and capital.

The Honor of Border Control

The ability to enforce migration laws was as much an indicator of national status as was their formal adoption. International pressure, lack of domestic resources, and the inability to mediate between demands for sovereign regulation and liberal intercourse often caused weaker nations to swing wildly from periods of harsh and absolute exclusion to periods of massive immigration through smuggling, special privileges, and poorly enforced laws. These states did not have the resources to put on the expensive and symbolically powerful performance of the U.S. exclusion laws. Despite their many practical failures, U.S. laws still engaged each individual applicant in a ritualized display of U.S. power and its vision of international order. These weaker nations could not even maintain a consistent performance at their own borders, much less project hegemony beyond their borders and lay claim to define the categories of global social order.

For example, after Peru abrogated its treaties with China in 1914, migration rates swung dramatically between months with no immigration and years with unprecedented high immigration rates in which Chinese gained entry through special permits obtained through personal connections within the Peruvian government. Periods of high migration were widely understood as evidence of the corruption and weakness of Peruvian institutions. But Chinese and other foreigners also criticized periods of complete exclusion as evidence of the failure of Peruvian institutions to regulate justly and fairly. As in Mexico, systematic restriction came only with the establishment of a populist government in 1930 that had a much stronger ideological and material commitment to exclusion.[18]

The open failure of local migration laws was also an invitation to foreign intervention, as was the case when Cuban officials failed to enforce the Chinese exclusion laws bequeathed to them by the U.S. occupation in 1902. As responsibility for the laws shifted from ministry to ministry through the 1920s, officials issued repeated decrees to clarify the law, strengthen it along the lines of U.S. exclusion, and remind officials that the old decrees were still in force. Certificates issued by Chinese and Cuban officials were repeatedly suspended and reinstated, as were the officials themselves. But regulation was continually undermined by corruption, loopholes, uncommitted and uncoordinated enforcement, and the pressure of sugar interests that succeeded in obtaining legislation from 1917 to 1921 that admitted more than twelve thousand Chinese laborers to take advantage of the growth in world sugar prices.[19]

These failures invited U.S. and Chinese interventions. In April 1924 the Chinese minister wrote to Cuban Secretary of State Miguel de Cespedes about the shortcomings of existing enforcement. He noted wryly that existing decrees that had been promulgated "with the expert advice of the authorities of the country which had originally introduced the Chinese Exclusion law into Cuba" should be "quite sufficient and ample enough to prevent the entry of Chinese of Chinese laborers if it is properly administered." He suggested that if Cuban officials found it difficult to enforce these laws, the Chinese government would be willing to engage in its own regime of self-restriction, and he suggested a model Cuban administrative decree to this effect.[20] The next month, U.S. Ambassador Enoch Crowder also wrote that even though U.S. and Cuban laws restricting Chinese were "strikingly similar," a great many Chinese were still entering Cuba. He demanded that reform measures be implemented so as to stop the flow of smuggled Chinese into the United States.[21] Under these pressures, the Cuban government continued to revise its laws, but generally with little effect. It did, however, successfully resist Chinese proposals for "mutual self-restriction" along the lines of Cuba's recent treaty with Japan. Claims of the sovereign right to control immigration still trumped the failure to properly enforce them.[22]

The relation of migration control to national honor was most vividly dramatized in struggles over illegal Chinese migration to Panama. In 1904, shortly after its U.S.-sponsored independence from Colombia, the Panamanian government passed a law prohibiting all Chinese, Syrians, and Turks except returning residents, agricultural laborers, and replacement employees from entering.[23] Panama was a stop on the newly established steamship lines from Hong Kong to Peru, and Chinese entries continued to grow despite repeated attempts to strengthen the decree over the next two decades. In the words of Secretary of Foreign Relations E. T. Lefevre in 1910, the original law of 1904 had inspired the Chinese to put in practice "every kind of subterfuge to make this legal mandate entirely diverted."[24] Major portions of the secretary's reports to the national assembly through the 1920s were devoted to diatribes against the Chinese and his own defense against accusations of corruption and incompetence in enforcing the laws.

The issue came to a head as a matter of international relations in March 1913, when a new law required reregistration and a monthly tax on all Chinese individuals and associations. Local Chinese refused to comply. In petitions to the Panamanian and Chinese governments, they complained that they were being singled out for discrimination and appealed to the rights guaranteed by international comity:

> Although the positive rules of International Law permit, from a theoretical point of view, that a State may prohibit immigration into its territories, in practice this does not happen. Because it is evident that the purpose of the Law of Nations is to regulate the relations between States, and it is indispensable that these relations begin and develop in virtue of reciprocal communication between members of distinct nations. Without the liberty of immigration the existence of an international community would be almost impossible.[25]

Lefevre drew on all available rhetorical resources in his response. He acknowledged that "The practice of closing the doors of a State to foreigners in general has tended to disappear," but he qualified this assertion with an appeal to the trans-Pacific civilizational divide by insisting that "the principle of free immigration tends to become general [only] between people with equal customs and equivalent civilization."[26] He pointed to the United States as a model for how Chinese could be excluded while still retaining good relationships with China. He went on to explain that the problem lay not in exclusion itself, but in the disrespectful attitude and criminal actions of the Chinese. The law was not intended to embarrass the members of a foreign colony, "but to impede the continuation of an immoral traffic, that could well be described by the label 'yellow traffic,' which found its first victims among the members of this race, treasonously, and like a plague, began to introduce its venom among certain sectors of society and above all in many of the employees of public administration."[27] The current Chinese "attitude of open rebellion" further compounded the threat posed by illegitimate migration and made the enforcement more difficult for the Executive Power, "which needs to defend not only the dignity of the National Government but the principle of authority that is seriously threatened."[28] The very enactment of a local law supposedly designed to protect the nation had helped to construct certain kinds of mobility as a threat to the nation.

Certain forms of international intervention also proved to be more legitimate than others. Chinese Consul General Ouyang Geng supported the Chinese refusal to register and their attempts to test the constitutionality of the law. He even made it impossible for any Chinese to reregister by holding all of their old *cédulas* (identity certificates) in his office under the pretext of a census. The Panamanian government expelled him from the country for encouraging noncompliance with the law. In response, Chinese residents engaged in a business shutdown and obtained the good offices of Cyrus Wicker, the secretary of the U.S. legation, to assist in their struggle (U.S. consuls had provided their "good offices" on behalf of Chinese in many Central American countries since the 1890s).[29] Wicker negotiated a lower tax, concessions on registration procedures, and improved return privileges. In agreeing to these terms, Panamanian officials and Chinese both implicitly agreed to the validity of sovereign control if set in moderate terms and conceded the expertise of the United States in setting the terms of that moderation.

But the problems remained unresolved in practice. In 1922 Secretary of Foreign Relations Narciso Garay (in an implicit critique of Lefevre) insisted that "Every time that a Secretary of Foreign Relations has proposed a new law about prohibited immigration, or drawn up a new decree regulating it, it has forged an illusion." His approach would be to reduce smuggling, "not by any theoretical system deserving of the name, but as a result of a personal and tenacious campaign of administrative morality."[30] Nonetheless, he continued to issue new decrees, and the Chinese continued to evade them. The resulting legal and political struggles generated debates very similar to those that had taken place in the white settler nations over the previous four decades about the finality of administrative law, the dangers of English habeas corpus, the validity of documents obtained through false statements and technicalities, and whether Panamanian migration law was based on race or citizenship.[31] Panama's inability to reach a definitive conclusion, formulate a lasting policy, and mask evasion under systematic procedure only entrenched the image of Panama as yet one more incompetent southern state.

Quotas

The U.S. quota law of 1924 was perhaps the most significant innovation law of the twentieth century. With quotas based on the proportions of current residents of each national "stock," it maintained the pretense of equal treatment to all nations while simultaneously claiming to protect and preserve the ethnic balance of the national population. The idea of quotas attracted wide-ranging support, from pro-Japanese lobbyist Sidney Gulick to eugenicist Harry Laughlin. Along the way, the new quota laws consolidated and perfected procedures developed through the exclusion of Chinese, such as the distinction between immigrants and nonimmigrants like merchants and students; the processes of appeal, deportation, and administrative finality; the techniques of remote control and status inspection; and the creation of the "illegal" alien. It set the global standard for the progressive and scientific management of migration.

The difficulties of dealing with Asian migration were the main inspiration behind the technical aspects of the quota laws. The 1905 Chinese boycott and Japanese crisis of 1906–1908 had left a lasting impression among diplomatic and executive officers concerned with projecting the international image of a nation that guaranteed equality for all. At least since 1907, the Bureau of Immigration had wanted to merge the Chinese exclusion laws into the general immigration laws. Political concerns over reviving Chinese immigration as a public issue blocked any attempt to do this, but much of the phraseology in draft immigration laws proposed by the bureau was incorporated into the general immigration laws and regulations of 1917, 1921, and 1924, particularly those stipulating deportation procedures, burden of proof, and the duties of consuls abroad.[32] The Japanese attempt to insert a racial equality clause in the League of Nations charter in 1919 emphasized that this problem still would not go away soon. The white settler countries remained opposed to the implications of such a clause because they thought it would undermine their power to control immigration as they wished. Japan ultimately dropped its demand for an equality clause, reportedly in return for the ex-German extraterritorial concessions in China. But concerns over Japanese immigration continued to be one of the main inspirations behind the revision of U.S. immigration laws into a quota system.[33]

Walter Husband, who would become commissioner general of immigration from 1921 to 1925, was an important early proponent of quotas. As part of the enormous report on immigration published by the Senate-appointed Dillingham commission in 1910, he proposed a quota based on existing ethnic proportions of current U.S. residents. This proposal was unable to sidetrack the push for a literacy test that had shaped the restrictionist agenda since the 1890s, but Husband remained committed to the idea of quotas as part of the ideal of "regulating" migrants according to the demands of the labor market, rather then "restricting" particular types.[34] As opposed to migration laws that revolved around standards of discrimination and selectivity, "The more modern theory . . . is that immigration *per se* may be undesirable even though the immigrants themselves are highly desirable persons. I am convinced that the immigration problem cannot be settled on the basis of the superiority or inferiority of the races involved, but I believe that it can be solved . . . if due weight is given to its purely economic aspects."[35]

Chinese and Japanese always hovered in the background of any talk about inferior races and quotas. Japanese officials never relented in their objections to discrimination, and U.S. officials always remained uncomfortable with the concession of regulatory power to Japan in the Gentleman's Agreement. Reverend Sydney Gulick's quota proposal, drafted at about the same time as Husband's, was directly motivated by the desire to uphold Japanese dignity while not exacerbating racial tensions in the United States.[36] An ex-missionary in Japan, Gulick promoted his idea tirelessly in his magazine, *Immigration Journal*. In 1914 he explained to the Immigration Restriction League that "The danger of overwhelming oriental immigration can be obviated by a general law allowing a maximum annual immigration from any land of a fixed percentage of those from that land already here and naturalized."[37] The desire to maintain a good image in China also drove quota proponents. In 1914 Husband also told the National Federation of Religious Liberals that "the Dillingham [quota] plan might be utilized in solving the troublesome problem of Asiatic immigration. We now have a rigid Chinese exclusion law, but it is questionable how long we can comfortably have one law for the Chinaman and another for the rest of mankind. Under the Dillingham plan, China might be put on the same basis with every other nation, and immigration from that country would still be limited to about 7,100 annually."[38]

The literacy test of 1917 (based not on the Natal formula but on a test in the migrant's native language) did not reduce immigration to the extent hoped for by its proponents. This opened the political space for the implementation of the quota law. The Bureau of Immigration had been collecting statistics on immigrant ethnicity and formulating a "list of races and peoples" since the 1890s. This list was the basis for the "experimental" quota law of 1921 that established a ceiling of 350,000 immigrants a year, proportioned according to the nationality of U.S. residents of foreign birth in the 1910 census.[39] Enforcement was plagued by serious administrative and conceptual difficulties. At the end of each month, ships raced into New York harbor trying to discharge their passengers before the monthly quota was filled. Losers would anchor off of New Jersey and wait for the next month. The law also established poor criteria for distinctions between "immigrants" and travelers not subject to quota. And, most importantly, the numbers and quota categories remained highly contentious.

Many of the technical problems were resolved in the extensive 1924 law. These included provisions for consular inspections abroad and detailed definitions of "immigrants," "nonimmigrants" (temporary visitors not subject to quotas), and "nonquota immigrants" (such as close family who were not included in the quota). Bureau of Immigration Law Officer A. Warner Parker remarked that "Casual inspection might lead one to conclude that the new law is remarkable for logical sequence, terseness, and artistic composition," but a practical analysis "makes it apparent that clearness of expression and certainty of terms have been sacrificed to sequence, brevity and artistic effects."[40] The kinks became quickly apparent over the next year of enforcement. But officials put great effort into ironing them out and, artistic or not, the categories and terms became the basic framework for the differential application of rights at the border.

The issue of determining specific quotas was more difficult to resolve, running into both conceptual and international difficulties. The point of quotas was to maintain the veneer of equal treatment of all migrants while simultaneously appeasing restrictionist demands to reduce the amount of "new" immigrants from southern and eastern Europe. Thus, the basis for quotas was to be the replication of the ethnic composition of the United States at a particular moment in time. The 1924 law had put off the final determination of quotas until 1927, pending an expert investigation into the national heritage of all U.S. citizens based on the census of 1920. In the meantime, proportions of migrants were determined according to the ethnic heritage of U.S. residents in the 1890 census (the first to record ethnicity). The task of categorization proved extremely difficult, and the results were delayed until 1929. The experts fretted over the many hybrid individuals and uncertain ethnicities that they encountered, but they never questioned that their fundamental assumptions were "scientific" and could be solved through proper method, categorization, and diligence.[41] Unsurprisingly, with the significant exceptions of Jews and nations such as Brazil that contained large white and nonwhite populations, ethnicity fell quite conveniently into national categories.

Many nations initially objected to the new law. Most objections, such as those from Cuba, Italy, Norway, Romania, and Salvador, focused on how the quota might impinge on their national sovereignty over emigration. The Italian government objected that the provisions for consular visas "practically invalidate the sovereign right of the Italian government to control the emigration of its citizens and interfere with the necessary national measure to safeguard public order with the regulations relating to passports." It also attacked the absolute power of administrative officials over the rights of individual migrants, insisting that the provisions laying the burden of proof on the alien contradict the "recognized procedure of law the world over."[42] But the Italians could not do much about it other than complain. Brazilian officials, on the other hand, protested not against the infringement on practical powers but against the way that quota categories denied a common ethnicity to their nation. The Bureau of Immigration also ignored repeated petitions for Brazilians to be counted as a single race rather than divided between blacks and whites.[43] Although Asian migration had driven many early formulations of the quota law, the final legislation only strengthened the Pacific divide by prohibiting the admission of "aliens ineligible to naturalization" (a formulation borrowed from a 1917 California landownership law) as immigrants. The Chinese exclusion law remained in force, while the superimposition of the quota law even narrowed the potential "exempt classes" through a more restrictive definition of merchants (now limited to those who engaged in international trade with their home country) and by forbidding the Chinese wives of U.S. citizens to immigrate. Even more significantly, the ineligible to naturalize clause effectively abrogated the Gentleman's Agreement. The House Committee on Immigration justified this unprecedented and diplomatically disastrous provision with the circular logic that "All must agree that nothing can be gained by permitting to be built up in the Untied States colonies of those who cannot, under the law, become naturalized citizens, and must therefore owe allegiance to another government."[44] The Japanese did not quite see it this way. For the next two decades, Japanese politicians and militarists would regularly refer to this unilateral action as a national humiliation that justified opposition to the West, militarism, and war.[45] For their part, the Chinese found themselves in the odd position of demanding a return to the sole jurisdiction of more lenient exclusion laws, which they claimed were already adequately serving their purpose.[46]

Despite the difficulties, the 1924 law became the gold standard of migration laws. Even countries that did not adopt the quota provisions admired and emulated the use of policy to define and create national character, as well as the refined distinctions among types of immigrants, nonimmigrants, and excludables. With more sophisticated discriminations at the border, domestic institutions could more easily proceed in the work of establishing equal treatment on the interior regardless of race, religion, or any characteristic other than legal immigration status. In the long run, quotas themselves would lose their attractiveness in the face of domestic and international pressures. But the procedures designed to enforce the quotas would endure.

International Organization

The consolidation of domestic immigration controls around the world came hand in hand with calls for an international regulatory regime. Even at the turn of the century, when border control was still more of a dream than a reality, critics insisted that the effective regulation of migration was impossible through the efforts of a single nation. But this international imagination was firmly grounded in the idea of a world of autonomous nation states that need cooperation in order to achieve their own best interests. By the 1920s, internationalist ideas were also grounded in the idea that strict and illiberal border controls were increasingly a thing of the past. Although this idea flew in the face of actual trends, it was indispensable for maintaining the basic narrative of progress and reform as something that would overcome existing inequities, not produce them.[47]

Internationalists argued that even from the perspective of practical enforcement, the best-policed borders would still leak without international cooperation and a better understanding of the causes of migration. As James Whelpley wrote in *The Problem of the Immigrant* (1905), "No nation can effectually control this movement single-handed, even in the matter of admission to its own territory. There is a more or less well-organized conspiracy to break down or evade barriers which may be erected, and it succeeds to a remarkable degree; for the influences at work are international, hence cannot be neutralized from a single, or national, point of operation."[48] The "conspiracy" referred to brokers and other informal networks that organized migration. He insisted that a binding international agreement was necessary to better regulate these undesirable processes. "The benefit of such an agreement would be mutual, and its results conducive to the safety, happiness, and prosperity not only of the strong but of the weak, not only of the free but of the oppressed."[49]

Most of this remained just talk until the 1920s, when a series of negotiations and conferences attempted to put it into practice. International conferences and associations already had a legacy of achievement since the 1860s in regulating and standardizing, among other things, weights and measures, telegraphic systems, postal service, marine signaling, fisheries, freight transportation, patents and trademark protections, tariff information, insurance, and scientific knowledge.[50] Not all the conferences were successful, but many were so effective that we have forgotten the enormous work put into creating a global infrastructure that we now take for granted.

Migration was not one of the many topics considered in prewar international conventions. The trend among progressive thinkers in most European countries before the 1890s was to think of migration as a natural process that needed to be liberated from regulation rather than a new technology that needed to be regulated in any aspect except travel conditions. The only conference to be held on migration before the 1920s was the International Congress on the Intervention of Public Powers in Immigration and Emigration at the 1889 Universal Exposition in Paris. Representatives from only eleven countries (Argentina, Belgium, Brazil, Chile, Spain, Hawaii, France, Guatemala, Paraguay, Salvador, and Venezuela) attended, and its impact was minimal. Much of the discussion revolved around exit policy and colonial governance rather than immigration policy or international management, reflecting concerns more rooted in the final dismantling of the old regime in Europe and rise of new empires than in the modern immigration policies then being forged in the Pacific. The plenary speaker M. Chandéze cited economist J. B. Say's assertion that "superabundant population that does not depart through the frontiers, will depart through the tombs" in support of his argument that the best way to manage migration was by resolving the domestic problems that caused emigration.[51]

The final resolutions confirmed the need to promote free migration as a self-regulating process rather than impose restrictions and management. Participants did, however, express faith in an idea that would shape most later attempts at international management—that the collection of data on the natural processes of migration would form the basis for a global information exchange about labor needs and conditions, and ultimately an international treaty. The final resolutions, however, only went as far as to call for future conferences and to assert that (1) emigration and immigration considered in themselves and released from all abnormal conditions have advantages for the state and for individuals; and (2) the state should not intervene directly in the movement of emigration but only to inform and protect the emigrant.[52]

The rise of immigration controls at the turn of the century led to more calls for international cooperation. The U.S. immigration law of 1907 even included a clause authorizing the president to call an international conference on migration. But no practical steps were taken until 1919, when the League of Nations charged the International Labour Organization (ILO) to gather information and develop model immigration laws for nations to adopt. The ILO created the International Emigration Commission in 1921.[53] Like many other postwar internationalists, ILO officials claimed to be the pioneers of a progressive new trend of global cooperation that would overcome the jealous sovereignties of the nineteenth century. In practice, however, they largely contributed to the continuing institutionalization and technical co-ordination of a competitive international system. Most of these organizations focused on the collection of information and dissemination of policy recommendations, a process that often seemed futile in the short run but ultimately contributed greatly to the global homogenization of national institutions. For example, the International Emigration Commission produced exhaustive volumes and papers on national migration statistics and laws and sponsored an International Conference on Migration Statisticians in 1932, which resulted in a 1936 volume on immigrant stock in countries around the world.[54] The very process of collecting data served to reinforce nationalized understandings of migration.

International conferences and organizations could also be used as platforms to disseminate ideas of national autonomy and self-determination. Immigrant-receiving states were reluctant to attend international migration conferences, but when they did they used the opportunity to hammer home the idea of migration control as a unilateral domestic policy. Beyond this, they generally refused to cooperate. This meant that their "domestic" policies became de facto international norms, as other countries were still required to generate documents and emigrants that fulfilled their requirements. For example, the United States and Australia refused to take part in the International Emigration Commission, and participants from South Africa and Canada used the absence of these major receiving countries as an excuse to argue that no action could be taken.[55] Representatives from emigrant countries nonetheless met in Rome in 1921 and produced resolutions about the need for international coordination of information on labor needs around the world, and for international conventions to regulate the transportation, contracts, and work conditions of migrants. In response, the representatives from immigrant countries met in Paris in 1923 and decided that it was best to avoid formal commitments and resolutions. If necessary, specific diplomatic agreements were preferable to general conventions. They especially worried about emigrant countries wanting to extend state power over their emigrants abroad, and that immigrants would take advantage of social insurance while not taking up corresponding obligations through naturalization.[56]

Each side brought these perspectives to the first international conference on migration, attended by representatives from fifty-seven countries in Rome in May 1924. The invitations from the Italian government promised that the issues to be considered were "strictly technical." The United States responded that it considered immigration to be a purely domestic matter but would send a small delegation as long as the issues remained technical.[57] Benito Mussolini opened the conference by saying that the time had come when migrants should no longer be treated like merchandise, and when existing conventions that already govern the exchange of riches can be augmented with conventions for the "effective protection of the workers."[58] The liveliest and longest of the subsequent discussions revolved around the very definition of an "emigrant." Emigration countries considered anybody who traveled abroad in search of a livelihood to be an emigrant. Immigration countries wanted to limit it to those who intended to settle permanently, as distinguished from businessmen, students, and other temporary travelers (remaining vague on the intentions of a migrant laborer). The final definition of an emigrant appeared to compromise, with an emphasis on both livelihood and family resettlement, but essentially reproduced the "immigrant" categories of the 1924 U.S. immigration law:

> Any person who leaves his country for the purpose of seeking work or who accompanies or goes to join his wife, or her husband, his or her relatives in the ascendant or descendant degree, his or her brothers or sisters, his or her uncles or aunts, nephews or nieces, or the wife or the husband of the latter, who have already emigrated with the same object, or who returns to the country to which he had previously emigrated in the same conditions.[59]

Upon the moment of arrival at the border, this person would become an "immigrant," and thus subject to local legislation.

The conference also generated forty-nine resolutions on methods to assure the safety of migrants during travel; principles for migration treaties; information sharing on labor markets, passports, the control of clandestine immigration; and supporting official and nonofficial aid associations for migrants. The United States did not vote in favor of most of the resolutions other than those for the sharing of information. Australia and New Zealand supported none. The resolutions concluded with a general charter for emigration, which asserted that the right to immigrate and emigrate should be recognized, "subject to the restrictions imposed in the interests of public order or for economic or social reasons, particularly the state of the labour market and the protection of the public health and morals of the immigration country . . . [and] so far as their respective legislation permits, persons to whom, on account of their condition, admission would be refused by the law of the country of intended destination, should be prohibited from emigrating thereto."[60] In other words, the right to migrate was a universal one that could be abrogated for nearly any reason that a state may find convenient. These were precisely the kinds of principles used to justify the exclusion of Asians, but the United States, Great Britain, and Japan refused to approve even this charter as a potential infringement on domestic prerogative. They voted in favor of only the clause asking emigrant countries to refuse exit to persons who would be refused admission abroad.

The resolutions were used as the basis for several migration treaties within Europe, many of which guaranteed legally recognized migrant laborers the same benefits and rights as citizens.[61] But the greatest result of the Rome conference was to establish the basic inutility of any broader collaboration. A 1926 attempt by the International Federation of Trade Unions to call an international conference on migration failed.[62] The follow-up to the Rome conference held in Havana in 1928 attracted only thirty-six participants and six international organizations.[63] The State Department instructed the U.S. delegation to remember that migration put people under a new flag, that the country of origin had no right to maintain sovereignty over its emigrants (an increasing trend among European nations), and that "you should in any discussion on international aspects of immigration problems, be careful to note any tendency to call this doctrine into question and should, if necessary, be prepared to combat such a tendency by clear and unequivocal statements based on the historic position of the United States."[64] The Australian observer reported happily to Canberra that the "complete aloofness" of the U.S. delegation and Japan's objections to any attempts to diminish the power of the home government over emigrants made it impossible to reconcile the differences between emigration and immigration countries. In any case most delegates believed that existing international practices were already sufficient.[65] Most of discussion focused on technical issues of interest to the receiving countries, such as the standardization of documentation and the means of distinguishing commercial travelers from "immigrants."

International conferences in 1920 and 1926 to standardize passports were much more successful. Most participants entered the first passport conference with expressions of regret over the proliferation of these documents under wartime conditions and of sincere hopes that passports would soon no longer be necessary. In the meantime, they felt that movement and commerce could be facilitated by the design of a standardized passport for temporary use. As many participants noted, the issuance of such a passport would require the centralization of passport-issuing authorities within each nation and a firm recognition of responsibility over all to whom the documents were issued. Ultimately, both sending and receiving countries appreciated the increased opportunities for surveillance. By the time of the 1926 conference, the most pressing issue was not whether the passport system would be abolished, but whether the British passport would be accepted as the universal model.[66]

Despite the increasingly bellicose assertions of sovereign prerogative in migration matters, many participants at international conferences continued to proclaim a dawning age of international cooperation and progressive advancement. For example, at the Second Conference of the Institute of Pacific Relations in 1927, the Japanese delegate extensively criticized the validity of the economic and assimilationist arguments used to justify discriminatory immigration laws. But he concluded with the assertion that "We are living in a new day when the notion of unlimited individualism is undergoing a decided change and the spirit of social sharing and co-operation is gradually gaining ground." The recognition of the right of free immigration will "be realized first in the most progressive and enlightened country."[67] During the roundtable, other delegates held up the British Empire as a model that pointed to the future of international cooperation in migration matters.[68] And another delegate summed up the mood with an assertion that "Questions reserved for 'domestic jurisdiction' are the remnants of what a comparatively short time ago was unlimited state sovereignty." This nineteenth-century emphasis on the rights of nation states was now being overcome, and "there is a clear tendency for questions to pass from the sphere of purely domestic interest and jurisdiction into the sphere of international agreement."[69] Conference participants apparently had no difficulty interpreting the entrenchment of national borders as a rising tide of international cooperation.

In a sense, this narrative of increased international collaboration was not entirely wrong. The focus on standardization of technical issues appeared to be a retreat from international cooperation, a de facto concession to the needs of immigrant states for standardized surveillance without binding policy commitments. But it also carried the appealing aura of pragmatic modern management and helped to create an international regime of common regulatory norms. The emigrant states developed an increasingly large stake in surveillance, not only to protect the welfare of emigrants but to enforce their growing anti-emigration policies and to extend political claims over people whom they now often referred to as overseas citizens rather than emigrants.[70] Even the guarantees of equal rights and benefits for labor immigrants in European migration treaties were dependent on the elaboration of nation-based surveillance that could better distinguish legitimate from illegitimate immigrants. U.S. distinctions between several types of immigrants, nonimmigrants, and illegals conveniently grounded those distinctions on the status under which a migrant crossed the border. In France, the surveillance took place inside the country through intensified registration, household inspections, and deportation proceedings. Very few of the deportation proceedings actually resulted in expulsion, and many French looked wistfully at the U.S. immigration law as a much better method. But the extensive effort devoted to issuing and confiscating papers served much the same purpose as border procedures that distinguished between aliens who did and did not deserve rights and benefits.[71]

Naturalizing Migration Control

By the late 1920s the proposals of internationalists often seemed little different from actual practices of migration control. They still claimed to be searching for a more just and effective regime of migration control, but rather than critique the fundamentals of existing practices, they framed their search as an extension of existing trends away from the arbitrary powers and discriminations found in history. Some couched their search in pragmatic terms; others, in idealistic terms. But all insisted that their visions were grounded in the progressive achievements of the present and formulated their understandings of migration history in ways that could make their claims seem true.

Practical efforts in the international sphere mostly worked to better define the scope and purpose of national regulation and thus limit the need for international intervention. In 1927 the ex-director of the ILO, Albert Thomas, explained that he understood his duties regarding migration to be limited to disseminating international rules of assimilation and naturalization, and helping regulate migrations that threatened to overwhelm a nation.[72] In 1931 delegates to the International Association for Social Progress resolved that migrants needed international legal protections, but that migration also needed to be regulated and that "control should aim to harmonize the rights of the individual with those of nations, that the right to protect their physique, economic equilibrium, and intellectual and moral and social standards cannot be refused to nations, but that in thus protecting themselves they avoid every appearance of discrimination based on nationality, race, origin, language, or religion."[73] The association did not suggest how these potentially contradictory imperatives could be resolved (although this was precisely the problem that the U.S. quotas claimed to solve). But by then the rhetoric had become so familiar that it did not need clarification. The problem of migration was routinely framed as a difficult conflict between the equally legitimate claims of free mobility and absolute sovereignty. The job of the progressive policy maker was to engage in the difficult and objective search for a reasonable and equitable compromise.

The reasonable compromise often turned out to be a confirmation of existing practice. But by framing history in terms of extremes, that practice could be depicted as a progressive step toward justice and rationalization. For example, in 1924 Paul Fachille, the founder and editor of *Revue générale de droit international public*, published an article in the ILO's *International Labour Review* that analyzed the place of migration in international law. After staking out the extremes of those who asserted the natural right of free movement and an absolute right of state self-protection, he placed himself in a lineage going back to Grotius and Vattel that accepted the legitimate claims of both sides and tried to find a more realistic compromise. The construction of this genealogy, however, entailed a reinterpretation and exclusion of predecessors who would have considered themselves as part of this same moderate lineage. For example, Fachille placed Oppenheim in the camp of those who insisted only on the rights of states because of his claim that there was no necessary right of migration. Fachille, in contrast, insisted that the rights to life and the pursuit of happiness were more fundamental than the rights of states, concluding that "Although there is a legal obligation on a state to open its frontiers to foreigners, it may legitimately close them, justifying its action not by its rights of sovereignty but solely by its right of self-preservation."[74] Despite the insistence on individual rights, however, his formulation actually differed little from Oppenheim's. Whereas Oppenheim had said there is no necessary right of migration but that no state would actually exclude migrants without good reason, Fachille insisted that an absolute right of migration existed but that no state was compelled to recognize it.

Fachille concluded with a list of the justifiable causes for exclusion. These included the usual categories of the diseased, aged, infirm, vagrants, impoverished, political subversives, criminals, and "foreigners who are a danger to the national well-being, life, honour or safety." He insisted that "To base the exclusion of foreigners merely on their nationality and not on personal defects would be to infringe a fundamental principle of international law: the equality of states." He then qualified this statement with the assertion that, "For its own preservation, a state might wish to prevent a fusion of races which might alter its ethnic character or obliterate its national culture. This does not really affect the self-preservation of the state, and the exclusion of members of a given race would only be justified if this race belonged to an absolutely different civilization and its members wished to enter the territory of the state in large numbers."[75] In other words, Fachille largely confirmed existing practice. Phrases such as "national well-being" and "honor" provided great lassitude of interpretation that could encompass existing restrictions. Indeed, similar lists of justifiable exclusions circulating in the 1920s expanded on Fachille's list in more detail. For example, geologist and explorer John Gregory added that a nation had a right to exclude if the migrants were more than it could comfortably absorb, to prevent a lowered standard of living, to protect itself from deterioration by racial intermixture (except for intermixture between the white races), to protect national institutions, and to protect the right of a class to organize for its own protection.[76] This list justified not only most existing practices but also some that would not be common until later in the century.

Other commentators altered the definition of migration in a way that made exclusions no longer appear to be exclusions. For example, in 1913 U.S. sociologist Henry Pratt Fairchild defined immigration as "a movement of people, individually or in families, acting on their own personal initiative and responsibility, without official support or compulsion, passing from one well-developed country to another well-developed country with the intention of residing there."[77] He contrasted immigration to other types of movement that he called invasion (by a less developed people), conquest (by a more developed people), and colonization (of empty lands). The former was no longer common except in the form of a peaceful invasion whereby a large number of less culturally developed immigrants move to a nation in large numbers. In a true immigration movement, by contrast, "Both of the two states concerned . . . are well established, and on approximately the same stage of civilization. "He went on to explain that it "is a distinctly individual undertaking" that takes place only within a single culture area that shares common climatic conditions and circumstances of life. "In fact, practically all immigration, historically speaking, has been between different countries in the temperate zone."[78] Fairchild was a strong critic of race prejudice and the actual methods of enforcing the Chinese exclusion. He supported the exclusion laws them-selves, however, and civilizational discourse helped him reframe exclusion in race-neutral vocabulary. In this way, he could justify exclusion in the very same terms that could still uphold a claim to live in the most "progressive and enlightened country."

Fairchild's four categories of mobility have fallen into disuse, but the idea of true migration being the relocation of free, self-willed individuals remains. And the historical memory of mass migration as an exclusively temperate-zone phenomenon is even more firmly entrenched, providing, as we shall see in the conclusion, justification for a range of obstacles against the supposedly unprecedented threats of recent migration flows. Both the explicitly racial and civilizational justifications of migration control would also fall away after World War II. But the enormous intellectual and administrative machinery set into motion by Asian exclusion would remain.

Education for Independence

Even as theorists were still justifying the exclusion of Asians, the logic of migration control was already spreading through Asia. Sovereign migration control was increasingly seen as a prerequisite of national independence. The existence of effective migration control tailored to local conditions was evidence that a nation possessed the institutions of modern population man-agement that befitted a sovereign state. This can be seen in the creation of migration laws as part of the tutorship for Philippine independence. From the very beginning of the American presence, the enforcement of Chinese exclusion was seen as inseparable from the preparation of Filipinos for partici-pation in the modern world. Over time, this expanded locally tailored general immigration laws based on U.S. models that were seen as an indispensable part of pending independence.

Until 1917, all U.S. migration laws were applied to the Philippines. But responsibility for enforcement was entrusted to the Philippine Department of Customs with the idea that they could be adapted to local conditions through judicial decisions and administrative regulations. In practice, U.S. Bureau of Immigration administrative rules were generally enforced in the Philip-pines, although a few local differences emerged, such as even fewer oppor-tunities for appeal, mostly due to unclear lines of authority in the Philippine government.[79]

For many colonial officials, training the locals in scientific administration was a key obligation of colonial tutorship. It was also an opportunity to build carefully managed progressive institutions in a way that was often difficult in the United States because of politics and the entrenched interests of existing officials. The first collector of customs, W. Morgan Schuster, charged with enforcing the exclusion laws, was among the most zealous of these progressive administrators. Many merchants complained that his punctilious enforcement of customs laws was unnecessary in a "backward" country such as the Philippines, where it worked to hamper trade and development.[80] In response, Schuster published a newspaper article in 1903 arguing that the literal interpretation of laws was necessary for the maintenance of democracy and the division of powers. Excessive flexibility and laxity would undermine stable governance by the people. Justice was even found in procedure itself, which operated according to a well-known canon of statutory interpretation. "To adopt any other principle of executive procedure is to invite chaos, injustice and fraud."[81] Firm foundations had to be laid for the tutorship of a new nation, including the honest management of migration under the Chinese exclusion laws.

The logic of "Philippines for the Filipinos" took a new twist after 1912, as U.S. officials and the public lost interest in the civilizing mission and the Wilson administration increasingly transferred political and administrative responsibilities over to Filipinos. Laws such as the 1917 literacy test and 1924 quotas, designed in their details to craft a particular nation rather than protect against undesirables per se, were not extended to the Philippines. In the wake of these changes, the Philippine media and legislature increasingly took up immigration as a key topic of debate, almost always with the Chinese in mind. Some called to strengthen existing laws, others called to drop restrictive laws altogether, while yet others urged turning exclusion on its head by proposing the admission of Chinese contract labor and the prohibition merchants. Most immigration bills foundered in struggles between sugar interests and labor groups, deadlocked in pro- and anti-Chinese arguments that had changed little since the 1850s. In the meantime, bookkeeping and registration laws designed to discriminate against Chinese were enacted, making colonial officials concerned that Filipinos were still incapable of regulating their nation as civilized men.[82]

While politicians debated Chinese exclusion, the legacy of Schuster had declined into a notoriously lax and idle ceremony. Smuggling and fraud scandals emerged in the 1910s and remained nearly constant through the 1930s. No section 6 certificates were denied in Manila from 1921 to 1940, arriving Chinese were frequently released on bonds and never inspected, no pre-investigations were made of departing migrants, and, most egregiously, the files were incomplete and disordered (one of the few people to be dismissed for these failings was a chief clerk charged with "infidelity in the custody of public documents"). Immigration decisions were frequently reversed in the courts on the basis of procedural flaws.[83] Rather than develop a systemic process for the creation of new identities, Philippine officials appeared to have lost control.

U.S. officials viewed the endless debates, domestic discrimination, and enforcement failures not as the exercise of self-government but as evidence of native disorder and incompetence. But, other than a broad agreement that an undeveloped Asian society needed its own distinct laws, they were no more able than the Filipinos to overcome their diverse opinions and engage in decisive intervention. In 1922 Chief of the Bureau of Insular Affairs Frank McIntyre, fretting over the failure of the 1916 land law to attract settlers on unused lands, wrote to Philippine Governor General Leonard Wood that "a proper immigration system" was key to the development of the islands and "a subject I deem of first importance in carrying out our full duty in the Philippine Islands."[84] Wood responded that a "certain amount of Chinese immigration is desirable" but then recited the long list of "well-justified fears" that the Filipinos held against the Chinese.[85]

The issue remained unresolved until the transformation of the Philippines into a commonwealth in 1934 with a ten-year independence schedule. The need for a national migration policy came to the forefront once again, and by now most politicians agreed that a national-origins quota was the best method.[86] But the legislation stalled until 1938 when Chinese immigration scandals broke out once more and the Philippine government requested an immigration adviser from the United States. The State Department first considered sending John Sawyer from Shanghai, who "understands Oriental psychology and gets along eminently well with Orientals."[87] But they worried he had been too long in the Orient and was no longer familiar with the U.S. perspective and policy. I. F. Wixon from the Labor Department and George Brandt from the State Department were sent instead. The instructions to Brandt explained that "the unsatisfactory situation results largely from the fact that the laws are unsuited to the needs of the Islands. They were enacted for the United States proper. They are complicated, intricate and involved and highly technical. Their proper administration requires special knowledge and experience on the part of the administrative officials."[88] The instructions proposed that a less technical version of the U.S. quota law would be the ideal solution.

Brandt and Wixon proposed a simple quota of one thousand per year from all countries of the world. But they soon found that Filipinos were not satisfied with a law that was but a pale imitation of the U.S. law. Wixon explained to the secretary of labor that they had arrived in the Philippines with the assumption that "we were dealing with a primitive people who understood pictures better than printing." But, he continued, "We were soon disillusioned in that respect. We were thrown into contact with highly educated persons representing the government; men who are graduates of our higher institutions of learning back home . . . men who have practiced law and are grounded in its fundamentals, and we are certain that they would have resented attaching less dignity to their immigration laws than we do in our own country."[89]

The final law expanded to fifty-five pages and ninety-four sections, based on the U.S. quota law but with extra provisions for contract immigration and family reunion. Wixon even thought the Philippine law to be an improvement on the U.S. law. They could not refrain, however, from lecturing President Manuel Quezon on the need for strict procedure and discipline, "It is universally true that any departure in the Immigration Service from established procedure, if they appear to adversely affect the public, meets with opposition."[90] The law was passed in August 1940. The power to grant quota visas was distributed to congressmen rather than consuls, who were reported to have made a tidy profit by selling them. But whatever the actual methods of administration, the adoption of the migration law was a diplomatic success. Both the Chinese and Japanese governments protested the absolute numbers (five hundred for each) but not the principle of quotas itself.[91]

Migration control had become an indispensable part of being a modern society. Even within parts of the British Empire that were not self-governing dominions, arguments for free and contract labor migration were increasingly trumped by the need to protect natives from competition and cultural dissonance. Hong Kong prohibited the migration of Chinese laborers to Pacific islands in 1913 and collaborated with Fiji to further restrict Chinese immigration to that island through visas and passports in 1920s.[92] Australia readily enforced its White Australia laws in nonwhite territories after Papua New Guinea came under its protection as a League of Nations mandate in 1921.[93] British administrators frequently considered policies to limit free Asian migration to colonies in eastern Africa, although emigration restrictions from India usually rendered them unnecessary.[94] Even in Singapore, one of the last bastions of laissez-faire and contract mobility in the world, a Chinese quota was established in 1930.

At the same time, the self-governing British dominions modified their laws to conform to international standards. Although the dictation test remained highly effective, most of these nations responded to pressures to temporarily admit individuals of the globalizing classes such as merchants, students, and teachers. Canada rewrote its Chinese immigration laws to resemble the U.S. law in 1923, although it was never able to abrogate its agreement with Japan.[95] Administrative changes in Australia also led to the admission of more students and merchants, largely as a result of trade talks and diplomatic pressure from an increasingly respected China.[96] Even South Africa enacted a quota law in 1930 that facilitated the repeal of the Cape Colony Chinese exclusion law in 1932, one of the few remaining provincial restrictions.[97] The populations that made up the international system of nation states were increasingly well managed in a standardized and mutually acceptable manner.

Conclusion

A Melancholy Order

"Don't misunderstand me," said the priest, "I am only showing you the various opinions. You must not pay too much attention to them. The scriptures are unalterable and the comments often enough merely express the commentators' despair. . . . The man is only seeking the Law. The doorkeeper is already attached to it. It is the Law that has placed him at his post; to doubt his dignity is to doubt the Law itself."

"I don't agree with that point of view," said K., "for if one accepts it, one must accept as true everything the doorkeeper says. But you yourself have sufficiently proved how impossible it is to do that."

"No," said the priest, "it is not necessary to accept everything as true, one must only accept it as necessary."

"A melancholy conclusion," said K. "It turns lying into a universal principle."   —Kafka, *The Trial*

A sense of crisis pervades public discussions of migration, both now and for the past two centuries. There is seemingly no end to the diverse events, tales of migrant suffering, stories of migrant success and migrant dreams, econometric calculations, policy adjustments, strange coalitions, unintended consequences, incommensurable interpretations and uncompromising polemics that are the raw material of these discussions. This material is worked into endlessly contentious arguments about the virtues, vices, assimilability and contributions of immigrants, the scope and meaning of rights, the obligations of asylum, and the nature of national community.[1] A belief in the transformative newness of contemporary migration adds urgency to these debates. Currently, that belief is expressed as unprecedented flows moving from unprecedented sources to unprecedented destinations; as globe-trotting cosmopolitans and low-wage laborers creating new diasporic spaces that are the fabric of a flexible and fragmented globalization; and as the emergence of new human rights and privatization regimes that threaten to remake the nation and dismantle citizenship. All of this combines powerfully dynamic debates, as if the very nature of society were at stake.

From the perspective of two hundred years, however, the arguments about migration are numbingly familiar. Like the endless ebb and flow of enforcement failure and reform, the intractable positions of migration debates seem to be trapped in an incestuous cycle of call and response that has little to do with the dynamics of migration itself. But this should not be read merely as a tedious story of folly and repetition. The passion and dynamism of this call and response highlights the extent to which it expresses the convictions and tensions of the modern world. The most basic of these tensions is the powerful belief in both individual and nation. Both are grounded in the same ideals of freedom and self-determination, both are the foundations of social order in the modern world, and both are constantly straining against each other in their striving for autonomy, precedence and survival. Whether framed as migrant rights vs. national interest, natural rights vs. positive law, intercourse vs. sovereignty, the rights of man vs. national self-determination, liberal states vs. despotic statism, free markets vs. national borders, homo economicus vs. the social animal, private vs. public, or as universal human rights vs. citizenship, this tension has been an extremely fertile source of conflict and change. Disagreements over the optimal proportions of each has produced endlessly innovative struggles between the proponents of social justice, free markets, individual rights, racial and ethnic dignity, international comity, self-preservation, economic growth, anti-colonialism, law and order, and the preservation of national identity

Although most of these tensions remain unresolved, some unambiguous trends have emerged out of the ebbs and flows of migration and migration control over the past two centuries. Some of the most notable (and potentially reversible) of these trends are the decline of caste, blood, race and discretionary dictation tests as legitimate modes of exclusion, the rise of remote control, and the continuing proliferation of occupation- and wealth-based preferences as favored categories of selectivity. Broadly, this can be seen as a shift from attributes to achievements as the basis of selection, the latter being a more acceptable mode of discrimination in a meritocratic world.[2] Some countries are even edging out family reunification provisions in favor of migrants who can better contribute to national economies. Although some of these trends might be interpreted as an infringement on human rights or national sovereignty, overall they create a sense of progressive change, even as they entrench the accident of territorial birth as the ultimate determinant of access to equal opportunity. They also mark a shift away from cruder and more sporadic exercises of power, such as mass expulsion and absolute exclusion, to a more pervasive regulation that examines, measures and arranges all possible applicants on an individual basis.

These trends are often cast as the evolutionary unfolding of liberal rights, or even as examples of the disjunctive newness of contemporary globalization. Either way, they are asserted to be distinct developments of late twentieth century liberalization as it overcomes the statist hegemonies of earlier age. But the machinery of identification and border control has a much longer pedigree, the product as much of mid-nineteenth century processes of privatization, self-government and free intercourse as it was of the nationalisms, administrative centralization and consolidation of a state-based international system that came into its own after the 1890s. The establishment of this machinery was framed in much the same liberatory terms of self-determination and rights that continue to frame our critiques of that machinery and projects to reform it. In short, these trends are the refinement of regulatory techniques established well over a century ago, not the overcoming of an earlier epoch of unchecked controls.

One of the most important of those techniques is the insistence on newness itself. Indeed, a call for more order will always flourish best when constructed as a response to new challenges and threats. For nearly two centuries, forgetting the past has been fundamental to the naturalization of border control. This forgetting can recast the mechanisms of regulation (and deregulation) as progressive solutions to our problems, rather than as the same old techniques that have already created the problems we want to solve. Forgetting also obscures the effects of human regulation in creating the many aspects of social organization that we now accept unquestioningly as the basic order of things, transforming a world historically created by human institutions into a universal principle. Whatever we think about that principle, we accept and further reproduce it as necessary when we continue to debate and strategize how to best work within it.

Border Education

Border controls have rarely succeeded in actually regulating movement according to their own standards and categories. They have nonetheless created the world in their own image. Lawyers, smugglers, and social networks around the world continue to organize alternative networks of mobility at the interstices between nations, using the tools of border control itself as a means of crossing and evading borders. Agents use legal and administrative channels to challenge decisions, train migrants to construct personas that adhere to administrative categories, and rely on the predictability of standardized procedures as a way to guarantee passage. These activities can be interpreted as the utilization of loopholes to claim new rights, or as a mockery of law and order. Either way, they still amount to participation in and further entrenchment of the regulatory system, as both enforcers and evaders become dependent on it to do their jobs. Whatever the actual terms of admission, the very act of engaging with border control institutions is the first step of incorporation into the world order that they define.

For example, *American Visa Tactics and Examples* (2000) a bilingual volume published in China by U.S. lawyer Richard Beaubien and his collaborator Zhang Chao, guides prospective immigrants into the cross-referenced files of the U.S. immigration bureaucracy.[3] One of many such handbooks printed in various languages around the world, it offers migration advice much like that given to Chinese for well over a century. The authors depict themselves as training prospective immigrants to fulfill U.S. bureaucratic needs:

> Regretfully, some ambitious applicants have some serious misunderstandings about the visa application. Some people think it depends on luck, i.e. if the visa officer likes you, you will get the visa, and if he or she doesn't, you will fail. The visa officers are humans—not computers—and they do react somewhat to their emotions, but more often, they have a strict set of rules and regulations to follow. These rules and regulations are very strong, and they will follow them exactly. . . . If you do not fully understand the principles—and follow them, your chances of getting a visa drop dramatically. (English preface, 1)

A successful applicant must be well prepared and understand the necessary tactics of visa applications. Proper self-presentation and adherence to form are crucial skills:

If you have an adequate situation and meet the requirements of the visa application, you should get the visa. If you have no favorable conditions, but you convince them that you meet the requirements of the INA [Immigration and Naturalization Act] you may also be granted a visa. To persuade the American visa officer and to be in line with the American INA you must use some tactics. This is an art based on facts, and it is not everyone who can do it well. (English preface, 2)

The "art based on facts" is an ability to choose and present facts in a way that conforms to detailed regulations. But given the high volume of applicants, the meaning of each "fact" is highly dependent on presentation and first impressions. The book contains dozens of sample letters and interviews with detailed analyses of how the slightest nuances of expression may influence an officer's decision. Unlike the earlier coaching books, these examples are not meant to be repeated verbatim and with a blank face. Applicants are expected to take a more active role in constructing their persona by selecting and adapting the phrases and formulas most appropriate to their own situation.

The art based on facts is only loosely related to the status of the applicant before he or she applies. Once an applicant is committed to a particular identity, he or she must not diverge from it. The visa officers are always looking to trap applicants in contradictions, and the more information they have the easier it is to catch an applicant. An unsuccessful application is dangerous because the information is stored on computers, and "The next time you apply, the visa officer will see it. It is impossible to revise this information, and it may bring trouble to you" (English preface, 2). The border encounter has generated a new identity that is hard to escape.

By confining his or her persona to standardized forms, the applicant satisfies the migration bureaucrats in two waysby fitting easily into carefully categorized and cross-referenced databases and by showing a willingness to adopt an identity that can be documented as true and appropriate for participation in U.S. society and a globalizing world. The authors claim that their advice is not merely deception or a practical means of overcoming red tape. It is training in a new mode of thinking, the first step of incorporation into "the most advanced country of the world" which is something that "every applicant desires":

The visa officers are Americans, and for Americans, the typical Chinese arguments do not work. Above all, America works under the rule of law, not the rule of *guanxi* [personal relations]. Normal Chinese style *guanxi* does not work, and anyone who tells you it that it does, is lying to you. Paying money to a liar is the same as throwing the money away. We use *guanxi*, but a different kind: we use expertise. We know what the visa officers think, the rules they must follow, and we know how to arrange your documents and make an argument that the visa officers will find convincing. (2)

Obtaining a visa is inseparable from having demonstrated an ability to comport oneself as the kind of rational and isolated individual who is appropriate to a nation characterized by rule of law. The authors further explain that a successful application must conform to what they call the CCC principles: clear, concise, and convincing. "CCC principles are derived from values in American culture. . . . They may seem strange to you at first, but after you enter the US, you will learn the culture and understand how correct these principles are" (English preface, 3).

CCC methods, the art based on facts, do not train people to misrepresent the truth, but to internalize new methods of producing truths. But however cynically an applicant may put together a case, success depends on that applicant's ability to create an identity that is transparent and replicable for the purposes of continued interaction with the "advanced" parts of the world. As the authors note, "China and America will maintain 'people to people' and commercial contacts. It is in the interest of both China and America to keep up good relations" (English preface, 3). The very possibility of a gap between a migrant's self-identity and his or her case-file identity only serves to emphasize the need for continued personal transformation to bridge the disparity between the migrant's consciousness and the embodiment of those higher truths that allow one to move freely into a nation that claims to best represent the truths of a globalizing world.

Free Nations, Free Individuals: Examples of Enforcement

Identities applied at borders have become an indispensable aspect of political action in a world divided between nations. As late as the mid-nineteenth century, citizenship still marked a membership in a certain kind of political community. A person could still be a subject, serf, slave, kinsman, townsman, tribe member, or member of an "uncivilized" nation incapable of self-government. Status applied during movement across borders was comparatively irrelevant beyond a particular journey. By the middle of the twentieth century, however, almost everybody in the world had become a "citizen," now understood loosely as a member of some particular nation. Movement between those nations is impossible without citizenship. But, subsidiary identities applied at the border have become a new source of ever-proliferating diversity in terms of rights and responsibilities. Ethnicity, gender, and criminal conviction still frame domestic political and legal distinctions in some places, and childhood and mental health do so in all places. But more than anything, status applied while crossing borders has become the key marker of legitimate discrimination, distinguishing a broad diversity of access to rights, bundled in diverse configurations for permanent residents, lawful immigrants, investors, students, undocumented immigrants, refugees, guest workers, or any number of other possible categories. The desirability of such categories is rarely challenged, just the precise contents and modes of application.

Numerous examples can illustrate the concrete and symbolic powers of migration law in the contemporary world. Taken as a whole, they represent a highly diverse constellation of institutions and mechanisms, as appropriate for a machinery devoted to the systematic production and categorization of infinite, individualized diversity.

The Asylum Regime

The foundational categories of nation and individual are most apparent in the asylum regime. Not only has the global consolidation of nation states been the main cause of exploding refugee movements in the twentieth century, but the ideals of both individual rights and national security have shaped most attempts to manage those movements, replacing the older norm of hospitality.[4] The many failures of the asylum regime have also highlighted both the mutual dependencies and the contradictions of individual rights and national sovereignty. As Hanna Arendt noted of stateless refugees over half a century ago, "It turned out that the moment human beings lacked their own government and had to fall back upon their minimum human rights, no authority was left to protect them and no institution was willing to guarantee them."[5] Many more recent authors believe that the subsequent spread of human rights norms, especially over asylum and other migration cases, is the main challenge to the "traditional" powers of state self-determination, one that may threaten to undermine sovereignty and rights altogether.[6] But in its present state, asylum has proven unable to protect either human rights or state sovereignty to the satisfaction of the proponents of either. Those who worry about sovereignty complain of the massive fraud and loopholes, while those who worry about human rights complain of the enormous difficulty of asylum and its subjection to the whims of foreign and domestic policy.

More than any other aspect of contemporary migration control, the asylum regime resembles Chinese exclusion in the complex web of bureaucratic regulation and ritual that has emerged from the nexus of lawyers, bureaucrats, judges, journalists, NGOs, politicians, and migrants. In the name of protection, millions of refugees queued in a backlog of cases are incarcerated in camps and prisons around the world. Others are released on their own recognizance without the right to support themselves except as "irregular" migrants. Public complaints that asylum undermines national self-determination proliferate alongside stories of individual suffering and humiliation at the hands of demeaning and arbitrary procedures, as well as more physical abuse from prison and border guards.[7] The asylum process is both a ceremonial and a starkly material confirmation of the powerlessness of the applicant who has fallen outside state institutions. In court, refugees are required to recount or fabricate the most traumatic and painful moments of their lives in order to fit into categories of "political" rather than "economic" migrants. The success of these accounts is dependent on heavy coaching in the clear, concise, and convincing presentation of victimhood. The effect is not to find the truth of each case, but to produce a ritualized public confession of humiliation, a plea for the mercy of the international order and reincorporation into the gentler regime of a new state.

Pressures toward uniformity in decision making continue to be an important factor in the creation of such a regime. A recent quantitative study of the asylum decisions of immigration judges around the United States found great variability in their decisions. The most consistent correlation is that cases represented by lawyers were most likely to receive asylum, from a low of 16 percent of cases not represented by counsel up to 96 percent for cases represented by large law firms working with Human Rights First. Even the individualism of judges will retreat in the face of properly constructed cases. The article concludes that "Accuracy, consistency, and public acceptance are among the most important goals of any adjudicative system. . . . the government must now take steps to achieve greater consistency in decision making."[8] The authors recommend greater peer communication among judges rather than more detailed codification as the best solution. But just as the intense public scrutiny of Chinese exclusion before 1905 led to the increased formalization of decisions, there is little reason to think that peer pressure and criticism from lawyers will produce anything other than standardized refugees with clear, concise, and convincing cases that conform to the predictable needs of standardized judges.

The Proliferation of Categories

The proliferation and perfection of administrative categories continues to be promoted as the key to the effective management of migration. Around the world, the categories of merchants, students, diplomats, tourists, ethnicities, and family reunification have expanded to include asylum seekers, working holidaymakers, guest workers, investors, professionals, and other categories and skill sets, many of which are framed in discretionary terms to make them even more adaptable to the needs of labor markets and political imperatives. This has been perfected in the point systems of Australia, New Zealand, and Canada in which each individual can be defined by his or her unique position in a matrix of standardized characteristics and arranged hierarchically against other individuals. Reformers extol the refinement of distinctions as the best means to simultaneously protect migrant interests, strengthen the border, and promote social inclusion. It will help sift out undesirable migrants, streamline procedure by eliminating gray areas, and gradually replace procedures such as asylum where the state may be losing control. Improved migrant selection will also dampen hate and intolerance of immigrants, promote incorporation, and serve a state's needs of globalization and economic competition.[9] At the same time, the ever-nuanced categories help justify certain discriminations within the border without undermining the ideal of equality before law. Through "impartial" identification and categorization at the border, immigration law can determine the rights that each applicant will enjoy according to their appropriate individual attributes.

Guest Workers

Programs to admit temporary workers who will depart upon completion of their job have supplanted indenture with schemes that involve even more direct government surveillance, taxation, and collaboration with private enterprises. With laws that often make it illegal to change jobs and limit access to other local rights, guest worker and other temporary work programs are the most straightforward attempt to simultaneously meet business demands for cheap and dispensable labor while policing membership of the nation. As with indenture, the migrants frequently find themselves heavily indebted (often for government taxes paid by recruiters), dependent on their employers (sometimes the recruiters themselves), and unable to move freely (although unlike the older requirement that they must obtain travel passes, this restriction is now largely obtained by confiscating existing travel documents like passports). But just as many indentured migrants remained permanently in their destinations despite discriminatory postindenture regulations, so are many guest workers likely to circumvent laws and remain as settlers [10] Even in the Persian Gulf states and Southeast Asia, where liberal norms are less entrenched and governments supposedly have a freer hand to regulate both migrants and employers, repeated asylums, deportations, employer and recruiter abuses, and black markets in migrant labor testify to the difficulty of enforcing the intentions of temporary migrant labor laws.[11]

Alongside the expanding government regulation of labor migration, the demonization of privately organized migration that evades official collaboration continues apace. It is now routinely labeled as trafficking and associated with smuggling and sex-work. The annual U.S. report on migrant trafficking explains that its root causes are "greed, moral turpitude," and political and economic instability, while the traffickers themselves have "little respect for the rights or dignity of their victims."[12] Frequently involved in other transnational crimes, traffickers are a threat to a just global order even as they are a relic of an outmoded past, a "modern-day form of slavery, which has persisted into the twenty-first century."[13] The report then shifts attention from private traffickers to international peer pressure by dividing the countries of the world in terms of their "good behavior" in suppressing trafficking.

The Undocumented, Irregular, and Illegal

Anybody who evades border surveillance or does not maintain the status imposed at the border is potentially a criminal and subject to discriminations that would be withheld from lawful immigrants. These irregular and undocumented are simultaneously the most visible and invisible products of border control. Uncontrollably porous borders and the large police presence that accumulates around them are prominent symbols of migration as problem, simultaneously reinforcing a sense of threat to the integrity of the nation and of the criminality of those who evade. The actual processes of capture and return at the border do little to limit these entries, but they are highly effective in marking the migrants themselves as outside the political community. But once these migrants arrive at the interior, they make up a great invisible underclass, ignored in statistics, and most (but not all) welfare projects. Even as they become an indispensable part of the economic community, they can obtain few legal or social protections and are scapegoated as the enemies of the political and social communities. Their invisibility makes it possible to maintain a public image of equality before law while still preserving the material benefits of unequal social and economic relations.[14]

My Family

My wife and I adopted a daughter from China in 2005. The four weeks of crying that accompanied her abrupt removal to the United States leave little doubt that it was a painful and coerced migration. But even more than guest workers, international adoption is the most highly regulated form of migration in the world (especially after scandals in the early 1990s). Accordingly, it is also one of the most moralized forms, couched in terms of love, family, and mutual benefit, especially toward those who are unable to provide for their own best interests. It is a discourse with strong similarities to that which promoted indentured migration in the nineteenth century. Also like indenture, international adoption is firmly situated within a global economy. Prospective parents collect information and compare the costs and (racially and gender coded) quality of children from competing countries around the world before making a choice.

During the adoption process, the Chinese government requested that my wife, who was born in China, demonstrate that the Zhu Zhi in her Chinese documents was identical to the Cecily McKeown in her U.S. documents. When she applied for her initial immigration visa after our marriage in China, the U.S. consul in Guangzhou readily accommodated our request to use her English name in U.S. documents. But then the Chinese government said that photographs on her Chinese and English documents were insufficient evidence of a link between the two people. When we asked the immigration service for documentation of that link, officials denied that they were in the business of changing names, insisting that only the courts could do that. Copies of her immigration files confirmed that they had no record of the name Zhu Zhi. The Chinese government was finally satisfied when we found that her U.S. alien number was written both on the U.S. visa in her Chinese passport and on her U.S. naturalization certificate, evidence of adequately cross-referenced files. As far as the U.S. immigration service is concerned, however, Cecily McKeown emerged fully formed from the tarmac of the San Francisco airport, x-ray in hand. Much like the identities built around Chinese immigrants a century ago, any link to a pre-existing Zhu Zhi is irrelevant now that she has been inserted into cross-referenced domestic files.

International Management

Proposals for the international management of migration represent the densest collaboration of scholars, bureaucrats, and activists working toward the refinement of ever more sophisticated forms of regulation. As in the 1920s, these proponents claim a bird's-eye view of the global problem, and international institutions function mostly as clearinghouses for knowledge about migration and migration laws. This knowledge is often presented within a framework of newness: of new kinds of migration that demand new forms of regulation that can augment and transcend poorly functioning national border controls. This insistence on newness helps to obscure the fact that their proposals are largely an expansion and intensification of existing regulation.

Migration scholars frequently insist that existing migration laws are based on a faulty understanding of migration. Appropriate regulation must be based on more accurate research and knowledge of the thing to be regulated. In answering the question posed by the title of his article, "Why Migration Policies Fail," Stephen Castles argues that national migration controls "still follow a national logic, while many of the forces driving migration follow a transnational logic."[15] This is the basis of calls for international cooperation that have remained much the same for over a century. As explained by Douglas Massey and Edward Taylor, "Policymakers should recognize immigration as a natural part of global economic integration and work multilaterally to *manage it more effectively*. Much as flows of capital, commodities, and goods are managed for the mutual benefit of trading partners by multilateral agreements and institutions such as Gatt and the WTO, labor migration can also be cooperatively managed to maximize the benefits and minimize the costs for both sending and receiving societies."[16] By situating migration as an aspect of the global political economy, proponents further argue that the management of migration cannot merely take place at borders because migration is inseparable from the problems of international inequalities in wages, development, and economic security that create emigrants in the first place. As Paul Peirce expressed it in 1910, "May we not hope from international agreements, or international pressure, some amelioration of the conditions and some relief from the oppressions which have driven people from their native lands, and so some modification of the very causes of immigration?"[17]

Much recent scholarship also insists that an understanding of migration should not be rooted in the mythical idea of isolated individuals making self-interested choices and engaging in monodirectional resettlement. Migration takes place in the context of dense social relationships. Families and personal networks are the most important sites of decision, but this quickly expands into friends, businesses, and other channels of information and assistance. In this context, migration is a multidirectional process of return voyages, varying durations, and geographically dispersed networks. Analysts disagree about the extent to which the "diasporic" and transnational spaces of contemporary migrations differ from earlier migrations, the extent to which they may undermine the state, and if a golden age of migration control ever really existed. But they nearly all agree that "Unilateral, domestic control over immigration is one of the cornerstones of traditional notions of sovereignty."[18] And if that is the case, these new ways of understanding migration imply that to better protect migrant rights, interests, and incorporation, we need new forms of regulation that go beyond these "traditional notions."

These analyses of the global and social contexts of migration are highly convincing correctives to the political imaginary of the free, monodirectional individual. But the overall effect is to isolate migration as something that exists largely in terms of its own dynamics, independent of and prior to regulation and political processes. As expressed in an influential article on the study of transnational networks, any understanding of migration must be grounded in the "individual and his/her support networks as the proper unit of analysis." This is the basic foundation on which "aggregate structural effects" are built "*in reaction* to government policies" (emphasis in original).[19] Other scholars even insist that existing migration controls have no appreciable affects on established patterns, although they may successfully block incipient flows.[20] Such an approach obscures the extent to which the categories through which we know migration, and even the migrants themselves, are already the product of nearly two centuries of regulation. The stereotype of "traditional" border controls further obscures the past century of innovative and progressive regulatory techniques that have created the world we know. Accordingly, most policy proposals generated from these understandings of migration turn out to be reformulations of long-standing techniques of national control. The exact mix varies, but even the more self-consciously innovative and research-

based proposals for international management tend to favor further proliferation of categories, refined surveillance techniques, temporary migrations and
greater regulation of the private organization of migration. The diversity of
individual cases, specificities, and forms of evasion generated by previous controls always require ever more intensive management to keep up with them.

For example, the 2003 report of the International Organization of Migration (IOM), the most prominent institutional proponent of global management, is well-grounded in contemporary migration research. Its activities and
aims are very similar to those of international organizations in the 1920s. It
strives to be a global clearinghouse of information and recommendations on
migration and its management. It aims not to transcend nations but to facilitate the harmonization of national policies. To this end, it calls for standardized statistics to help coordinate global labor markets, facilitate multilateral
agreements, and promote successful policies for migrant control and incorporation. It favors the point systems of Australia and Canada as ideal methods of
satisfying the needs of both states and individuals, because they can evaluate
migrants according to a diverse range of standardized categories and produce
a single, unique and quantitative value for each one. It also stresses the need
for surveillance technologies, extensive information, expert knowledge, consistent definitions, and cross-referenced files. To this end, it promotes fingerprinting, databases, biometric identification, and monitoring employers.[21]

The IOM frames these policies not as the erection of barriers but as an
attempt to protect the interests of migrants and nations. Expressed in the
languages of multiculturalism and economic liberalism, their purpose is to
"maximize migrant contributions to social diversity, through integration"
(289). Global regulation and suppression of the private organization of migration is key to making this possible. "In the long run, only the establishment of
an international immigration management framework will make migration—
and indeed mobility—safe, fair and constructive, failing which the principle
beneficiaries risk being those who are more opportunistic and the smuggling
rings" (23). In sum, a successful international regime will

> create a system that permits and encourages voluntary migration through
> authorized channels, restoring the element of choice to individuals and
> governments. A fully and effectively functioning international migration
> management system would facilitate voluntary migration to meet the
> needs of the global economy and mobile populations. At the same time,

vulnerable persons would be protected and forced and irregular migration would decrease. (110)

Whatever its continuities with past practices and concerns, the IOM claims that the context is entirely different because the world is now experiencing a "migration governability crisis" (195). As evidence, it draws a clear line between "classic" migration patterns and modern mobility. Traditional migration was largely between Europe and the four "traditional countries of immigration," the United States, Canada, Australia, and New Zealand (nary a mention of Argentina and Brazil, not to mention Singapore, Malaysia, or other Asian countries).[22] In contrast, new patterns bring migrants from distant places beyond the North Atlantic into new destinations that include Europe, the Middle East, and Southeast Asia. This new migration also moves through diasporic and transnational formations qualitatively different from the old migrations. More than anything, this description does not describe actual shifts in migration itself so much as the shifting definitions of migration, from Henry Fairchild to contemporary sociologists:

Migration movements were long confined to relatively straightforward and linear relations between closely linked poles—a sending country automatically had its receiving country, based on age-old ties that were mostly cultural, emotional, economic or historical in nature; however, these special ties are rapidly giving way to an unprecedented widening of the migration landscape. This broadening is moving hand-in-hand with the evolution of types of migration. The classical, long-term migration model will dominate less and less in the future as other types of migration— including short-term and circulatory migration—come to the fore. One thing is beyond doubt: migration is gradually eroding the traditional boundaries between languages, cultures, ethnic groups and nation-states. A transnational flow par excellence, it therefore defies cultural traditions, national identities and political institutions, contributing in the long run to curtailing nation-state autonomy and to shaping a global society. No longer simply the result of identifiable push and pull factors, human mobility is developing a life of its own. (4)

In addition to the intrinsic challenges of regulating this new migration, the spread of supranational human rights norms also impinges upon the power of nations to establish and enforce regulations. In consequence, argues the IOM, "states feel they have lost the sovereign right to determine who enters and remains in their territories. This feeling of loss of control has real consequences for the health, safety and stability of society and has led to an increase in public anger and frustration both at the government and at the migrant level" (103). Thus new forms of international management are not only justified, but necessary to help states preserve their own sovereignty.

Although the nation is supposedly under threat, it is still the source of the most reliable knowledge about migration. The IOM even insists that citizenship is the most "objective" measure of migration because it requires a migrant to produce tangible evidence such as a passport.[23] Ironically, a measurement based on fixity rather than mobility is necessary because the very proliferation of categories recommended by the IOM has created much undocumented migration and made statistics of actual movement noncomparable across nations, if not indecipherable. The IOM recognizes this problem and interprets it as a need to generate ever more standardized methods of management. Whether or not borders are effectively patrolled is less relevant than the continued need to refine management techniques to generate the kinds of identities required by national states and global capitalism. Any statement about the challenges of global migration is, at heart, an assertion of expansive ambitions to govern mobility and identities.

Newness and History

This cycle of regulation creating conditions that demand more regulation is grounded in the rhetoric of newness and forgetting. This rhetoric naturalizes previous regulation so the world seems not like the product of regulation at all, or at least the product of an entirely different and more objectionable kind of regulation. It also obscures the long-term dynamism of tension between individuals and states, so that each substantial assertion of rights, international organization, privatization, or centralized management can be depicted as pioneering reform, even a brave new age. The rhetoric of newness also works on a geographic scale, constantly repositioning the world beyond the North Atlantic as somehow outside of history, only now being incorporated. This is best exemplified by the series of concepts used to project North Atlantic history as the trajectory of world history: natural rights, civilization, family of nations, modernization, the community of liberal states, and, as often as not, globalization itself.[24] Each of these ideas helps naturalize global difference and justify new projects of expansive regulation, often through the very medium of a critique of the inequalities and hegemonies embodied in earlier progressive new ages.

In terms of migration and its regulation, current chronologies of newness usually piggyback on some mix of two general narratives of globalization. The first—I'll call it the "liberal narrative"—was common in sociological and political science analyses of migration control in the 1980s and 1990s. It describes the period since the 1950s as the unfolding and diffusion of liberal norms that had been germinating since the eighteenth century. Freer mobility, human rights, international organizations, and the expansion of asylum are some of the hallmarks of this unfolding. But they have had the unfortunate byproduct of undermining the liberal states and citizenship ideals that produced them in the first place and are still their main guarantors. The second account, the "globalization narrative," posits a break in the 1970s or 1980s in which a new era of globalization, transnational interactions, and privatization began to reconfigure - stable borders, dismantle citizenships, and generate new configurations of postnational membership and deterritorialized identities.[25] The liberal narrative has stalled since the late 1990s, as it has become harder to interpret North Atlantic migration control trends in terms of unfolding liberal ideals. But the continued expansion of joint private-government ventures in the organization of migration and the continued proliferation of categories have been readily incorporated into both narratives as a new age that transcends the statist totalities of the past.

These two narratives share much in common: a conception of the world from the sixteenth century to 1950s as dominated by totalizing state initiatives (while simultaneously nurturing liberal ideals in Europe an America); a weak understanding of the extensive privatization, ideals of free intercourse, ad hoc citizenship practices, denationalized rights of, man and world-transforming networks of the nineteenth century; and a Eurocentric history of the "global." Their differences can best be encapsulated in their periodizations. The liberal narrative tends to see the world of states before the 1950s as a hangover of illiberal ideals and conservatism. It took more than two centuries of germination for liberal ideals to really set root in the late twentieth century. The globalization narrative, on the other hand, tends to see the mid-twentieth century world of states as the pinnacle of liberalism—at least the version of liberalism encapsulated in the welfare state and progressive era management. Those states are now being undermined, but private ownership is an ideal that has continued to flourish across the transformation from an international system to globalization that began in the 1970s. Both the entanglement and divergence of these two narratives are captured in the idea of "neoliberalism," a word that encompasses many of the recent transformations that make up a new age in the globalization narrative, while preserving a memory of the common roots of both welfare state progressivism and privatization in the ideals of - mid-nineteenth century "liberalism."

The liberal narrative of migration control often revolves around the idea of a "liberal paradox."[26] This idea recognizes some of the tensions within liberalism but, like "civilization" before it, is framed as a quality that is simultaneously universal and limited to a distinct group of "liberal" nations. Indeed, a threat from outside is crucial to the conceptualization of the paradox. It begins with the assertion that the laws and institutions of the liberal state are the very things that make those states the most attractive for migrants. In the words of one scholar, "The migration state is almost by definition a liberal state inasmuch as it creates a legal and regulatory environment in which migrants can pursue individual strategies of accumulation."[27] But this very attraction is also the source of threats that may undermine liberality. An excess of migrants can swamp democratic institutions through sheer numbers or undermine the political and social community through the inequalities that may accumulate, especially when migrants remain unnaturalized. But restriction is difficult if procedural and political commitments to individual rights are to be maintained. In practice, a mix of constitutional commitments, transnational norms, and special-interest lobbying results in toothless and confused laws and halfhearted enforcement. The resulting porous border allows even more migrants to enter on questionable grounds and the greater entrenchment of special interests, thus threatening the very rule of law that made the nation attractive and the border porous in the first place.

This cycle is generally situated as a product of the spread of liberal states, human rights norms, and the challenge of new migrations since World War II. Chinese exclusion is a "relic of a different era," a period of traditional enforcement by governments committed to plenary powers at the expense of individual rights and insensitive to international pressures.[28] Since then, constitutional commitments to rights in liberal states have been reinforced by supranational norms and institutions. All of these processes have come together to generate the massive legal and procedural difficulties that now inhibit effective enforcement and the delegation of much enforcement power to localities and private organizations. This has inspired "illiberal" reactions in many nations that demand a return to traditional understandings of sovereignty and border control. It has even inspired ambivalence from more self-consciously liberal commentators, worried about the dangerous implications for national sovereignty, which, for better or worse, is still the main guarantor of civil rights. In the words of David Jacobson, "If the distinction between citizens and alien erodes, and the boundary defining the national community consequently is blurred, the civil connection between state and society becomes frayed. The state abdicates its role as the political organization of the community because there is less of a community to represent."[29]

Here, the significant overlap with the globalization narrative becomes obvious. Both narratives project a global order of sovereign border control that was achieved only in the 1930s (if even then) into a foundational truth of the international system and sovereign nationhood. Both project the experiences of a few core states into a universal experience. The globalization narrative is more likely to acknowledge that much migration, migration control problems, and the proliferation of rights and categories takes place outside the realm of liberal states. But the insistence on newness plays a similar role of projecting a bounded North Atlantic history as the terms of a world-consuming present. By casting past migration control as a remnant of illiberal or traditional practices, the liberal/civilized state forgets the extent to which those freedoms and progressive ideals were built on the erection of borders to exclude the rest of the world from participating. By ignoring the importance of diplomatic pressures from that world in mitigating the extremes of border control, the liberal/civilized states also create a self-valorizing history as pioneers of freedom and progress (or privatization and exploitation) that extend universal values rather than receive or react. By forgetting the past, these historical narratives dress old policies in new clothes and embrace them as the forefront of innovation and transformation in response to unprecedented challenges.

Rather than a history of breaks or unfolding, we can read the past two centuries as a story of dynamic and unresolved tensions, in which assertions of newness are political tactics. The ideals of intercourse and self-determination in the mid-nineteenth century established a powerful imaginative framework for those tensions. State centralization of identities emerged out of both self-rule and the imperatives of international interaction. Certain forms of private and local organization were suppressed in favor of others, mostly corporate and philanthropic, that were willing to collaborate in regulation and the entrenchment of the individual as the object of rights and surveillance. This collaboration helped make the international system of nation states and the society–individual opposition into institutional realities at the turn of the twentieth century. The technologies of border control and identification were a crucial aspect of this consolidation. Once justified largely as a way to exclude people from participation in the family of nations and grounded in particular political formations of self-rule, they became part of the very fabric of the international system of self-determining nation states, a prerequisite of participation. The racial and civilizational ideals that once framed these laws were ultimately denounced even as the institutions, categories, and justifications that they spawned continued to be refined under the veneer of new progressive internationalisms and other projects in the service of justice and good management. The creation of an international system of centralized states was largely achieved by the 1960s, accompanied by genocides, expulsions, war, purifications and other promises of a new age. By the end of the century, this fragile construction was already being characterized as the "traditional," "illiberal," or "liberal" baseline of stable and totalizing identities now under challenge by the disruptions of globalization, mobility and privatization.

New ages and disruptions continue to proliferate, as do claims for the final unfolding of liberal ideals and rights. These are also claims to power, truth and control in this world. They are rooted in the imagination of temporal and geographic breaks, and enforced by institutions that have made those breaks into political realities. These breaks help map the world into hierarchies of difference and progress, creating spaces and epochs of truth that justify the extension of power to liberate others from savagery, barbarism, backwardness, immobility, despotism, tradition, heathenism, unfree markets, bad governance or any number of other qualities that imply exclusion from universal values. By the same token, these breaks help identify the "thems" that impose power—be they governments, corporate structures, militarists, wasteful and self-absorbed Americans, colonialism the lingering influence of traditional institutions, or the liberal, illiberal or neoliberal institutions of today. We may be skeptical of the reality of such categories and the possibility of actually labeling any individual as us, they or other. But we nonetheless all take part in the continued refinement of the techniques of categorization through our necessary participation in regulatory institutions and the constant adjustments we make in the name of resistance, order, liberation, protection, development, compromise and knowledge.

Primary Sources and Abbreviations Used in Notes

Australia

National Archives, Canberra

Au-NCEA   Records of the Department of External Affairs, Series A1, Correspondence File.

National Archives, New South Wales Branch, Chester Hill

Au-NNOC Outward Letter Books, Collector of Customs, A1016.
Au-NNOI   Outward Letter Books, Correspondence in Connection with the Immigration Restriction Act, A1026.

New South Wales State Archives, Kingswood

Au-NSW   Correspondence of the Colonial Secretary, Special Bundles.

Canada

Published Government Documents

Ca-CRAI   *Correspondence Regarding Asiatic Immigration*, Ottawa, 1907–1925 (Confidential publications, found in Ca-NEA, 1002/33896).
Ca-DCER *Documents on Canadian External Relations*. 4 vols. (Ottawa: Department of External Affairs, 1967–1971).

National Archives, Ottawa

Ca-NEA   Records of the Department of External Affairs, RG 25.
Ca-NIB   Records of the Immigration Branch, RG 76.

China

Institute of Modern History, Academia Sinica, Taipei

Ch-AFA   Archives of the Foreign Affairs Office (Zongli Yamen, Waiwubu, and Waijiaobu).

Number One Historical Archives, Beijing

Ch-AGC   Archives of the Grand Council (Junjichu).

Published Document Collections

Ch-CYS   *Chouban yiwu shimo: Tonggzhi chao* [Account of the management of barbarian affairs, Tongzhi reign] (Taipei: Wenhai, 1972).

Ch-GCDL   *Guangxu chao donghua lu* [Records of the Guangxu dynasty]. 5 vols. Edited by Zhu Shoupeng (Beijing: Zhonghua Shuju, 1958).

Ch-HCS   *Huagong chuguo shiliao huibian* [Collected documents on the emigration of Chinese laborers]. 4 vols. Edited by Chen Hansheng (Beijing: Zhonghua Shuju, 1980).

Ch-JHDY   *Jianada Huagong ding yue shiliao,* [Documents on the Chinese labor treaty with Canada]. Edited by Chen Shangeng and Jiong Zhenghua (Taipei: Academica Sinica, Modern History Research Institute, 1998).

Ch-JZX   *Jindai Zhongguo dui xifang ji lieqiang renshi ziliao huibian* [Collected material on knowledge of the Western penetration into China] (Taipei: Academia Sinica, Modern History Research Institute, 1986).

Ch-QW   *Qingji waijiao shiliao* [Qing foreign relations materials]. Edited by Wang Yanwei and Wang Liang (Taipei: Wenhai, 1985 [1932]).

Ch-ZMG   *Zong Mei guanxi shiliao* [Documents on Chinese-American relations]. 5 vols. Edited by Huang Jiamo (Taipei: Academia Sinica, Modern History Research Institute, 1988–90).

Great Britain

GB-CP   Foreign Office Confidential Prints.
GB-PP   Parliamentary Papers.

Hawaii

Archives of the State of Hawaii, Honolulu

H-FO   Foreign Office and Executive, Hong Kong.

H-MI   Ministry of the Interior, Immigration-Chinese.

United States

Asian American Studies Library, University of California, Berkeley

US-AJY   Judy Yung Collection.

Bancroft Library, University of California, Berkeley

US-BIEL   Ira and Edwar Lee Interview, Asian American Oral History Composite.

US-BJBS   John Birge Sawyer Diaries.

Chicago Historical Society

US-CWH   Walter William Husband Papers, 1891–1926.

Published Government Documents

US-DE   Executive documents.

US-DH   House documents.

US-DS   Senate documents.

US-FR   *Papers Relating to the Foreign Relations of the United States* (Washington, DC: Government Printing Office, 1872–1929).

US-IR   *Report of the Commissioner-General of Immigration.* U.S. Treasury Department, 1894–1902; U.S. Department of Commerce and Labor, 1903–1912; U.S. Department of Labor, 1913–1932.

National Archives, College Park, MD

RECORDS OF THE BUREAU OF INSULAR AFFAIRS, RG 350

US-NCCF   Classified Files Relating to Customs Matters in the Island Possessions, 1898–1941.

US-NCCG   General Classified Files, 1898–1945.

RECORDS OF THE STATE DEPARTMENT, RG 59

US-NCD   Decimal Files, 1910–1929.

US-NCDA Despatches from U.S. Consuls in Amoy, 1844–1906 (Microfilm M100).

US-NCDC Despatches from U.S. Consuls in Canton, 1790–1906 (Microfilm M101).

US-NCDH Despatches from U.S. Consuls in Hong Kong, 1844–1906 (Microfilm M108).

US-NCDS Despatches from U.S. Consuls in Shanghai, 1847–1906 (Microfilm M112).

US-NCDU Despatches from U.S. Ministers to China, 1843–1906 (Microfilm M92).

US-NCR   Inspection Reports on Foreign Service Posts.

US-NCNC Notes from the Chinese Legation in the United States to the Department of State, 1868–1906 (Microfilm M98).

US-NCNM Numerical and Minor Files, 1906–1910 (Microfilm M862).

US-NCR   Records Relating to Charges against John Goodnow and Robert McWade.

National Archives, Great Lakes Region, Chicago, IL

RECORDS OF THE IMMIGRATION AND NATURALIZATION SERVICE, RG 85

US-NGCC Chicago Chinese Case Files, 1898–1940.

US-NGCD Correspondence of Chinese Division, 1893–1924.

National Archives, Mid-Atlantic Region, Philadelphia, PA

RECORDS OF THE IMMIGRATION AND NATURALIZATION SERVICE, RG 85

US-NMC   Chinese Letters Sent, 1895–1903, Philadelphia Collector of Customs.

US-NML   Letters Concerning Chinese, 1904–1911.

National Archives, New England Region, Waltham, MA

RECORDS OF THE IMMIGRATION AND NATURALIZATION SERVICE, RG 85

US-NNM   Montreal Chinese Case Files, 1900–1952.

National Archives, Northeast Region, New York, NY

RECORDS OF THE IMMIGRATION AND NATURALIZATION SERVICE, RG 85

US-NNYC Chinese Exclusion Case Files, 1880–1960.

National Archives, Pacific Sierra Region, San Bruno, CA

RECORDS OF THE IMMIGRATION AND NATURALIZATION SERVICE, RG 85
US-NPD   Chinese Coaching Material (Densmore Investigation) 1906–1940.
US-NPH   Chinese Immigration Case Files, Honolulu, 1903–1915.
US-NPO   Outgoing Correspondence, Inspector in Charge at Honolulu, 1903–1904.

National Archives, Washington, DC

RECORDS OF THE IMMIGRATION AND NATURALIZATION SERVICE, RG 85
US-NWCD Chinese Division File.
US-NWCG Chinese General Correspondence, 1898–1908.
US-NWCS Chinese Smuggling Files, 1914–1921.
US-NWCu Customs Case File, no. 3359D, Related to Chinese Immigration, 1877–1891.
US-NWSC Subject Correspondence.

RECORDS OF THE STATE DEPARTMENT, RG 59
US-NWVC Visa Division Correspondence Regarding Immigration, 1910–1939 (Entry 702).
US-NWVD Visa Division, General Visa Correspondence, 1914–1940 (Entry 704).

Notes

Introduction: The Globalization of Identities

1. John Torpey, *The Invention of the Passport: Surveillance, Citizenship and the State* (Cambridge: Cambridge UP, 2000), 13.

2. Guy Goodwin-Gill, *International Law and the Movement of Persons Between States* (Oxford: Clarendon Press, 1978), 24–26, 24–28; Mark Salter, *Rights of Passage: The Passport in International Relations* (Boulder: Lynne Rienner, 2003), 1–6; Daniel Turack, *The Passport in International Law* (Lexington, MA: Lexington Books, 1972), 1, 17–20.

3. John Torpey, "States and the Regulation of Migration in the Twentieth-Century North Atlantic World," in *The Wall Around the West: State Borders and Immigration Controls in North America and Europe*, ed. Peter Andreas and Timothy Snyder, 31–54 (Lanham, MD: Rowman and Littlefield, 2000); and "Coming and Going: On the State Monopolization of the Legitimate 'Means of Movement,'" *Sociological Theory* 16 (1998): 239–59.

4. Richard Plender, *International Migration Law* (Leiden: Sijthoff, 1972), 48–52; Aristide Zolberg, "Global Movements, Global Walls: Responses to Migration: 1885–1925," in *Global History and Migrations*, ed. Wang Gungwu, 297–307 (Boulder: Westview, 1997); and "The Great Wall Against China: Responses to the First Immigration Crisis, 1885–1925," in *Migration, Migration History, History: Old Paradigms and New Perspectives*, ed. Jan and Leo Lucassen, 291–305 (Bern: Peter Lang, 1999.

5. Torpey, *Invention of the Passport*, 159–64.

6. See Adam McKeown, "Periodizing Globalization," *History Workshop Journal* 63 (2007): 218–30.

7. David Ludden, "Presidential Address: Maps in the Mind and the Mobility of Asia," *Journal of Asian Studies* 62 (2003): 1062.

8. Arjun Appadurai, *Modernity at Large: Cultural Dimensions of Globalization* (Minneapolis: University of Minnesota Press, 1996), 3–9; Linda Basch, Nina Glick Schiller, and Cristina Sztanton Blanc, *Nations Unbound: Transnational Projects, Post-*

colonial Predicaments and Deterritorialized Nation-States (Amsterdam: Gordon and Breach, 1994); Manuel Castells, *The Rise of Network Society*, vol. 1 of *The Information Age* (Oxford: Basil Blackwell, 1996); Saskia Sassen, *Territory, Authority, Rights: From Medieval to Global Assemblages* (Princeton: Princeton UP, 2006).

9. Francis Fukuyama, *The End of History and the Last Man* (New York: Perennial, 1993); Michael Hardt and Antonio Negri, *Empire* (Cambridge: Harvard UP, 2001); Bruce Mazlish, "Comparing Global History to World History," *Journal of Interdisciplinary History* 28 (1993): 385–95; Roland Robertson, *Globalization. Social Theory and Global Culture* (London: Sage, 1992), 58–59.

10. David Held, *Democracy and the Global Order: From the Modern State to Cosmopolitan Governance* (Cambridge: Polity Press, 1995), 32–47, 78–83; Sassen, *Territory, Authority, Rights.* Thomas Biersteker and Cynthia Weber, eds., *State Sovereignty as Social Construct* (Cambridge: Cambridge UP, 1996), 3, criticizes the Westphalian emphasis but offers essays about an expansive Europe.

11. Anthony G. Hopkins, *Globalization in World History* (New York: Norton, 2002); Adam McKeown, "Global Migration, 1846–1940," *Journal of World History* 15 (2004): 155–89; Kevin O'Rourke and Jeffrey Williamson, *Globalization and History: The Evolution of a Nineteenth-Century Atlantic Economy* (Cambridge: MIT Press, 1996); Andreas Wimmer and Nina Glick Schiller, "Methodological Nationalism, the Social Sciences, and the Study of Migration: An Essay in Historical Epistemology," *International Migration Review* 27 (2003): 576–610.

12. Dennis Flynn and Arturo Giráldez, "Path Dependence, Time Lags and the Birth of Globalization: A Critique of O'Rourke and Williamson," *European Review of Economic History* 8 (2004): 81–108, argues against the market-based definition of globalization in Kevin O'Rourke and Jeffrey Williamson, "When Did Globalization Begin?" *European Review of Economic History* 6 (2002): 23–50, developing a perspective that still emphasizes interactions but with less emphasis on quantity.

13. Appadurai, *Modernity at Large*; Michael Geyer and Charles Bright, "World History in a Global Age," *American Historical Review* 100 (1995): 1034–60; Sassen, *Territory, Authority, Rights.*

14. Robertson, *Globalization*, 26–27. Nonetheless, Robertson sees globalization as a linear process that began in Europe and is still tending toward "unicity."

15. Charles Maier, "Consigning the Twentieth Century to History: Alternative Narratives for the Modern Era," *American Historical Review* 105 (2000): 807–31; John Meyer et al., "World Society and the Nation-State," *American Journal of Sociology* 103 (1997): 144–81; George Thomas et al., *Institutional Structure: Constituting State, Society and the Individual* (London: Sage, 1987).

16. O'Rourke and Williamson, *Globalization and History.*

17. Thomas Gallant, "Brigandage, Piracy, Capitalism, and State-Formation," in *States and Illegal Practices*, ed. Josiah Heyman and Alan Smart, 25–62 (Oxford: Berg,

1999); Janice Thomson, *Mercenaries, Pirates and Sovereigns* (Princeton: Princeton UP, 1995).

18. Michael Walzer, *Spheres of Justice: A Defense of Pluralism and Equality* (New York: Basic Books, 1983), 35–51; Frederick Whelan, "Citizenship and Freedom of Movement: An Open Admission Policy?" in *Open Borders? Closed Societies? The Ethical and Political Issues*, ed. Mark Gibney, 3–39 (Westport, CT: Greenwood, 1988).

19. Mae Ngai, *Impossible Subjects: Illegal Aliens and the Making of Modern America* (Princeton: Princeton UP, 2004).

20. Uday Mehta, *Liberalism and Empire: A Study in Nineteenth-Century British Liberal Thought* (Chicago: University of Chicago Press, 1999).

21. Immanuel Wallerstein, "Culture as the Ideological Battleground of the Modern World-System," *Theory, Culture and Society* 7 (1990): 31–55.

22. Thomas Klevin, "Why International Law Favors Emigration over Immigration," *Inter-America Law Review* 33 (2002): 69–100.

23. James Madison, *The Federalist Papers*, ed. Clinton Rossiter (New York: Mentor, 1961), 46; Jean-Jacques Rousseau, "On the Social Contract," in *The Basic Political Writings*, ed. Peter Gay, 156 (Indianapolis: Hackett, 1987); Adam Smith, *The Wealth of Nations* (New York: Modern Library, 2000 [1776]), 148–49.

24. Jane Caplan and John Torpey, eds., *Documenting Individual Identity: The Development of State Practices in the Modern World* (Princeton: Princeton UP, 2001); Dieter Hoffman-Axthelm, "Identity and Reality: The End of the Philosophical Immigration Officer," in *Modernity and Identity*, ed. Scott Lash and Jonathan Friedman, 196–217 (Oxford: Blackwell, 1992); Matt Matsuda, *The Memory of the Modern* (New York: Oxford UP, 1996), 122–39; Radhika Singha "Settle, Mobilize, Verify: Identification Practices in Colonial India," *Historical Studies* 16 (2000): 151–98.

25. Simon Cole, *Suspect Identities: A History of Fingerprinting and Criminal Identification* (Cambridge: Harvard UP, 2001); William Roff, "Sanitation and Security: The Imperial Powers and the Nineteenth Century Hajj," *Arabian Studies* 4 (1982): 143–60.

26. For transnational histories of migration control centered on race, see Matthew Guterl and Christine Skwiot, "Atlantic and Pacific Crossings: Race, Empire and 'the Labor Problem' in the Late Nineteenth Century," *Radical History Review* 91 (2005): 40–61; Marilyn Lake and Henry Reynolds, *Drawing the Global Colour Line: White Men's Countries and the International Challenge of Racial Equality* (Cambridge: Cambridge UP, 2008); Erika Lee "Orientalisms in the Americas: A Hemispheric Approach to Asian American History," *Journal of Asian American Studies* 8 (2005): 235–56.

27. Eithne Luibhéid, *Entry Denied: Controlling Sexuality at the Border* (Minneapolis: University of Minnesota Press, 2002); Erica Rand, *Ellis Island Snow Globe* (Durham: Duke UP, 2005). For a general discussion of Foucault and race, see Ann Stoler,

Race and the Education of Desire: Foucault's History of Sexuality and the Colonial Order of Things (Durham: Duke UP, 1995).

28. Michel Foucault, *Discipline and Punish: The Birth of the Prison*, trans. Alan Sheridan (New York: Vintage, 1979), 26–27.

29. Ibid., 307. See also Timothy Mitchell, "Everyday Metaphors of Power," *Theory and Society* 19 (1990): 545–77; and "Society, Economy, and the State Effect," in *State/Culture: State Formation after the Cultural Turn*, ed. George Steinmetz, 76–97 (Ithaca: Cornell UP, 1999).

30. Aristide Zolberg, "The Archaeology of 'Remote Control,'" in *Migration Control in the North Atlantic World: The Evolution of State Practices in Europe and the United States from the French Revolution to the Inter-War Period*, ed. Andreas Fahrmeir, Olivier Faron, and Patrick Weil, 195–222 (New York: Berghahn, 2003).

1. Consolidating Identities, Sixteenth to Nineteenth Centuries

1. Francisco de Vitoria, "On the American Indian," in *Vitoria: Political Writings*, ed. Anthony Pagden and Jeremy Lawrence, 278–79 (Cambridge: Cambridge UP, 1992). Also see Antony Anghie, *Imperialism, Sovereignty and the Making of International Law* (Cambridge: Cambridge UP, 2004), chap. 1.

2. José de Acosta, *De Natura novi' orbis* (Salamanca, 1588), 256. Translation in Walter Demel, "Trade Aspirations and China's Policy of Isolation: European Views, Mainly in the Eighteenth Century," in *Maritime Asia: Profit Maximisation, Ethics and Trade Structure c, 1300–1800*, ed. Karl Anton Sprengard and Roderich Ptak, 108–9 (Wiesbaden: Harrassowitz Verlag, 1994).

3. Hugo Grotius, *The Freedom of the Seas*, trans. Ralph Magoffin, 12 (Kitchner, Ont.: Baroche Books, 2000 [1613]).

4. Samuel Pufendorf, *The Law of Nature and Nations in Eight Books*, trans. C. H. and W. A. Oldfather (Oxford: Clarendon Press, 1934 [1688]), bk. 7:2, §20. See also Christian Wolff, *The Law of Nations Treated According to a Scientific Method*, trans. Joseph Drake (Oxford: Clarendon Press, 1934 [1764]), §300–304.

5. Demel, "Trade Aspirations," 107–10.

6. Wolff, *Law of Nations*, §187.

7. Emerich de Vattel, *The Law of Nations or the Principles of Natural Law Applied to the Conduct and to the Affairs of Nations and of Sovereigns*, trans. G. Fenwick (Washington, DC: Carnegie Institution, 1916 [1758]), 1:§15.

8. Wolff, *Law of Nations*, §154.

9. Aristide Zolberg, *A Nation by Design: Immigration Policy in the Fashioning of America* (New York: Russell Sage Foundation, and Cambridge: Harvard UP, 2006), 43–47.

10. John Locke, "Second Treatise of Government," in *Political Writings of John Locke*, ed. David Wooton, §115–21 (New York: Mentor Books, 1993). Also see Vattel,

Law of Nations, 1:§220; Frederick Whelan, "Citizenship and the Right to Leave," *American Political Science Review* 75 (1981): 636–53.

11. Hugo Grotius, *The Law of War and Peace*, trans. Francis Kelsey (Oxford: Clarendon Press, 1925 [1646]), bk. 2:4, §23.

12. G. F. von Martens, *The Law of Nations: Being the Science of National Law, Covenants, Power, &c*, 4th ed., trans. William Cobbett (London: William Cobbett, 1829 [1788]), 86.

13. Bryan Garner, ed., *Black's Law Dictionary* (St. Paul: Thomson West, 2004), 865.

14. Philip Curtin, *Cross-Cultural Trade in World History* (Cambridge: Cambridge UP, 1984); Leslie Page Moch, *Moving Europeans: Migration in Western Europe Since 1650* (Bloomington: Indiana UP, 1992), 25–89; G. William Skinner, "Mobility Strategies in Late Imperial China: A Regional Systems Analysis," in *Regional Analysis*, vol. 1, *Economic Systems*, ed. Carol A, Smith, 327–64 (New York: Academic Press, 1976).

15. Natalie Zemon Davis, *The Return of Martin Guerre* (Cambridge: Harvard UP, 1983); Valentin Groebner "Describing the Person, Reading the Signs in Late Medieval and Renaissance Europe: Identity Papers, Vested Figures, and the Limits of Identification, 1400–1600," in *Documenting Individual Identity: The Development of State Practices in the Modern World*, ed. Jane Caplan and John Torpey, 15–27 (Princeton: Princeton UP, 2001).

16. Yash Ghai, "Migrant Workers, Markets, and the Law," in *Global History and Migrations*, ed. Wang Gungwu, 149–57 (Boulder: Westview, 1997).

17. Jeffrey Burds, *Peasant Dreams and Market Politics: Labor Migration and the Russian Village, 1861–1905* (Pittsburgh: University of Pittsburgh Press, 1998); David Moon, "Peasant Migration, the Abolition of Serfdom, and the Internal Passport System in the Russian Empire, c, 1800–1914," in *Coerced and Free Migration: Global Perspectives*, ed. David Eltis, 324–60 (Stanford: Stanford UP, 2002).

18. Ge Jianxiong, Cao Shuji, and Wu Songdi, *Jianming Zhongguo yimin* [Concise history of Chinese migration] (Fuzhou: Fujian Renmin Chubanshe, 1993), 391–93; L. Eve Armentrout Ma, "Fellow-Regional Associations in the Ch'ing Dynasty: Organizations in Flux for Mobile People, a Preliminary Survey," *Modern Asian Studies* 18 (1984): 307–30,

19. Roger Bartlett, *Human Capital: The Settlement of Foreigners in Russia 1762–1804* (Cambridge: Cambridge UP, 1979); Richard Hellie, "Migration in Early Modern Russia, 1480s–1780s," in *Coerced and Free Migration*, 292–323; Peter Kolchin, *Unfree Labor: American Slavery and Russian Serfdom* (Cambridge: Belknap Press of Harvard UP, 1987), 4–30.

20. Turrell Wylie, "Notes on Csoma de Körös's Translation of a Tibetan Passport," in *Silver on Lapis: Tibetan Literary Culture and History*, ed. Christopher I. Beckwith, 111–21 (Bloomington: Tibet Society, 1987).

21. Gaillard Hunt, *The American Passport: Its History and a Digest of Laws, Rulings, and Regulations Governing Its Issuance by the Department of State* (Washington, DC: Government Printing Office, 1898), 37–38.

22. Salter, *Rights of Passage*, 13–15.

23. Linda and Marsha Frey, *The History of Diplomatic Immunity* (Columbus: Ohio State UP, 1999), 93–99; Martin Lloyd, *The Passport: The History of Man's Most Traveled Document* (Phoenix Mill, UK: Sutton, 2003), 35–58; United States Passport Office, *The United States Passport: Past, Present and Future* (Washington, DC: Passport Office, Department of State, 1976), 1–14; Turrel Wylie, "Tibetan Passports: Their Function and Significance," *Central Asian Studies* 12 (1968): 149–52.

24. Kenneth Robinson, "From Raiders to Traders: Border Security and Border Control in Early Choson, 1392–1450," *Korean Studies* 16 (1992): 94–115.

25. Laura Newby, *The Empire and the Khanate: A Political History of Qing Relations with Khoqand c. 1760–1860* (Leiden: Brill, 2005), 192–98.

26. Fan Zhenshui, *Zhongguo huzhao* [Chinese passport] (Beijing: Shijie Zhishi Chubanshe, 2003), 140–57.

27. N. W. Sibley, "The Passport System," *Journal of the Society of Comparative Legislation* 7 (1906): 30.

28. C. Henry Alexandrowicz, *An Introduction to the History of the Law of Nations in the East Indies* (Oxford: Clarendon Press, 1967); Lauren Benton, *Law and Colonial Cultures: Legal Regimes in World History, 1400–1900* (Cambridge: Cambridge UP, 2002).

29. Fan, *Zhongguo huzhao*, 73, 100–101.

30. Robinson, "Raiders to Traders."

31. Tamar Herzog, *Defining Nations: Immigrants and Citizens in Early Modern Spain and Spanish America* (New Haven: Yale UP, 2003), 96–97.

32. For China, see Philip Kuhn, *Soulstealers: The Chinese Sorcery Scare of 1768* (Cambridge: Harvard UP, 1992).

33. Josiah Henry Benton, *Warning Out in New England, 1656–1817* (Boston: Clarke, 1911).

34. Edith Abbot, ed., *Historical Aspects of the Immigration Problem: Select Documents* (Chicago: University of Chicago Press, 1926), 542–58; and *Immigration: Select Documents and Case Records* (Chicago: University of Chicago Press, 1924), 102–10; Gerald Neuman, "The Lost Century of American Immigration Law (1776–1875)," *Columbia Law Review* 8 (1993): 1833–1901.

35. Abbot, *Historical Aspects*, 543.

36. Ibid., 580–93; Abbot, *Immigration*, 122–39; Benjamin Klebaner, "State and Local Immigration Regulation in the United States before 1882," *International Review of Social History* 3 (1958): 269–75.

37. Keechang Kim, *Aliens in Medieval Law: The Origins of Modern Citizenship* (Cambridge: Cambridge UP, 2000), 26–58.

38. Robinson, "Raiders to Traders."

39. U.S. Passport Office, *United States Passport*, 8.

40. Nancy Green, "The Politics of Exit: Reversing the Immigration Paradigm," *Journal of Modern History* 77 (2005): 263–89.

41. Fan, *Zhongguo hùzhao*, 107–10; Lo-shu Fu, *A Documentary Chronicle of Sino-Western Relations (1644–1820)*, 2 vols. (Tuscon: University of Arizona Press, 1966), 1:28–30, 38, 157–59, 174; Ng Chin-Keong, "Liturgical Services and Business Fortunes: Chinese Maritime Merhcants in the Eighteenth and Early Nineteenth Centuries," in *Maritime Asia: Profit Maximisation, Ethics and Trade Structure c, 1300–1800*, ed. Karl Anton Sprengard and Roderich Ptak, 75–96 (Wiesbaden: Harrassowitz Verlag, 1994); and "Maritime Frontiers, Territorial Expansion and *Hai-fang* during the Late Ming and High Ch'ing," in *China and Her Neighbours: Borders, Visions of the Other, Foreign Policy 10th to 19th Century*, ed. Sabine Dabringhaus and Roderich Ptak, 211–57 (Wiesbaden: Harrassowitz Verlag, 1997).

42. C.A. Bayly, *Imperial Meridian: The British Empire in the World, 1780–1830* (London: Longman, 1989); Victor Lieberman, *Strange Parallels: Southeast Asia in Global Context, c.800–1800* (Cambridge: Cambridge UP, 2003).

43. Herzog, *Defining Nations.*

44. Ibid., 178–83.

45. Zolberg, *Nation by Design*, 24–26.

46. Gérard Noiriel, "The Identification of the Citizen: The Birth of Republican Civil Status in France," in *Documenting Individual Identity: The Development of State Practices in the Modern World*, ed. Jane Caplan and John Torpey, 28–49 (Princeton: Princeton UP, 2001); Peter Sahlins, "The Eighteenth-Century Citizenship Revolution in France," in *Migration Control in the North Atlantic World: The Evolution of State Practices in Europe and the United States from the French Revolution to the Inter-War Period*, ed. Andreas Fahrmeir, Olivier Faron, and Patrick Weil, 11–24 (New York: Berghahn Books, 2003).

47. Andreas Farhmeir, "Passports and the Status of Aliens," in *The Mechanics of Internationalism: Culture, Society, and Politics from the 1840s to the First World War*, ed. Martin Geyer and Johannes Paulmann, 95–96 (Oxford: Oxford UP, 2001); Gérard Noiriel, *The French Melting Pot: Immigration, Citizenship, and National Identity*, trans. Geofroy de Laforcade (Minneapolis: University of Minnesota Press, 1996 [1988]), 45–59; John Torpey, *The Invention of the Passport: Surveillance, Citizenship and the State* (Cambridge: Cambridge UP, 2000), 27–48.

48. Frank Caestecker, *Alien Policy in Belgium, 1840–1940: The Creation of Guest Workers, Refugees and Illegal Aliens* (New York: Berghan Books, 2000), 39–45; Andreas Fahrmeir, *Citizens and Aliens: Foreigners and Law in Britain and the German States 1789–1870* (New York: Berghan Books, 2000), 20–28; Torpey, *Invention of the Passport*, 60–86.

49. Fahrmeir, *Citizens and Aliens*, 101–8; Leo Lucassen, "Revolutionaries into Beggars: Alien Policies in the Netherlands, 1814–1914," in *Migration Control in the*

North Atlantic, 178–91; Matt Matsuda, The Memory of the Modern (New York: Oxford UP, 1996), 121–32; Maarten Prak, "Burghers into Citizens: Urban and National Citizenship in the Netherlands during the Revolutionary Era (c, 1800)," in Extending Citizenship, Reconfiguring States, ed. Michael Hanagan and Charles Tilly, 17–36 (Lanham, MD: Rowman and Littlefield, 1999); Zolberg, Nation by Design, 72–76, 88–96.

50. Fahrmeir, Citizens and Aliens, 118–23.

51. Daniel Panzac, Quarantines et Lazarets: L'Europe et la Peste D'Orient (Aix-en-Provence: Édisud, 1986).

52. Abbot, Immigration, 21–58; Oliver MacDonagh, A Pattern of Government Growth 1800–1860: The Passenger Acts and Their Enforcement (London: MacGibbon and Kee, 1961); Zolberg, Nation by Design, 105, 111–12, 145–47.

53. Lloyd, Passport, 115.

54. Burds, Peasant Dreams.

55. Hunt, American Passport, 15–17.

56. Caestecker, Alien Policy, 39–45; Leo Lucassen, "A Many-Headed Monster: The Evolution of the Passport System in the Netherlands and Germany in the Long Nineteenth Century," in Documenting Individual Identity: The Development of State Practices in the Modern World, ed. Jane Caplan and John Torpey, 235–55 (Princeton: Princeton UP, 2001).

2. Global Migration, 1840–1940

1. Sucheta Mazumdar, "Chinese and Indian Migration: A Prospectus for Comparative Research," in Chinese and Indian Diasporas: Comparative Perspectives, ed. Wong Siu-lun, 139–67 (Hong Kong: Centre of Asian Studies, University of Hong Kong, 2004).

2. Virginia Yans-McLaughlin, "Introduction," in Immigration Reconsidered: History, Sociology, and Politics, ed. Virginia Yans-McLaughlin, 3 (New York: Oxford UP, 1990).

3. Ira Glazier and Luigi De Rosa, "Introduction," in Migrations across Time and Nations: Population Mobility in Historical Context, ed. Ira Glazier and Luigi De Rosa, 5 (New York: Holmes and Meier, 1986).

4. Douglas Massey, "Why Does Immigration Occur? A Theoretical Synthesis," in The Handbook of International Migration: The American Experience, ed. Charles Hirschman, Philip Kasinitz, and Josh DeWind, 35 (New York: Russell Sage Foundation, 1999).

5. Timothy Hatton and Jeffrey Williamson, The Age of Mass Migration: Causes and Economic Impact (New York: Oxford UP, 1998), 249. In their more recent book, Global Migration and the World Economy: Two Centuries of Policy and Performance

(Cambridge: MIT Press, 2005), Hatton and Williamson pay much more attention to Asian migrations but take pains to downplay the volume and significance of that migration beyond the Atlantic. This chapter will refute their arguments.

6. Pieter Emmer, "European Expansion and Migration: The European Colonial Past and Intercontinental Migration; An Overview," in *European Expansion and Migration: Essays on the Intercontinental Migration from Africa, Asia, and Europe*, ed. Pieter Emmer and Magnus Mörner, 3, 10–11 (New York: Berg, 1992).

7. Pieter Emmer, "Was Migration Beneficial?" in *Migration, Migration History: Old Paradigms and New Perspectives*, ed. Jan and Leo Lucassen, 113 (Bern: Peter Lang, 1999).

8. Lynn Pann, *Encyclopedia of Chinese Overseas* (Cambridge: Harvard UP, 1999), 62; Lydia Potts, *The World Labour Market: A History of Migration* (London: Zed Books, 1990), 70; and Walton Look Lai, "Asian Contract and Free Migrations to the Americas," in *Coerced and Free Migration: Global Perspectives*, ed. David Eltis, 230 (Stanford: Stanford UP, 2002). Dirk Hoerder, *Cultures in Contact: World Migrations in the Second Millennium* (Durham: Duke UP, 2002), 366–67, 377, and 389, has inconsistent numbers and notes that free migrants are not included in most estimates. But over two-thirds of his chapter on Asian migration from the 1830s to 1920s focuses on indentured migration to European plantations.

9. Chen Ta, *Chinese Migrations, with Special Reference to Labor Conditions* (Washington, DC: Government Printing Office, 1923); Chen Zexuan, "Shijiu shiji cheng xing de tiaoyue huagong zhi" [The nineteenth-century Chinese contract labor system], *Lishi yanjiu*, no. 1 (1963); Arnold Meagher, "The Introduction of Chinese Laborers to Latin America: The 'Coolie Trade,' 1847–1874" (Ph.D. dissertation, University of California at Davis, 1975). David Northrup, *Indentured Labor in the Age of Imperialism, 1834–1922* (Cambridge: Cambridge UP, 1995), 56, counts 386,901 indentured Chinese and 1,336,030 Indians. He does not count indenture in Southeast Asia.

10. Imre Ferenczi and Walter Willcox, eds., *International Migrations*, vol. 1, *Statistics* (New York: National Bureau of Economic Research, 1929).

11. Hoerder, *Cultures in Contact*, 12.

12. See the division of topics in Ge Jianxiong, Cao Shuji, and Wu Songdi, *Jianming Zhongguo yimin* [Concise history of Chinese migration] (Fuzhou: Fujian Renmin Chubanshe, 1993), 391–93. Also personal communication with Qiu Liben, December 2001.

13. Sources for all quantitative data are listed in Adam McKeown, "Global Migration, 1846–1940," *Journal of World History* 15 (2004): 185–89. Major and additional sources are in notes 15–20 below.

14. Ferenczi and Willcox, *International Migrations*, vol. 2, *Analysis*; J. D. Gould, "European Inter-Continental Emigration 1815–1914: Patterns and Causes," *European Journal of Economic History* 8 (1979): 598–605.

15. Susan Carter et al., eds., *Historical Statistics of the United States: Earliest Times to the Present* (New York: Cambridge UP, 2006), 1:247–87; Ferenczi and Willcox, *International Migrations*, vol. 1; B. R. Mitchell, *International Historical Statistics: Europe 1750–1993*, 4th ed. (New York: Macmillan Reference, 1998); Jose Moya, *Cousins and Strangers: Spanising Immigrants in Buenos Aires, 1850–1930* (Berkeley: University of California Press, 1998), 46; Walter Nugent, *Crossings: The Great Transatlantic Migrations, 1870–1914* (Bloomington: Indiana UP, 1992).

16. Kingsley Davis, *The Population of India and Pakistan* (New York: Russell and Russell, 1951), 99–100; Ferenczi and Willcox, *International Migrations*, 1:900–907, 915; Frank Heidemann, *Kanganies in Sri Lanka and Malaysia: Tamil Recruiter-cum-Foreman as a Sociological Category in the Nineteenth and Twentieth Century* (Munich: Anacon, 1992), 99–110: Claude Markovits, *The Global World of Indian Merchants, 1750–1947* (Cambridge: Cambridge UP, 2000), 17; and "Indian Merchant Networks Outside India in the Nineteenth and Twentieth Centuries: A Preliminary Survey," *Modern Asian Studies* 33 (1999): 895; Kernial Singh Sandhu, *Indians in Malaya: Some Aspects of Their Immigration and Settlement (1786–1957)* (Cambridge: Cambridge UP, 1969).

17. Data provided by Elizabeth Sinn from her Hong Kong Research Grants Council funded project, "The Impact of Chinese Emigration on Hong Kong's Economic Development, 1842–1941"; sources in McKeown, "Global Migration," 188–89.

18. Chen, *Chinese Migrations*, 84–86. See also Anthony Reid, "Early Chinese Migration into North Sumatra," in *Studies in the Social History of China and South-east Asia: Essays in Memory of Victor Purcell*, ed. Jerome Ch'en and Nicholas Tarling, 289–320 (Cambridge: Cambridge UP, 1970); Elizabeth Sinn, "Emigration from Hong Kong before 1941: Organization and Impact," in *Emigration from Hong Kong: Tendencies and Impacts*, ed. Ronald Skeldon, 35–50 (Hong Kong: Chinese University Press, 1995).

19. Eugene Kulischer, *Europe on the Move: War and Population Changes, 1917–1947* (New York: Columbia UP, 1948), 74–84; Donald Treadgold, *The Great Siberian Migration: Government and Peasant in Resettlement from Emancipation to the First World War* (Princeton: Princeton UP 1957).

20. Thomas Gottschang and Dana Lary, *Swallows and Settlers: The Great Migration from North China to Manchuria* (Ann Arbor: University of Michigan, Center for Chinese Studies, 2000), 64, 171; Alan Moriyama, *Imingaisha: Japanese Emigration Companies and Hawaii 1894–1908* (Honolulu: University of Hawaii Press, 1985), xvii; James Reardon-Anderson, *Reluctant Pioneers: China's Expansion Northward, 1644–1937* (Stanford: Stanford UP, 2005), 71–99; Michael Weiner, *Race and Migration in Imperial Japan* (London: Routledge, 1994), 53, 63, 121–22.

21. Hatton and Williamson, *Global Migration*, 23, 138.

22. Nugent, *Crossings*, 43.

23. Population data for China are from Gottschang and Lary, *Swallows and Settlers*, 172–73; Robert Marks, *Tigers, Rice, Silk, and Silt: Environment and Economy in Late Imperial South China* (Cambridge: Cambridge UP, 1998), 280.

24. Hoerder, *Cultures in Contact*, 217, 355–56; Daniel Johnson and Rex Campbell, *Black Migration in America: A Social Demography* (Durham: Duke UP, 1981); Bruno Ramirez, *Crossing the 49th Parallel: Migration from Canada to the United Sates, 1900–1930* (Ithaca: Cornell UP, 2001).

25. Orlando Patterson, "Migration in Caribbean Societies: Socioeconomic and Symbolic Resource," in *Human Migration: Patterns and Policies*, ed. William McNeill and Ruth Adams, 106–45 (Bloomington: Indiana UP, 1978).

26. Graves, Adrian, "Colonialism and Indentured Labour Migration in the Western Pacific, 1840–1915," in *Colonialism and Migration: Indentured Labour before and after Slavery*, ed. Pieter Emmer, 237–59 (Dordrecht: Martinus Nijhoff, 1986); Potts, *World Labour Market*, 71.

27. Jeffrey Burds, *Peasant Dreams and Market Politics: Labor Migration and the Russian Village, 1861–1905* (Pittsburgh: University of Pittsburgh Press, 1998); David Moon, "Peasant Migration, the Abolition of Serfdom, and the Internal Passport System in the Russian Empire, c, 1800–1914," in *Coerced and Free Migration*.

28. Davis, *Population of India*, 107–23; Arjan de Haan, "Migration on the Border of Free and Unfree Labour: Workers in Calcutta's Jute Industry, 1900–1990," in *Migration, Migration History: Old Paradigms and New Perspectives*, ed. Jan and Leo Lucassen, 197–222 (Bern: Peter Lang, 1999); Hoerder, *Cultures in Contact*, 380–83.

29. Ge, Cao and Wu, *Jianming Zhongguo yimin*, 460–92.

30. Ferenczi and Willcox, *International Migrations*, 1:1028.

31. Philip Curtin, *Why People Move: Migration in African History* (Baylor, TX: Baylor UP), 33–39; Patrick Harries, *Work, Culture, and Identity: Migrant Laborers in Mozambique and South Africa, c. 1860–1910* (Portsmouth, NH: Heinemann, 1994); François Manchuelle, *Willing Migrants: Soninke Labor Diasporas, 1848–1960* (Athens: Ohio UP, 1997); Patrick Manning, *Slavery and African Life: Occidental, Oriental and African Slave Trades* (Cambridge: Cambridge UP, 1990), 171–78.

32. Calvin Goldscheider, "Israel," in *Handbook on International Migration*, ed. William Serow et al., 132–35 (New York: Greenwood Press, 1990); Gülten Kazgan, "Migratory Movements in the Ottoman Empire and the Turkish Republic from the End of the 18th Century to the Present Day," in *Les Migrations Internationales: de la fin du XVIIIème siècle à nos jours*, ed. CIDMSS, 212–13 (Paris: Editions du CNS, 1980); Roger Portal, "Phénomènes migratoires en Russe et à partir de Russie au XIXème siècle," in *Les Migrations Internationales*, 207–25.

33. *Statistisch Jaaroverzicht* (Batavia: Centraal Kantoor voor de Statistiek in Nederlandsch Indie, 1938), 140.

34. Linda Boxberger, *On the Edge of Empire: Hadhramawt, Emigration, and the Indian Ocean, 1880s–1930s* (Albany: State University of New York Press, 2002); Christine Dobbin, *Asian Entrepreneurial Minorities: Conjoint Communities in the Making of the World-Economy 1570–1940* (Richmond: Curzon, 1996); Markovits, *Global World of Indian Merchants*; Adam McKeown, "From Opium Farmer to Astronaut: A Global History of Diasporic Chinese Business," *Diaspora* 9 (2000): 317–60.

35. Moya, *Cousins and Strangers*.

36. Hatton and Williamson, *Global Migration*, 23, 138, 146.

37. Sources for these and subsequent calculations are in notes 13 and 15–17.

38. Donna Gabaccia, "Women of the Mass Migrations: From Minority to Majority, 1820–1930," in *European Migrants: Global and Local Perspectives*, ed. Dirk Hoerder and Leslie Page Moch, 90–111 (Boston: Northeastern UP, 1996).

39. Hatton and Williamson, *Global Migration*, 146–47.

40. J. D. Gould, "European Inter-Continental Emigration: The Road Home: Return Migration from the U.S.A.," *European Journal of Economic History* 9 (1980): 57; Mark Wyman, *Round Trip to America* (Ithaca: Cornell UP, 1993), 11.

41. Leslie Page Moch, *Moving Europeans: Migration in Western Europe Since 1650* (Bloomington: Indiana UP, 1992), 130–46.

42. Nugent, *Crossings*, 35–46.

43. Anthony Reid, "South-East Asian Population History and the Colonial Impact," in *Asian Population History*, ed. Ts'ui-jung Liu, 45–62 (Oxford: Oxford UP, 2001).

44. McKeown, "From Opium Farmer."

45. Gottschang and Lary, *Swallows and Settlers*, 47, 69–79, 180.

46. Qiu Liben, *Cong shijie kan huaren* [Looking at Chinese from a world perspective] (Hong Kong: Nandao, 2000).

3. Creating the Free Migrant

1. Frank Sargent, "Problems of Immigration," *Annals of the American Academy of Political and Social Science* 24 (1904): 153.

2. Aristide Zolberg, *A Nation by Design: Immigration Policy in the Fashioning of America* (New York: Russell Sage Foundation, and Cambridge: Harvard UP, 2006), 35–38.

3. Fernando de Trazegnies, *En el País de las Colinas de Arena*, vol. 1 (Lima: Pontificía Universidad Católica del Perú, Fondo Editorial, 1994), 241–71; Robert Steinfeld, *The Invention of Free Labor: The Employment Relation in English and American Law and Culture, 1350–1870* (Chapel Hill: University of North Carolina Press, 1991).

4. Edith Abbot, ed., *Historical Aspects of the Immigration Problem: Select Documents* (Chicago: University of Chicago Press, 1926), 440.

5. Panchanan Saha, *Emigration of Indian Labour (1834–1900)* (Delhi: People's Publishing House, 1970), 12.

6. Robert Steinfeld, *Coercion, Contract, and Free Labor in the Nineteenth Century* (Cambridge: Cambridge UP, 2001), esp. 243–46 on legislation around Europe.

7. The arguments in this section rely heavily on Marina Carter, *Servants, Sirdars and Settlers: Indians in Mauritius 1834–1874* (Delhi: Oxford UP, 1995); Madhavi Kale, *Fragments of Empire: Capital, Slavery and Indian Indentured Labor in the British Caribbean* (Philadelphia: University of Pennsylvania Press, 1999); and Radhika Mongia, "Regimes of Truth: Indentured Indian Labour and the Status of the Inquiry," *Cultural Studies* 18 (2004): 749–68.

8. Carter, *Servants, Sirdars and Settlers*, 4.

9. Evelyn Hu-Dehart, "Chinese Coolie Labour in Cuba in the Nineteenth Century: Free Labour or Neo-Slavery?" *Slavery and Abolition* 14 (1993): 67–86; Humberto Rodríguez Pastor, *Hijos del Celeste Imperio en el Perú* (Lima: Instituto de Apoyo Agrario, 1989); Fernando de Trazegnies, *En el País de las Colinas de Arena*, vol. 2 (Lima: Pontificía Universidad Católica del Perú, Fondo Editorial, 1994).

10. Quoted in Kale, *Fragments of Empire*, 31–32.

11. Carter, *Servants, Sirdars and Settlers*, 84.

12. W. A. Green, "Was British Emancipation a Success? The Abolitionist Perspective," in *Abolition and Its Aftermath: The Historical Context, 1790–1916*, ed. David Richardson, 183–202 (London: Frank Cass, 1985).

13. Oliver MacDonagh, *A Pattern of Government Growth 1800–1860: The Passenger Acts and Their Enforcement* (London: MacGibbon and Kee, 1961); Singha "Settle, Mobilize, Verify," 164–73.

14. Quoted in Thomas Metcalf, "Hard Hands and Sound Healthy Bodies: Recruiting 'Coolies' for Natal, 1860–1911," *Journal of Commonwealth and Imperial History* 30, 3 (2002): 22.

15. Quoted in Saha, *Emigration of Indian Labour*, 150.

16. Quoted in K. O. Laurence, *A Question of Labour: Indentured Immigration into Trinidad and British Guiana, 1875–1917* (Kingston: Ian Randle, 1994), 51.

17. Basdeo Mangru, *Benevolent Neutrality: Indian Government Policy and Labour Migration to British Guiana 1854–1884* (Hertford: Hansib, 1987), 81–95; Saha, *Emigration of Indian Labour*, 78–94.

18. Dharmapriya Wesumperuma, *Indian Immigrant Plantation Workers in Sri Lanka: A Historical Perspective 1880–1910* (Colombo: Vidyalandara Press, 1986), 28.

19. J. C. Jha, *Aspects of Indentured Inland Emigration to North-East India 1859–1918* (New Delhi: Indus, 1996), 34–35; Adapa Satyanarayana, "Birds of Passage': Migration of Southern Indian Laborers to Southeast Asia," *Critical Asian Studies* 34 (2002): 100–102.

20. Ravindra Jain, "South Indian Labour in Malaya, 1840–1920: Asylum, Stability and Involution," in *Indentured Labour in the British Empire 1834–1920*, ed. Kay Saun-

ders, 171–74 (London: Croom Helm, 1984); Tiffany Trimmer, "Solving Migration "Problems": Trans-Atlantic and Trans-Indian Ocean Approaches, 1890-1930" (Ph.D. dissertation, Northeastern University, 2007), 155–69.

21. The following two sections are drawn from Persia Crawford Campbell, *Chinese Coolie Emigration to Countries within the British Empire* (London: King and Son, 1923); Robert Irick, *Ch'ing Policy toward the Coolie Trade 1847–1878* (Taipei: Chinese Materials Center, 1982); Arnold Meagher, "The Introduction of Chinese Laborers to Latin America: The 'Coolie Trade,' 1847–1874" (Ph.D. dissertation, University of California at Davis, 1975); Wang Sing-wu, *The Organization of Chinese Emigration, 1848–1888: With Special Reference to Chinese Emigration to Australia* (San Francisco: Chinese Materials Center, 1978); Yen Ching-hwang, *Coolies and Mandarins: China's Protection of Overseas Chinese during the Late Ch'ing Period (1851–1911)* (Singapore: Singapore UP, 1985).

22. "Annual Remittances by Chinese Immigrants in Singapore to Their Families in China," *Journal of the Indian Archipelago and Eastern Asia* (hereafter *JIAEA*) 1 (1847): 35–37; H. Crockwell, "The Tin Mines of Malacca," *JIAEA* 8 (1854): 112–33; GB-PP, *Correspondence Respecting Emigration from China* (1852–53), 25–26; "Notes on the Chinese of Pinang," *JIAEA* 8 (1854): 1–27; "Notes on the Chinese in the Straits," *JIAEA* 9 (1855): 109–24.

23. US-FR 1876, 63–65.

24. GB-PP, *Correspondence Respecting Emigration*, 1–20.

25. Ibid., 71–72, 92–94.

26. Ibid., 31.

27. GB-PP, *Correspondence upon the Subject of Emigration from China* (1855), 2.

28. Quoted in Yiching Wu, "Prelude to Culture: Interrogating Colonial Rule in Early British Hong Kong," *Dialectical Anthropology* 24 (1999): 153–54.

29. GB-PP, *Correspondence Respecting Emigration*, 3.

30. GB-PP, *Chinese Emigration* (1853), 74, 79. See also Gyan Prakash, "Terms of Servitude: The Colonial Discourse on Slavery and Bondage in India," in *Breaking the Chains: Slavery Bondage, and Emancipation in Modern Africa and Asia*, ed. Martin Klein , 64–82 (Madison: University of Wisconsin Press, 1993).

31. GB-PP, *Correspondence upon the Subject*, 20.

32. Ibid., 25.

33. Ibid., 52–53.

34. GB-PP, *Correspondence Regarding Emigration from Canton* (1860), 127.

35. GB-CP 894, *Correspondence Regarding Emigration from China* (1860), 21.

36. Ch-CYS, 39:6a, trans. in Yen, *Coolies and Mandarins*, 106.

37. Irick, *Ch'ing Policy*, 146; Yen, *Coolies and Mandarins*, 96–98.

38. GB-PP C328, *Coolie Emigration* (1868), 8–9, 19.

39. Ibid., 13.

40. Ibid., 15.

41. Trazegnies, *En el País*, 621–24.

42. Irick, *Ch'ing Policy*, 234, 263; Wang, *Organization of Chinese Emigration*, 104.

43. Trazegnies, *En el País*, 626–34, 651–53.

44. GB-PP, *Correspondence upon the Subject*, 62.

45. *Daily Press* (Hong Kong), 24 Aug. 1881, clipping in Au-SNSW 4/829.1.

46. Campbell, *Chinese Coolie Emigration*, 2–24; Elizabeth Sinn, "Emigration from Hong Kong before 1941: Organization and Impact," in *Emigration from Hong Kong: Tendencies and Impacts*, ed. Ronald Skeldon, 32 (Hong Kong: Chinese University Press, 1995).

47. Moon-ho Jung, *Coolies and Cane: Race, Labor, and Sugar in the Age of Emancipation* (Baltimore: Johns Hopkins UP, 2006), 120–21.

48. Russell Conwell, *Why and How: Why The Chinese Emigrate, and the Means they Adopt for the Purpose of Reaching America, with Sketches of Travel, Amusing Incidents, Social Customs, &c* (Boston: Lee and Shepard, 1871), 213–15.

49. Ibid., 190–95.

50. Ch-HCSH, 1/4:1503–9; H-FO 404–12–205; H-MI 1877–1890; Elizabeth Sinn, *Power and Charity: The Early History of the Tung Wah Hospital, Hong Kong* (Hong Kong: Oxford UP, 1989), 110–11.

51. Straits Settlements, *Proceedings of the Legislative Council* (1874), app. 33, 146. More generally, see Anthony Reid, *An Indonesian Frontier: Acehnese and Other Histories of Sumatra* (Singapore: Singapore UP, 2005), 194–225; Eunice Thio, "The Singapore Chinese Protectorate: Events and Conditions Leading to Its Establishment, 1823–1877," *Journal of the South Seas Society* 26 (1960): 40–80; Carl Trocki, *Opium and Empire: Chinese Society in Colonial Singapore, 1800–1910* (Ithaca: Cornell University Press, 1990).

52. Straits Settlements, *Proceedings* (1876), app. 22, "Report of the Committee Appointed to Consider and Take Evidence upon the Condition of Chinese Labourers in the Colony," 244.

53. Straits Settlements, *Proceedings* (1891), app. 33, "Report of the Commissioners Appointed to Enquire into the State of Labour in the Straits Settlements and Protected Native States," 32.

54. Ibid., 20.

55. GB-PP C3815, *Correspondence Respecting the Alleged Existence of Chinese Slavery in Hong Kong* (1882), 58.

56. Ronald Takaki, *Strangers from a Different Shore* (Boston: Little, Brown, 1989), 18.

57. Sucheng Chan, *This Bittersweet Soil: The Chinese in California Agriculture, 1860–1910* (Berkeley: University of California Press, 1986), xx.

58. For continued difficulties in finding a middle ground, see Patricia Cloud and David Galenson, "Chinese Immigration and Contract Labor in the Late Nineteenth

Century," *Explorations in Economic History* 24 (1987): 22–42; and Charles McClain, "Chinese Immigration: A Comment on Cloud and Galenson," *Explorations in Economic History* 27 (1990): 363–78.

4. Nationalization of Migration Control

1. David Kennedy, "International Law and the Nineteenth Century: History of an Illusion," *Quinnepiac Law Review* 17 (1997): 99–138; Lassa Oppenheim, "The Science of International Law: Its Task and Method," *American Journal of International Law* 2 (1908): 313–56.

2. Georg Freidrich von Martens, *The Law of Nations: Being the Science of National law, Covenants, Power, &c, Founded upon the Treaties and Customs of Modern Nations in Europe*, 4th ed., trans. William Cobbett (London: William Cobbett, 1829 [1788]), 146.

3. Lassa Oppenheim, *International Law: A Treatise*, vol. 1, *Peace* (London: Longmans, Green, 1905), 351.

4. Edwin Borchard, *The Diplomatic Protection of Citizens Abroad, or The Law of International Claims* (New York: Banks Law Publishing, 1915), 44; Guy Goodwin-Gill, *International Law and the Movement of Persons Between States* (Oxford: Clarendon Press, 1978), 233–62; Oppenheim, *International Law*, 191–92, 369; Plender, *International Migration Law* (Leiden: Sijthoff, 1972), 38–54.

5. Theodore Woolsey, *Introduction to International Law: Designed as an Aid in Teaching, and in Historical Studies*, 3rd ed. (New York: Charles Scribner's, 1871), 87.

6. Quoted in Borchard, *Diplomatic Protection*, 44.

7. Oppenheim, *International Law*, 192.

8. Ibid., 369.

9. Martti Koskenniemi, *The Gentle Civilizer of Nations: The Rise and Fall of International Law, 1870–1960* (Cambridge: Cambridge UP, 2004).

10. Alan Dowty, *Closed Borders: The Contemporary Assault on Freedom of Movement* (New Haven: Yale UP, 1987); Thomas Klevin, "Why International Law Favors Emigration over Immigration," *Inter-America Law Review* 33 (2002): 69–100; Daniel Turack, *The Passport in International Law* (Lexington, MA: Lexington Books, 1972), 1.

11. This section builds on Mary Bilder, "The Struggle over Immigration: Indentured Servants, Slaves, and Articles of Commerce," *Missouri Law Review* 61 (1996): 743–824; and Gerald Neuman, "The Lost Century of American Immigration Law (1776–1875)," *Columbia Law Review* 8 (1993): 1833–1901.

12. *Gibbon v. Odgen*, 22 U.S. 1, 189–90 (1824).

13. Philip Hamer, "Great Britain, the United States, and the Negro Seamen Acts, 1822–1848," *Journal of Southern History* 1 (1935): 3–28.

14. *City of New York v. Miln*, 36 U.S. 102, 142 (1837).

15. *Groves v. Slaughter*, 40 U.S. 449, 649, 653 (1841).

16. *Passenger Cases: Smith v. Turner* and *Norris v. City of Boston*, 48 U.S. 283, 492–94 (1849).

17. Aristide Zolberg, *A Nation by Design: Immigration Policy in the Fashioning of America* (New York: Russell Sage Foundation, and Cambridge: Harvard UP, 2006), 168–75.

18. Neuman, "Lost Century," 1843.

19. Thomas Wuil Joo, "New 'Conspiracy Theory' of the Fourteenth Amendment: Nineteenth Century Chinese Civil Rights Cases and the Development of Substantive Due Process Jurisprudence," *University of San Francisco Law Review* 29 (1994–95): 360.

20. *Henderson v. Mayor of New York*, 92 U.S. 259, 270 (1876).

21. Ibid.

22. *Chy Lung v. Freeman*, 29 U.S. 275, 278–79 (1876).

23. Ibid., 279–80.

24. George Peffer, *If They Don't Bring Their Women Here: Chinese Female Immigration before Exclusion* (Urbana: University of Illinois Press, 1999).

25. Andreas Fahrmeir, *Citizens and Aliens: Foreigners and Law in Britain and the German States, 1789–1870* (New York: Berghan Books, 2000), 135–40.

26. United States Passport Office, *The United States Passport: Past, Present and Future* (Washington, DC: Passport Office, Department of State, 1976), 13–14.

27. Henry Wheaton, *Elements of International Law*, ed. Richard Henry Dana (Boston: Little, Brown, 1866), 249–50.

28. Henry Wheaton, *Elements of International Law*, ed. William Beach Lawrence (London: Sampson Low, Son, 1857), 389–91.

29. Nancy Green and François Weil, eds., *Citizenship and Those Who Leave: The Politics of Emigration and Expatriation* (Urbana: University of Illinois Press, 2007).

30. Eileen Scully, *Bargaining with the State from Afar: American Citizenship in Treaty Port China, 1844–1942* (New York: Columbia UP, 2001), 57–59.

31. Gaillard Hunt, *The American Passport: Its History and a Digest of Laws, Rulings, and Regulations Governing Its Issuance by the Department of State* (Washington, DC: Government Printing Office, 1898), 41–57, 136–39.

32. Martin Lloyd, *The Passport: The History of Man's Most Traveled Document* (Phoenix Mill, UK: Sutton, 2003), 16–8; N. W. Sibley, "The Passport System," *Journal of the Society of Comparative Legislation* 7 (1906): 30.

33. Hunt, *American Passport*, 75–76.

34. US-FR 1893, 24.

35. US-FR 1895, 522.

36. Wheaton, *Elements*, 1866 ed., 250.

37. Hunt, *American Passport*, 5. Also Borchard, *Diplomatic Protection*, 488.

38. US-FR 1895, 1:xxxii. Also Charles Cheney Hyde, *International Law: Chiefly as Interpreted and Applied by the United States*, 2 vols. (Boston: Little, Brown, 1922), 2:692–99.

39. US-DH 59/847, *Compilation from the Records of the Bureau of Immigration Concerning the Enforcement of the Chinese-Exclusion Laws*, 59th Cong., 1st ses. (1906), 109–10. See also Estelle Lau, *Paper Families: Identity, Immigration Administration, and Chinese Exclusion* (Durham: Duke UP, 2006), 35.

40. John Bassett Moore, *A Digest of International Law*, 8 vols. (Washington, DC: Government Printing Office, 1906), 3:856.

41. Richard Plender, *International Migration Law* 71; John Torpey, "Coming and Going: On the State Monopolization of the Legitimate 'Means of Movement,'" *Sociological Theory* 16 (1998): 250–55; Turack, *Passport in International Law*, 15–18.

42. Charlotte Erickson, ed., *Emigration from Europe 1815–1914: Select Documents* (London: Adam and Charles Black, 1976), 137–42, 155–65.

43. Edith Abbot, ed., *Historical Aspects of the Immigration Problem: Select Documents* (Chicago: University of Chicago Press, 1926), 557–58, and *Immigration: Select Documents and Case Records* (Chicago: University of Chicago Press, 1924), 23–24; Benjamin Klebaner, "State and Local Immigration Regulation in the United States before 1882," *International Review of Social History* 3 (1958): 279–80.

44. Abbot, *Historical Aspects*, 638–41.

45. William Mulder, "Immigration and the 'Mormon Question': An International Episode," *Western Political Quarterly* 9 (1956): 416–33.

46. Katja Wüstenbecker, "Hamburg and the Transit of East European Emigrants," in *Migration Control in the North Atlantic World: The Evolution of State Practices in Europe and the United States from the French Revolution to the Inter-War Period*, ed. Andreas Fahrmeir, Olivier Faron, and Patrick Weil, 223–24 (New York: Berghahn Books, 2003).

47. Kathryn Cronin, *Colonial Casualties: Chinese in Early Victoria* (Carlton, Vic,: Melbourne UP, 1982), 20–22; Adam McKeown, *Chinese Migrant Networks and Cultural Change: Peru, Chicago and Hawaii, 1900–1936* (Chicago: University of Chicago Press, 2001); Elizabeth Sinn, "*Xin Xi Guxiang*: A Study of Regional Associations as a Bonding Mechanism in the Chinese Diaspora, the Hong Kong Experience," *Modern Asian Studies* 31 (1997): 375–97.

48. Peffer, *If They Don't Bring*, 43–45; Elizabeth Sinn, "Emigration from Hong Kong before 1941: Organization and Impact," in *Emigration from Hong Kong: Tendencies and Impacts*, ed. Ronald Skeldon, 46–49 (Hong Kong: Chinese University Press, 1995); "A History of Regional Associations in Pre-war Hong Kong," in *Between East and West: Aspects of Social and Political Development in Hong Kong*, ed. Elizabeth Sinn, 159–86 (Hong Kong: Centre of Asian Studies: University of Hong Kong, 1990); and *Power and Charity: The Early History of the Tung Wah Hospital, Hong Kong* (Hong Kong: Oxford UP, 1989), 71–72; 101–13, 275.

49. US-BJBS 3, 30 June 1918.

50. Erickson, *Emigration from Europe*, 143–46, 186–212.

51. David Feldman, "Was the Nineteenth Century a Golden Age for Immigrants? The Changing Articulation of National, Local and Voluntary Controls," in *Migration Control in the North Atlantic*, 171.

52. GB-PP Cd1741, *Report of the Royal Commission on Alien Immigration*, vol. 1, *Reports from Commissioners, Inspectors and Others* (1903), 8–10; GB-PP Cd1742, *Report of the Royal Commission on Alien Immigration*, vol. 2, *Minutes of Evidence Taken before the Royal Commission on Alien Immigration* (1903), 463–64.

53. GB-PP Cd1742, 464. See also Simo Belkin, *Through Narrow Gates: A Review of Jewish Immigration, Colonization and Immigrant Aid Work in Canada (1840–1940)* (Montreal: Eagle Publishing, 1966).

54. Robert Zeidel, *Immigrants, Progressives, and Exclusion Politics: The Dillingham Commission* (DeKalb: Northern Illinois UP, 2004), 66.

55. Erickson, *Emigration from Europe*, 247–54; Klebaner, "State and Local," 283–85.

56. Abbot, *Historical Aspects*, 580–93, and *Immigration*, 122–41; Erickson, *Emigration from Europe*, 269–81; Oliver MacDonagh, *A Pattern of Government Growth 1800–1860: The Passenger Acts and Their Enforcement* (London: MacGibbon and Kee, 1961), 307.

57. Nancy Green, "The Politics of Exit: Reversing the Immigration Paradigm," *Journal of Modern History* 77 (2005): 275–78; Green and Weil, *Citizenship and Those Who Leave*; Alan Moriyama, *Imingaisha: Japanese Emigration Companies and Hawaii 1894–1908* (Honolulu: University of Hawaii Press, 1985), 8–58; Torpey, *Invention of the Passport*, 103–5; James Whelpley, *The Problem of the Immigrant* (London: Chapman & Hall, 1905), 28–38.

58. US-FR 1904, 57. See also Julianna Puskás, *From Hungary to the United States, 1880–1914* (Budapest: Akadémiai Kiadó, 1982), 92–115.

59. Michael Low, "The Twin Infection: Pilgrims, Plagues, and Pan-Islam under British Surveillance, 1865-1924," *International Journal of Middle East Studies* 40 (2008): 269–90.

60. Edwin Jones Clapp, *The Port of Hamburg* (New Haven: Yale UP, 1912), 67–69; Wüstenbecker, "Hamburg and the Transit."

61. GB-PP Cd1742, 462.

62. United States Immigration Commission, *Reports of the Immigration Commission* (Washington, DC: Government Printing Office, 1907–1910), 4:69–94; Dorothee Schnieder, "The United States Government and the Investigation of European Emigration in the Open Door Era," in *Citizenship and Those Who Leave*, 195–210; Zeidel, *Immigrants*, 55–67.

63. Amy Fairchild, *Science at the Borders: Immigrant Medical Inspection and the Shaping of the Modern Industrial Labor Force* (Baltimore: Johns Hopkins UP, 2003), 62; US-NWSC 52495/49.

64. Among many historical and theoretical works on migration networks, see Teó-filo Altamirano, *Presencia Andina en Lima Metropolitana* (Lima: Pontificía Universidad Católica del Perú, Fondo Editorial, 1984); Monica Boyd, "Family and Personal Networks in International Migration: Recent Developments and New Agendas," *International Migration Review* 23 (1989): 638–70; Madeline Hsu, *Dreaming of Gold, Dreaming of Home: Transnationalism and Migration Between the United States and South China, 1882–1943* (Stanford: Stanford UP, 2000); James H. Jackson and Leslie Page Moch, "Migration and the Social History of Modern Europe," *Historical Methods* 22 (1989): 27–36; Ivan Light, Parminder Bachu, and Stavros Karageoris, "Migration Networks and Immigrant Entrepreneurship," in *Immigration and Entrepreneurship*, ed. Ivan Light and Parminder Bachu, 25–49 (New Brunswick, NJ: Transaction Publishers, 1993); Charles Tilly, "Migration in Modern European History," in *Human Migration: Patterns and Policies*, ed. William McNeill and Ruth Adams, 48–72, and "Transplanted Networks," in *Immigration Reconsidered: History, Sociology, and Politics*, ed. Virginia Yans-McLaughlin, 79–95 (New York: Oxford UP, 1990).

65. US-FR 1894, 367.

66. Abbot, *Immigration*, 186.

67. Ibid., 182–88.

68. US-FR 1894, 368.

69. Quoted in Broughton Brandenburg, *Imported Americans: The Story of the Experiences of a Disguised American and His Wife Studying the Immigration Question* (New York: Frederick A. Stokes, 1904), 294.

70. Ibid., 296.

71. Gunther Peck, *Reinventing Free Labor: Padrones and Immigrant Workers in the North American West, 1880–1930* (Cambridge: Cambridge UP, 2000), 61–62, 93–94, 183–85.

72. U.S. Immigration Commission, *Reports*, 2:432.

73. Abbot, *Immigration*, 498–539.

5. Experiments in Border Control, 1852–1887

1. *Chinese Exclusion Case: Chae Chan Ping v. United States*, 130 U.S. 581, 598 (1889).

2. *Case of the Chinese Merchant: In re Low Yam Chow*, 13 F. 605, 616 (D. Ca. 1882).

3. US-DS 48/62, *Letters from the Secretary of the Treasury Transmitting in Compliance with Senate Resolution of the 7th Instant, copies of all papers relating to the subject of the extension of the act of May 6, 1882, to execute certain treaty stipulations relating to Chinese*, 48th Cong., 1st ses. (1884), 28.

4. The literature on anti-Chinese movements is vast. See Andrew Markus, *Fear and Hatred: Purifying Australia and California 1850–1901* (Sydney: Hale & Iremonger,

1974); Stuart Creighton Miller, *The Unwelcome Immigrant: The American Image of the Chinese, 1785–1882* (Berkeley: University of California Press, 1969); Charles Price, *The Great White Walls Are Built: Restrictive Immigration to North America and Australia, 1836–1888* (Canberra: Australian Institute of International Affairs and Australian National UP, 1974); Patricia Roy, *A White Man's Province: British Columbia Politicians and Chinese and Japanese Immigrants, 1858–1914* (Vancouver: University of British Columbia Press, 1989); Elmer Sandmeyer, *The Anti-Chinese Movement in California* (Urbana: University of Illinois Press, 1973); Alexander Saxton, *The Indispensable Enemy: Labor and the Anti-Chinese Movement in California* (Berkeley: University of California Press, 1971); Peter Ward, *White Canada Forever: Popular Attitudes and Public Policy toward Orientals in British Columbia* (Montreal and Kingston: McGill-Queen's UP, 2002 [1978]).

5. Aristide Zolberg, *A Nation by Design: Immigration Policy in the Fashioning of America* (New York: Russell Sage Foundation, and Cambridge: Harvard UP, 2006), 43–57.

6. Edith Abbot, ed., *Historical Aspects of the Immigration Problem: Select Documents* (Chicago: University of Chicago Press, 1926), 704–5.

7. Chester Holcombe, "Chinese Exclusion," *Outlook* 76, no. 17 (1904): 975.

8. Quoted in Michael Hunt, *The Making of a Special Relationship: The United States and China to 1914* (New York: Columbia UP, 1983), 381.

9. Gabriel Chin, "Regulating Race: Asian Exclusion and the Administrative State," *Harvard Civil Rights-Civil Liberties Law Review* 37 (2002): 1–64; Lucy Salyer, *Laws Harsh as Tigers: Chinese Immigrants and the Shaping of Modern Immigration Law* (Chapel Hill: University of North Carolina Press, 1995).

10. Mark Kanazawa, "Immigration, Exclusion, and Taxation: Anti-Chinese Legislation in Gold Rush California," *Journal of Economic History* 65 (2005): 779–805.

11. Kathryn Cronin, *Colonial Casualties: Chinese in Early Victoria* (Carlton, Vic,: Melbourne UP, 1982), 82–99.

12. Golden Dragon Museum Volunteers, *The Walk from Robe* (Bendigo: Golden Dragon Museum, 2001), 12–15; Wang Sing-wu, *The Organization of Chinese Emigration, 1848–1888: With Special Reference to Chinese Emigration to Australia* (San Francisco: Chinese Materials Center, 1978), 273–74.

13. Au-NSW 4/829.1, Newcastle to John Young, 26 February 1862; Also Price, *Great White Walls*, 74–87.

14. Au-NSW 4/829.1, Colonial Secretary to Officer Administering Government of New South Wales, 12 February 1868.

15. Markus, *Fear and Hatred*, 96; Ward, *White Canada Forever*, 47.

16. Richard Huttenback, *Racism and Empire: White Settlers and Colored Immigrants in the British Self-Governing Colonies 1830–1910* (Ithaca: Cornell UP, 1976), 79–92; Michael Williams, "Anglo-Saxonizing Machines: Exclusion America, White Australia," *Chinese America: History and Perspectives* 17 (2003): 23–46.

17. Cronin, *Colonial Casualties*, 7–8; John Fitzgerald, *Big White Lie: Chinese Australians in White Australia* (Sidney: UNSW Press, 2007).

18. Myra Willard, *History of the White Australia Policy to 1920* (Melbourne: Melbourne UP, 1923), 41–50.

19. Au-NSW 4/829.1, Parkes to Chief Secretaries, 11 June 1880.

20. Ibid., petition to Earl of Kimberly, 31 January 1881.

21. Ernest Cashmore, "The Social Organization of Canadian Immigration Law," *Canadian Journal of Sociology* 3/4 (1978): 409–29.

22. Stanislaw Andracki, *Immigration of Orientals into Canada with Special Reference to Chinese* (New York: Arno, 1978), 14–21.

23. Canada Parliament, *Debates of the House of Commons* (1879), 1251.

24. Ca-CRAI, 1:2.

25. Roy, *White Man's Province*, 55.

26. Ca-CRAI, 1:5–11.

27. *Report of the Royal Commission on Chinese Immigration* (Ottawa, 1885), 409.

28. H-MI Acts to Regulate Chinese Immigration; US-FR 1884, 282; 1888, 1:864–65; Clarence Glick, *Sojourners and Settlers: Chinese Migrants in Hawaii* (Honolulu: Hawaii Chinese History Center and University Press of Hawaii, 1980), 10–20, 209–23; Ralph Kuykendall, *The Hawaiian Kingdom*, vol. 3, *1874–1893: The Kalakaua Dynasty* (Honolulu: University of Hawaii Press, 1967), 117–22, 147–52, 176–78.

29. US-NWCU, clipping "The Chinese Question!" 14 October 1889.

30. H-FO 404–14–223, 224.

31. John Hayakawa Torok, "Reconstruction and Racial Nativism," *Asian Law Journal* 3 (1996): 79–85.

32. Andrew Gyory, *Closing the Gate: Race, Politics and the Chinese Exclusion Act* (Chapel Hill: University of North Carolina Press, 1998).

33. *New York Times*, 25 February 1871, 2. See also Shirley Hune, "Politics of Chinese Exclusion: Legislative-Executive Conflict 1876–1882," *Amerasia Journal* 9 (1982): 5–27.

34. US-DS 57/106 *Immigration of Chinese into the United States*, 57th Cong., 1st ses. (1902), 12.

35. US-FR 1878, 130.

36. US-FR 1880, 301–2.

37. US-FR 1881, 171. Chinese version in Ch-HCS, 1/4:1324–6. See also Shih-shan Henry Tsai, *China and the Overseas Chinese in the United States* (Fayetteville: University of Arkansas Press, 1983), 53–59.

38. US-FR 1881, 173–74.

39. Ibid., 175.

40. Ibid., 178.

41. Ibid., 184.

42. Ibid., 186–89.

43. US-DS 57/106, 17.

44. J. Thomas Scharf, "The Farce of the Chinese Exclusion Laws," *North American Review* 166 (1898): 91. See also Kitty Calavita, "The Paradoxes of Race, Class, Identity, and 'Passing': Enforcing the Chinese Exclusion Acts, 1882–1910," *Law and Social Inquiry* 25 (2000): 1–40.

45. US-DS 48/62, 43.

46. *In re Ho King*, 14 F. 724, 725 (D. Or. 1883).

47. *Bulletin*, 21 November 1883, clipping in US-NWCu.

48. Ca-NIB 827821, O'Hara to Newcombe, 9 November 1909.

49. Ibid., 11 June 1909.

50. *Case of the Chinese Wife: Ah Moy on Habeas Corpus*, 21 F. 785 (D. Ca. 1884). See also Sucheng Chan, "The Exclusion of Chinese Women, 1870–1943," in *Entry Denied: Exclusion and the Chinese Community in America*, ed. Sucheng Chan, 94–146 (Philadelphia: Temple UP, 1991).

51. US-NWCu, petition to Chester A. Arthur, 27 October, 1884, 9–10.

52. *In re Chung Toy Ho*, 42 F. 398, 399–400 (D. Or. 1889).

53. *San Francisco Chronicle*, 13 April 1887, 1; US-DH 59/847, 71–6; US-DS 57/776, *Chinese Exclusion: Report and Testimony Taken before the Committee on Immigration*, 2 vols., 57th Cong., 1st ses. (1902), 2:317–9; US-NWCu, Hagar to Manning, 26 July 1886; Withers to Porter, 21 February 1887, 5 April 1887

54. US-NWCu, Beecher to Fairchild, 4 September 1887; Quincy to Brooks, 2 September 1887.

55. Cole, *Suspect Identities*, 122–27; Estelle Lau, *Paper Familes: Identity, Immigration Administration, and Chinese Exclusion* (Durham: Duke UP, 2006), 94–102.

56. Au-NSW 4/884.1, Gillies to Governor, 11 April 1888; personal communication from Paul Jones, 22 June 2006.

57. Au-NSW 4/884.1, memorandum from W. J. Walker, 30 November 1887.

58. Ca-NIB 827821, Department of Trade and Commerce Memorandum, 18 May 1893.

59. US-IR 1916, xvii–iii. For more descriptions of such schemes, see US-NWCD 212; US-DH 59/847, 60–70; US-IR 1901, 51.

60. US-DE 49/103, *Letter from the Secretary of the Treasury, Transmitting, in response to Senate resolution of March 9, reports of Special Agent Spaulding relative to the charge of fraudulent importation of Chinese*, 49th Cong., 1st ses. (1886), 2–8.

61. US-DS 48/62, 31–32; US-NWICU, Spaulding to Manning, 5 November 1885.

62. US-NWCU, Beecher to Fairchild, 2 July 1887; Beecher to Hobson, 15 June 1887; Sears to Folger, 23 May 1884.

63. Au-NNOC, Collector to Stevens, 12 September 1883.

64. Ca-NIB 826734, Parmalee to Minister of Customs, 25 May 1892.

65. Quoted in Shirley Fitzgerald, *Red Tape, Gold Scissors: The Story of Sydney's Chinese* (Sydney: State Library of New South Wales Press, 1997), 29.

66. Ca-NIB 826734, Parmalee to Minister of Customs, 25 May 1892.

67. Ca-NIB 827821, Controller in Victoria to Parmalee, 17 February 1900.

68. US-NWCU, Beecher to Fairchild, 12 November 1887.

69. US-DS 48/62, 16, 23, 52–54, 57–58, 66–67; 74–78; US-NWCU, Beecher to Manning, 23 September 1885; Horr to Folger, 4 November 1882; Tibbits to Folger, 15 December 1883; Beecher to Fairchild, 7 July 1887; Jerome to Fairchild, 13 February 1888.

70. US-DE 49/103, 5.

71. George Paulson "Abrogation of the Gresham-Yang Treaty," *Pacific Historical Review* 40 (1971): 457–77; US-DH 51/4048, *Immigration*, 51st Cong., 2nd ses. (1890), 2:593–94; US-DS 48/62, 6–11, 39–40.

72. Robert Chao Romero, "Transnational Chinese Immigrant Smuggling to the United States via Mexico and Cuba, 1882–1916," *Amerasia Journal* 30 (2004/2005): 1–16; Scharf, "Farce of the Chinese Exclusion Laws," 91–95.

73. US-FR 1890, 357.

74. Ibid., 655.

75. Ibid., 656.

76. US-FR 1892, 309.

77. Amy Fairchild, *Science at the Borders: Immigrant Medical Inspection and the Shaping of the Modern Industrial Labor Force* (Baltimore: Johns Hopkins UP, 2003), 150–59; US-FR 1892:309–25; Erika Lee, *At America's Gates: Chinese Immigration during the Exclusion Era, 1882–1943* (Chapel Hill: University of North Carolina Press, 2003), 176–80; US-NCNM 223/64–5; US-NWSC 51436/B.

78. US-DE 49/103, 8 US-NWCu, Beecher to Manning, 23 September 1885, Beecher to Fairchild, 7 July 1887, Gowan to Fairchild, 30 August 1888.

79. US-NWCu, Brooks to Windom, 10 March 1890.

80. US-NWCu, Jerome to Manning, 16 July 1886; McCay to Windom, 20 August 1890.

81. US-NWCu, Miller to Foster, 30 June 1891; Spaulding to Detroit collector, 10 July 1891; US-NWVC 151.0637/5.

82. CA-CRAI, 5:58–60, 65–66.

83. Christian Fritz, "Due Process, Treaty Rights, and Chinese Exclusion, 1882–1891," in *Entry Denied*, 29–30.

84. Salyer, *Laws Harsh as Tigers*, 18–30; *San Francisco Chronicle*, 13 April 1887, 1; US-NWCu, Brooks to Fairchild, 29 May 1888; Man to Windom, 1 October 1890.

85. US-NCDC, 12 March 1883; US-NCDU, 17 October 1882, no. 42.

86. US-NCDC, 8 June 1882, no. 208.

87. US-DS 48/62, 13–14.

88. US-NCDU, 17 October 1882, no. 42; 27 November 1882, no. 63.

89. US-FR 1883, 214–15.

90. Christian Fritz, ""A Nineteenth Century 'Habeas Corpus Mill': The Chinese before the Federal Courts in California," *American Journal of Legal History* 32 (1988): 361; US-DS 48/62, 60–61, 67–68.

91. US-DS 48/62, 64.

92. Ibid, 65–66.

93. US-NCDC 31 January 1884, no. 44; US-NWCu, Cheshire to Freylinghuysen, 6 April 1884; US-FR 1884, 105;

94. US-DS 48/62, 5–6.

95. Ibid., 14.

96. Ibid.

97. US-FR 1884, 107.

98. US-NWICU, Morton to Miller, 18 March 1884; Stevens to Porter, 22 April 1885; Cheng to Bayard, 4 December 1885, 9 March 1886, 24 March 1886.

99. US-NWICU, Hagar to Manning, 16 December 1885; US-FR 1884, 105–9, 115–18.

100. US-NWICU, Tsai to Frelinghuysen, 8 October 1884; Folger to Frelinghuysen, 13 October 1884; Manning to Hagar, 6 April 1886.

101. US-NCSDCH, 4 April 1885, no. 376; 15 April 1885, no. 379.

102. US-NWICU, Stevens to Manning, 10 December 1885.

103. US-NCSNC, Memorandum, 20 June 1884.

104. Ibid., Bayard to Cheng, 30 March 1886.

105. US-NWISC 52704/2, "A Few Observations on the Chinese Exclusion Situation," 2.

6. *Civilization and Borders, 1885–1895*

1. Michel Foucault, "Governmentality," in *The Foucault Effect: Studies in Governmentality*, ed. Colin Gordon, Graham Burchell, and Peter Miller (Chicago: University of Chicago Press, 1991), 87–104.

2. C. Henry Alexandrowicz, *An Introduction to the History of the Law of Nations in the East Indies* (Oxford: Clarendon Press, 1967), 97–124; Lauren Benton, *Law and Colonial Cultures: Legal Regimes in World History, 1400–1900* (Cambridge: Cambridge UP, 2002); Pär Cassel, "Excavating Extraterritoriality: The 'Judicial Sub-Prefect' as a Prototype for the Mixed Court in Shanghai," *Late Imperial China* 24/2 (2003): 156–82; John Fairbank, "The Early Treaty System in the Chinese World Order," in *The Chinese World Order*, ed, John Fairbank, 257–75 (Cambridge: Harvard UP, 1968); Linda and Marsha Frey, *The History of Diplomatic Immunity* (Columbus: Ohio State UP, 1999); Shih Shun Liu, *Extraterritoriality: Its Rise and Decline* (New York: Faculty of Political Science at Columbia University, 1925); Laura Newby, *The Empire and the Khanate: A Political History of Qing Relations with Khoqand c. 1760–1860* (Leiden: Brill, 2005), 189–99.

3. Michael Auslin, *Negotiating with Imperialism: The Unequal Treaties and the Culture of Japanese Diplomacy* (Cambridge: Harvard UP, 2004); Pär Cassel, "Rule of Law or Rule of Laws: Legal Pluralism and Extraterritoriality in Nineteenth Century East Asia" (Ph.D. diss., Harvard University, 2006); James Hevia, *English Lessons: The Pedagogy of Imperialism in Nineteenth-Century China* (Durham: Duke UP, 2003); Richard Horowitz, "International Law and State Transformation in China, Siam, and the Ottoman Empire during the Nineteenth Century," *Journal of World History* 14 (2004): 445–86; Eiichi Motono, *Coflict and Cooperation in Sino-British Business, 1860–1911: The Impact of the Pro-British Commercial Network in Shanghai* (New York: St, Martin's Press, 2000); Mary Wright, *The Last Stand of Chinese Conservatism: The T'ung-Chih Restoration, 1862–1874* (Stanford: Stanford UP, 1957), 232–38.

4. R. P. Anand, "Family of 'Civilized' States and Japan: A Story of Humiliation, Assimilation, Defiance and Confrontation," in his *Studies in International Law and History*, 24–79 (Leiden: Martinus Nijhoff, 2004); Thomas Franck, "Legitimacy in the International System," *American Journal of International Law* 82 (1988): 705–59; Gerrit, Gong, *The Standard of "Civilization" in International Society* (Oxford: Clarendon Press, 1984).

5. Christian Wolff, *The Law of Nations Treated According to a Scientific Method*, trans. Joseph Drake (Oxford: Clarendon Press, 1934 [1764]), §53.

6. Ibid., §54.

7. Henry Wheaton, *Elements of International Law* (Philadelphia: Carey, Lea & Blanchard, 1836), 45.

8. Henry Wheaton, *Elements of International Law*, ed. William Beach Lawrence (London: Sampson Low, Son, 1857), 22.

9. Theodore Woolsey, *Introduction to International Law: Designed as an Aid in Teaching, and in Historical Studies*, 3rd ed. (New York: Charles Scribner's, 1871), 103.

10. Martti Koskenniemi, *The Gentle Civilizer of Nations: The Rise and Fall of International Law, 1870–1960* (Cambridge: Cambridge UP, 2004), 131–36.

11. Anand, "Family of 'Civilized' States," 107–22; Lydia Liu, *The Clash of Empires: The Invention of China in Modern World Making* (Cambridge: Harvard UP, 2004); John Peter Stern, *The Japanese Interpretation of the "Law of Nations," 1854–1874* (Princeton: Princeton UP, 1979), 66–71; Tian Tao, "19 Shiji xia banqi Zhongguo zhishi jie de guoji fa guannian" (Chinese intellectuals' ideas about international law in the second half of the 19th century), *Jindai shi yanjiu*, no. 2 (2000): 108–10.

12. Cassel, "Rule of Law," 149–47.

13. Alexis Dudden, *Japan's Colonization of Korea: Discourse and Power* (Honolulu: University of Hawaii Press, 2004); Gong, *Standard of "Civilization,"* 27–41; John Holland, "International Law in the War between Japan and China," in his *Studies in International Law*, 112–20 (Oxford: Clarendon Press, 1898); F. E. Smith and N. W. Sibley, *International Law as Interpreted during the Russo-Japanese War* (Boston: Boston

Book Co., 1905); Sakuyé Takahashi, *Cases on International Law during the Chino-Japanese War* (Cambridge: Cambridge UP, 1899).

14. Gong, *Standard of "Civilization,"* 30; Lassa Oppenheim, *International Law: A Treatise,* vol. 1, *Peace* (London: Longmans, Green, 1905), 30–34.

15. Antony Anghie, *Imperialism, Sovereignty and the Making of International Law* (Cambridge: Cambridge UP, 2004); Jorg Fisch, "International Civilization by Dissolving International Society: The Status of Non-European Territories in Nineteenth Century International Law," in *The Mechanics of Internationalism: Culture, Society, and Politics from the 1840s to the First World War,* ed. Martin Geyer and Johannes Paulmann, 235–58 (Oxford: Oxford UP, 2001).

16. Woolsey, *Introduction to International Law,* 90.

17. Oppenheim, *International Law,* 370.

18. Ibid., 373.

19. Edwin Borchard, *The Diplomatic Protection of Citizens Abroad, or The Law of International Claims* (New York: Banks Law Publishing, 1915), 406.

20. Ibid., 221.

21. For other narratives of these events, Michael Hunt, *The Making of a Special Relationship: The United States and China to 1914* (New York: Columbia UP, 1983); Henry Tsai, *China and the Overseas Chinese in the United States* (Fayetteville: University of Arkansas Press, 1983).

22. Cassel, *Rule of Law,* 21–22.

23. US-FR 1875, 1:334.

24. US-NCNC, memorandum, 28 February 1880.

25. US-DH 49/102, *Message from the President of the United States Relative to Chinese Treaty Stipulations,* 49th Cong., 1st ses. (1886), 4.

26. US-NCNC, Chen to Evarts, 21 January 1881.

27. US-DH 49/102, 8–9.

28. Ibid., 1.

29. Ibid., 3.

30. Ibid., 64.

31. Ibid., 63–64.

32. Ibid., 71.

33. Thomas Bayard, "State Rights and Foreign Relations," *Forum* 11 (1891): 245.

34. Ibid., 248.

35. US-DH 49/102, 3.

36. *Baldwin v. Franks,* 120 U.S. 678 (1887). Also Charles McClain, *In Search of Equality: The Chinese Struggle against Discrimination in Nineteenth-Century America* (Berkeley: University of California Press, 1994), 173–90.

37. Ch-HCS, 1/4:1404–5.

38. Ch-JZX, 3/2:758.

39. Elizabeth Sinn, *Power and Charity: The Early History of the Tung Wah Hospital, Hong Kong* (Hong Kong: Oxford UP, 1989), 87, 137–49; Andrew Wilson, *Ambition and Identity: Chinese Merchant Elites in Colonial Manila, 1880–1916* (Honolulu: University of Hawaii Press, 2004), 99–107.

40. Ch-HCS, 1/1:267–70.

41. Ibid., 1/4:1349.

42. Ibid., 1/4: 1351, 1370. Also US-DS 50/272, *Message from the President of the United States Responding to Senate Resolution of Sept, 11, 1888 about Pending Treaty*, 50th Cong., 1st ses. (1888), 21.

43. Ibid., 1/4:1357.

44. US-DS 50/272, 16. Also Ch-HCS 1/4:1374–75; US-FR 1888, 368–69

45. US-DS 50/272, 17.

46. For other accounts, see Richard Huttenback, *Racism and Empire: White Settlers and Colored Immigrants in the British Self-Governing Colonies 1830–1910* (Ithaca: Cornell UP, 1976), 99–125; Charles Price, *The Great White Walls Are Built: Restrictive Immigration to North America and Australia, 1836–1888* (Canberra: Australian Institute of International Affairs and Australian National UP, 1974), 186–97; Wang Sing-wu, *The Organization of Chinese Emigration, 1848–1888: With Special Reference to Chinese Emigration to Australia* (San Francisco: Chinese Materials Center, 1978), 282–301; Myra Willard, *History of the White Australia Policy to 1920* (Melbourne: Melbourne UP, 1923), 71–98.

47. Marquis Tseng, "China: The Sleep and the Awakening," *Chinese Recorder* (April, 1887): 146–53.

48. GB-PP C5448, *Correspondence Relating to Chinese Immigration into the Australasian Colonies, with a Return of Acts Passed by the Legislatures of those Colonies and of Canada and British Columbia on the Subject* (1888), 2.

49. Au-NSW 4/884.1, Parkes to Colonial Secretaries, 8 November 1887.

50. Ibid., Gillies to Parkes, 22 March 1888; Parkes to Gillies, 30 March 1888.

51. GB-PP C5448, 2–6, 36–38.

52. Au-NSW 4/884.1, Telegram Carrington to Knutsford, 31 March 1887.

53. *New South Wales Law Reports* 9 (1888): 221.

54. *Victorian Law Reports* 14 (1888): 349.

55. Quoted in Price, *Great White Walls*, 195.

56. *New South Wales Law Reports* 9 (1888): 493, 496.

57. Quoted in Richard Jebb, "The Imperial Problem of Asiatic Immigration," paper presented to the Colonial Section of the Royal Society of Arts, 7 April 1908, in Ca-NIB 729921, 2.

58. *Sydney Morning Herald*, 5 May 1888.

59. GB-CP6018, 9–11; GB-PP C5448, 35.

60. Ch-HCS, 1/4:1376, 1539–40, 1555–57. See also Tsai, *China and the Overseas Chinese*, 90

61. Ch-HCS, 1/4:1394.

62. Ibid., 1/4:1376–78.

63. Ibid., 1/4:1541, also 1379.

64. Ibid., 1/4:1541–45; GB-CP6018, 10.

65. Ch-QW, 77:3a–b, trans. in Tsai, *China and the Overseas Chinese*, 90. See also US-FR 1888, 1:350–4.

66. Tsai, *China and the Overseas Chinese*, 93.

67. *San Francisco Examiner*, 2 October 1888.

68. US-NWCu, Grover Cleveland's Message, 1 October 1888.

69. Ibid., Asst. Sect. Treasury to Hip Lung, 9 May 1889; Asst. Sect. Treasury to Harris, August 1889.

70. Ibid., San Francisco Collector to Sect. of Treasury, 24 November 1888.

71. *In re Ah Ping*, 23 F. 329, 331 (D. Ca. 1885).

72. Charles Denby, *China and Her People: Being the Observations, Reminiscences, and Conclusions of an American Diplomat*, 2 vols. (Boston: Page, 1906), 1:100; Tsai, *China and the Overseas Chinese*, 95; US-FR 1889, 132–39; 1890, 187–219.

73. Ch-HCS, 1/4:1399–1403.

74. Ibid., 1/4:1383–85.

75. Ch-ZMG, 4:2229.

76. Ch-HCS, 1/4:1429–31; George Paulson, "The Gresham-Yang Treaty," *Pacific Historical Review* 37 (1968): 281–97; US-FR 1896, 91; 1897, 104.

77. Ch-HCS, 1/4:1436.

78. Ibid., 1/4:1439.

79. *China Mail*, 3 May 1888, 8 September 1888.

80. Quoted in Ralph Mooney, "Matthew Deady and the Federal Judicial Response to Racism in the Early West," *Oregon Law Review* 63 (1984): 634. See also Christian Fritz, "A Nineteenth Century 'Habeas Corpus Mill': The Chinese before the Federal Courts in California," *American Journal of Legal History* 32 (1988); Thomas Wuil Joo, "New 'Conspiracy Theory' of the Fourteenth Amendment: Nineteenth Century Chinese Civil Rights Cases and the Development of Substantive Due Process Jurisprudence," *University of San Francisco Law Review* 29 (1994–95): 363; McClain, *In Search of Equality*; Lucy Salyer, *Laws Harsh as Tigers: Chinese Immigrants and the Shaping of Modern Immigration Law* (Chapel Hill: University of North Carolina Press, 1995), 26–54.

81. *Congressional Globe*, 141st Cong., 2nd ses. (1870), 3658.

82. Stephen Kens, *Justice Stephen Field: Shaping Liberty from the Gold Rush to the Gilded Age* (Lawrence: University Press of Kansas, 1997).

83. Carl Swisher, *Stephen J. Field: Craftsman of the Law* (Washington, DC: Brookings Institution, 1930), 207–8.

84. Joo, "New 'Conspiracy Theory.'"

85. Charge to Grand Jury, 2 Sawy. 667, 680–81 (D. Ca. 1872).

86. *In re Ah Fong*, 3 Sawy. 144, 148 (D. Ca. 1874).

87. *Chew Heong v. United States*, 112 U.S. 536, 578 (1884).

88. *Head Money Cases*, 112 U.S. 536 (1884).

89. *Chinese Exclusion Case*, 604.

90. US-NWCu, Miller to Foster, 30 June 1891.

91. *Nishimura Ekiu v. United States*, 142 U.S. 651 (1892).

92. *Lau Ow Bew v. United States*, 144 U.S. 47 (1892).

93. *Fong Yue Ting v. United States*, 149 U.S. 698, 712 (1893).

94. Kens, *Stephen J. Field*, 213.

95. *Yick Wo v. Hopkins*, 118 U.S. 356, 396 (1886).

96. *Baldwin v. Franks*, 704.

97. *In re Ross*, 140 U.S. 453, 465 (1891).

98. *Fong Yue Ting v. U.S.*, 743.

99. *Chinese Exclusion Case*, 756.

100. *Fong Yue Ting v. U.S.*, 755.

101. *Church of the Holy Trinity v. United States*, 143 U.S. 457, 471 (1892).

102. *Fong Yue Ting v. U.S.*, 744; *United States v. Sing Tuck*, 194 U.S. 161, 182 (1904).

103. *Lochner v. People of State of New York*, 198 U.S. 45 (1905).

104. *United States v. Ju Toy*, 198 U.S. 253 (1905).

105. *Japanese Immigrant Case: Yamataya v. Fisher*, 169 U.S. 649 (1903); *Lem Moon Sing v. United States*, 158 U.S. 538 (1895); *Wong Kim Ark v. United States*, 169 U.S. 649 (1898).

106. Quoted in Linda Przybyszewski, *The Republic According to John Marshall Harlan* (Chapel Hill: University of North Carolina Press, 1999), 120–22. See also Gabriel Chin, "The *Plessey* Myth: Justice Harlan and the Chinese Cases," *Iowa Law Review* 82 (1996–97): 151–82.

107. *Wong Wing v. United States*, 163 U.S. 228 (1896).

108. Hiroshi Motomura, *Americans in Waiting: The Lost Story of Immigration and Citizenship in the United States* (New York: Oxford UP, 2006), 100–14; *Ng Fung Ho v. White*, 259 U.S. 276 (1922).

109. Charles Cheney Hyde, *International Law: Chiefly as Interpreted and Applied by the United States*, 2 vols. (Boston: Little, Brown, 1922), 1:101.

110. Bayard, "State Rights," 249.

111. Louis Post, "Administrative Decisions in Connection with Immigration," *American Political Science Review* 10 (1916): 253.

112. Quoted in Harley McNair, *The Chinese Abroad: Their Position and Protection, a Study in International Law and Relations* (Shanghai: Commercial Press, 1924), 301.

113. Borchard, *Diplomatic Protection*, 201, also 44.

114. Siegfried Hesse, "The Constitutional Status of the Lawfully Admitted Permanent Resident Alien: The Pre-1917 Cases," *Yale Law Journal* 68 (1959): 1578–1625.

115. Hyde, *International Law*, 1:104.

7. The "Natal Formula" and the Decline of the Imperial Subject 1888–1913

1. Maurice Olliver, ed., *The Colonial and Imperial Conferences from 1887 to 1937*, 2 vols. (Ottawa: Queen's Printer and Controller of Stationery, 1954), 2:411–12.

2. Minutes by Curzon, 27 January 1903, cited in Robert Huttenback, *Gandhi in South Africa* (Ithaca: Cornell UP, 1971), 141.

3. GB-PP C5448, 42; Ch-HCS, 1/4:1558–63.

4. GB-CP6018, 12–15.

5. *Law Times Reports of Cases Decided* (March, 1891), 378–80.

6. GB-CP6039, *Report on the Chinese Question by Under Secretary of State, E. H. Parker of the Chinese Consular Service* (1888), 8–9.

7. *Daily Press*, 24 August 1881, clipping in Au-NSW 4/829.1.

8. GB-CP6039, 6.

9. Ibid., 6, 10.

10. For other narratives of events in South Africa, see Huttenback, *Gandhi in South Africa*; and Iqbal Narain, *The Politics of Racialism: A Study of the Indian Minority in South Africa Down to the Gandhi-Smuts Agreement* (Delhi: Shiva Lal Agarwala, 1962).

11. GB-PP C7911, *Papers Relating to Grievances of Her Majesty's Indian Subjects in the South African Republic* (1895), 52.

12. Ibid., 24.

13. Ibid., 26–27.

14. Ibid, 46–49.

15. GB-PP C8423, *Further Correspondence Relating to Affairs in the South African Republic* (1897), 64–69.

16. Ibid., 105, 113–15.

17. GB-PP C8721, *Further Correspondence Relating to Affairs in the South African Republic* (1898), 6–14.

18. Ibid., 19.

19. For other accounts, see Marilyn Lake, "From Mississippi to Melbourne via Natal: The Invention of the Literacy Test as a Technology of Racial Exclusion," in *Connected Worlds: History in Transnational Perspective*, ed. Ann Curthoys and Marilyn Lake, 215–22 (Canberra: ANU EPress, 2005); Jeremy Martens, "A Transnational History of Immigration Restriction: Natal and New South Wales 1896–97," *The Journal of Imperial and Commonwealth History* 34 (2006): 323–44.

20. Quoted in Martens, "Transnational History," 332. See also Myra Willard, *History of the White Australia Policy to 1920* (Melbourne: Melbourne UP, 1923), 108–11.

21. Lake, "From Mississippi to Melbourne," 221.

22. *Collected Works of Mahatma Gandhi* (Delhi: Ministry of Information and Broadcasting, Government of India, 1959), 2:327

23. Ibid., 2:326

24. Ibid., 2:328

25. Ibid., 2:329

26. *Report of the Immigration Restriction Officer at the Port* (Colony of Natal, 1897), 1–4.

27. Olliver, *Colonial and Imperial Conferences*, 1:138–9.

28. Richard Huttenback, *Racism and Empire: White Settlers and Colored Immigrants in the British Self-Governing Colonies 1830–1910* (Ithaca: Cornell UP, 1976), 164.

29. Ca-CRAI, 1:56.

30. Quoted in Huttenback, *Racism and Empire*, 282.

31. Government of Australia, *Parliamentary Papers* (1901–2), 2:845–46.

32. Ca-NEA 8565; Huang Tsen-ming, *The Legal Status of the Chinese Abroad* (Taipei: China Cultural Service, 1954 [1936]), 52, 135, 147; Tung Miao, *Legal Status of Chinese in the Union of South Africa* (Johannesburg: Chiao Cheng Pao, 1947), 8–14.

33. Laura Tabili, *"We Ask for British Justice": Workers and Racial Difference in Late Imperial Britain* (Ithaca: Cornell UP, 1994), 88.

34. Manning Clark, *Sources of Australian History* (London: Oxford UP, 1957), 494.

35. A. T. Yarwood, *Asian Migration to Australia: The Background to Exclusion 1896–1923* (Melbourne: Melbourne UP, 1967), 19–52.

36. Australia, *Parliamentary Papers* (1901–2), 2:850–55.

37. Ca-NEA 4324, Sec. of External Affairs to Frederic Jones, 4 July 1905. See also Au-NNOI, circular from the Department of External Affairs, 31 August 1904; Willard, *History of the White Australia Policy*, 116, 127; Yarwood, *Asian Migration*, 87–89, 98–100.

38. Ca-NEA 4324, Nathan to Northcote, 17 Aug. 1905, 23 November 1905, Deakin to Northcote, 9 October 1905.

39. Ca-NEA 14282, 14383, 14923; Paul Jones, "What Happened to Australia's Chinese Between the World Wars?" in *After the Rush: Regulation, Participation and Chinese Comunities in Australia*, ed. Sophie Couchman, John Fitzgerald, and Paul Macgregor, special edition of *Otherland Literary Magazine* 9 (2004): 217–36; Andrew Markus, "Reflections on the Administration of the 'White Australia' Immigration Policy," in *After the Rush*, 51–9; Michael Williams, "Would Not This Help Your Federation?" in *After the Rush*, 35–50; Yarwood, *Asian Migration to Australia*.

40. McNair, *Chinese Abroad*, 172.

41. Narain, *Politics of Racialism*, 181–203.

42. Mohandas Gandhi, *Satyagraha in South Africa*, trans. Valji Govindji Desai (Ahmedabad: Navajivan, 1950 [1928]), 86–89.

43. Quoted in Huttenback, *Gandhi in South Africa*, 163.

44. Ibid., 342.

45. On events in Canada, see also Stanislaw Andracki, *Immigration of Orientals into Canada with Special Reference to Chinese* (New York: Arno Press, 1978); Patricia Roy, *A White Man's Province: British Columbia Politicians and Chinese and Japanese Immigrants, 1858–1914* (Vancouver: University of British Columbia Press, 1989); Peter Ward, *White Canada Forever: Popular Attitudes and Public Policy toward Orientals in British Columbia* (Montreal and Kingston: McGill-Queen's UP, 2002 [1978]).

46. Bruce Ryder, "Racism and the Constitution: The Constitutional Fate of British Columbia Anti-Asian Immigration Legislation, 1884–1909," *Osgoode Hall Law Journal* 29 (1991): 641.

47. *Vancouver Daily News-Advertiser*, 12 July 1899, in Ca-CRAI, 1:56.

48. Ca-CRAI, 2:189. Also 2:140, 182, 189; *Documents Relating to Commercial Relations Between China and Japan* (Ottawa: Government Printing Bureau, 1913), 104.

49. Ca-CRAI, 1:27–29.

50. Andracki, *Immigration of Orientals*, 89–90, 114–16; Amy Fairchild, *Science at the Borders: Immigrant Medical Inspection and the Shaping of the Modern Industrial Labor Force* (Baltimore: Johns Hopkins UP, 2003), 144–50; Gunther Peck, *Reinventing Free Labor: Padrones and Immigrant Workers in the North American West, 1880–1930* (Cambridge: Cambridge UP, 2000), 93–95; Mabel Timlin, "Canada's Immigration Policy, 1896–1910," *Canadian Journal of Economics and Political Science* 26 (1960): 517–32.

51. Ch-HCS, 1/4:1476–79. See also Ca-CRAI, 6:128–30, 151–52; 9:202; 17:292–94; 21:378–81.

52. Michael Auslin, *Negotiating with Imperialism: The Unequal Treaties and the Culture of Japanese Diplomacy* (Cambridge: Harvard UP, 2004); Douglas Howland, *Translating the West: Language and Political Reason in Nineteenth-Century Japan* (Honolulu: University of Hawaii Press, 2002).

53. Eric Han, "1899 and the End of the Treaty Port: Mixed Residence and Nationalism," chap. 3 of forthcoming Columbia University Ph.D. dissertation.

54. Ibid. See also GB-CP9112, *Immigration of Japanese Labourers into the United States of America* (1908), 16–17; Andrea Vasishth, "A Model Minority: The Chinese Community in Japan," in *Japan's Minorities: The Illusion of Homogeneity*, ed. Michael Weiner, 125 (London: Routledge, 1997); George Wilson and Edward Wynne, *Immigration Laws: Australia, Canada, New Zealand, Japan* (New York: Institute of Pacific Relations, 1927), 115–16.

55. Raymond Buell, "The Development of the Anti-Japanese Agitation in the United States," *Political Science Quarterly* 37 (1922): 605–83.

56. Ca-NEA 40, part 1, McInnis to Oliver, 2 October 1907; 33896, confidential memorandum, 3; *Report of the Royal Commission Appointed to Inquire into the Methods by Which Oriental Labourers Have Been Induced to Come to Canada* (Ottawa: Government Printing Bureau, 1908).

57. US-FR 1901, 372–73.

58. *Report of Mr. Justice Murphy Royal Commissioner Appointed to Investigate Alleged Chinese Frauds and Opium Smuggling on the Pacific Coast 1910–11* (Ottawa, 1913).

59. Ca-CRAI, 2:152–53.

60. Buell, "Development of the Anti-Japanese Agitation," 634–36; Ca-CRAI, 2:179–200; GB-CP9112.

61. *Documents Relating to Commercial Relations*, 103.

62. Ca-CRAI, 2:210–14.

63. Quoted in Donald Avery and Peter Neary, "Laurier, Borden and a White British Columbia," *Journal of Canadian Studies* 12 (1977): 30.

64. Ibid., 29.

65. GB-CP9337, *Memorandum Respecting Japanese Immigration into Canada and the United States* (1908), 1–2.

66. Quoted in Roy, *White Man's Province*, 217.

67. Ca-CRAI, 2:221–24, 3:255–56; US-FR 1924, 2:362–66.

68. Ch-JHDY, 11–12; Ca-CRAI, 3:305, 5:31–40; Ca-DCER, 1:597–607.

69. Jones, "What Happened to Australia's Chinese," 222; Yarwood, *Asian Migration to Australia*, 107–9.

70. Ch-JHDY, 26–47.

71. *Boletín de Relaciones Exteriores* 55 (Lima, 1914): 29.

72. Ca-NIB 23635, Robertson to Cory, 3 January 1914, 13 January 1914; Ca-CRAI, 20:343–45, 26:15–17; Ch-JHDY, 99, 133–38.

73. Paul Peirce, "The Control of Immigration as an Administrative Problem," *American Political Science Review* 4 (1910): 388.

74. Elihu Root, "The Basis of Protection to Citizens Residing Abroad," *American Journal of International Law* 4 (1910): 519.

75. Ca-NEA Series D1/84, Farrell to Yamasaki, 16 October 1930; Melanie Yap and Dianne Leong Man, *Colour Confusion and Concessions: The History of the Chinese in South Africa* (Hong Kong: Hong Kong UP, 1996), 248–50, 376–79.

76. For accounts of events surrounding Indian migration, see Joan Jensen, *Passage from India: Asian Indian Immigrants in North America* (New Haven: Yale UP, 1988); Radhika Mongia, "Race, Nationality, Mobility: A History of the Passport," *Public Culture* 11 (1999): 527–56.

77. Ca-CRAI, 3:279. See also *Report by L. Mackenzie King on Mission to England to Confer with the British Authorities on the Subject of Immigration to Canada from the Orient and Immigration from India in Particular* (Ottawa: S. E. Dawson, 1908).

78. Ca-CRAI, 2:210–11, 3:248–50.

79. Ca-DCER, 1:611.

80. Andracki, *Immigration of Orientals*, 110–13, 169.

81. Ca-CRAI, 18:309. See also Ca-CRAI, 8:192; Ca-DCER, 1:232.

82. Ca-CRAI, 3:306–9, 5:2–10; 8:152–55, 183–90, 23:396–97, 26:1–2.

83. Ca-CRAI, 18:306.

84. Ca-DCER, 1:660.

85. Ca-DCER, 1:323; Olliver, *Colonial and Imperial Conferences*, 2:265.

86. Narain, *Politics of Racialism*, 243–48.

87. GB-Cd6940, *Further Correspondence (Respecting) Bill to Regulate Immigration into the Union of South Africa: With Special Reference to Asiatics* (1913), 2, also 21–24.

88. Huttenback, *Gandhi in South Africa*, 313.

89. P. S. O'Conner, "Keeping New Zealand White, 1908–1920," *New Zealand Journal of History* 2 (1968): 59–64.

90. Quoted in Ryder, "Racism and the Constitution," 672.

91. Jensen, *Passage from India*, 108–11, 147–50.

92. US-FR 1913, 641.

93. John Edward Kendle, *The Colonial and Imperial Conferences 1887–1911: A Study in Imperial Organization* (London: Longmans, 1967).

94. Olliver, *Colonial and Imperial Conferences*, 2:200.

95. Ibid., 2:253.

96. Richard Jebb, "The Imperial Problem of Asiatic Immigration," paper presented to the Colonial Section of the Royal Society of Arts, 7 April 1908, in Ca-NIB 729921: 8.

97. *United Empire* 2/12 (1911): 852.

98. *United Empire* 3/1 (1912): 68.

99. *United Empire* 3/5 (1912): 367.

100. Ibid., 375.

101. Melisa Cheung, "The Legal Position of the Ethnic Chinese in Indochina under French Rule," in *Law and the Chinese in Southeast Asia*, ed. M, Barry Hooker, 32–64 (Singapore: Institute of Southeast Asian Studies, 2002); Charles Coppel, "The Indonesian Chinese: 'Foreign Orientals', Netherlands Subjects, and Indonesian Citizens," in *Law and the Chinese*, 131–49; J. De Galembert, "The Status of Aliens in Indo-China," in *The Legal Status of Aliens in Pacific Countries: An International Survey of Law and Practice Concerning Immigration, Naturalization and Deportation of Aliens and Their Legal Rights and Disabilities*, ed. Norman MacKenzie, 159–81

(London: Oxford UP, 1937); Huang, *Legal Status of the Chinese*, 12–15, 67–69, 162–72; Netherlands Council of the Institute of Pacific Relations, "The Legal Status of Foreigners in Netherlands India," in *The Legal Status of Aliens in Pacific Countries*, 240–61; W. E. Willmott, "Congregations and Associations: The Political Structure of the Chinese Community in Phnom-Penh, Cambodia," *Comparative Studies in Society and History* 11 (1969): 284–89.

102. Wayne Patterson, *The Korean Frontier in America: Immigration to Hawaii, 1896–1910* (Honolulu: University of Hawaii Press, 1988), 135–38, 169–71.

103. Clark Alejandrino, *A History of the 1902 Chinese Exclusion Act: American Colonial Transmission and Deterioration of Filipino-Chinese Relations* (Manila: Kaisa Para Sa Kaunlaran, 2003); Katharine Bjork, "Race and the Right Kind of Island: Immigration Policy in Hawaii and Cuba under US Auspices, 1899–1912," in *Studies in Pacific History: Economics, Politics and Migration*, ed. Dennis Flynn, Arturo Giráldez, and James Sobredo, 140–54 (Aldershot: Ashgate, 2002); US-NCCG 184; 185; 370/83, 43, 69, 86–87; US-NWSC 51830/199.

104. United States Congress, *Congressional Record* (1904) 35:4159.

105. Mae Ngai, *Impossible Subjects: Illegal Aliens and the Making of Modern America* (Princeton: Princeton UP, 2004), 96–126; James Sobredo, "The 1934 Tydings—McDuffie Act and Filipino Exclusion: Social, Political and Economic Context Revisited," in *Studies in Pacific History*, 155–69.

8. Experiments in Remote Control, 1897–1905

1. US-DH 59/847, 5–6.

2. For accounts of enforcement in the United States, see Kitty Calavita, "The Paradoxes of Race, Class, Identity, and 'Passing': Enforcing the Chinese Exclusion Acts, 1882–1910," *Law and Social Inquiry* 25 (2000): 1–40; Estelle Lau, *Paper Families: Identity, Immigration Administration, and Chinese Exclusion* (Durham: Duke UP, 2006); Erika Lee, *At America's Gates: Chinese Immigration during the Exclusion Era, 1882–1943* (Chapel Hill: University of North Carolina Press, 2003); Lucy Salyer, *Laws Harsh as Tigers: Chinese Immigrants and the Shaping of Modern Immigration Law* (Chapel Hill: University of North Carolina Press, 1995). On the politics of immigration reform, see Delber McKee, *Chinese Exclusion versus the Open Door Policy 1900–1906: Clashes over China Policy in the Roosevelt Era* (Detroit: Wayne State UP, 1977).

3. J. Thomas Scharf, "The Farce of the Chinese Exclusion Laws," *North American Review* 166 (1898): 96–97.

4. US-NWSC 52730/84, Greenhalge to Walter Chance, 28 February 1899.

5. Terence Powderly, *The Path I Trod: The Autobiography of Terence V. Powderly*, ed. Harry Carman, Henry David, and Paul Guthrie (New York: Columbia UP, 1940), 234.

6. US-NWSC 53990/52, 116.

7. *Terence Vincent Powderly Papers, 1864–1937*, ed. John A, Turcheneske (Glen Rock, NJ: Microfilming Corporation of America, 1974), Series B, Part 4, "With the Board of Review: A Plea for Better Immigration Laws."

8. US-IR 1899, 32.

9. Lee, *At America's Gates*, 55–57, 64; McKee, *Chinese Exclusion*, 33–34.

10. US-NWCG 6386, James Dunn to Frank Sargent, 26 January 1903.

11. Darrell Smith and H. Guy Herring, *The Bureau of Immigration, Its History, Activities and Organization* (Baltimore: Johns Hopkins UP, 1924), 10, 22, 71, 109; US-IR 1901, 46–52; 1904, 137, 141.

12. *Chin Yow v. United States*, 208 U.S. 8 (1908).

13. United States Treasury Department, Bureau of Immigration, *Digest of the Chinese-Exclusion Laws and Decisions* (1899), and *Laws, Treaties and Regulations Relating to the Exclusion of the Chinese* (1902); U.S. Department of Commerce and Labor, *Treaty, Laws and Regulations Governing the Admission of Chinese* (1903–1910).

14. US-DH 59/847, 23.

15. Ibid., 25–28; US-NWCD, "Court Opinions Rendered in Chinese Cases."

16. US-FR 1899, 194–95.

17. US-FR 1901, 68–75; US-NCDU, 1 March 1904.

18. US-IR 1903, 108.

19. US-NWSC 52704/2, James Dunn to Frank Sargent, 3 December 1902.

20. US-NPO 179.

21. US-NWSC 5704/2, "Memorandum from Commissioner General."

22. Ibid., "MEMORANDUM." See also US-NWVC 151.01/16; James Reynolds, "Enforcement of the Chinese Exclusion Law," *Annals of the American Academy of Political and Social Science* 34/2 (1909): 153.

23. US-DH 59/847, 52.

24. Wilbur Carr, "The American Consular Service," *American Journal of International Law* 1 (1907): 891–913; Waldo Heinrichs, "Bureacuracy and Professionalism in the Development of American Career Diplomacy," in *Twentieth C, American Foreign Policy*, ed. John Braeman, Robert Bremner, and David Brody (Columbus: Ohio State UP, 1971), 119–206; US-DH 59/665, Herbert Peirce, *Report on Inspection of United States Consulates in the Orient*, 59th Cong., 1st ses. (1906).

25. Gerald Neuman, "Qualitative Migration Controls in the Antebellum United States," in *Migration Control in the North Atlantic World: The Evolution of State Practices in Europe and the United States from the French Revolution to the Inter-War Period*, ed. Andreas Fahrmeir, Olivier Faron, and Patrick Weil, 108 (New York: Berghahn Books, 2003).

26. Broughton Brandenburg, *Imported Americans: The Story of the Experiences of a Disguised American and His Wife Studying the Immigration Question* (New York: Frederick A. Stokes, 1904), 222.

27. Immigration Restriction League, *Digest of Immigration Statistics, Effects of Immigration upon the United States and Reasons for Further Restriction* (Boston, 1902), 19.

28. Robert Zeidel, *Immigrants, Progressives, and Exclusion Politics: The Dillingham Commission* (DeKalb: Northern Illinois UP, 2004), 15, 17, 55–67.

29. George Peffer, *If They Don't Bring Their Women Here: Chinese Female Immigration before Exclusion* (Urbana: University of Illinois Press, 1999), 52–54; US-NCDH, 4 April 1885, 15 April 1885, 16 July 1885.

30. US-NCD, 21 September 1887.

31. US-NCDH, 21 February 1887.

32. Ibid., 21 August 1885, 22 January 1886, 18 April 1888; Elizabeth Sinn, "Emigration from Hong Kong before 1941: Organization and Impact," in *Emigration from Hong Kong: Tendencies and Impacts*, ed. Ronald Skeldon, 41 (Hong Kong: Chinese University Press, 1995).

33. US-NCDC, 22 August 1889.

34. US-FR 1890, 177, 186–87.

35. Ch-ZMG, 2:1908; US-NCDS, 21 July 1891, 11 August 1891, 6 October 1891, 11 November 1891.

36. Ch-ZMG, 3:2185, 4:2264, 5:3125; US-NCDU, 26 June 1896, 24 July 1896, 7 September 1896.

37. US-NCDH, 8 June 1897 and subsequent dispatches.

38. US-NCDC, 23 May 1899.

39. US-NCDH, 6 October 1897, 18 November 1897, 16 February 1898, 27 May 1899.

40. US-NCDC, 2 November 1899.

41. Charles Denby, "Chinese Exclusion," *Forum* 34 (1902): 133.

42. Ibid., 132–33.

43. Ibid., 135.

44. US-NCDC, 26 February 1906.

45. US-NCCG 370/156.

46. US-NGCC 467.

47. US-NCDC, 7 July 1898 (emphasis in original).

48. Ch-ZMG, 4:2344, 2347, 2350, 2362; US-NCDS, 13 October 1898 and enclosures.

49. Ch-ZMG, 4:2384.

50. US-NCDC, Bedloe to Jackson, 30 August 1899; Chung to U.S. Consul, 16 June 1899.

51. Ibid., 10 September 1898; US-NCDS, 13 October 1898.

52. Accusations are in US-DS 57/776, 2:315, 479.

53. US-NCDH, 27 May 1899.

54. Ibid., 15 June 1904, enclosed letter to George Courtelyou.

55. Roger Thompson, *China's Local Councils in the Age of Constitutional Reform 1898–1911* (Cambridge: Council on East Asian Studies, Harvard University, 1995).

56. Ch-HCS, 1/1:296.

57. Lee Lai To, "Chinese Consular Representatives and the Straits Government in the Nineteenth Century," in *Early Chinese Immigrant Societies: Case Studies from North America and British Southeast Asia*, ed. Lee Lai To, 84–85 (Singapore: Hienemann Asia, 1988).

58. Ch-GCDL, 4:4365. Another account of these events is in Yen Ching-hwang, *Coolies and Mandarin: China's Protection of Overseas Chinese during the Late Ch'ing Period (1851–1911)* (Singapore: Singapore UP, 1985), 269–77.

59. Ch-GCDL, 4:4368.

60. Ibid., 4:4476–77.

61. US-NCDA, Lupton to Rockhill, 11 April, 1906.

62. Ch-GCDL, 5:5001–2. See also US-NCDU, 21 March 1903.

63. US-NCDU, 5:5115–16.

64. Ibid., 5:5376–78.

65. Ch-AFA 02–29.4.6/2.

66. Ch-ZMG, 3:2498–9, 5:3086–88, 3231–32; Clarence Glick, *Sojourners and Settlers: Chinese Migrants in Hawaii* (Honolulu: Hawaii Chinese History Center and University Press of Hawaii, 1980), 274–81.

67. US-DH 59/665, 38–39; US-NCDA, 25 July 1905, no. 39; 8 August 1905, Anderson to Rockhill; 16 August 1905, 28 August 1905, 12 December 1905, Lupton to Rockhill; 11 April 1906; US-NCDC, Li Ung Bing to Fesler, 19 November 1903; Andrew Wilson, *Ambition and Identity: Chinese Merchant Elites in Colonial Manila, 1880–1916* (Honolulu: University of Hawaii Press, 2004), 126–37.

68. Ch-ZMG, 5:3128–33, 3263–65, 3404–8.

69. Ibid., 5:3408.

70. US-DH 59/665, 65. See also US-NCDC, 19 November 1903, 9 December 1903.

71. US-DH 59/665, 39.

72. Ibid., 136.

73. Ibid., 52.

74. Ibid.

75. Ch-ZMG, 5:3402.

76. US-DH 59/665, 42–60.

77. Ibid., 13.

78. Ibid., 270–71.

79. Ibid., 80–93.

80. Eileen Scully, "Taking the Low Road to Sino-American Relations: 'Open Door' Expansionists and the Two China Markets," *Journal of American History* 82 (1995): 62–83.

9. The American Formula, 1905–1913

1. US-NCDC, 3 November 1903, 9 December 1903. See also US-NWCu, Brooks to Windom, 6 February 1890.

2. US-IR 1907, 107.

3. Delber McKee, *Chinese Exclusion versus the Open Door Policy 1900–1906: Clashes over China Policy in the Roosevelt Era* (Detroit: Wayne State UP, 1977), 68–102; Michael Hunt, *The Making of a Special Relationship: The United States and China to 1914* (New York: Columbia UP, 1983), 231–35; Henry Tsai, *China and the Overseas Chinese in the United States* (Fayetteville: University of Arkansas Press, 1983), 104–8; US-DH 59/847, 38–50; Wang Guanhua, *In Search of Justice: The 1905–1906 Chinese Anti-American Boycott* (Cambridge: Harvard University Asia Center, 2001), 50–89; Wong Sin Kiong, *China's Anti-American Boycott Movement in 1905: A Study in Urban Protest* (New York: Peter Lang, 2002), 25–9; Zhang Cunwu, *Guangxu san-shiyi nian Zhong Mei gong yue fengchao* [Tide against the Chinese-American worker treaty in 1905] (Taipei: Institute of Modern History, Academia Sinica, 1966), 8–35.

4. US-DH 59/847, 148–9. A version in US-NML, 19 May 1905, contains this sentence in all capital letters.

5. Quoted in McKee, *Chinese Exclusion*, 128. See also Hunt, *Making of a Special Relationship*, 242–44.

6. US-NWSC 5704/2, "Memorandum from Commissioner General."

7. US-NWSC 51881/85.

8. McKee, *Chinese Exclusion*, 141, 172.

9. Ibid., 205–9; US-DH 59/847, 28–35.

10. US-NWSC 52702/2, undated memorandum, 13–15.

11. Quoted in James Reynolds, "Enforcement of the Chinese Exclusion Law," *Annals of the American Academy of Political and Social Science* 34/2 (1909): 144–45.

12. US-DH 59/847, 125.

13. US-IR 1905, 78–79.

14. US-IR 1904, 137.

15. US-NWSC 5704/2, Alford Cooley to President, 29 April 1907.

16. Victor Safford, *Immigration Problems: Personal Experiences of an Official* (New York: Dodd, Mead, 1925), 88–89.

17. On similar changes in San Francisco between 1895 and 1905, see Estelle Lau, *Paper Families: Identity, Immigration Administration, and Chinese Exclusion* (Durham: Duke UP, 2006), 80–81.

18. US-NMC, especially McLaughlin to Rodgers, 24 June 1903, 22 September 1903, 4 November 1903, 19 November 1903; US-NML, McLaughlin to Rodgers, 7 January 1904; Rodgers to Chinese Officer in Charge in NY, May 1904.

19. US-NML, several letters dated May to August 1904.

20. Ibid., McLaughlin to Rodgers, 9 September. 1905. Cases in Hawaii show a similar shift in late 1905; see US-NPH 500–50. Cases in Chicago show no marked shift until Chinese Inspector Lorenzo Plummer was transferred to Montana under a cloud of suspicion in 1910.

21. US-NGCC 2005/418, 949; US-NML, Benkhart to Hughes, 23 November 1909; US-NPO 1414.

22. US-NML, Rodgers to Commissioner of Immigration at Baltimore, 23 October 1906.

23. US-NWSC 52516/10.

24. US-NCCG 12177/66.

25. US-NCDC, 26 February 1906.

26. US-NCDA, 22 May 1905.

27. US-NCCG 370/129, Anderson to Taft, 14 October 1905.

28. Ibid., 370/139, 142; US-NCDA, 12 March 1906, 13 March 1906.

29. US-NCDA Lupton to Rockhill, 11 April 1906; US-NCIR, Amoy, December 1908, "Note—Chinese Returning."

30. US-NCNM 3121/9–1/2.

31. Ibid., 8534/2.

32. Ibid., 3121/30.

33. Ibid., 3121/10–14, Hanna to Hung, 24 December 1906.

34. Ng Chin-Keong, *Trade and Society: The Amoy Network on the China Coast, 1683–1735* (Singapore: Singapore UP, 1983), 171.

35. US-NCNM 8534/1.

36. Ibid., 3121/7–9. See also Ch-AFA 02–29.4.6/2l

37. Ibid., 3121/14.

38. Ibid., 3121/18.

39. Ibid., 8534/1.

40. Ibid., 3121/39–40. See also 4058/21.

41. US-NCCG 12177/66.

42. US-NWSC 53990/52, "Minutes of the Immigration Consultation," 13.

43. Max Kohler, *Immigration and Aliens in the United States: Studies of American Immigration Laws and the Legal Status of Aliens in the United States* (New York: Block, 1936), 131.

44. US-NWSC 52516/10, Sargent to Dunn, confidential, 10 June 1908.

45. Ibid., Larned to Keefe, 12 June 1909.

46. US-IR 1909, 128.

47. US-IR 1910, 131.

48. US-IR 1908, 220.

49. US-IR 1909, 123, 133, 153–74.

50. US-NWSC 52227/1C.

51. Erika Lee, *At America's Gates: Chinese Immigration during the Exclusion Era, 1882–1943* (Chapel Hill: University of North Carolina Press, 2003), 70–87.

52. US-IR 1909, 128–29.

53. US-IR 1912, 62.

54. US-NPH 2305.

55. Ibid.

56. Michael Churgin, "Immigration Internal Decision Making: A View from History." *Texas Law Review* 78 (2000): 1633–59.

57. US-IR 1910, 133; US-NWSC 52961/23; US-NWVC 151.08/12; 151.10/15.

58. Hunt, *Making of a Special Relationship*, 247–49; US-NCNM 803/228; US-NWSC 52320/1; 52363/14; 51830/199–199A; 5208/52; 52961/23C; 52961/24C; US-NWVC 151.08/1–53.

59. US-NWVC 151.08/12.

60. US-NWSC 53059/52B; US-NWVC 151.lo/1–16.

61. US-NCIR, Amoy, 13 June 1913, February 1921; Canton, April 1913, "Treatment of Sec. VI Certificates," February 1917, April 1921; Hong Kong, 29 June 1909, memorandum by Vice-Consul Fuller, December 1915; Shanghai, May 1916; US-NWVC 151.10/14, 215, 231, 828, 841.

62. US-NWVC 151.10/487.

63. Ibid., 151.10/360, 905. See also US-NGCD 2/38.

64. US-NCIR, Hong Kong, June 1909, "Note on Chinese Immigration." See also Clifford Perkins, *Border Patrol: With the U.S. Immigration Service on the Mexican Boundary 1910–54* (El Paso: Texas Western Press, 1978), 48.

65. US-NWVC 151.10/101.

66. Ibid., 151.10/165, 278.

67. Ibid., 151.10/110

68. US-NWVC 151.10/197.

69. US-NWSC 53775/245, Report to the Commissioner General, 7 March 1914, 4–5.

70. US-NWVC 151.10/215. For official Chinese efforts to protect against fraudulent certificates, see US-NCNM 803/60–62 and 88–90.

71. US-NWVC 151.10/531.

72. US-NCIR, Hong Kong, December 1915; Shanghai, May 1916; US-NWVC 151.10/143, 231.

73. US-BJBS 2:22 October 1917

74. Perkins, *Border Patrol*, 53.

75. US-NGCC 2072.

76. Ibid., 767; US-NGCD 2/223.

77. US-NGCD 6/260

78. US-NPO 531.

79. US-IR 1913, 247.

80. US-NWVC 151.10/841.

81. Ibid., 151.05/40; 151.10/1378, 1398, 1435, 1474.

82. US-NWSC 53990/52, "Minutes of Immigration Consultation at San Francisco," 4, 323–7. See also Lucy Salyer, *Laws Harsh as Tigers: Chinese Immigrants and the Shaping of Modern Immigration Law* (Chapel Hill: University of North Carolina Press, 1995), 217–33.

83. US-NWSC 53990/52A, 2, 11.

84. Quoted in Chen Wen-hsien, "Chinese under Both Exclusion and Immigration Laws" (Ph.D. diss., University of Chicago, 1940), 135–36.

85. US-NWSC 53990/52, 316.

86. US-NGCD 20/1.

87. US-BJBS 3: late 1925.

88. US-IR 1920: 48.

89. Joan Jensen, *Passage from India: Asian Indian Immigrants in North America* (New Haven: Yale UP, 1988), 146–60.

90. US-NPD.

91. US-NWSC 53620/203, Secretary of Labor to Attorney General, 23 July 1915, 4. See also US-NWVC 151.10/442.

92. US-NWCS; US-NWSC 52229/1; 52320/1; 52803/1; 537881/1; 53990/52, 18–28, 49–9, 296–98; US-NWVC 151.0637/10–17; US-IR 1913, 177.

93. US-NCD 123 W 156

94. Chen, "Chinese under Both," 104, 334–42.

95. Kohler, *Immigration and Aliens*, 252.

96. US-NWVC 151.08/14.

97. Ibid., 151.08/137.

98. Ibid., 151.08/139.

99. Ibid., 151.08/164.

100. Neil Thomsen, "No Such Sun Yat-sen: An Archival Success Story," *Chinese America: History and Perspectives* 11 (1997): 23.

101. US-NWSC 5181/85; US-NWVC 151.05/2; 151.08/87, 92; 151.08/1–35.

102. Amy Fairchild, *Science at the Borders: Immigrant Medical Inspection and the Shaping of the Modern Industrial Labor Force* (Baltimore: Johns Hopkins UP, 2003), 209–15.

103. US-NWSC 55452/385, Nagle to Husband, 15 January 1925.

104. Ibid., Husband to Nagle, 19 March 1925.

105. US-IR 1911, 3.

106. Melissa Macauley, *Social Power and Legal Culture: Litigation Masters in Late Imperial China* (Stanford: Stanford UP, 1998).

107. US-NWSC 55452/385, Shaughnessy to Husband, 13 June 1925.

108. AUPS-DI 54184/138 File 21, Memoranda.

109. US-NPD 52961/23A.

110. US-AJY, "Mr. Dea, etc.," 6.

111. US-NWSC 53775/245, Report to the Commissioner General, 7 March 1914, 17.

112. US-IR 1911, 136.

10. Files and Fraud

1. US-IR 1908, 220.

2. US-IR 1911, 134.

3. Estimates can be found in Chen Wen-hsien, "Chinese under Both Exclusion and Immigration Laws" (Ph.D. diss., University of Chicago, 1940), 136, 421; US-AJY, "Immigration Inspector 1," 2; US-NWVC 151.01/16, 151.10/3.

4. See similar arguments in Kitty Calavita, "The Paradoxes of Race, Class, Identity, and 'Passing': Enforcing the Chinese Exclusion Acts, 1882–1910," *Law and Social Inquiry* 25 (2000): 1–40; and Amy Fairchild, *Science at the Borders: Immigrant Medical Inspection and the Shaping of the Modern Industrial Labor Force* (Baltimore: Johns Hopkins UP, 2003), 64–82.

5. US-IR 1903, 97.

6. Mary Douglas, "The Contempt of Ritual," in her *In the Active Voice* (London: Kegan Paul, 1982), 4–8.

7. The literature on ritual is vast. I have been most influenced by Catherine Bell, *Ritual: Perspectives and Dimensions* (Oxford: Oxford UP, 1997), and *Ritual Theory, Ritual Practice* (Oxford: Oxford UP, 1993); Maurice Bloch, *Ritual History and Power: Selected Papers in Anthropology* (London: Berg, 1989); Stanley Tambiah, "A Performative Approach to Ritual," *Proceedings of the British Academy* 65 (1979): 113–16; and Victor Turner, *The Forest of Symbols: Aspects of Ndembu Ritual* (Ithaca: Cornell UP, 1970).

8. The variety of approaches to ritual in secular and industrialized contexts is apparent from a list of typical titles: Robert Bocock, *Ritual in Industrial Society: A Sociological Analysis of Ritualism in Modern England* (London: Allen and Unwin, 1974); Terence Deal and Alan Kennedy, *Corporate Cultures: The Rites and Rituals of Corporate Life* (Reading, MA: Perseus, 1982); Erving Goffman, *Interaction Ritual: Essays on Face to Face Behavior* (New York: Pantheon Books, 1967); Julian Huxley, ed., *A Discussion on Ritualization of Behavior in Animals and Man*, special edition of *Philosophical Transactions of the Royal Society of London, Series B* 251 (1966); Peter McClaren, *Schooling as a Ritual Performance* (Lanham, MD: Rowman and Littlefield, 1999); Sally Falk Moore, and Barbara Meyerhoff, eds., *Secular Ritual* (Amsterdam: Van Gorcum, 1977); Dennis Rook, "Ritual Dimension of Consumer Behavior," *Journal of Consumer Research* 12 (1985): 251–63.

9. Bell, *Ritual Theory*, 88–93; Philippe Buc, *The Dangers of Ritual: Between Early Medieval Texts and Social Scientific Theory* (Princeton: Princeton UP, 2001); Max

Gluckman, *"Les Rites de Passage"*, in *Essays on the Ritual of Social Relations*, ed. Max Gluckman (Manchester: Manchester UP, 1962), 1–52; Jack Goody, "Against 'Ritual': Loosely Structured Thoughts on a Loosely Defined Topic," in *Secular Ritual*, 25–35.

10. Pierre Bourdieu, *Language and Symbolic Power*, ed. John Thompson (Cambridge: Harvard UP, 1999), 170.

11. Some nuanced approaches include Randall Collins, *Interaction Ritual Chains* (Princeton: Princeton UP, 2005); John Meyer and Brian Rowan, "Institutionalized Organizations: Formal Structure as Myth and Ceremony," *American Journal of Sociology* 83 (1977): 340–63; and Victor Turner, *Drama, Fields and Metaphors* (Ithaca: Cornell UP, 1974). Studies of political ritual in premodern societies are also not so dependent on the secular-sacred divide. See David Cannadine and Simon Price, eds., *Rituals of Royalty: Power and Ceremonial in Traditional Societies* (Cambridge: Cambridge UP, 1987); Kai-wing Chow, *The Rise of Confucian Ritualism in Late Imperial China* (Stanford: Stanford UP, 1994); Clifford Geertz, *Negara: The Theatre State in Nineteenth Century Bali* (Princeton: Princeton UP, 1980); Joseph McDermott, ed., *State and Court Ritual in China* (Cambridge: Cambridge UP, 1999)..

12. Bell, *Ritual Theory*, 106, 110.

13. US-NWCu, Carey to Attorney General, 27 October 1888.

14. US-NNYC 29/50. See also US-DH 59/847, 17–19, 92–107; US-DS 55/120, *Alleged Illegal Entry into the United Sates of Chinese Persons: Letter from the Attorney-General*, 55th Cong., 1st ses. (1897); US-IR 1904, 138–9; US-NWSC 5326/58; 52074.

15. These include John Young in Vermont, and Frederick Paddock and William Badger in Malone, New York. See US-DH 59/847, 97; US-NNM 938/44–151; US-NNYC 6/1040, 1051; 14/3721–3800.

16. US-DH 59/847, 123.

17. Quoted in J. Thomas Scharf, "The Farce of the Chinese Exclusion Laws," *North American Review* 166 (1898): 96.

18. US-NML, Rodgers to CGI, 14 March 1904, also 3 April 1905.

19. US-BJBS, 1:58; US-DH 59/847, 97; US-NGCC 2084; US-NGCD 1/95; US-NML, Thomas to Rodgers, 31 March 1905.

20. Marcus Braun, "How Can We Enforce Our Exclusion Laws?" *Annals of the American Academy of Political and Social Science* 34/2 (1909): 141.

21. US-DH 59/847, 13–14, 91–110, 119–24; US-IR 1901, 52; 1902, 76–77; 1903, 100–1; 1904, 138.

22. US-IR 1904, 46–47; 1907, 107; 1925, 22–23. My calculation, based on native-born citizens who made a trip to China, estimates that a minimum of six male children must have been born to every Chinese woman residing in the United States before 1906.

23. US-NNM 938/44–151; US-NWSC 53560/225.

24. Braun, "How Can We Enforce," 141.

25. US-IR 1916, 201. Some Chinese used deportation as a free trip home. See US-IR 1929, 18.

26. Clifford Perkins, *Border Patrol: With the U.S. Immigration Service on the Mexican Boundary 1910–54* (El Paso: Texas Western Press, 1978), 10.

27. US-IR 1932, 37–8; US-NWSC 55452/385, Nagle to Husband 15 January 1926.

28. Other descriptions of "paper son" techniques include Chin Tung Pok, *Paper Son: One Man's Story* (Philadelphia: Temple UP, 2000); Madeline Hsu, *Dreaming of Gold, Dreaming of Home: Transnationalism and Migration between the United States and South China, 1882–1943* (Stanford: Stanford UP, 2000), 69–89; Estelle Lau, *Paper Families: Identity, Immigration Administration, and Chinese Exclusion* (Durham: Duke UP, 2006), 47–60; Erika Lee, *At America's Gates: Chinese Immigration during the Exclusion Era, 1882–1943* (Chapel Hill: University of North Carolina Press, 2003), 203–7; Mae Ngai, *Impossible Subjects: Illegal Aliens and the Making of Modern America* (Princeton: Princeton UP, 2004), 205–10.

29. Chen, "Chinese under Both," 29.

30. Robert Bard and Gustavo Bobonis, "Detention at Angel Island: First Empirical Evidence," *Social Science History* 30 (2006): 107, calculates a median stay of four days and an average stay of ten days from 1913 to 1917. Previous residents passed through much more quickly.

31. US-NGCD 1/2.

32. Copies of coaching papers and contracts in are in US-DH 59/847, 9–10, 107; US-DS 57/776, 2:122–24; US-NGCC 2142; US-NGCD 21/1; US-NPD 12016/1076–3; US-NPH 739; US-NWSC 55452/385; US-NWVC 151.06/118; 151.10/360.

33. US-NWSC 55452/385.

34. Compiled from papers in US-NPD 39262/11–16; US-NWVC 151.06/118.

35. Hsu, *Dreaming of Gold*, 84; US-AJY, "Inspector #3," line 0602.

36. US-BJBS, 2: 22 Oct. 1917; US-NPD 54184/138.

37. Perkins, *Border Patrol*, 8–10.

38. US-NWCG, Power to Sect. of Treasury, 8.

39. Ibid., Dunn to Power, 1 December 1899.

40. US-NPH 312.

41. Ibid., 2305.

42. Ibid., 2198.

43. US-NWSC 53990/52A, 115.

44. US-AJY, "Immigration Inspector #3," line 0413; US-BIEL, 20.

45. US-NCCG 370/220.

46. US-NWVC 151.10/11.

47. US-AJY, "Inspector #2," 9; US-NML, Rodgers to W. R. Morton, 4 January 1907; US-NPD 12016/1076–1.

48. Lau, *Paper Families*, 89–90.

49. US-NNM 939/3.

50. US-NWVC 151.05/40, 6–8.

51. US-NWVC 151.05/40, 11–13.

52. US-DS 57/776, 2:478–79.

53. US-NPH 1727, 1748.

54. US-NPH 2303.

55. US-NGCC 2014.

56. AUCP-CH, 21 February 1887; US-NWVC 151.08/16; 151.10/360, 531; US-IR 1909, 127.

57. For examples, see US-IR 1907, 60; 1911, 135–39; US-NGCC 1/169, 2028/20D; US-NGCD 10/56; US-NPD folder 2; US-NWCS 309/14; US-NWVC 151.06/55, 23.

58. *New China News*, 12 August 1911. Clipping and translation in US-NPH 2426, also Adam McKeown, *Chinese Migrant Networks and Cultural Change: Peru, Chicago and Hawaii, 1900–1936* (Chicago: University of Chicago Press, 2001), 258–59. On Sun Yat-sen, see Thomas Ganschow, "Sun Yat-sen: An American Citizen," *Chinese Studies in History* 25/3 (1992): 18–39.

59. *Liberty News*, 21 August 1911.

60. *New China News*, 22 August 1911.

61. Zeng Cangling, "Meidi zhu Xiamen lingshiguan dui fu pai huaqiao de qiwu" [The bullying of Chinese migrants by the American imperialist consulate in Xiamen], *Xiamen Wenshi Ziliao* 1 (1963): 60.

62. Him Mark Lai, Genny Lim, and Judy Yung, eds., *Island: Poetry and History of Chinese Immigrants on Angel Island* (Seattle: University of Washington Press, 1980), 100.

63. Ng Poon Chew, *The Treatment of the Exempt Classes of Chinese in the United States: A Statement from the Chinese in America* (San Francisco: Chung Sai Yat Po, 1908), 8.

64. Chen, "Chinese under Both," 425.

65. Bell, *Ritual*, 93–99; Thomas Peterson, "Initiation Rite as Riddle," *Journal of Ritual Studies* 1 (1987): 73–84; Victor Turner, *The Ritual Process: Structure and Antistructure* (London: Routledge and Kegan Paul, 1969).

66. Lai, Lim, and Yung, *Island*.

67. Wu Yangcheng, *Shenghuo zai Niuyue tangren jie* [Life in New York Chinatown] (Hong Kong: Jiwen Chubanshe, 1959), 5–6.

68. Quoted in Madeline Hsu, "Gold Mountain Dreams and Paper Son Schemes: Chinese Immigration under Exclusion," *Chinese America: History and Perspectives* 11 (1997): 47.

69. Paul Siu, *The Chinese Laundryman: A Study of Social Isolation*, ed. John Kuo Wei Tchen (New York: New York UP, 1987), describes the isolation of Chinese migrants, unable to fit in either abroad or in China.

70. Chin, *Paper Son*, 71; Charles Choy Wong and Kenneth Klein, "False Papers, Lost Lives," in *Origins and Destinations: 41 Essays on Chinese America* (Los Angeles:

Chinese Historical Society of Southern California and UCLA Asian American Studies Center, 1994), 355–74.

71. Lau, *Paper Families*, 120–30; Ngai, *Impossible Subjects*, 206–24.

72. Lai, Lim, and Yung, *Island*, 137.

73. Gary Okihiro, *Margins and Mainstreams: Asians in American History and Culture* (Seattle: University of Washington Press), ix.

74. Ibid., 3.

75. Christian Fritz, "Due Process, Treaty Rights, and Chinese Exclusion, 1882–1891," in *Entry Denied: Exclusion and the Chinese Community in America*, ed. Sucheng Chan (Philadelphia: Temple UP, 1991); Charles McClain, *In Search of Equality: The Chinese Struggle against Discrimination in Nineteenth-Century America* (Berkeley: University of California Press, 1994), 279–81; Lucy Salyer, *Laws Harsh as Tigers: Chinese Immigrants and the Shaping of Modern Immigration Law* (Chapel Hill: University of North Carolina Press, 1995), 69–93, 248.

76. Peter Schuck, *Citizens, Strangers and In-Betweens: Essays on Immigration and Citizenship* (Boulder: Westview, 1998), 19. On the divorce from "social reality," see Calavita, "Paradoxes of Race." For a critique of the idea of immigration law as outside the norm, see Gabriel Chin, "Regulating Race: Asian Exclusion and the Administrative State," *Harvard Civil Rights-Civil Liberties Law Review* 37 (2002): 1–64.

11. Moralizing Regulation

1. In addition to works cited below, see Delber McKee, "The Chinese Boycott of 1905–6 Reconsidered: The Role of Chinese Americans," *Pacific Historical Review* 55 (1986): 165–91; Shih-shan Henry Tsai, "Reaction to Exclusion: The Boycott of 1905 and Chinese National Awakening," *Historian* (November 1976): 95–110; Wang Lixin, "Zhongguo jindai minzuzhuyi de xingqi yu dizhi Mei huo yundong" [The rise of modern Chinese nationalism and the Anti-American boycott] *Lishi Yanjiu*, no. 1 (2000): 21–33.

2. Ch-ZMGS, 2:1784.

3. "Chinese and Mixed Residence," *Japan Weekly Mail*, 1 July 1899. Thanks to Eric Han for this reference.

4. L. Eve Armentrout Ma, *Revolutionaries, Monarchists and Chinatowns* (Honolulu: University of Hawaii Press, 1990), 45–51, 90–94; K. Scott Wong, "Liang Qichao and the Chinese of America: A Re-evaluation of His *Selected Memoir of Travels in the New World*," *Journal of American Ethnic History* 11, 4 (1992): 3–24.

5. John Fitzgerald, *Big White Lie: Chinese Australians in White Australia* (Sidney: UNSW Press, 2007), chap. 5.

6. Liang Qichao, *Xin Dalu you ji* [Record of travels in the New World] (Shanghai: Shangwu Yinshuguan, 1922), 194–203.

7. Ibid., preface, 1.

8. Ibid., 169.

9. Ibid., 48–53.

10. Jane Leung Larson, "The Chinese Empire Reform Association (Baohuanghui) and the 1905 Anti-American Boycott: The Power of a Voluntary Association," in *The Chinese in America: A History from Gold Mountain to the New Millenium*, ed. Susie Lan Cassel, 195–216 (Walnut Creek: AltaMira Press 2002).

11. "Bai Aozhou zhi fandiulun" [A theory to counter White Australia], *Xinmin congbao*, 24 June 1903, 69–70.

12. Liang, *Xin dalu*, appendix; Wang Guanhua, *In Search of Justice: The 1905–1906 Chinese Anti-American Boycott* (Cambridge: Harvard University Asia Center, 2001), 56–58.

13. Translation in Wang, *In Search of Justice*, 148.

14. Wong Sin Kiong, *China's Anti-American Boycott Movement in 1905: A Study in Urban Protest* (New York: Peter Lang, 2002), 70–102; Zhang Cunwu, *Guangxu sanshiyi nian Zhong Mei gong yue fengchao* [Tide against the Chinese-American worker treaty in 1905] (Taipei: Institute of Modern History, Academia Sinica, 1966), 136–44.

15. Wang, *In Search of Justice*, 96, 123–26.

16. Ng Poon Chew, *The Treatment of the Exempt Classes of Chinese in the United States: A Statement from the Chinese in America* (San Francisco: Chung Sai Yat Po, 1908), 14. More generally, see K. Scott Wong, "Cultural Defenders and Brokers: Chinese Responses to the Anti-Chinese Movement," in *Claiming America: Constructing Chinese American Identities during the Exclusion Era*, ed., K. Scott Wong and Sucheng Chan, 3–40 (Philadelphia: Temple UP, 1998).

17. *New China News*, 20 May 1905.

18. Henry Tsai, *China and the Overseas Chinese in the United States* (Fayetteville: University of Arkansas Press, 1983), 150; US-NCDC, 19 December 1905; telegram, 30 December 1905.

19. Wang, *In Search of Justice*, 144–55.

20. Translated in Tsai, *China and the Overseas Chinese*, 148.

21. Zhu Shijia, ed., *Meiguo pohai huagong shiliao* [Materials on the U.S. persecution of Chinese laborers] (Shanghai: Zhonghua Shuju, 1958), 149.

22. Zhang, *Guangxu sanshiyi nian*, 78.

23. A Ying, ed., *Fan Mei huagong jinyue wenxue ji* [Literature in opposition to the exclusion treaty] (Beijing: Zhonghua Shuju, 1962), 6; trans. in Wang, *In Search of Justice*, 155.

24. Quoted in Zhang, *Guangxu sanshiyi nian*, 23.

25. US-NCDC, 12 September 1905.

26. Zhang, *Guangxu sanshiyi nian*, 167–75.

27. US-NCDC, 9 August 1905; 10 August 1905; US-NCDU, 27 September 1905.

28. Michael Hunt, *The Making of a Special Relationship: The United States and China to 1914* (New York: Columbia UP, 1983), 235–54; US-NCDC, 12 September 1905, 15 September 1905, Rockhill to Lay; 30 December 1905, memorandum.

29. Ch-GCDL, 5:5389.

30. US-NCDC, 16 August 1905. Also 9 August 1905, 24 August 1905.

31. Ch-AGC 7722.42–43; Zhang, *Guangxu sanshiyi nian*, 64.

32. Zhang, *Guangxu sanshiyi nian*, 246–47.

33. Ch-AGC 7722.44. Wang's official title is not preserved.

34. Translation in Wang, *In Search of Justice*, 187–8.

35. Ch-JZX 4/1:225–26; *Waijiao bao*, 2:507–10.

36. Elihu Root, "The Real Questions under the Japanese Treaty and the San Francisco School Board Resolution," *American Journal of International Law* 1 (1907): 273–74.

37. Mohandas Gandhi, *Hind Swaraj or Indian Home Rule* (Ahmedabad: Navajivan, 1938), 68.

38. *Collected Works of Mahatma Gandhi* (Delhi: Ministy of Information and Broadcasting, Government of India, 1959), 2:12–13. See also Paul Power, "Gandhi in South Africa," *Journal of Modern African Studies* 7 (1969): 441–55.

39. *Collected Works*, 6:5.

40. Ibid., 5:390, 6:54, 7:397; Karen Harris, "Gandhi, the Chinese and Passive Resistance," in *Gandhi and South Africa: Principles and Politics*, ed. Judith Brown and Martin Prozesky, 69–95 (New York: St. Martin's Press, 1996).

41. Gandhi, *Satyagraha in South Africa*, 72–73.

42. *Collected Works*, 7:2.

43. Ibid., 4:142.

44. Gandhi, *Satyagraha in South Africa*, trans. Valji Govindji Desai (Ahmedabad: Navajivau 1950 [1928]) 206.

45. *Collected Works*, 6:5.

46. Ibid., 8:109

47. Gandhi, *Satyagraha in South Africa*, 94–95.

48. Ibid., 100–1.

49. Mohandas Gandhi, "The Doctrine of the Sword," in *Penguin Gandhi Reader*, ed. Rudrangshu Mukherjee, 98 (New York: Penguin, 1993).

50. Gandhi, *Satyagraha in South Africa*, 87–88.

51. Ibid., 105–6.

52. *Collected Works*, 8:77–78

53. Ibid., 8:78

54. Ibid., 8:80. Also Gandhi, *Satyagraha in South Africa*, 162.

55. *Collected Works*, 8:79.

56. Gandhi, *Satyagraha in South Africa*, 123, 146.

57. GB-PP Cd7111, *Correspondence Relating to the Immigrants Regulation Act and Other Matters Affecting Asiatics in South Africa* (1913); Huttenback, *Gandhi in South Africa*, (Ithaca: Cornell UP, 1971) 324–29.

12. *Borders Across the World, 1907–1939*

1. Harry Laughlin, *The Codification and Analysis of the Immigration-Control Law of Each of the Several Countries of Pan America*, analysis volume (New York: Report of the Eugenics Record Office of the Carnegie Institution, 1936), 95.

2. Ibid., 151–60.

3. Diego Lin Chou, *Chile y China: inmigración y relaciones bilaterales (1845–1970)* (Santiago: Instituto de Historia and Centro de Investigaciones Diego Barros Arana, 2004), 208–14; Adam McKeown, "Inmigración china al Perú, 1904–1937: Exclusión y negociación," *Histórica* 20 (1997): 59–91.

4. Ch-AFA 02–23.5.2; Diego Lin Chou, *Los Chinos en Hispanoamérica* (San José, Costa Rica: Sede Académica, FLASCO, 2002), 42–43; US-FR 1907, 593–98;

5. My understanding of institutional diffusion is based on Paul DiMaggio and Walter Powell, "The Iron Cage Revisited: Institutional Isomorphism and Collective Rationality in Organizational Fields," *American Sociological Review* 48 (1983): 147–60; Zachary Elkins and Beth Simmons, "On Waves, Clusters, and Diffusion: A Conceptual Framework," *The Annals of the American Academy of Political and Social Science* 598 (2005): 33–51; Thomas Franck, "Legitimacy in the International System," *American Journal of International Law* 82 (1988): 705–59; David Levi-Faure, "The Global Diffusion of Regulatory Capitalism," *Annals of the American Academy of Political and Social Science* 598 (2005): 12–32; John Meyer and Brian Rowan, "Institutionalized Organizations: Formal Structure as Myth and Ceremony," *American Journal of Sociology* 83 (1977): 340–63; and George Thomas et al., *Institutional Structure: Constituting State, Society and the Individual* (London: Sage, 1987).

6. Frank Caestecker, *Alien Policy in Belgium, 1840–1940: The Creation of Guest Workers, Refugees and Illegal Aliens* (New York: Berghan Books, 2000); Leo Lucassen, "The Great War and the Origins of Migration Control in Western Europe and the United States (1880–1920)," in *Regulation of Migration: International Experiences*, ed. Anita Böcker et al., 45–72 (Amsterdam, 1998).

7. David Strang and John Meyer, "Institutional Conditions for Diffusion," *Theory and Society* 22 (1993): 506.

8. On categories and networks, see Charles Tilly, *Durable Inequality* (Berkeley: University of California Press, 1999).

9. US-FR 1905, 704–5; 1906, 1186–88.

10. US-FR 1909, 245.

11. US-FR 1914, 286.

12. US-FR 1905, 393–404, 532–50.

13. US-FR 1912, 534.

14. US-NWSC 52541/44; 53588/1B; Kevin Cott, "Mexican Diplomacy and the Chinese Issue, 1876–1910," *Hispanic American Historical Review* 67 (1987): 63–85; Amy Fairchild, *Science at the Borders: Immigrant Medical Inspection and the Shaping of the Modern Industrial Labor Force* (Baltimore: Johns Hopkins UP, 2003), 150–59; Erika Lee, *At America's Gates: Chinese Immigration during the Exclusion Era, 1882–1943* (Chapel Hill: University of North Carolina Press, 2003), 179–84.

15. Quoted in Cott, "Mexican Diplomacy," 76.

16. Quoted in Fairchild, *Science at the Borders*, 150.

17. José Jorge Gómez Izquierdo, *El Movimiento antichino en México (1871–1934): Problemas del racismo y del nacionalismo durante la Revolución Mexicana* (Mexico City: Instituto Nacional de Antropología e Historia, 1991), 111, 140–43; Humberto Monteón González and José Luis Trueba Lara, *Chinos y Antichinos en México: Documentos para su estudio* (Guadalajara: Gobierno de Jalisco, Secretaría General, Unidad Editorial, 1988), 23–25, 60–63.

18. McKeown, "Inmigración china."

19. Duvon Clough Corbitt, *A Study of the Chinese in Cuba, 1847–1947* (Wilmore, KY: Asbury College, 1971), 95–106; *Gaceta de La Habana*, 1902–1927; Juan Jiménez Pastrana, *Los Chinos en la historia de Cuba: 1847–1930* (Havana: Editorial de Ciencias Sociales, 1983), 133–42; Kathleen Lopez, "Migrants between Empires and Nations: The Chinese in Cuba, 1874–1959" (Ph.D. diss., University of Michigan, 2005), 189–97; Zou Guangwan, "Zhongguo Guba zhi waijiao guanxi [Foreign relations of China and Cuba]" (Ph.D. diss., National Taiwan University, 1963), 11–43; US-NWVC 151.0637/10–32.

20. US-NWVC 151.0637/25, memorandum from Chinese Minister to Cuban Foreign Office, 29 April 1924.

21. US-NWVC 151.0637/23, Crowder to de Cespedes, 22 May 1924.

22. Zou, "Zhongguo Guba," 24.

23. Ch-AFA 02–23.4.7, 03–12.2.1; Chou, *Chinos en Hispanoamérica*, 28–34; US-FR 1907, 933–36; 1913, 1105–39.

24. *Memoria presentada por el señor Secretario de Relaciones Exteriores, áe la Asamblea Nacional de Panamá* (Panamá: Imprenta Nacional, 1910), xxv.

25. *Memoria presentada por el señor Secretario de Relaciones Exteriores, áe la Asamblea Nacional de Panamá* (Panamá: Imprenta Nacional, 1914), 99–100.

26. Ibid., 104.

27. Ibid., xxiv.

28. Ibid., xxii.

29. Ch-AFA 03–12.12.2; US-FR 1896, 379–80; 1903, 262, 318–19.

30. *Memoria presentada por el señor Secretario de Relaciones Exteriores, áe la Asamblea Nacional de Panamá* (Panamá: Imprenta Nacional, 1922), 157.

31. Ibid., 157–91.

32. Darrell Smith and H. Guy Herring, *The Bureau of Immigration, Its History, Activities and Organization* (Baltimore: Johns Hopkins UP, 1924), 13–14, 23–24; US-IR 1909, 123, 153–74; 1917, xxi; 1919, appendix 5; US-NCNM 4739.

33. Sean Brawley, *The White Peril: Foreign Relations and Asian Immigration to Australasia and North America, 1919–1978* (Sydney: UNSW Press, 1995), 15–29.

34. Robert Zeidel, *Immigrants, Progressives, and Exclusion Politics: The Dillingham Commission* (DeKalb: Northern Illinois UP, 2004), 131–33.

35. US-CWH, "Address by W. W. Husband," 11 March 1912,21, 25.

36. Sidney Gulick, *American Democracy and Asiatic Citizenship* (New York: Charles Scribner's Sons, 1918), 113–14, and *The American Japanese Problem* (New York: Charles Scribner's Sons, 1914), 281–307; Zeidel, *Immigrants, Progressives,* 134–37.

37. Quoted in Zeidel, *Immigrants, Progressives,* 134.

38. US-CWH, "Immigration Restriction," 23 February 1914, 19.

39. Patrick Weil, "Races at the Gate, Racial Distinctions in Immigration Policy: A Comparison between France and the United States," in *Migration Control in the North Atlantic World: The Evolution of State Practices in Europe and the United States from the French Revolution to the Inter-War Period,* ed. Andreas Fahrmeir, Olivier Faron, and Patrick Weil, 271–91 (New York: Berghahn Books, 2003).

40. A. Warner Parker, "The Ineligible to Citizenship Provision of the Immigration Act of 1924," *American Journal of International Law* 19 (1925): 27.

41. Mae Ngai, *Impossible Subjects: Illegal Aliens and the Making of Modern America* (Princeton: Princeton UP, 2004), 21–55.

42. US-FR 1924, 1:225–26.

43. Weil, "Races at the Gates," 277–78.

44. Quoted in Parker, "Ineligible to Citizenship," 24.

45. Izumi Hirobe, *Japanese Pride, American Prejudice: Modifying the Exclusion Clause of the 1924 Immigration Act* (Stanford: Stanford UP, 2001), 7–9; Akira Iriye, *Pacific Estrangement: Japanese and American Expansion, 1897–1911* (Cambridge: Harvard UP, 1972), 106.

46. Roderick McKenzie, *Oriental Exclusion* (New York: Institute of Pacific Relations, 1927), 42–43, 124–25; Harley McNair, *The Chinese Abroad: Their Position and Protection, a Study in International Law and Relations* (Shanghai: Commercial Press, 1924), 195–201.

47. I am indebted to discussions with Tiffany Trimmer for many of the ideas and sources in the next two sections. See her "Solving Migration 'Problems': Trans-Atlantic and Trans-Indian Ocean Approaches, 1890–1930" (Ph.D. diss., Northeastern University, 2007).

48. James Whelpley, *The Problem of the Immigrant* (London: Chapman & Hall, 1905), 6.

49. Ibid., 5.

50. Madeleine Herren, "Governmental Internationalism and the Beginning of a New World Order in the Late Nineteenth Century," in *The Mechanics of Internationalism*, 121–44; Craig Murphy, *International Organization and Industrial Change: Global Governance since 1850* (New York: Oxford UP, 1994), 56–59; Paul Reinsch, "International Unions and Their Administration," *American Journal of International Law* 1 (1907): 579–623.

51. *Congrès International de L'Intervention des Pouvoirs Publics dans L'Émigration et L'Immigration* (Paris: Bibliothèque des Annales Economiques, 1890), 14.

52. Ibid., 142.

53. Leah Haas, "Migration and International Economic Institutions," in *Global Migrants, Global Refugees: Problems and Solutions*, ed. Aristide Zolberg and Peter Benda, 271–96 (New York: Berghahn Books, 2001); Ellen Percy Kraly and K. S. Gnanasekaran, "Efforts to Improve International Migration Statistics: A Historical Perspective," *International Migration Review* 21 (1987): 969–74.

54. *Emigration and Immigration: Legislation and Treaties* (Geneva: International Labour Office, 1922); and *World Statistics of Aliens: A Comparative Study of Census Returns, 1910–1920–1930* (Geneva: International Labour Office, 1936).

·55. Brawley, *White Peril*, 76–77; Yash Ghai, "Migrant Workers, Markets, and the Law," in *Global History and Migrations*, ed. Wang Gungwu, 164–65 (Boulder: Westview, 1997).

56. D. Christie Tait, "International Aspects of Migration," *Journal of the Royal Institute of International Affairs* 6 (1927): 32–35.

57. US-FR 1923, 1:115–20.

58. Quoted in Miguel Angel Cárcano, "La conferencia internacional de Roma y la política inmigratoria Argentina," *Revista de economia Argentina* 13 (1924): 29.

59. *Conference Internationale de L'Emigration et de L'Immigration*, 3 vols. (Rome: Commissariat General Italien de l'Emigracion, 1924), 3:159.

60. Ibid., 3:160.

61. *Segunda Conferencia Internacional de Emigracion e Inmigracion, Diario Oficial*, 2 vols. (Havana, 1928), 1:13; Gérard Noiriel, *The French Melting Pot: Immigration, Citizenship, and National Identity*, trans. Geofroy de Laforcade, 81–83 (Minneapolis: University of Minnesota Press, 1996 [1988]).

62. Brawley, *White Peril*, 94.

63. *Segunda Conferencia*, 1:45–52.

64. US-FR 1928, 1:566.

65. Au-NCEA 1928/4912.

66. Martin Lloyd, *The Passport: The History of Man's Most Travelled Document* (Phoenix Mill, UK: Sutton, 2003), 120–30; John Torpey, *The Invention of the Passport: Surveillance, Citizenship and the State* (Cambridge: Cambridge UP, 2000), 111–21.

67. J. B. Condliffe, ed., *Problems of the Pacific: Proceedings of the Second Conference of the Institute of Pacific Relations* (Chicago: University of Chicago Press, 1928), 32.

68. Ibid., 159.

69. Ibid., 158.

70. Nancy Green and François Weil, eds., *Citizenship and Those Who Leave: The Politics of Emigration and Expatriation* (Urbana: University of Illinois Press, 2007).

71. Clifford Rosenberg, *Policing Paris: The Origins of Modern Immigration Control between the Wars* (Ithaca: Cornell UP, 2006).

72. Donald Taft, *Human Migration: A Study of International Movements* (New York: Ronald Press, 1936), 43–44.

73. Ibid., 411.

74. Paul Fachille, "The Rights of Emigration and Immigration," *Internatonal Labour Review* 9 (1924): 325.

75. Ibid., 325–26.

76. John Gregory, *Human Migration and the Future: A Study of the Causes, Effects & Control of Emigration* (London: Seeley Service, 1928), 198–205.

77. Henry Pratt Fairchild, *Immigration: A World Movement and Its American Significance* (New York: Macmillan, 1913), 26.

78. Ibid., 20–21.

79. US-NCCF 1093/70, 86; US-NCCG 370/93–103, 175, 258–62, 295–99; US-NWVD 811b.111/152.

80. US-NCCF 60/84; US-NCCG 370/124–27, 143, 172, 204.

81. *Manila American*, 28 October 1903.

82. Antonio Tan, *The Chinese in the Philippines, 1898–1935: A Study of Their National Awakening* (Quezon City: R. P. Garcia, 1972), 182–201; US-NCCF 1093/102–11.

83. *La Opinión*, 17 October 1938, 21 October 1938, 31 October 1938, and through December; *Manila Daily Bulletin*, 21 October 1938, 31 October 1938; US-NCCG 370/295, 340, 12177/125; US-NCR, Amoy 13 June 1913, March 1917; US-NWVD 811b.55/1, Wixon to President of Philippines, 23 February 1939; 811b.111/395.

84. US-NCCF 1093/130.

85. Ibid., 1093/132.

86. Ibid., 1093/191.

87. US-NWVD 811b.55/1, memorandum by Jacobs, 2 July 1938.

88. Ibid., memorandum by Brandt, 7 October 1938.

89. Ibid., Wixon to Houghteling, 30 January 1939.

90. Ibid., Wixon to President, 23 February 1939, 17.

91. Ibid., Brandt to Messersmith, 22 April 1939.

92. Bessi Ng Kumlin Ali, *Chinese in Fiji* (Suvia: Institute of Pacific Studies, 2002), 65–68.

93. David Wu, *Chinese in Papua New Guinea, 1880–1980* (Hong Kong: Chinese UP, 1982), 29–30.

94. Robert Gregory, *India and East Africa: A History of Race Relations within the British Empire 1890–1939* (Oxford: Clarendon Press, 1971), 247.

95. Ca-DCER, 3:703- 6, 724–43; 4:94–104, 881–87.

96. Paul Jones, "What Happened to Australia's Chinese Between the World Wars?" in *After the Rush: Regulation, Participation and Chinese Communities in Australia*, ed. Sophie Couchman, John Fitzgerald, and Paul Macgregor, special edition of *Otherland Literary Magazine* 9 (2004): 224–28.

97. Melanie Yap and Dianne Leong Man, *Colour Confusion and Concessions: The History of the Chinese in South Africa* (Hong Kong: Hong Kong UP, 1996), 180, 184.

Conclusion: A Melancholy Order

1. Keith Fitzgerald, *The Face of the Nation: Immigration, the State, and the National Identity* (Stanford: Stanford UP, 1996); Leo Lucassen, *The Immigrant Threat: The Integration of Old and New Migrants in Western Europe since 1850* (Urbana: University of Illinois Press, 2005); Cheryl Shanks, *Immigration and the Politics of American Sovereignty, 1890–1990* (Ann Arbor: University of Michigan Press, 2001); Daniel Tichenor, *Dividing Lines: The Politics of Immigration Control in America* (Princeton: Princeton UP, 2002); Aristide Zolberg, *A Nation by Design: Immigration Policy in the Fashioning of America* (New York: Russell Sage Foundation, and Cambridge: Harvard UP, 2006).

2. Christian Joppke, *Selecting by Origin: Ethnic Migration in the Liberal State* (Cambridge: Harvard UP, 2005), 2–3.

3. Richard Beaubien and Zhang Chao, *Meiguo qianzheng jiqiao he shili* [American visa tactics and examples] (Haikou: Nanhai Chuban Gongsi, 2000).

4. Gil Loescher, "Protection and Humanitarian Action in the Post-Cold War Era," in *Global Migrants, Global Refugees: Problems and Solutions*, ed. Aristide Zolberg and Peter Benda, 171–205 (New York: Berghahn Books, 2001); Aristide Zolberg, "The Formation of New States as a Refugee-Generating Process," *Annals of the American Academy of Political and Social Sciences* 467 (1983): 24–38.

5. Hannah Arendt, *The Origins of Totalitarianism* (Cleveland: Meridian Books, 1958 [1951]), 292.

6. Virginie Guiraudon and Christian Joppke, "Controlling a New Migration World," in *Controlling a New Migration World*, ed. Virginie Guiraudon and Christian Joppke, 1–27 (London: Routledge, 2001); David Jacobson, *Rights across Borders: Immigration and the Decline of Citizenship* (Baltimore: Johns Hopkins UP, 1996); Saskia Sassen, *Globalization and Its Discontents* (New York: New Press, 1998).

7. Mark Dow, *American Gulag: Inside U,S, Immigration Prisons* (Berkeley: University of California Press, 2004); International Organization for Migration, *World Migration 2003: Managing Migration—Challenges and Responses for People on the Move* (Geneva: International Organization for Migration, 2003), 97–108; Jeanette Money, "Human Rights Norms and Immigration Control," *UCLA Journal of International Law and Foreign Affairs* 3, 2 (1998–99): 497–25; Rosemary Sales, "Secure Borders, Safe Haven: A Contradiction in Terms?" *Ethnic and Racial Studies* 28 (2005): 445–62.

8. Jaya Ramji-Nogales, Andrew Schoenholts, and Philip Shrag, "Refugee Roulette: Disparities in Asylum Adjudication," *Stanford Law Review* 60 (2008): 389.

9. Don Flynn, "New Borders, New Management: The Dilemmas of Modern Immigration Policies," *Ethnic and Racial Studies* 28 (2005): 463–90; Lydia Morris, *Managing Migration: Civic Stratification an Migrants' Rights* (London: Routledge, 2002); Kathleen Newland and Demetrios Papademetriou, "Managing International Migration: Tracking the Emergence of a New International Regime," *UCLA Journal of International Law and Foreign Affairs* 3, 2 (1998–99): 637–57; Sales, "Secure Borders."

10. Cindy Hahamovitch, "Creating Perfect Immigrants: Guest Workers of the World in Historical Perspective," *Labor History* 44 (2003): 70–94; Ulrich Herbert, *A History of Foreign Labor in Germany, 1880–1980: Seasonal Workers/Forced Laborers/Guest Workers*, trans William Templer (Ann Arbor: University of Michigan Press, 1990); James Hollinger, *Immigrants, Markets, and States: The Political Economy of Postwar Europe* (Cambridge: Harvard UP, 1992).

11. See almost any issue of *Asian Migration News*, available at http://www.smc.org. ph/amnews/amnarch.htm.

12. United States Department of State, *Trafficking in Persons Report: Victims of Trafficking and Violence Protection Act of 2000* (Washington, DC: U.S. Government Printing Office, 2001), 1.

13. Ibid., 2.

14. Didier Bigo, "Migration and Security," in *Controlling a New Migration World*, 212–49; Wayne Cornelius, "Death at the Border: Efficacy and Unintended Consequences of US Immigration Control Policy," *Population and Development Review* 27 (2001): 61–85; Nicholas DeGenova, "Migrant 'Illegality' and Deportation in Everyday Life," *Annual Review of Anthropology* 31 (2002): 419–47; Godfried Engbersen, "The Unanticipated Consequences of Panopticon Europe: Residence Strategies of Illegal Migrants," in *Controlling a New Migration World*, 222–46; Joseph Nevins, *Operation Gatekeeper: The Rise of the "Illegal Alien" and the Making of the U.S.-Mexico Boundary* (New York: Routledge, 2002).

15. Stephen Castles, "Why Migration Policies Fail," *Ethnic and Racial Studies* 27 (2004): 212.

16. Douglas Massey and J. Edward Taylor, "Back to the Future: Immigration Research, Immigration Policy, and Globalization in the Twenty-first Century," in *International Migration: Prospects and Policies in a Global Market*, ed. Douglas Massey and J. Edward Taylor, 387 (Oxford: Oxford University Press, 2004).

17. Paul Peirce, "The Control of Immigration as an Administrative Problem," *American Political Science Review* 4 (1910): 388.

18. Christopher Rudolph, "Globalization, Sovereignty, and Migration: A Conceptual Framework," *UCLA Journal of International Law and Foreign Affairs* 3 (1998–99): 355. See also Hollinger, *Immigrants, Markets and States*, 12; Jacobson, *Rights across Borders*, 4–10; Shanks, *Immigration and the Politics*, 2–4; Tichenor, *Dividing Lines*, 50–53, 147.

19. Alejandro Portes, Luis Guarnizo, and Patricia Landolt, "The Study of Transnationalism: Pitfalls and Promise of an Emerging Research Field," *Ethnic and Racial Studies* 22 (1999): 220.

20. Douglas Massey, "Why Does Immigration Occur? A Theoretical Synthesis," in *Handbook of International Migration: The American Experience*, ed. Charles Hirschman, Philip Kasinitz, and Josh DeWind, 34–52 (New York: Russell Sage Foundation, 1999).

21. *World Migration 2003*, 64–69, 144–51, 253–54. See also Money, "Human Rights Norms."

22. *World Migration 2003*, 142. Note 1 also includes Israel as a TCI.

23. Ibid., 287; Hania Zlotnik, "The Concept of International Migration as Reflected in Data Collection Systems," *International Migration Review* 21 (1987): 925–46.

24. A famous statement of the community of liberal states is Anne-Marie Slaughter, "International Law in a World of Liberal States," *European Journal of International Law* 6 (1995): 503–38. For an empirical critique, see José Alvarez, "Do Liberal States Behave Better: A Critique of Slaughter's Liberal Theory," *European Journal of International Law* 12 (2001): 183–246. On newness and globalization, see Adam McKeown, "Periodizing Globalization," *History Workshop Journal* 63 (2007): 218–30.

25. Linda Basch, Nina Glick Schiller, and Cristina Sztanton Blanc, *Nations Unbound: Transnational Projects, Postcolonial Predicaments and Deterritorialized Nation-States* (Amsterdam: Gordon and Breach, 1994); Aihwa Ong, "Mutations in Citizenship," *Theory, Culture & Society* 23 (2006): 499–531; Saskia Sassen, *Territory, Authority, Rights: From Medieval to Global Assemblages* (Princeton: Princeton UP, 2006), 277–322.

26. Gary Freeman, "Can Liberal States Control Unwanted Migration?" *Annals of the American Academy of Political and Social Science* 534 (1994): 17–30, and "Modes of Immigration Politics in Liberal Democratic States," *International Migration Review* 29 (1995): 881–902; Guiraudon and Joppke, "Controlling a New Migration World," 8–9; Christian Joppke, "Why Liberal States Accept Unwanted Immigration," *World Politics* 50 (1998): 266–93; James Hollifield, "Migration, Trade and the Nation-State:

The Myth of Globalization," *UCLA Journal of International Law and Foreign Affairs* 3, 2 (1998–99): 595–636.

27. James Hollifield, "The Emerging Migration State," *International Migration Review* 38 (2004): 901.

28. Louis Henkin, "The Constitution and United States Sovereignty: A Century of *Chinese Exclusion* and Its Progeny," *Harvard Law Review* 100 (1986–87): 862.

29. Jacobson, *Rights across Borders*, 8. Also Peter Schuck, *Citizens, Strangers, and In-Betweens: Essays on Immigration and Citizenship* (Boulder: Westview, 1998), 163–75.

Index